GW00862947

Victorian Subjects

Victorian Subjects

J. Hillis Miller
University of California at Irvine

New York London Toronto Sydney Tokyo Singapore

First published 1990 by

Harvester Wheatsheaf,
66 Wood Lane End, Hemel Hempstead,
Hertfordshire, HP2 4RG
A division of
Simon & Schuster International Group

Printed and bound in Great Britain by
BPCC Wheatons Ltd., Exeter

British Library Cataloguing in Publication Data

Miller, J. Hillis (Joseph Hillis), *1928–*
Victorian subjects.
1. English literature, 1837–1900 – Critical studies
I. Title
820.9008

ISBN 0–7450–0820–8

1 2 3 4 5 94 93 92 91 90

Contents

Contents

Preface

"Victorian subjects": the phrase names simultaneously three nodes around which these essays gather, in spite of their manifest disparities. All but one are on "Victorian subjects," that is, on topics within Victorian literature. All are concerned with "Victorian subjects" in the sense of subjectivity, consciousness, or selfhood as it was expressed in Victorian literature. All interpret works by "Victorian subjects," meaning now those who were subject to Queen Victoria, that is, subject to the reigning ideologies of the time, among them prevalent ideologies about subjectivity. To be a "Victorian subject" meant to be subjected to specific social, historical, and material conditions, including the economic and technological conditions under which literature was then written, published, distributed, and consumed. Victorian subjectivities as constituted and recorded in novels and poems were subject to those conditions, "haled" or "interpellated" by them, as Althusser puts it. These essays, taken together, sketch the outlines of ideological assumptions in the Victorian period about the self, interpersonal relations, nature, literary form, the social function of literature, and other Victorian subjects.

But these three meanings of the phrase "Victorian subjects" do not name concepts of a priori intellectual mastery. They do not define things the critic knows already, conceptual paradigms into which a given author or work is then fitted. "Victorian subjects," in all its meanings, is rather a set of questions for interrogation, including the question of the relations among the various meanings of "subject": as topic, as subjectivity, and as one who is subjected or subaltern. Are these meanings merely contingent homonyms, or is there some deeper connection, some hierarchy among them or some level at which the three "nodes" come together in a single knot? In any case, the nodes in question here are not command points from which the work of criticism can exercise sovereignty, but points absent or distant that the work of reading in each case attempts to reach. They are sites of displacement or dislocation rather than unifying centers.

This means, among other things, that the reader would be in error if he were to expect to find some teleological unity in these essays, for example a movement from a phenomenological "criticism of consciousness" to a deconstructive "rhetorical criticism," and, beyond that, to the premonitory signs of a criticism focusing on a performative, positional ethics of writing and reading. The earliest essay here speaks of the "creation" of the self, and the latest still ranges thought under the proper name of an author. What the reader will find here is not so much a clear-cut shift from phenomenological "criticism of consciousness" to so-called "deconstruction" as an uneasy co-presence throughout, in different proportions, of the reliving from within of ideological formations and their redisplaying through citation and commentary, on the one hand, and the critique of ideology by way of rhetorical criticism, on the other. But ironic displacement through citational miming is already an implicit critique. Citation is incitation or solicitation, through which heretofore unseen implications folded into a text come into the open. Such displacement through repetition is a fundamental part of the strategy of so-called deconstruction. Moreover, the asymmetry between method and the results of the application of method, between theory and reading, is displayed throughout these essays, though that may be easier for me to see now than it was when I wrote them. This asymmetry resists any totalizing formulations about them individually or collectively.

Each of the three senses of the phrase "Victorian subjects" is a way of alluding to the displacement that occurs when reading disqualifies the presuppositions of theory. To say "Victorian subjects" in the first sense presupposes a homogeneity or spirit of the age that these essays in one way or another put in question. This happens in part through identification of heterogeneities and discontinuities among works and authors in the same "period," in part through evidence that the work of a writer such as Gerard Manley Hopkins is inhabited by ideas and figures that are not "Victorian." These discoveries of reading cast doubt on the notion that there is such a thing as a unified "Victorian period." They cast doubt, that is, on those basic paradigms of periodization in literary history that were one of the products of nineteenth-century aesthetic ideology.

To say "Victorian subjects" in the second sense appears to presuppose that subjectivity or "consciousness" can be taken for granted as a starting and ending place for the analysis of literature. But the word "subject" means "thrown under." It names the way the self is always subject to something other than itself, something beneath it or beyond it that may be experienced more as an abyss than as a ground, as when Cathy, in *Wuthering Heights*, says of Heathcliff, "He's more myself than I am." The exploration in these essays of the ways subjectivity is created in literature leads in various ways to the recognition that subjectivity is not a perdurable monad. It is rather a virtuality constantly being transformed by its relation to those various others that are thrown beneath it: language, other people, nature, and most of all that evasive other within the self that one can never glimpse except out of the corner of the eye, at the moment of its disappearance.

To say "Victorian subjects" in the third sense, finally, is by no means to assume that these various authors can be understood as straightforwardly "subject" to a Victorian ideology that can be identified and understood as a starting point for analysis. Each author is interpellated, brought into being by pre-existing reigning ideologies, but never simply their subaltern. The act of writing in each case works toward the creation of new versions of those ideologies and toward their putting in question. Works of literature enter history not as mere reflections of what was already there, but function creatively, performatively. Literature, for better or for worse, helps to make history. These essays display the way Victorian subjects were not merely subjected to social, historical, and ideological forces, but reworked and transformed them.

The latest of these essays appeared in 1986. I have published two more books since then, and my work has continued to change. But it remains still a response to solicitations from literature that were already putting questions to me in 1955 about Victorian subjects.

J. Hillis Miller
December 26, 1989
Irvine, California

Acknowledgements

I am grateful to the publishers and editors for permission to reprint the following essays:

"The Creation of the Self in Gerard Manley Hopkins," *ELH*, XXII (1955). A few sentences from this essay were later incorporated in the chapter on Hopkins in *The Disappearance of God* (Cambridge, Mass: Harvard University Press, 1963).

"'Orion' in 'The Wreck of the Deutschland,'" *Modern Language Notes*, LXXVI (1961).

"Introduction," Charles Dickens, *Oliver Twist* (New York: Holt, Rinehart, and Winston, 1962).

"The Theme of the Disappearance of God in Victorian Poetry," *Victorian Studies* (March 1963). Some paragraphs from this essay were later incorporated in revised form in *The Disappearance of God* (Cambridge, Mass: Harvard University Press, 1963).

"Afterword," Charles Dickens, *Our Mutual Friend*, (New York: New American Library, 1964).

"Some Implications of Form in Victorian Fiction," G. A. Panichas, ed., *Mansions of the Spirit; Essays in Religion and Literature* (New York: Hawthorne Books, 1964). Also in *Comparative Literature Studies*, III, 2, copyright 1966.

"Three Problems of Fictional Form: First Person Narration in *David Copperfield* and *Huckleberry Finn*," *Experience in the Novel*, ed. R. H. Pearce, English Institute Essays for 1967, copyright *c.* 1968, Columbia University Press, New York. Used by permission.

"The Sources of Dickens' Comic Art: From *American Notes* to *Martin Chuzzlewit*," reprinted from *Nineteenth-Century Fiction*, XXIV, 4, March 1970. © 1970 by The Regents of the University of California.

"The Fiction of Realism: *Sketches by Boz, Oliver Twist*, and Cruikshank's Illustrations," *Charles Dickens and George Cruikshank* (William Andrews Clark Memorial Library, University of California, 1971). Reprinted in *Dickens' Centennial Essays*, ed. Ada Nisbet and Blake Nevius. © 1971 by The Regents of the University of California.

"Introduction," Charles Dickens, *Bleak House*, ed. Norman Page (Middlesex, England: Penguin, 1971).

"Nature and the Linguistic Moment," *Nature and the Victorian Imagination*, ed. U. C. Knoepflmacher and G. B. Tennyson. © 1977 The Regents of the University of California. Several paragraphs on Gerard Manley Hopkins from this essay were later incorporated in revised form in the chapter on Hopkins in J. Hillis Miller, *The Linguistic Moment: From Wordsworth to Stevens*, © 1985 by Princeton University Press.

"Beguin, Balzac, Trollope et la Double Analogie Rédoublée," trans. Georges Poulet, *Albert Beguin et Marcel Raymond*, Colloque de Cartigny (Paris: Corti, 1979).

"*Middlemarch*, Chapter 85," reprinted from *Nineteenth-Century Fiction*, XXXV, 3, December 1980. © 1980 by The Regents of the University of California.

"The Ethics of Reading: Vast Gaps and Parting Hours," *American Criticism in the Post-structuralist Age*, ed. Ira Konigsberg, *Michigan Studies in the Humanities* (1981).

"Introduction" to Anthony Trollope, *Cousin Henry*, I (New York: Arno Press, 1981). Arno Press is now Ayer Company, Salem, New Hampshire.

"Introduction" to Anthony Trollope, *Lady Anna*, I (New York: Arno Press, 1981). Arno Press is now Ayer Company, Salem, New Hampshire.

"Trollope's Thackeray," reprinted from *Nineteenth-Century Fiction*, XXXVII, 3, 1982. © 1982 by The Regents of the University of California.

"Theology and Logology in Victorian Literature," *American Critics at Work: Examinations of Contemporary Literary Theories*, ed. Victor A. Kramer (Whitston Publishing Co., 1984). Also in *Journal of the American Academy of Religion*, XLVII 2 Supplement (June 1979).

"The Two Rhetorics: George Eliot's Bestiary," *Writing and Reading Differently: Deconstruction and the Teaching of Composition and Literature*, ed. G. Douglas Atkins and Michael L. Johnson, © 1985 by the University Press of Kansas, "The Two Rhetorics: George Eliot's Bestiary," © 1985 by J. Hillis Miller.

"'Hieroglyphical Truth' in *Sartor Resartus*: Carlyle and the Language of Parable," *Victorian Perspectives*, ed. John Clubbe and Jerome Meckier (London: Macmillan Press, 1989).

1

The creation of the self in Gerard Manley Hopkins

Seen from one point of view Hopkins' work is some dozen nearly perfect lyrics.* Seen from another perspective it is a heterogeneous collection of documents: poems, fragments of poems, letters, notebooks, undergraduate papers, lecture notes, incomplete commentaries, sermons, and so on. But within this seemingly chaotic mass we can detect a certain persistent structure. It is not a structure of abstract thought, nor is it a pattern of concrete images. To create this structure the world of sense perception has been transformed, through its verbalization, into the very substance of thought, and, one may say, into the very substance of Hopkins himself. This paper has as its limited objective the attempt to reveal this pervasive imaginative structure. One of its chief limitations is the necessity of describing discursively and seriatim what is really the non-temporal interior world of Hopkins, the total context in which any single poem exists and has its real meaning.

I

> I find myself both as man and as myself something most determined and distinctive, at pitch, more distinctive and higher pitched than anything else I see.[1]

It would seem that the problem of individuation is solved for Hopkins with his first awareness of himself. No one has had a more intense apprehension of the uniqueness and substantiality of his own identity. Hopkins' version of the Descartean *Cogito* is: "I taste myself, therefore I exist." "My selfbeing," says Hopkins, "my consciousness and feeling of myself, that taste of myself, of *I* and *me* above and in all things . . . is more distinctive than the taste of ale or alum, more distinctive than the smell of walnutleaf or camphor, and is incommunicable by any means to another man (as when I was a child I used to ask myself: What must it be to be someone else?)."[2]

The self for Hopkins, in the very first moment in which it recognizes itself, recognizes itself not as a lack, an appeal, but as a plenitude. It does not need to seek something outside of itself as a source of its life, because that life has already been given. One finds oneself, from the beginning, a "throng and stack of being, so rich, so distinctive."[3] No one could be less like Mallarmé, for whom the moment of self-consciousness was the moment of a paralyzing sense of emptiness. Nor does self-awareness for Hopkins depend, as it does in the long tradition coming down from Locke, on sense perception of the external world. Much less does it depend on a *relation* to that world. No, Hopkins' *Cogito* is neither a purely intellectual self-consciousness arrived at by putting in doubt and separating from oneself everything which seems to come from the outside, nor is it the Lockean self-awareness which springs out of psychological nothingness in the moment of sensation. It is, like the first, entirely interior, entirely independent of the exterior world, since, for Hopkins, "when I compare myself, my being myself, with anything else whatever, all things alike, all in the same degree, rebuff me with blank unlikeness; so that my knowledge of it, which is so intense, is from itself alone."[4]

The first moment of self-awareness is, then, not a thought, but a deeply organic sense experience which permeates the whole being, as in the famous formula of Condillac: "I am odor of rose." But it is a "taste of *oneself*," not of anything whatsoever which comes from the outside: "The development, refinement, condensation of nothing shows any sign of being able to match this to me or give me another taste of it, a taste even resembling it."[5] The self is already fully existent as soon as one is aware of oneself at all, and seems to form an eternally subsisting tasting of oneself which prolongs itself from moment to moment as long as one endures. Since it remains exactly the same through time, it is apparently indestructible. If it extends beyond disembodied consciousness, it is only to include a minimal sense of one's incarnation, minimal because it is a sense of incarnation in a simple, spaceless body which is wholly undifferentiated, wholly made up of a single taste.

The Hopkinsian self is, then, positive and definite, and it is vividly *sensed*, in the same way that objects in the exterior world are sensed. Intrinsic identity is a primary datum for man. He does not need to *do* anything at all to come into existence or to guarantee himself continued existence. And this intense possession of the sensation of self is the occasion of an elated joy at one's interior richness and at one's independence. If Hopkins' "taste of myself" reminds one of Sartre's "nausea," it is more because of the striking difference than because of the similarity. Sartre's nausea is disgust at the deeply organic sense of one's contingency, of the fact that one is not a free spirit, but is trapped in the flesh and enmeshed in a world of meaningless things. What is in Sartre a sickening sense of imprisonment in one's own unjustifiable material form is in Hopkins cause for rejoicing. For Hopkins the fact that "human nature" is "more highly pitched, selved, and distinctive than anything in the world" is proof that man is "life's pride and cared-for crown."[6] Man is, it seems, sufficient unto himself, like God.

But beneath the rejoicing in Hopkins at the uniqueness and self-subsistence of each human individual there is another current of thought, a current of wonder at this uniqueness, a wonder which shades off into a question, one of the fundamental metaphysical questions, a question which reinstates all the problems. If nothing "explains" or "resembles" this "unspeakable stress of pitch," if I "taste self but at one tankard, that of my own being," "from what then do I with all my being and above all that taste of self, that selfbeing, come?"[7]

II

The proof of the existence of God for Hopkins is neither from the evidence of the external world, nor from direct intuition. It is a logical deduction from the fact of one's own uniqueness:

> Nothing finite then can either begin to exist or eternally have existed of itself, because nothing can in the order of time or even of nature act before it exists or exercise function and determination before it has a nature to "function" and determine, to selve and instress, with.[8]

And if this is true for all created things, how much more true for human beings is it that they cannot be self-created and self-existent. In a radical about-face Hopkins sees that his apparently so independent self must, on the evidence of its very nature, depend on something outside of itself, must draw its existence from "one of finer or higher pitch and determination than itself."[9] So here, almost in the moment of rejoicing over the distinctiveness of the "taste of oneself," strikes the "terror" of God.[10] For if the Creator could do so much, so can he undo, or do with his creatures as he wishes. For Hopkins, "a self is an absolute which stands to the absolute of God as the infinitesimal to the infinite."[11] The question becomes, then, "What relation do I or should I have to this Being who is so infinitely my superior and so 'dangerous'[12] to me?"

The answer is simple and total: "Man was created. Like the rest then to praise, reverence, and serve God; to give him glory."[13] But how do God's creatures "give him glory"? Merely by being themselves, by *doing* themselves. Selfhood is not a static possession, but an activity:

Each mortal thing does one thing and the same:
Deals out that being indoors each one dwells;
Selves – goes itself; myself it speaks and spells;
Crying *What I do is me: for that I came.*[14]

But it is just here that a radical division among God's creatures appears. Each non-human creature exists in the absolute security of being unable to do other than what it came for. It cannot choose *not* "to fling out broad its name,"[15] and, in doing so, "make [God] known," "tell of him," "give him glory."[16] "What they can *they always do*."[17] But if man can *mean* to give God glory, he can, necessarily, mean *not* to give him glory. His complete fulfillment of his nature, the selving for which he came, is radically contingent. If the full accomplishment of his being puts him "beyond all visible creatures,"[18] so also he can, because of his free will and its accompanying self-consciousness utterly fail to be, in a way no other of God's creatures can. So then, within the very development of Hopkins' apprehension of the nature of his self-being an amazing transformation takes place. What had seemed so solid and definite turns out to be merely a "positive infinitesimal,"[19] something that both exists and does not exist, like a point on a line. It is the mere potentiality of being, a self "intrinsically different from every other self," but a self to which a "nature" must be added.[20] What had seemed so self-subsistent is really very much like the Mallarméan "néant"; it is "nothing, a zero, in the score or account of existence":[21] "For the self before nature is no thing as yet but only possible; with the accession of a nature it becomes properly a self, for instance a person."[22]

Now we can see how the fearful experience recorded in the "terrible sonnets," utter paralysis of the will, and the accompanying spiritual vertigo, is possible, perhaps even necessary, given the premises of Hopkins' universe. Only the self-conscious mind of man can utterly fail to be and plunge downward into the abyss of complete nothingness, and only the mind of man can experience the terror of that plunge:

O the mind, mind has mountains; cliffs of fall
Frightful, sheer, no-man-fathomed. Hold them cheap
May who ne'er hung there. Nor does long our small
Durance deal with that steep or deep.[23]

And if it is only man who can taste himself, can be aware of his own being, it is also only man for whom that self-taste can be a terrifying experience of his isolation from God and from all things, an experience of complete enclosure within the prison of his own self-tormenting self:

I am gall, I am heartburn. God's most deep decree
Bitter would have me taste: my taste was me.[24]

The self which had seemed so solid, so enduring and self-subsistent discovers not only that it is created, but that it absolutely requires help from outside itself in order to be, since to be necessarily means being able to selve, to *do* one's proper being. Without some relation to something outside oneself, man may remain paralyzed, a mere "positive infinitesimal," unable to transform possibility into actuality. Exiled within itself, caged in itself, the self discovers that far from sufficing to itself, it is, in its isolation, entirely impotent, as impotent as a eunuch. It is "time's eunuch,"[25] that is, it is wholly unable to project into the future an action and then carry that action out. Instead of a growth, change, accomplishment matching the passage of time and filling it, such as we find in non-human creatures, man in his desolation finds that he is plunged into a subterranean darkness where time has lengthened out into an endless succession of empty moments, each one of which, because of its emptiness, seems itself to be lifelong:

> What hours, O what black hoürs we have spent
> This night! what sights you, heart, saw; ways you went!
> And more must, in yet longer light's delay.
> With witness I speak this. But where I say
> Hóurs I mean years, mean life.[26]

In this extremity, any possibility of help will be grasped. Perhaps that non-human world of creatures who "always do what they can," even though it rebuffs man with "blank unlikeness," may serve in some way to rescue man from his dizzy plunge into the abyss, from the utter cessation of the forward movement of his life. What is the relation of man to nature in Hopkins?

III

There is evident in Hopkins, from the earliest fragmentary notebooks onward, an interest in the exact nature of things in the external world which is extraordinary even in a century to which nature meant so much.

Hopkins' primary relation to nature was what perhaps remains man's most profound reaction to the external world: it was simply the astonished recognition that each perceived object is *there*, exists as a stubborn, irreducible fact. "But indeed," says Hopkins, "I have often felt . . . that nothing is so pregnant and straightforward to the truth as simple *yes* and *is*."[27] No one has felt more deeply and consciously this wonder at the mere existence of things, and no one has tried more earnestly to cherish that wonder and make it persist throughout as the basic ingredient of his relation to the world.

This attitude toward nature reminds one, of course, of the fidelity to the minute particulars of nature in Hopkins' contemporaries, the

Pre-Raphaelites. Hopkins' own beautiful landscape drawings are very Pre-Raphaelite in their ornate realism. Often a sketch will accompany a detailed verbal description in the *Journal*. And the *Journal* itself is largely made up of the impersonal recording of observed phenomena:

> Clouds however solid they may look far off are I think wholly made of film in the sheet or in the tuft. The bright woolpacks that pelt before a gale in a clear sky are in the tuft and you can see the wind unravelling and rending them finer than any sponge till within one easy reach overhead they are morselled to nothing and consumed – it depends of course on their size.[28]

There is in this a naturalism, an empiricism, even a nominalism, which seems to exclude any theory that objects in nature are parts of a coherent whole. What is, is what it is, and there seems to be nothing more to say about it. In any individual act of perception the whole world is reduced to the self and the observed scene, and one can only assert truthfully what one has oneself experienced. There is an implicit rejection of authority, of a priori ideas, the same rejection that was behind the growth of modern science, the same rejection that is one of the central motivations of romanticism. The Hopkins who wrote such passages in his journal might have said, with Keats, "O for a Life of Sensations rather than of Thoughts," and "I can never feel certain of any truth but from a clear perception of its Beauty." In order to reach truth one must begin all over again each time, reject all received opinions and make oneself energetically passive.

But what does Hopkins find outside of himself through this process of long and hard *looking?* He discovers that each thing is uniquely itself, that each thing has its own distinct nature, a nature which is never repeated. This individuality is manifested in things by the freshness and sharpness of their outline or pattern. Hopkins' nature is a nature with clearly defined edges. It is a nature without blurring or smudging, a nature in which each thing stands out vividly as though it were surrounded by perfectly translucid air. And air can reach all the surfaces of even the smallest and most intricate object, so abrupt is the frontier between the object and its surroundings:

> Wild air, world-mothering air,
> Nestling me everywhere,
> That each eyelid or hair
> Girdles; goes home betwixt
> The fleeciest, frailest-flixed
> Snowflake[29]

Hopkins' word for the design or pattern which is the perceptible sign of the unique individuality of a thing is "inscape." I give only one example among a great many: "Below at a little timber bridge I looked at some delicate fly shafted ashes – there was one especially of single sonnet-like inscape."[30] But an "inscape" need not be a single object. It can be a *group* of objects which together form a pattern. Nevertheless, this form of inscape, too, is not a mere extrinsic organization of disparate parts, but is the manifestation of an inner, organic unity. Nor is inscape only discovered through the sense of sight (although that sense certainly predominates in Hopkins). The use of synesthesia in Hopkins' poetry is matched by an explicit analysis in the *Journal* of the way the unitary inscape of a single object may be perceived by all the senses. The passage begins: "The bluebells in your hand baffle you with their inscape, made to every sense."[31] "Inscape," then, is always used in contexts wherein the oneness, the organic unity, of a single object or group of *composed* objects is seen. And it is always associated with distinctness of outline, with words like "sharp," "wiry" and "crisp." Each object in Hopkins' world is distinctly itself, separated starkly from every other object in the universe. And it is not, like the nature of Tennyson and Rilke, seen as suspended statically and mutely in an eternal and fateful present which seems to be in the very act of fading suddenly away into non-existence. Nature in Hopkins is neither static nor does it hauntingly slip beyond the observer's immediate grasp. It is seen as present to the observer and as acting directly upon him without any intervening distance or vacancy. It does not somehow escape the spectator by withdrawing in upon itself. And even a natural scene which might seem to ask to be treated as static and inanimate is perceived by Hopkins as the center of a vital activity, even of a *personal* activity: "The mountain ranges, as any series or body of inanimate like things not often seen, have the air of persons and of interrupted activity."[32]

Natural objects, then, are not dead, but are sustained from within by a vital pressure. They are not static but ceaselessly active, even when they are apparently motionless. It is this inner pressure, permeating all nature, which is the true source of inscape and what is actually manifested by it. The word is *in*-scape, the outer manifestation or "scape" of an inner principle or activity – not the mere external pattern which things make and which is pleasing to the eye as design: "*All the world is full of inscape* and chance left free to act falls into an order as well as purpose: looking out of my window I caught it in the random clods and broken heaps of snow made by the cast of a broom."[33] "There lives the dearest freshness deep down things."[34] "Fineness, proportion of feature, comes from a moulding force which succeeds in asserting itself over the resistance of cumbersome or restraining matter."[35] Some of Hopkins' drawings are startlingly like Chinese paintings: their swirling whirlpool patterns seem to manifest an ubiquitous spiritual force rolling through all nature. Hopkins' nature, as much as Coleridge's or Whitehead's, is the locus of a vital process, the explosive meeting-point of a spiritual elan and the stubborn resistance of matter. It is a nature which is in ceaseless activity and which manifests an extreme tension between the inner energy and the restraining outward form. The inscape is the meeting place of these two.

But for the inner energy itself Hopkins uses another word, a word which suggests not the outer design or pattern of a thing, but that very energy which upholds it from within: "all things are upheld by instress and are meaningless without it," wrote Hopkins in an undergraduate essay on Parmenides.[36] Just as the apparently unique and solid "taste of self" which was discovered in the first moment of awareness turned out to be a mere "positive infinitesimal," so nature, apparently so full of sharply defined distinctive objects, turns out to be upheld by a single permeating spirit. This spirit is God himself: "As we drove home the stars came out thick: I leant back to look at them and my heart opening more than usual praised our Lord to and in whom all that beauty comes home."[37] Even more striking is a passage from Hopkins' unpublished retreat notes of 1882. In this passage all the solid world is dissolved into expression of God. It is a passage which seems at the furthest possible remove from the naturalism, the humble scientific observation of nature with which Hopkins began: "God's utterance of Himself in Himself is God the Word, outside Himself in this world. The world then is word, expression, news of God. Therefore its end, its purpose, its purport, its meaning and its life and work is to name and praise him."[38] Nature, then, for Hopkins as for the Middle Ages, is the "book of nature" in which we may read "news of God." But there is one crucial difference: the medieval doctrine of analogy has almost disappeared from Hopkins. For the Christian of the Middle Ages each object in the natural world repeated some particular aspect of the supernatural world. It was thus a means of knowing that supernatural world in detail. For Hopkins all the world is "charged with the grandeur of God," and we know through the things of this world simply the power and presence of God, not details of the supernatural world.

It is easy to see now why Hopkins was so elated when in 1872 he discovered Duns Scotus' *Commentaries on the Sentences of Peter Lombard*, and why in that year he could write: "just then when I took in any inscape of the sky or sea I thought of Scotus."[39] Hopkins found in Scotus confirmation of the theory of nature and of the human self which he already held. Hopkins had always felt that the unique individuality of a thing or person was really a part of it, part of its form and not merely a result of the matter in which the form was actualized as Aristotle and

St Thomas maintained. He had always felt that one knows in the act of perception not, by means of the Aristotlean or Thomistic *species intelligibilis*, the mere *quidditas* or "whatness" of a thing, but its distinctive individuality, its "thisness." In the Scotian doctrine of the *haecceitas* or individualizing form, which makes an object not simply a member of a species, a pine tree, for example, but this particular unrepeatable pine tree, Hopkins found his own deepest apprehension of the world systematized. And perhaps even more importantly Hopkins felt that through the immediate sense perception of things in the world he could know God directly as the "instress" that upheld each thing. He did not want a world of abstract "ideas" or "forms" ("pinetreeness," "bluebellness" and so on) to intervene between himself and God. Paradoxically, the Scotian metaphysic, which, from one perspective at least, seems perilously close to nominalism,[40] was actually a much better basis for Hopkins' view of the universe as "news of God" than would have been the Aristotlean theory of forms. Only a world in which God himself is directly present without intermediary in each one of his creatures can be "expression, news of God" in the way Hopkins deeply felt it to be: "All things," he wrote, "therefore are charged with love, are charged with God and if we know how to touch them give off sparks and take fire, yield drops and flow, ring and tell of him."[41]

IV

"*If* we know how to touch them." The perception of the instress in natural objects, then, is contingent on something in the observer. The true theme of Hopkins' *Journal* and of his nature poems is not nature alone but the man–nature relationship. Hopkins has a striking phrase for the "bridge," the dynamic interaction, he felt to exist between subject and object: he called it the "stem of stress between us and things."[42] This tension, as between two magnets, is absolutely necessary to "bear us out and carry the mind over."[43] Subject and object share one thing at least in common: their possession of the inward energy of instress. This intrinsic spiritual force flashes out from objects; it rays forth from them. Each object is not merely the tense withholding of a spiritual charge. This charge leaps out at the slightest provocation, and all objects are thereby potentially in touch with one another. The world in Hopkins is a vast network of electrical discharges given and received by objects which are an inexhaustible source of the divine energy:

> The world is charged with the grandeur of God.
> It will flame out, like shining from shook foil.[44]

But human beings too are charged with energy: "Honour is flashed off exploit," says Hopkins,[45] and "self flashes off frame and face."[46]

Perception, as in Whitehead, is only a special case of the dynamic interaction between all objects. In the moment of perception a "stem of stress" is created between subject and object to which the subject contributes as much as does the object: "What you look hard at seems to look hard at you."[47] Hopkins' epistemology, like that of the Pre-Socratics (whom he had read), is based ultimately on the "theory of sensation by like and like."[48] Only if the beholder is able to return stress for stress will the moment of knowledge, the moment of the coalescence of subject and object, take place.

Hopkins almost always mentions both subject and object in his descriptions of nature. He not only describes the bluebells, he says: "I caught as well as I could while my companions talked the Greek rightness of their beauty."[49] "I caught." It is an active verb, suggesting the energetic grasp of the mind on things. The phrase echoes through the *Journal* and the poetry; it is Hopkins' special term for the strenuous activity of perception: "I caught this morning morning's minion, kingdom of daylight's dauphin, dapple-dawn-drawn Falcon."[50]

Just as Hopkins' self-awareness is an organic taste of himself, not a dry lucidity, so his grasp of the external world in the dynamic moment of instress is as much emotional as intellectual. It is a total possession of the object by the thinking, feeling, sensing subject. The object is internalized by the subject. Hence Hopkins speaks repeatedly of instress as something deeply *felt*, not merely intellectually realized: "But such a lovely damasking in the sky as today I never felt before."[51] "Looking all round but most in looking far up the valley I felt an instress and charm of Wales."[52] One gathers from the constant use of this word and of the word "caught" a strong sense of the precariousness of these experiences. They are reported with a tone of elation, as though they were rare occurrences of success among many failures.

And sometimes indeed the instress does fail to come. It depends on just the proper conditions in the perceiver and in what is perceived: in the perceiver a certain freshness of vision and a singleness of concentration on the object perceived: "Unless you refresh the mind from time to time you cannot always remember or believe how deep the inscape in things is."[53] For the instress to come it must be as if there were nothing else in the world but the present moment of ecstatic communication with what is directly present to the senses. Hopkins differs from the romantic poets generally in that there is in his writings almost no interest in affective memory, in the linkage to a moment in the past by means of intense perception in the present. Each moment recorded in the *Journal* and in the poems is sufficient unto itself. There is a kind of radical discontinuity in Hopkins' temporal existence. It proceeds by a series of vivid perceptions. Each is distinct from all the others and each fades away almost immediately to be replaced by another or sometimes by mere vacancy and lassitude. If a relation between past and present via memory appears in Hopkins at all it is almost always in the form of a lament for the irretrievable fading away of the ecstacy of instress when it is past: "Saw a lad burning big bundles of dry honey-suckle: the flame (though it is no longer freshly in my mind) was brown and gold."[54] The *Journal* entries were often written down long after the event recorded from notes made at the time. In the few cases where the notes themselves exist we can sense a frantic attempt to capture some portion at least of what is known to be fleeting and fragile. And are not the *Journal* and the poems themselves ultimately to be defined as the attempt to give through words some form of permanence to what were actually unique, instantaneous and unrepeatable experiences? There is implicit in the very form of the *Journal* and of the poems a deep anguish at the inevitable passing away of these moments. The loss of these experiences is painful because it is the loss of what the person himself is at that moment. We can detect in the *Journal* both the anxious attempt to give these fleeting moments some permanence in words *and* the obsessive urge to have more and more and more of them. Hopkins can think of no more painful form of self-mortification and penance than to deprive himself of the repetition of one of these experiences.[55]

But sometimes even if the precious activity of instressing is permitted and desired it will not come. Not only must one banish the past and future and live wholly in the moment, one must also banish the awareness that any other person exists: "Even with one companion ecstacy is almost banished: you want to be alone and to feel that, and leisure – all pressure taken off."[56] One can see clearly and explicitly here what is sometimes obscured in other projects of founding one's self-identity on a direct relationship to nature: such a project is, strictly speaking, amoral. It does not exist in what Kierkegaard called the "ethical" realm. For Hopkins, as for Keats and Wordsworth, the self is formed not through inter-personal relations but through experiences of non-human nature, experiences which simply ignore the existence of other human beings. Hopkins' *Journal* and his greatest poems are the record of experiences of absolute isolation from other people.

But even to be alone, in the moment, isolated from past and future and from all other human beings, is not always enough. There may be simply a failure of the sensibility, a failure which in some people is total and permanent: "I thought how sadly beauty of inscape was unknown and buried away from simple people and yet how near at hand it was if they had eyes to see it and it could be called out everywhere again."[57]

And sometimes it is the *object* which for one reason or another fails to offer itself to perception, fails to flash itself outwards in the stress that can be counterstressed by the poet. This fact is perceived when a change in a natural object makes it possible to detect an inscape that has been present all the time, but hidden: "This is the time to study inscape in the spraying of trees, for the swelling buds carry them to a pitch which the eye could not else gather."[58] "I caught as well as I could [in the bluebells] . . . a notable glare the eye may abstract and sever from the blue colour of light beating up from so many glassy heads, which like water is good to float their deeper instress in upon the mind."[59] "Float their deeper instress in upon the mind"! How different this is from the perception, at a *distance*, that each individual thing is its distinct self and has an inscape. Now Hopkins wants to possess that external perception, to internalize it, to "float it in upon the mind" across the stem of stress between subject and object.

When the communication is total perceiver and perceived come into intimate contact, interpenetrate and coalesce. This experience is the true theme of the early nature poems, of "Spring," "The Starlit Night," "The Sea and the Skylark," and "Hurrahing in Harvest." The effect of this experience on the self is, in the etymological sense of the word, "ecstacy": the self leaps outside of itself and creates a new self by means of a substantial identification with all of perceived nature:

> These things, these things were here and but the beholder
> Wanting; which two when they once meet,
> The heart rears wings bold and bolder
> And hurls for him, O half hurls earth for him off under
> his feet.[60]

V

> Another night from the gallery window I saw a brindled heaven, the moon just marked – I *read* a broad careless inscape flowing throughout.[61]
>
> The [elms'] tops are touched and *worded* with leaf.[62]

On the one hand, natural objects are intelligible; they can be read by man as though they were not simply objects, but *signs*. On the other hand, they are *mute* signs. They only speak when there is a human being present to read them. Man gives natural objects a voice and a language. In "reading" them, and in bodying forth that meaning in words man gives nature something it does not possess, self-consciousness and a tongue to speak that awareness:

> And what is Earth's eye, tongue, or heart else, where
> Else, but in dear and dogged man?[63]

The true "stem of stress" between man and nature is the word itself. At the point of fusion, where subject meets object and coalesces with it, is born the word. Words have for Hopkins a magic quality of attaining the object, wresting from it its meaning and making that meaning a permanent possession for man. "To every word meaning a thing and not a relation," wrote Hopkins in a brief paper on words dated 1868, "belongs a passion or prepossession or enthusiasm which it has the power of suggesting or producing, but not always or in everyone."[64] In one sense, all Hopkins' efforts in his poetry were towards the creation of a continuum of words which would, like a proper name, convey the "prepossession," to use his word, of a unique individual experience. All Hopkins' poetry is based on the fundamental discovery that words can imitate things, re-present them in a different form, rescue them from the ceaselessly moving realm of nature and translate them into the permanent realm of words. Words can, Hopkins' discovered, "catch" things, "stall" them, as he said,[65] and transform them into spiritual stuff. Metaphors were not, for him, "poetic lies," nor were words arbitrary signs. Hopkins discovered what certain contemporary poets, philosophers and anthropologists are making their central theme: in the word subject and object merge and we touch the object in a way we never can without naming it. The word is not an arbitrary label; it carries the object alive into the heart. Each different word for the "same thing" transmits to the mind a slightly (or radically) different aspect of reality. Each new word is a window through which a new portion of reality is revealed. To name a thing is to perceive it. This thing is not subjective, not "imposed" by the mind "outwards."[66] It is "really there," but is only perceived when it is so named. We only truly *see* the world when we have represented it in words. Metaphor, onomatopoeia, compound words, inversion, functional shift, and all the other special techniques of verbal representation are only modes of the universal operation of verbal *mimesis*. All the seemingly idiosyncratic methods of Hopkins' poetry are, in one way, directed towards the perfect imitation in words of the object perceived in all its concreteness and in all its energetic activity.

But if words for Hopkins face outwards towards the object, they also face inwards towards the mind. Even in the earliest of Hopkins' writings we can see another fundamental obsession: a fascination for words in themselves, for their etymology, for their multiplicity of meanings, for their abstract "prepossession" without any reference to particular experiences. Hopkins was very sensitive to the inscape of words in themselves, taken in isolation from their meaning. He was fascinated by the fact that the same word can in different contexts carry the "prepossession" of entirely different realities: "Sky peak'd with tiny flames. . . . Altogether peak is a good word. For sunlight through shutter, locks of hair, rays in brass knobs etc. Meadows peaked with flowers."[67] If Hopkins was the most nature-intoxicated poet of the Victorian period, he was also the poet most fascinated by words in themselves, by words not as the signs of an external reality but as the signs of certain definite spiritual states.

Accordingly, alongside the theory and practice of poetry as *mimesis* we can observe a very different notion, a notion of poetry as a thing to be contemplated for its own sake and without any reference to the external world: "But as air, melody, is what strikes me most of all in music and design in painting, so design, pattern or what I am in the habit of calling 'inscape' is what I above all aim at in poetry."[68] Inscape, said Hopkins, is "the very soul of art."[69] It is what makes a work of art "beautiful to individuation," that is, it gives a poem or a painting the kind of distinctness, uniqueness, *haecceitas*, possessed by a natural object. "Inscape," then, has two very different meanings. It can refer to the willed design of a human artifact as well as to the pattern into which natural objects fall without any human intervention.

Hopkins sought to achieve in his poetry an organic unity in which each part would be interrelated to all the other parts, and thus transcend its isolation as the name of an external object: "Repetition, *oftening, over-and-overing, aftering* of the inscape must take place in order to detach it to the mind and in this light poetry is speech which alters and oftens its inscape, speech couched in a repeated figure and verse as spoken sound having a repeated figure."[70] "Tout le mystère est la," said Mallarmé, in terms that Hopkins himself might have used, "établir les identités secrètes par un deux à deux qui ronge et use les objêts, au nom d'une centrale pureté" (All the mystery is there, to establish secret identities by a two by two that gnaws and wears away the objects, in the name of a central purity).[71] For Hopkins, as for Mallarmé, the repetition or parallelism which establishes "secret identities" between one part of a poem and another was for the sake of a "central purity," a central purity which Hopkins called the total inscape of the poem. Here we have moved very far indeed from the notion of poetry as the *mimesis* of the external world, as the violent point of contact between subject and object. All the density of texture in Hopkins' verse is as much for the sake of creating its own self-sufficient durée or "sliding inscape," as it is to express the packed energy and radiance which some event in nature contains. If the extreme use of various forms of "over-and-overing" in Hopkins, assonance, alliteration, internal rhyme, Welsh *cynghanedd* and so on, is in one sense all for the purpose of representing nature, it is in another sense wholly indifferent to external nature and all calculated to "detach the mind" and "carry" the "inscape of speech for the inscape's sake."

Inscape in poetry is "the essential and only lasting thing";[72] it is "species or individually distinctive beauty of style."[73] But it is only attained via the individuality of the poet himself: "Every poet," says

Hopkins, "must be original and originality a condition of poetic genius; so that each poet is like a species in nature (*not* an *individuum genericum* or *specificum*) and can never recur."[74] Each poet, then, is very like each inanimate object in that he is a *species*, not a *genus*, a *haecceitas*, not a *quidditas*. "No doubt my poetry errs on the side of oddness," wrote Hopkins, ". . . Now it is the virtue of design, pattern, or inscape to be distinctive and it is the vice of distinctiveness to become queer. This vice I cannot have escaped."[75] We can see now that when Hopkins said that he aimed above all at "inscape" in poetry he meant not simply that he aimed at pattern, design, organic unity, but that he aimed at these because only through them could poetry be the affirmation and actualization of his own identity. So in the headnote of the sonnet to Henry Purcell, Purcell is praised for having "uttered in notes the very make and species of man as created in him and in all men generally."[76] But in the poem itself the bow to St Thomas is forgotten and Purcell's music is praised not as manifesting "man generally," but as the expression of an absolutely unique self, Purcell's own "arch-especial . . . spirit":

> It is the forgèd feature finds me; it is the rehearsal
> Of own, of abrúpt sélf there so thrusts on, so throngs the ear.[77]

But at the center of the project of individuation by means of "poeting" there lies a double flaw, a flaw which leads to the faltering and ultimate total collapse of the project. In this collapse, Hopkins is left bare again, "no one, nowhere," enclosed within the unpierced walls of his own impotent taste of self.

VI

This collapse can be seen from two perspectives. The poet, it is true, however much he may be apparently imitating the external world in his poetry, is actually speaking himself, *doing* himself. The poet poets. But this "poeting" is accomplished after all through words that have meanings, that remain signs even when they are used for the sake of their own inscapes. A poem is not an act of absolute self-creation. Without the external world it could not exist; however independent it may be it must remain, to be successful, a faithful representation of the external world. The success of this reliance on the external world will depend on the stability and solidity of that world itself.

Hopkins' nature, so densely packed with distinctly singular objects, each sustained by the instress of an inexhaustible energy, would seem perfectly suited to such a dependence on it. Nevertheless, we can see a disastrous transition in Hopkins' apprehension of nature. At first it seems full of solid, static, enduring objects, objects which cannot help but be themselves and which cannot cease to be themselves. But it becomes apparent that these things are in continual movement. Nature is not only full of kinetic energy, it is also a nature in process which is the dynamic expending of that energy. One remembers the clouds in "Hurrahing in Harvest" which are continually made and unmade, "moulded ever and melted across skies."[78] It is only in some kind of movement that things can radiate their inexhaustible energy outwards. But there seems nothing ominous about the discovery that things are not fixed eternally in a single inscape.

Yet in two magnificent poems of Hopkins' maturity, "Spelt from Sibyl's Leaves" and "That Nature is a Heraclitean Fire and of the Comfort of the Resurrection," there is a complete reversal of the earlier feeling of the permanent distinctiveness of things. What had begun as the simple perception that the inscapes of things are in a continual process of change becomes an anguished recognition that the "forgéd features" of things are ultimately utterly destroyed. Never has the perception of nature as a shifting flux of birth and death been expressed with more intensity. As in Parmenides, "unmeaning (ἀδαῆ) night, thick and wedgèd body"[79] which inevitably follows day and hides the perceptible forms of things is taken as the symbol of that absolute non-being which will inevitably overtake all created things, all *mortal* beauty:

> Earnest, earthless, equal, attuneable, ' vaulty, voluminous, . . .
> stupendous
> Evening strains to be tíme's vást, ' womb-of-all, home-of-all,
> hearse-of-all night.
>
> . . . For earth ' her being has unbound, her
> dapple is at an end, as –
> tray or aswarm, all throughther, in throngs; ' self ín self
> steepèd and páshed – qúite
> Disremembering, dísmémbering ' áll now.[80]

Only if we know how much Hopkins cherished the "original definiteness and piquant beauty of things"[81] can we understand fully what violence of regret, what "pity and indignation,"[82] there is in the image of "self ín self steepèd and páshed." It is a dynamically experienced image of the return of all individuated forms to the "thick and wedgèd body" of primordial chaos. In that chaos every self will be blurred, smeared, inextricably mixed in the other selves. Nature will be, in Hopkins' striking coinage, "all throughther." The suggestion that a complete phrase such as "each interpenetrated through and through with the others" has been collapsed into "throughther" makes it a perfect *mimesis* of the event described. One feels the forms of the collapsed words straining to differentiate themselves, just as the identities being crushed into chaos resist desperately the unbinding of their being.

In the poem called "That Nature is a Heraclitean Fire" another of the

Pre-Socratic symbols is used, fire, the symbol of the energy of being, "ethery flame of fire" as Hopkins calls it in his essay on Parmenides.[83] In this poem all the thousand forms in which this energy manifests itself are seen to be impermanent as clouds or as straws in a bonfire, and are continually being destroyed and replaced by other forms. "God gave things," wrote Hopkins, "a forward and perpetual motion."[84] If "Spelt from Sibyl's Leaves" is the frightening vision of night as dismembering, the later poem is a hymn to day as destructive fire, a fire in which 'million-fuèled, nature's bonfire burns on."[85] The very energy of Being, its fire, what seemed to inhere within things and to sustain them in selfhood turns out to be itself the source of their undoing. For that energy drives things on to an activity of selving that eventually consumes them, unselves them, transforms them out of all resemblance to their former selves. Only the "ethery flame of fire" remains constant, that and the activity of change itself, the ceaseless metamorphosis of one form into another.

How, then, can an identification of oneself with external nature be used to establish a permanent identity if nature is as unstable as the day which moves every moment closer towards the tomb of night, as quick to change and as destructive as fire, and if it is to this universal flux that we must testify in our poems?

VII

The evidence from the other side is equally fatal. If nature fails man, man fails nature and fails himself even more totally. His relation to nature can be far different from the reverent and concentrated attention which "floats its instress in upon the mind." If natural objects lack stability and permanence, so even more completely does man. In non-human nature the law is transformation, flux, but the law for man is absolute destruction, since his identity, though incarnated, is too subtle, too spiritual, to retain its distinctness through even so many changes as a tree or flower will endure. The final lesson man learns from nature is that he, too, is part of nature and that this means but one thing for him: death. If all objects are burned in nature's bonfire, man is simply annihilated in that same fire:

> But quench her bonniest, dearest ' to her, her clearest-
>   selvèd spark
> Man, how fast his firedint, ' his mark on mind, is gone!
> Both are in an unfathomable, all is in an enormous dark
> Drowned.[86]

Even if a man could achieve through the poetizing of his perception of nature an unwavering and permanent identity, it would be all dismembered and unbound in a moment at his death.

But even within the limits of earthly life the project is bound to fail. As we have seen, the ability to "instress" nature is intermittent and can be replaced in a moment by the most agonizing spiritual impotence. If the self is unable to selve, as it often is, it will be cut off entirely from the world which can give it such delight. In times of spiritual dryness, of spiritual paralysis, the self is locked entirely within its self-torment and cut off entirely from the outside world:

> I cast for comfort I can no more get
> By groping round my comfortless, than blind
> Eyes in their dark can day or thirst can find
> Thirst's all-in-all in a world of wet.[87]

The proper image of spiritual aridity is not of a thirsty man in a desert but of a thirsty man in the midst of water he cannot drink; it is not the image of a man straining to see in the darkness but of a blind man in the midst of light which he cannot see.

There was something ominous in the double orientation of words, and in the split in Hopkins between poetry as *mimesis* and poetry as "the inscape of speech for the inscape's sake." Words can become not the point of fusion of subject and object, but the locus of their most absolute and permanent division. Words, instead of reaching out to things, touching them, and *giving* them over to man, can become merely the opaque walls of his interior prison:

> . . . Only what word
> Wisest my heart breeds dark heaven's baffling ban
> Bars or hell's spell thwarts. This to hoard unheard
> Heard unheeded, leaves me a lonely began.[88]

Cast outwards by the mind to capture the object, words may fall endlessly through a shadowy void and never touch anything at all, neither things nor the God within things:

> . . . my lament
> Is cries countless cries like dead letters sent
> To dearest him that lives alas! away.[89]

The end point of Hopkins' long dialogue with nature is a complete reversal of the ecstatic mood of "Hurrahing in Harvest." He is cut off entirely from nature and lives in the utter isolation of his spiritual inertia, "this tormented mind / With this tormented mind tormenting yet."[90] His state is very like that of the damned who are also imprisoned in the corrosive contemplation of their own limits. "Against these acts of its own," wrote Hopkins, "the lost spirit dashes itself like a caged beast and is in prison, violently instresses them and burns, stares into them and is the deepest darkened."[91]

VIII

If all the positive ways of self-affirmation fail, perhaps there is one final way, a way through the center of the deepest despair and spiritual abnegation: the creation of one's true self by self-sacrifice. The crucifixion, central moment of history, was the act whereby Christ "annihilated himself."[92] Christ was most Christ, the Mediator and Saviour of mankind, when he thus sacrificed himself, just as the windhover is most windhover when it renounces its sovereignty of the air and dives earthward.

Hopkins in his later years planned a treatise on sacrifice. It was never published, but it is clear from texts scattered throughout his work what he would have said. Non-human things can praise God simply by being themselves, by "dealing out that being indoors each one dwells." Only man in order to praise God and win salvation must cease to be himself. Only through such a total change of his essential being can man escape the damnation of being "no one, nowhere, / In wide the world's weal," exiled within himself, separated from all, dwelling in "the barren wilderness outside of God,"[93] condemned to taste his own self eternally. Only by ceasing to be oneself and becoming Christ can a man avoid an existence which is a continual dizzy falling away in time:

> I am soft sift
> In an hourglass – at the wall
> Fast, but mined with a motion, a drift,
> And it crowds and it combs to the fall.[94]

In the subtle and elaborate investigation of free will and grace in the "Commentary on the Spiritual Exercises of St Ignatius Loyola" Hopkins devises a brilliant metaphor to define this transformation. The actual pitch of self existing at any moment in each person is only one self out of an infinity of possible selves. It is like one cross-section out of all the possible ones of a three-dimensional solid. It is one "cleave of being" out of the total "burl of being." This "burl of being" is as much really part of a person, though only potential, as his actual self. The transformation of the self when it becomes Christ is the abandonment of one cleave of being and the actualizing of another potential one. For every man, and even Satan himself, has at least one potential cross-section which coincides with Christ.

But how can this transformation be brought about? For man of his own power can do absolutely nothing to move himself from one "cleave of being" to another. There is only one answer: by God's grace, "which lifts the receiver from one cleave of being to another and to a vital act in Christ."[95] Hopkins' concept of grace seems to relate him rather to Post-Reformation theologies than to Thomistic Catholicism. For a Thomist, the initial act of creation gives a man's soul an indestructible permanence. He cannot cease to be himself, even if he veers to one of the extremes of mortal sin or sainthood. Grace, in the Thomistic view, does not exert its power on the permanent identity of a man's being, but only upon the variations of his temporal existence. But grace for Hopkins is precisely a *transubstantiation* of the person's innermost being. It is "an exchange of one whole for another whole, as they say in the mystery of Transubstantiation, a conversion of the whole substance into another substance, but here it is not a question of substance; it is a lifting him from one self to another self, which is a most marvellous display of divine power."[96] "It is not a question of substance," says Hopkins, but it is difficult to say what else it is, this total transformation from one self to another self, "through the gulf and void between pitch and pitch of being."[97]

Where then is free will? It would seem that there is nothing left for God's creature to do but to pray for grace. But in what Hopkins calls the "least sigh of desire," the "aspiration,"[98] of man towards God a tiny corner is left for man's free will. "Correspondence" is the key word in Hopkins' theory of grace. Just as man's salvation is won by achieving a correspondence to Christ, so the only action on man's part that makes this occur is the minute movement of volition whereby he wills to correspond with God's grace: "and by this infinitesimal act the creature does what in it lies to bridge the gulf fixed between its present actual and worser pitch of will and its future better one."[99] This "correspondence with grace and seconding of God's designs"[100] is man's tiny bit contributed towards the creation of his own best self.

But even when transubstantiated into Christ a man still remains himself, since it is that mere positive infinitesimal which the man is aware of in his first self-consciousness which is so filled with Christ. The proper figure for the achieved transformation is of a hollow shell or vessel which is everywhere inhabited by Christ and brought into positive being by Christ: "This too," writes Hopkins, "but brings out the nature of the man himself, as the lettering on a sail, or the device upon a flag are best seen when it fills."[101]

However, this metamorphosis of man into Christ remains until his death contingent, in jeopardy. It depends on God's continual gift of fresh grace and on man's continual "saying Yes"[102] to God.[103] Only at the Resurrection will man be securely and permanently transformed, soul and body, into Christ: whence the "comfort of the Resurrection," the only real comfort for man:

. . . Flesh fade, and mortal trash
Fall to the residuary worm; ' world's wildfire, leave but ash:
In a flash, at a trumpet crash,
I am all at once what Christ is, ' since he was what I am, and

> This Jack, joke, poor potsherd, ' patch, matchwood, immortal
> diamond,
> Is immortal diamond.[104]

We must leave Hopkins here, at the extreme point of his despair and hope, turned far from nature and from poetry, standing aghast at the sight of a world that is visibly disintegrating and being consumed, as at the last trump. We leave him with nothing but the "comfort of the Resurrection," the hope of that miracle of transubstantiation which will change man from the mere impure carbon of matchwood to immortal diamond, change him, that is, from one allotropic form of himself to another so different that if there is any secret continuity between the two it is only in that the same null potentiality of being, is, in each case, actualized by God, actualized by God in ways that are as far apart as the whole distance from hell to heaven.

Notes

* A few sentences from this essay were later incorporated in the chapter on Hopkins in my *The Disappearance of God* (Cambridge, Mass.: Harvard University Press, 1963).

1. *The Notebooks and Papers of Gerard Manley Hopkins*, Humphry House, ed. (London, 1937), p. 309.
2. *idem.*
3. *idem.*
4. *idem.*, p. 310.
5. *idem.*
6. *Poems of Gerard Manley Hopkins*, W. H. Gardner, ed., third edition (New York, 1948), p. 73.
7. *Notebooks*, p. 310.
8. *idem.*, p. 312.
9. *idem.*, p. 309.
10. *Poems*, p. 56.
11. *Notebooks*, p. 331.
12. *Poems*, p. 73.
13. *Notebooks*, p. 303.
14. *Poems*, p. 95.
15. *idem.*
16. *Notebooks*, p. 303.
17. *idem.*
18. *idem.*, p. 303.
19. *idem.*, p. 322.
20. *idem.*
21. *idem.*
22. *idem.*, p. 325.
23. *Poems*, p. 107.
24. *idem.*, p. 110.
25. *idem.*, p. 113.

26. *idem.*, p. 109.
27. *Notebooks*, p. 98.
28. *idem.*, p. 140.
29. *Poems*, p. 99.
30. *Notebooks*, p. 211.
31. *idem.*, p. 145.
32. *Poems and Prose of Gerard Manley Hopkins*, W. H. Gardner, ed. (London, 1953), p. 115.
33. *Notebooks*, pp. 173, 174.
34. *Poems*, p. 70.
35. *Further Letters of Gerard Manley Hopkins*, C. C. Abbott, ed. (London, 1938), p. 159.
36. *Notebooks*, p. 98.
37. *idem.*, p. 205.
38. Quoted in W. A. M. Peters, S. J., *Gerard Manley Hopkins* (London, 1948), p. 175.
39. *Notebooks*, p. 161.
40. See Bernard Landry, *La Philosophie de Duns Scot* (Paris, 1922), *passim.*
41. *Notebooks*, p. 342.
42. *idem.*, p. 98.
43. *idem.*
44. *Poems*, p. 70.
45. *idem.*, p. 112.
46. *idem.*, p. 104.
47. *Notebooks*, p. 140.
48. *idem.*, p. 102.
49. *idem.*, p. 174.
50. *Poems*, p. 73.
51. *Notebooks*, p. 143.
52. *idem.*, p. 210.
53. *idem.*, p. 140.
54. *idem.*, p. 159.
55. See *idem.*, p. 199.
56. *idem.*, p. 111.
57. *idem.*, p. 161.
58. *idem.*, p. 141.
59. *idem.*, p. 174.
60. *Poems*, p. 75.
61. *Notebooks*, p. 158, my italics.
62. *idem.*, p. 190, my italics.
63. *Poems*, p. 96.
64. *Notebooks*, p. 95.
65. For a use of this word, see *Notebooks*, p. 127: "these images . . . once lodged there are stalled by the mind like other images."
66. *idem.*, p. 154.
67. *idem.*, p. 32.
68. *Letters of Gerard Manley Hopkins to Robert Bridges*, C. C. Abbott, ed. (London, 1935), p. 60.
69. *Correspondence of Gerard Manley Hopkins and Richard Watson Dixon*, C. C. Abbott, ed. (London, 1935), p. 135.
70. *Notebooks*, p. 249.

71. Letter to Vielé Griffin, August 8, 1891, quoted in G. Poulet, *La Distance Intérieure* (Paris, 1952), p. 343.
72. *Further Letters*, p. 225.
73. *idem.*
74. *idem.*, p. 222.
75. *Letters to Bridges*, p. 60.
76. *Poems*, p. 84.
77. *idem.*, p. 85.
78. *Poems*, p. 74.
79. *Notebooks*, p. 102.
80. *Poems*, p. 104.
81. *Further Letters*, p. 72.
82. *Poems*, p. 112.
83. *Notebooks*, p. 102.
84. *idem.*, p. 347.
85. *Poems*, p. 112.
86. *idem.*
87. *idem.*, p. 111.
88. *idem.*, p. 109.
89. *idem.*
90. *idem.*, p. 110.
91. Peters, *op. cit.*, p. 177.
92. *Letters to Bridges*, p. 175.
93. *Notebooks*, p. 344.
94. *Poems*, p. 56.
95. *Notebooks*, p. 337.
96. *idem.*, p. 329.
97. *idem.*, pp. 334, 335.
98. *idem.*, p. 333.
99. *idem.*, p. 333.
100. *idem.*, p. 344.
101. *idem.*, p. 343.
102. *idem.*, p. 333.
103. See Hopkins' beautiful image for God's continual *sustaining* of man in stanza four of "The Wreck of the Deutschland" (*Poems*, p. 56).
104. *Poems*, p. 112.

2

"Orion" in "The Wreck of the Deutschland"

The passage in question is in the twenty-first stanza of the poem:

Thames would ruin them;
Surf, snow, river and earth
Gnashed: but thou art above, thou Orion of light;
Thy unchancelling poising palms were weighing the worth,
Thou martyr-master: in thy sight
Storm flakes were scroll-leaved flowers, lily showers – sweet
heaven was astrew in them.[1]

The general meaning of the lines is clear enough. Hopkins has told us how the nuns have been exiled from Germany, and cannot find haven in England. Now he returns to the storm. The elements too are "unkind" (st. 13), and seem to be hunting the nuns down, as if they were dogs with gnashing teeth.[2] But even in the midst of the storm Christ is present, as the constellation Orion still shines above the clouds. It is Christ who has driven the nuns westward from their sanctuary. He has "unchancelled" them.[3] He is the master of martyrs, the ruler who commands and judges them, but he can be their leader only because he is himself the master-martyr, the archetypal example of the unmerited suffering which they must re-experience. "The martyrs," says Hopkins in a sermon, "follow [Christ] through a sea of blood."[4] Christ can see the storm as evil and a cause of suffering, but he can also see it as blessed because of the outcome of this suffering. The Prince of the Power of Air seems to have been liberated in the storm, and the wind from a "cursed quarter" (st. 13) seems to have been raised by the devil. But the storm is really from God. It is "the dark side of the bay of [his] blessing" (st. 12). In Christ's sight the storm-flakes are showers of lilies to crown the martyrs. And these flowers are "scroll-leaved," that is, they are "worded." They speak for Christ, and express his judgment of the nuns, just as in the next stanza the fact that there are five nuns is symbolic of the five wounds of Christ which "letter the lamb's fleece." However evil the storm seems, the passage says, it has an ultimately good purpose, for whatever happens in nature is from God or is turned to his uses.

But why Orion? Is it simply because Orion is a constellation forming an heroic human figure and therefore an apt image of Christ? Is there any traditional justification for using Orion in this way? Perhaps Hopkins has merely gone on from the metaphor of "surf, snow, river and earth" as gnashing dogs, to suggest that Orion (i.e. Christ) is the mighty hunter of souls directing these dogs and controlling them. (The constellation Orion, after all, is associated with two constellations of dogs, *canis major* and *canis minor.*) This is certainly part of the meaning. And it would be supported by Hopkins' general theory of classical myth,[5] and by his notion that the stars are a "piece-bright paling" through which heaven shines – "Christ and his mother and all his hallows."[6] But a great deal more than this is working in the reference to Orion. And this more suggests that in some cases at least Hopkins must be read not simply in the light of Scotus or St Ignatius, but also in the light of the general tradition of classical–Christian symbolism. In Hopkins is still alive that way of writing poetry which we associate, say, with Donne, Herbert, or Vaughan, or with medieval and renaissance poetry generally.

The standard classical, medieval, and renaissance tradition about Orion derives from meteorological notions. The constellation rises in the late fall and sets in the spring. Throughout the tradition, from Virgil to the seventeenth century, Orion is seen as a bringer of storms and rain. Virgil calls him *nimbosus* and *aquosus.*[7] Horace associates him with "Notus," the South wind, and with shipwreck: *Me quoque devexi rabidus comes Orionis / Illyricis Notus obruit undis* (Me also has the raging South Wind, companion of setting Orion, sunk in the Illyrian waves).[8] Gregory,[9] Rabanus Maurus,[10] the second Vatican mythographer,[11] Honorius Augustodunensis,[12] Cornelius a Lapide,[13] Milton,[14] and Alexander Ross[15] all tell us with monotonous regularity that Orion stirs up tempests, and brings rain, hail and snow. The traditional belief was that if Orion was visible, fine weather would follow; if he was obscured, storms would come. This association with storms and rain is derived not only from the fact that Orion rises during the stormy weather of late fall, but also from the myth of Orion's birth. Orion, so the story goes, was conceived from the urine of Jupiter, Mercury, and Neptune. And the name "Orion" was often etymologized from "urine."[16] So Honorius Augustodunensis says: *Inde est Orion, qui ab urina natus, inter sidera est translatus. Hujus stellœ si fulgent, serenum erit; si obscurentur, tempestas* (After this comes Orion who, born from urine, was translated up among the constellations. If his stars shine, it will be fair; if they are clouded over, stormy). Cornelius a Lapide repeats Honorius almost word for word, and Alexander Ross keeps the tradition going.

The wreck of the Deutschland occurred on the night of December 7, 1875, at a time when Orion would have been shining in full force, though obscured by cloud. Hopkins' use of Orion in a poem about a winter storm is thus perfectly justified by the tradition.

But is there any more to it than this? The meteorological interpretation seems hardly enough to justify the identification of Orion with Christ. The fact is, however, that there is a long tradition associating Orion specifically with the martyrs of the Church. The ultimate sources of this tradition are the passages in the Bible which mention Orion, especially Amos 5:8 and Job 9:9. Biblical commentators from Gregory to Cornelius a Lapide interpret the Old Testament references to Orion as tropological foreshadowings of the martyrs. The basic text here seems to be Gregory's commentary in the *Moralia* on Job 9:9: *Qui facit Arcturum, et Orionas, et Hyadas, et interiora Austri* (Which maketh Arcturus, Orion, and Pleiades, and the chambers of the south [King James translation]). Arcturus, says Gregory, is the Church. Orion the martyrs, and the Hyades the doctors of the Church.[17] Gregory's interpretation and his explanation of it is echoed through the centuries, and appears to have been the standard exegesis. Rabanus Maurus in his *De Universo*, for example, quotes Gregory almost word for word without reference to him,[18] and hundreds of years later Cornelius a Lapide quotes him directly in his commentary on Amos.[19] Of the three commentaries Hopkins is perhaps most likely to have seen either Gregory or Cornelius. Perhaps he saw one or the other at St Beuno's College, in North Wales, where he wrote "The Wreck" while he was in the midst of his theological studies. Gregory was a basic authority, and Cornelius was a Jesuit whose commentaries were often reprinted. The works of either would have been likely to be in the library at St Beuno's. In any case, the association of Orion with the martyrs is such a persistent tradition that it seems very likely that Hopkins may have encountered it somewhere.

This seems even more likely when we turn to Gregory's development of his identification of Orion and the martyrs, and see how it illuminates the passage in "The Wreck of the Deutschland":

> Quid igitur post Arcturum per Orionas nisi martyres designantur? Qui, dum sancta Ecclesia ad statum prædicationis erigitur, pondus persequentium molestiasque passuri, ad cœli faciem quasi in hieme venerunt. His etenim natis, mare terraque turbata est, quia dum gentilitas mores suos destrui, apparente illorum fortitudine doluit, in eorum necem non solum iracundos ac turbidos, sed etiam placidos erexit. Ex Orionibus itaque hiems inhorruit, quia, clarescente sanctorum constantia, frigida mens infidelium ad tempestatem se persecutionis excitavit. Orionas ergo cœlum edidit, cum sancta Ecclesia martyres misit. Qui dum loqui recta rudibus ausi sunt, omne pondus ex frigoris adversitate pertulerunt.

(Beyond Arcturus, therefore, what do the stars of Orion signify if not the martyrs? When the holy Church rose to the status of public proclamation, these had to suffer the weight of persecution and the injuries, and they took on their aspect in the sky as it were in wintry weather. For when these emerged on the horizon, land and sea were disturbed, because the pagan world, lamenting that its moral core was being weakened even as the courage of these martyrs shone forth, stirred up not only wrathful and troublesome men, but peaceful men too, to slaughter them. So from the stars of Orion the winter storms raged, because the shining constancy of the saints caused the cold minds of the heathens to stir themselves up into a storm of persecution. Therefore the sky brought forth the stars of Orion when the holy Church commissioned its martyrs. When they dared to speak the truth to the ignorant, they suffered the whole weight of this affliction of cold.)[20]

The storms of winter, then, are symbols of the persecution the martyrs arouse by their very sanctity. At a time when the pagan culture is losing its moral fiber, the fortitude of the martyrs is more than the unbelievers can stand. Even the peaceful among the heathen, as well as the rabble-rousers, are stirred up to murderous rage in this wintertime of the Church. Gregory is here turning the meteorological tradition about Orion to his own uses. Orion causes storms, Gregory is saying, not because it is evil but because it is good, just as the martyrs stir up storms of persecution because their very courage and goodness is intolerable to the wicked and degenerate disbelievers. So the martyrs are sent by the Church, as Orion is sent by heaven, for the martyrs must bear upon themselves all the weight of persecution, just as Orion must endure the weight of winter. "The blood of the martyrs is the seed of the Church." The suffering of the martyrs is a witness to Christ and spreads the faith at a time when it is just establishing itself. But the death of the martyrs also appeases the wrath of persecution and bears it away, leaving the Church more free to act, just as Christ, the martyr-master, took upon himself the sins of the world, appeased the wrath of God against mankind, and thus made it possible for man to escape from the original sin. So, in Cornelius, Orion is a harbinger of spring with its flowers, as well as a bringer of storms.[21] The storms of persecution, and the martyrdom they cause, are necessary to the triumph of the Church in the spring.

All this is immediately applicable to the passage in "The Wreck of the Deutschland." We can see now that the storm which wrecks the Deutschland is a kind of extension of the persecution which has driven them from Germany. And Christ, the martyr-master, is indeed "weighing the worth" of the nuns' suffering in his "poising palms," just as Orion poises the club and sword in his hands. He is testing the pain of the nuns to see if it is great enough to appease the divine wrath of the storm and bring on the spring, with its flowers, its showers of grace, and its resultant salvation for others. The suffering of afflictive grace is a necessary prelude to the sweet descent of elevating grace.

And the suffering of the nuns is indeed great enough. It transforms the malign storm into the freshening showers of grace, in which sweet heaven is astrew. Just as Christ's death at Easter makes possible the lilies of Spring and the salvation of mankind, so Hopkins suggests (st. 31) that the death of the nuns may have made possible the salvation of the fallen souls on board the Deutschland: ". . . is the shipwrack then a harvest, does the tempest carry the grain for thee?" In the sight of Christ, the Orion of light, evil is transformed into good, and the storm flakes are indeed "scroll-leaved flowers, lily showers," in all the multiplicity of meanings we have found for this transformation.

The symbolism of stanza 21 of "The Wreck of the Deutschland" derives from traditional sources, particularly from the tradition of medieval and renaissance Biblical commentary. The interpretation of this passage in the light of the tradition does not produce a meaning inconsistent with Hopkins' general attitude toward classical myth, with his notions about stars, or with the Ignatian drama of the poem. But merely to recognize the presence of these constant Hopkinsian assumptions does not lead to a full understanding of the passage. It is possible that many other passages in Hopkins must be interpreted in the same way, and that we must often refer to the tradition of Biblical commentary, as well as to the *Exercises* of St Ignatius or to the *Opus Oxoniense* of Scotus, for a complete reading of Hopkins' poems.

Notes

1. *Poems of Gerard Manley Hopkins*, W. H. Gardner, ed., third edition (New York and London, 1948), p. 62.
2. See Gardner's note, *op. cit.*, p. 224.
3. See Gardner's note in *Gerard Manley Hopkins: A Selection of His Poems and Prose* (Harmondsworth, 1953), p. 218. One might add that the chancel is the area in the eastern side of a church near the altar. Only priests and the choir can go there during service. It is called "chancel" from the crisscross fretwork of barrier lattices which shuts it in.
4. *The Sermons and Devotional Writings of Gerard Manley Hopkins*, Christopher Devlin, ed. (London, 1959), p. 35.
5. For Hopkins classical myth is valid, if at all, only as a veiled allegory, a shadowy parallel or anticipation of the Christian story, especially that part of the Christian story having to do with Christ's defeat of the devil. So, in a letter to Dixon, after damning the Greek gods as "not gentlemen and ladies," he goes on to say: "But I grant that the Greek mythology is very susceptible of fine treatment, allegorical treatment for instance, and so treated gives rise to the most beautiful results" (*The Correspondence of Gerard Manley Hopkins and Richard Watson Dixon*, Claude Colleer Abbott, ed.

[London, 1955], p. 147.) And so Hopkins writes a poem giving a Christian interpretation to the story of Perseus and Andromeda (*Poems*, p. 89); he refers in "The Wreck" to the "beat of endragonèd seas" (st. 27); and in his analysis of the Apocalypse in his spiritual writings he discusses the way a Dragon is a proper symbol of the Devil, bringing in evidence from "the religions of heathendom" as well as from Scripture (*The Sermons and Devotional Writings*, p. 199). It is even possible that Hopkins remembered Orion in "The Wreck" because the story of Orion's defeat by the earth-scorpion was an ironic reversal of the stories of Perseus or St George. But Hopkins' Orion is an "Orion of *light*," and therefore victorious, whereas the proud pagan hunter was defeated. (See Hyginus [*Poet. Astron.*, 2, "*Scorpius*"], where we are told that the constellation Scorpio was originally the scorpion which killed Orion, and that it has been placed in the heavens by Jupiter as a warning against too great self-confidence.)

6. "The Starlight Night," *Poems*, pp. 70, 71. And see also *The Journals and Papers of Gerard Manley Hopkins*, Humphry House and Graham Storey, eds, (London, 1959), p. 47, where Hopkins speaks of the "lantern of night, pierced in eyelets," and p. 254, where he says: "As we drove home the stars came out thick: I leant back to look at them and my heart opening more than usual praised our Lord to and in whom all that beauty comes home."
7. *Aen.*, 1: 535; 4: 52.
8. *Carm.*, 1: 28: 21.
9. *PL*, 75: 866.
10. *PL*, 111: 273, 274.
11. *Scriptores rerum Mythicarum Latini tres Romae nuper reperti*, G. H. Bode, ed. (Gottingen, 1834), p. 118.
12. *PL*, 172: 145.
13. 'Commentaria in Amos Prophetam," *Commentaria in Duodecim Prophetas Minores* (Venice, 1703), p. 216.
14. *Paradise Lost*, 1: 305, 306.
15. *Mystagogus Poeticus, or the Muses Interpreter* (London, 1653), pp. 334, 335.
16. For example, by the second Vatican mythographer (*loc. cit.*), and by Alexander Ross (*op. cit.*, p. 335).
17. *loc. cit.*, pp. 865–8.
18. *loc. cit.*
19. *op. cit.*, p. 217.
20. *loc. cit.*, p. 866; Cornelius quotes this passage exactly, but omits the second and third sentences.
21. *op. cit.*, p. 216.

3

What the lonely child saw: Charles Dickens' *Oliver Twist*

Oliver Twist is the earliest full expression of Dickens' vision of the world. It was first published in monthly instalments in *Bentley's Miscellany*, of which Dickens was then editor, and ran from February, 1837, to April, 1839. Dickens was just twenty-five when the first installment was published. Less than a year earlier he had leaped to national fame with *Pickwick Papers*. But *Oliver Twist*, though no less popular, was to be a very different sort of novel. Begun while *Pickwick Papers* was still appearing in monthly numbers, *Oliver Twist* is the first novel by Dickens to be planned as an integrated whole, rather than written as a series of disconnected episodes. And *Oliver Twist* presents in a pure and vivid form most of the characteristic scenes, figures, and motifs of Dickens' later novels. It could be said that Dickens' career as a novelist is an exploration or a gradual bringing to the surface of the implications and inner complexities of *Oliver Twist*. The complete meaning of such later masterpieces as *Great Expectations* and *Our Mutual Friend* can only be understood when they are set against the earlier novels; and all Dickens' novels, taken together, form an organic whole, a single great work which, as T. S. Eliot said of Shakespeare's plays, dramatizes, but in no obvious form, an action or struggle for harmony in the soul of the writer.[1]

I

Dickens' prefaces to *Oliver Twist*, however, tend to underplay the relation of the novel to its author's own life. In the various prefaces (written or revised in 1841, 1850, and 1867) Dickens had most in mind the need to defend his novel from the attacks of Thackeray and others. The attacks had come from two opposite directions. Some reviewers found *Oliver Twist* too ugly and sordid in its characters and scenes. Other readers associated Dickens' work with the "Newgate novels" of Bulwer and Ainsworth, novels which romanticized the life of thieves and outcasts. Dickens' defense against these attacks is to insist on the absolute truth-to-life of his portraits of Sikes, Nancy and the rest. In defending his novel on the grounds of its factual accuracy, Dickens uses the strategy traditional for English novelists. *Oliver Twist*, he says, is a faithful and exact reproduction of reality, and its virtue and utility lie in this alone. He has not imposed any preconceptions on what he has seen. He has neither added to reality nor distorted it in any way, but has made himself a perfect mirror reflecting reality as it is. English literature, from *The Beggar's Opera* down to the low-life novels of Dickens' own day, has presented thieves "as leading a life which is rather to be envied than otherwise." In place of romanticized highwaymen in lace neckcloths and polished jackboots, Dickens will present thieves as they really are, "in all the squalid misery of their lives," "for ever skulking uneasily through the dirtiest paths of life, with the great black ghastly gallows closing up their prospect, turn them where they [may]." The best defense of Fagin, Sikes, and Nancy, in all their sordidness and vice, is that they are "God's truth," and the purpose of the novel is that of all good journalistic reporting. Dickens will uncover hidden aspects of English life and persuade his readers to recognize a shocking situation. Since his purpose is to hold an undistorted mirror up to reality, he will not "abate one hole in the Dodger's coat, or one scrap of curl-paper in Nancy's dishevelled hair." Seen from this point of view, *Oliver Twist* continues the journalistic method Dickens learned as a newspaperman and used in his first work, the *Sketches by Boz*.[2] And coming as it does in 1837, the year of the queen's accession to the throne, *Oliver Twist* might be said to be the first important Victorian novel. It applies the traditional realism of European fiction to the new conditions of life coming into existence in England.

The aesthetic theory of Victorian fiction was usually based on the notion of what might be called "moralistic realism."[3] Novelists like George Eliot, Thackeray, and Trollope all tended to agree with Dickens that fiction is morally useful because it presents a sincere and accurate picture of things and people as they really are. Such fiction, in theory at least, was moralistic in the sense that it assumed undistorted pictures of real life would show us the consequences of bad or good acts, and persuade us to choose the good. And Victorian novelists thought of "realism" not as one convention among others. They saw it as objective mirroring or reporting of reality. They would have found dangerous or mistaken Henry James's idea of fiction as a house of many windows, each inhabited by a novelist with a unique view of reality.

Oliver Twist is in fact rooted in the reality of the eighteen-thirties. Saffron Hill, Bethnal Green, and the other slums mentioned in *Oliver Twist* were real places in London, notorious in Dickens' day as the dens of thieves and pickpockets. Dickens had seen these places with his own eyes, both as a newspaper reporter and during long walks to every corner of London. The streets through which the Artful Dodger leads Oliver when he first comes to London, the route followed by Sikes when he takes Oliver out in the country to rob the Maylie's house, the wanderings of Sikes after he has murdered Nancy – all these are scrupulously accurate itineraries and can be followed on an old map or retraced in the London of today. And other nineteenth-century reports corroborate Dickens' descriptions of the filth of London, the drunken, brawling crowds in the streets, the sordid rooms, so dark and dirty that they seem far underground, the fog, the mud, the rain, the somber river flowing through the city and bringing more dirt than it takes away. The London of *Oliver Twist,* which seems to a modern reader like the dream of an urban hell, is a literal representation of the city as it was in the early nineteenth century. Mr Fang, for example, the terrifying magistrate who nearly sentences Oliver to prison, is modeled on a real judge, a Mr Laing, well known at the time. Dickens had visited his court, and imitates his mannerisms and speech in this novel.

Not merely the décor, the scenic background, of *Oliver Twist* is based on historical reality. The situation of the hero springs no less from the reality of the time. As Humphry House has shown,[4] *Oliver Twist* is topical. The original subtitle of the novel was: "The Parish Boy's Progress." The story of little Oliver, the workhouse foundling, is based on the operations of the new Poor Law of 1834, and it attacks the Malthusian theory of society which lay behind that law. According to Malthus and the economists who followed him, the population of a country will always increase faster than the means of subsistence. Therefore there will always be a part of the population living in misery and unable to support itself. But this did not mean, to the "philosophers" Dickens attacked, that we should love our poor neighbors and feed and cherish them. If the poor persisted in breeding, they should be given relief in the most unpleasant way possible, and under conditions in which they could not breed at all. So, by the Act of 1834, workhouses were set up for the indigent. Life was made deliberately harsh in these houses. The food was barely enough to keep the paupers alive. (Oliver's diet of gruel is scarcely an exaggeration.) Husbands and wives were separated. Children were thrown in with adults. The poor were treated like criminals and outcasts, "millstones around the Parochial throat." To be in the workhouse was hardly better than being in prison.

Just as *Nicholas Nickleby* was to be directed against provincial schools, *Bleak House* against the Court of Chancery, and *Little Dorrit* against imprisonment for debt, so *Oliver Twist* is a propagandistic novel. Against the abstract theories of the economists, it sets the actual experiences of someone born into the workhouse system. Dickens' novel is in part a piece of literary journalism, an outcry against an objectively existing condition. It is a fictional transposition of real conditions for the purposes of preaching reform. The voice of the narrator is that of Dickens himself. This narrator is detached from the events he describes. He speaks with alternate irony and sentiment, deliberately manipulating his materials for effect. The very tone of his voice tells us that he is himself safe, one of the lucky and well-to-do. His own life is not in danger. He writes out of sympathy for the sufferings of others, and describes with objective anger, from a distance, the experiences of one of the victims of social injustice. This detachment of the narrator from the events he describes is a necessary part of the realistic method Dickens employs. As Ian Watt has shown,[5] realism in the novel is associated with the appearance of modern philosophical realism in Descartes and Locke. The philosophical realist who puts all in doubt and the objective narrator of a realistic novel both adopt the stance of the scientist, rejecting traditional assumptions, effacing their own preconceptions, and confronting reality as directly and immediately as possible. Dickens uses this stance in *Oliver Twist* to persuade the reader of the truth-to-life of the scenes and characters he presents. His propagandistic purpose can best be served if he persuades his readers of the detached objectivity of his vision.

Life in the slums of London is rendered in *Oliver Twist* with such a combination of realistic detail and the grotesque twistings or exaggerations of the inimitable Dickensian imagination that the novel, in the end, has come to determine our idea of what Victorian London was like. For many people Victorian London *is* Dickensian London, and to think of one is to think of the other.

II

But *Oliver Twist* is more than simply an extension of the realistic reporting of the *Sketches by Boz*, though the germ of many aspects of the novel may be found in the earlier work. Against the dark background of the new Poor Law workhouses and the thieves' kitchens of Saffron Hill, Dickens presents the story of Oliver Twist, the parish foundling, "the humble, half-starved drudge – to be cuffed and buffeted through the world – despised by all, and pitied by none." Only if a dramatic action is presented against the realistic background can the book become a novel at all, and not a mere series of sketches.

The dramatic action of *Oliver Twist* has a double source. On the one hand it is the age-old story of the dispossessed heir. It has connections with fairy tales, with religious allegory, and with such characteristic eighteenth-century novels as *Tom Jones*. Tom Jones too is an illegitimate child who after many adventures discovers his parents and recovers his rightful inheritance. From this point of view *Oliver Twist* might be said to be an adaptation of this traditional plot to the particular situation of industrialized man in nineteenth-century England. It is old wine in a new bottle. Dickens is affirming his sense of the continuity of human experience. Even in the changed circumstances of modern life, even in the slums of London, life is still the same, and we can still see the same eternal laws of human destiny in operation. But on the other hand the melodramatic plot of *Oliver Twist* is a shadowing-forth of Dickens' own experiences as a child. It is no mere stylized repetition of an archetypal plot. Dickens can tell Oliver's story with such vividness and intensity because it is an imaginative expression of his sense of his own life. In *Oliver Twist*, as in most great art, the particular is universalized.

For Dickens himself had experienced the anguish of the outcast, the terror of the abandoned child, passive victim of incomprehensible cruelties and unjust punishments. And in most of Dickens' novels, the lonely child, orphan or illegitimate or both, holds the center of the stage. In an autobiographical fragment, written at the time of *David Copperfield*, and shown to his friend John Forster, Dickens tells the story of the traumatic experience of his childhood, the imprisonment of his father in the Marshalsea debtors' prison, and his own "imprisonment" as a drudge in a blacking factory. This experience fixed forever in Dickens' mind the fear of becoming once again abandoned and excluded from happiness. And in novel after novel he tried to exorcise this fear, to find some believable way to escape from it.

The autobiographical fragment gives us an important clue to the meaning of the motif of the lonely child in Dickens' novels. Dickens' experiences in Warren's blacking factory might not have seemed so bad to another child. What made the experience so catastrophic was that Dickens had been led to expect something better. His parents had treated him as a child of great talent, as indeed he was, and had led him to expect a gentleman's education and career. Now, with the fall of his family, all those great expectations are gone forever, and he sinks into the situation of the outcast. "No words," says Dickens,

> can express the secret agony of my soul as I sunk into this companionship; compared these everyday associates with those of my happier childhood; and felt my early hopes of growing up to be a learned and distinguished man, crushed in my breast. The deep remembrance of the sense I had of being utterly neglected and hopeless; of the shame I felt in my position; of the misery it was to my young heart to believe that, day by day, what I had learned, and thought, and delighted in, and raised my fancy and my emulation up by, was passing away from me, never to be brought back any more; cannot be written. My whole nature was so penetrated with the grief and humiliation of such considerations, that even now, famous

> and caressed and happy, I often forget in my dreams that I have a dear wife and children; and even that I am a man; and wander desolately back to that time of my life.[6]

The center of this experience is a spiritual change which seems to the young Dickens to be caused in him by the change in his surroundings. Before, he had felt certain that he would grow up to be a learned and distinguished man. Already he possessed in anticipation the reality of that future self. Now he feels himself literally ceasing to be what he was. It is as though the reality and solidity of his life, the very substance of what he has been, is slipping away, and he is falling into an abyss of nonentity. The language Dickens uses to describe this change is significant. He says he *sank* into the companionship of the other factory boys, that he felt his old identity *passing away*, never to be recovered, and that he was *penetrated* with the grief and humiliation of his condition. He felt as if the very stuff of his being were slipping away and being replaced by the new selfhood of the outcast. His identity was slipping away not so much because of his new surroundings as because he felt that he had been abandoned to them by his parents. "It is wonderful to me," he writes,

> that, even after my descent into the poor little drudge I had been since we came to London, no one had compassion enough on me – a child of singular abilities, quick, eager, delicate, and soon hurt, bodily or mentally – to suggest that something might have been spared, as certainly it might have been, to place me at any common school. Our friends, I take it, were tired out. No one made any sign. My father and mother were quite satisfied. They could hardly have been more so if I had been twenty years of age, distinguished at a grammar-school, and going to Cambridge.[7]

Dickens' experience in the blacking factory is a prolonged endurance of the nightmare of the lost child, the child who looks around in a crowd and suddenly realizes that his parents are no longer there. Dickens never really escapes from this sense of abandonment. Even when he is famous and happy, with a wife and children, he wanders back to that desolate condition in his dreams. In his novels the experience is usually projected in the situation of a hero who has never known any parents at all, and who, as long as he can remember, has been unwanted and unloved by all the world.

The dramatic action of *Oliver Twist* is more than simply a means by which Dickens can accomplish his propagandistic aim. It is also an early example of Dickens' expression in his fiction of the central experience of his own life. This doubleness in the novel may be seen in the doubleness of point of view. For *Oliver Twist*, after all, does not give us merely the attitude of the narrator. The novel is made of the superimposition of two consciousnesses: the consciousness of the narrator, safely above all Oliver's sufferings, and the consciousness of Oliver himself, trapped in his situation without apparent hope of escape. The novel fluctuates between these two consciousnesses, sometimes commenting, with a wise irony far beyond Oliver's power, on the experiences of the hero, sometimes plunging us directly into the hero's blind suffering and fear. It is certainly true that the direct presentation, from the inside, of Oliver's suffering aids Dickens' moralistic intent. Through our identification with Oliver's experiences, we are led to pity him and to feel righteous indignation against the unjust institutions which have made him suffer. And to see Fagin and Sikes through Oliver's eyes is to see them as all the more frightening and terrible, all the more a danger to the nation. But the detached objectivity of the narrator is perhaps more obviously associated with the stance of Dickens the reformer, and the presentation of Oliver's inner experiences becomes in the novel something transcending its propagandistic uses, something we find interesting for its own sake.

But the two points of view, Oliver's and the detached narrator's, are similar as well as different. It is impossible simply to oppose them, and in their similarity we may perhaps catch a glimpse of the origin of Dickens' comic gift. Oliver sees the world through the eyes of a frightened child. Things appear to him as ferocious and sinister, distorted by his youth and his fear into something larger than life, as the rooms in the old house where Fagin imprisons him have "great high wooden chimney-pieces and large doors, with panelled walls and cornices to the ceiling," or as Fagin gliding stealthily along the streets on a black night seems "like some loathsome reptile, engendered in the slime and darkness through which he moves." But this particular vision of Fagin as a primeval monster is not seen through Oliver's eyes at all. It is presented directly by the adult narrator. The narrator too sees the world as ferocious and sinister, and heightens reality with fantasy. Nevertheless, it might be said that Dickens' special innovation in literature is the presentation of the realities of city life as seen through the eyes of a lonely child. The adult narrator shares this transforming vision, the power to see modern reality as something strange or grotesque, something with the heightened menace or attraction of scenes in a fairy tale or dream. Indeed Dickens' genius for comedy can be seen as a permutation of the child's vision. Mr Bumble in *Oliver Twist*, like Jingle, Sairey Gamp, Mr Micawber, or a host of characters in other novels, is seen with the same exaggerating child's perspective that creates Fagin or Sikes. But in the comic characters the terrified vision of the child, generated out of the very passivity and hopelessness of his fear, is transformed into the perspective of the humorist who sees people from the safety of his detachment. Mr Bumble, in fact, is seen both from Oliver's point of view and from that of the narrator. The vision of Oliver and the vision of the narrator are subtly continuous, just as the novel itself is both an objective plea for reform and an imaginative re-creation of Dickens' own experiences as a child.

III

But though the personal impetus behind the story of Oliver's adventures may be Dickens' own early life, the dramatic action of *Oliver Twist* has its own form and meaning, a form and meaning which far transcend their source.

We may notice, first of all, that Dickens makes the situation of his hero significantly different from his own situation. The orphan is in one way in a better position than was Dickens in the blacking factory. The real bitterness of Dickens' experience was the feeling that his parents did not care, that they had willingly abandoned him to his degradation. He felt not only hopeless, but intentionally neglected. But Oliver Twist has never been known by his parents at all. Dickens' own sense of being treated unjustly by his parents is transformed into the situation of someone who has been deprived of his parents since birth. But in another way Oliver's situation is worse than Dickens' own, for Oliver is treated far more cruelly than Dickens ever was. In *Oliver Twist* the whole world is a bad parent, a kind of collective wicked stepmother bent on destroying the helpless foundling.

The key to the meaning of the novel is a sentence in the preface of 1841 in which Dickens says that he "wished to show, in little Oliver, the principle of Good surviving through every adverse circumstance, and triumphing at last." The novel dramatizes the situation of the naturally good soul cast out into what seems to him a world of complete evil. As Graham Greene has suggested,[8] there is something Manichean in this situation. Not that a good God does not exist for Oliver. God exists all right, but not, apparently, in *this* world. This world seems entirely dark, entirely evil. As Oliver himself says: "Heaven is a long way off; and they are too happy there, to come down to the bedside of a poor boy." Oliver is as it were a spark of divine goodness exiled and imprisoned in what appears to be a realm of complete evil. This idea of the good soul in an evil world, like much else in *Oliver Twist*, is of course derived from the traditional Christian view of man's lot, or perhaps one should say that it comes from Christianity as sentimentalized by Rousseau and Wordsworth. For in two ways it deviates from the central Christian tradition: in the rejection of original sin implied in the notion of Oliver's perfect and incorruptible goodness, and in the way the world is seen, at least initially, as bereft of the immanent presence of God. Like other nineteenth-century works which grew out of Protestantism (*Wuthering Heights* is an excellent example), *Oliver Twist* pushes to an extreme certain aspects of Christianity and minimizes others.

In *Oliver Twist* happiness and escape from suffering tend to be associated with death. Happiness is possible only somewhere out of this world. Rose Maylie, for example, is too good for earthly existence. Just as Dickens' seventeen-year-old sister-in-law Mary Hogarth died while Dickens was writing *Oliver Twist*, so, in the novel, Rose Maylie nearly dies of an illness which seems to express more than anything else her sheer unfitness for this world. She is "as fair and innocent of guile as one of God's own angels," and therefore, asks Dickens, "who could hope, when the distant world to which she was akin, half opened to her view, that she would return to the sorrow and calamity of this?" In the same way, Oliver, when he is rescued by Mr Brownlow, falls into a deep sleep, a sleep which is a kind of rehearsal of death. Again Dickens associates escape from suffering with escape from the world: "Who, if this were death, would be roused again to all the struggles and turmoils of life; to all its cares for the present; its anxieties for the future; more than all, its weary recollections of the past!" And when Oliver is rescued once more by the Maylies, Dickens says: "He felt calm and happy, and could have died without a murmur."

This world, then, seems to be totally bad, a place of sorrows and calamities, struggles and turmoils. *Oliver Twist* expresses this assumption very powerfully in the experiences of its hero. Oliver finds himself in a world full of an inexplicable malevolence. He is "the victim of a systematic course of treachery and deception." There seems to be a general conspiracy to destroy him out of hand, to starve him, or smother him, or crush him, or terrify him by imprisonment into hanging himself. And when he escapes from the cruelties of the Sowerberrys and Bumble, he is drawn by a kind of fatality into the center of the world's evil: London. The London of *Oliver Twist* is indeed a kind of urban hell, and Oliver's adventures there are probably what most readers remember longest from the novel. The city is presented as an infernal labyrinth, dirty, dark, choked in fog and rain. Oliver is as effectively imprisoned there when he is out in the streets as when he is locked in one of the thieves' dens. And at the center of the labyrinth crouches Fagin, the evil genius of this underworld. As other critics have noted, Fagin is constantly presented in ways that associate him with the devil.[9] We see him crouching over the fire with a toasting fork, or gloating over his hidden treasure, or creeping along the muddy streets, like a hideous monster "crawling forth, by night, in search of some rich offal for a meal."

The inevitable effect of this environment, and of the deliberate efforts of Fagin and his associates, will apparently be to quench the divine goodness in Oliver, and make him, like the others, an evil soul in an evil world. "In short," says Dickens,

> the wily old Jew had the boy in his toils. Having prepared his mind, by solitude and gloom, to prefer any society to the companionship of his own sad thoughts in such a dreary place, he was now slowly instilling into his soul the poison which he hoped would blacken it, and change its hue for ever.

And in another place we hear Fagin boasting of the success of his plans: "Once let him feel that he is one of us; once fill his mind with the idea that he has been a thief; and he's ours!"

"Desolate and deserted," "alone in the midst of wickedness and guilt," "hedged round and round," Oliver's reaction to his experiences is uncomprehending bewilderment. We see him "stunned," his senses "confounded," by a tumult of disordered sights and sounds in Smithfield, or "quite overpowered by fatigue and the fumes of the tobacco," or "scarcely knowing where he is, or what is passing around him," and, in any case, "completely stupefied" by his experiences. Oliver's world is either an empty solitude or a confused mass of sense impressions, but in either case it is incomprehensible to him. He can find no way to understand it or relate himself to it. He can only passively endure whatever happens to him. Perhaps the passage which best expresses his state is the description of Oliver's imprisonment in an old empty house when he is recaptured by Fagin. Here a duration of passive suffering made up of the alternation of solitude and bewildering multiplicity is perfectly epitomized:

> there was neither sight nor sound of any living thing; and often, when it grew dark, and he was tired of wandering from room to room, he would crouch in the corner of the passage by the street-door, to be as near living people as he could; and would remain there, listening and counting the hours, until the Jew or the boys returned. . . . There was a back-garret window with rusty bars outside, which had no shutter; and out of this, Oliver often gazed with a melancholy face for hours together; but nothing was to be descried from it but a confused and crowded mass of housetops, blackened chimneys, and gable-ends.

Oliver can defend himself from the malevolence of the world only because "nature or inheritance" has "implanted a good sturdy spirit" in his breast. He is "a child of a noble nature and a warm heart," and "that Power which has thought fit to try him beyond his years, has planted in his breast affections and feelings which would do honour to many who have numbered his days six times over." Again Dickens' language is significant. Oliver's goodness is *implanted* in him by God, *planted* in his breast ineradicably as something which is part of his very substance, and yet comes from beyond him. His goodness is his way of participating in the universal power of good. He is naturally and inalterably good, though he dwells in a world of evil. Whatever happens to him, this goodness will be unstained, untainted.

Oliver's incorruptible goodness is a combination of the Rousseauistic doctrine of the natural goodness of man and the Protestant doctrine of election. For in *Oliver Twist* some people are more naturally good than others. Sikes the brutal housebreaker and Nancy his mistress were, like Oliver, naturally good at birth. Though Sikes is one of those "insensible and callous natures, that do become utterly and incurably bad," nevertheless this badness is what he has become, not what he was at the beginning. His badness is the corruption of an originally good nature. And Nancy's betrayal of Sikes, which saves Oliver, is "the last fair drop of water at the bottom of the weed-choked well." Like Rose Maylie herself, Nancy was once a well of purity and innocence. But the world, powerless against Oliver, has corrupted Nancy, though her good acts manifest "a soul of goodness in things evil." Here many readers have seen a conflict between the propagandistic intent and the dramatic action of the novel. One of Dickens' strongest arguments against the new Poor Law is the way it breeds criminality. Pauper orphans thrown together with hardened adults grow up to be thieves and prostitutes themselves. Dickens' sociological theory depends on the idea that a bad environment produces bad people. The evil and injustice of the world is the work of man and can be ameliorated by man. But the story of the novel depends on the opposite notion: the image of an invulnerable goodness persisting unstained through all attempts to deprave it. The context here is not sociological but religious. The dramatic action of *Oliver Twist* is, as Kathleen Tillotson says, a "moral fairytale," "the necessary embodiment of [Dickens'] moral optimism – and, less consciously, of his impulse towards fairytale and romance in his heroes and heroines."[10] Sikes and Nancy are good propaganda against heartless treatment of the poor, but the life of Oliver is no argument against slums and workhouses, except as it arouses our pity for his unmerited suffering. And this suffering, from the religious point of view, is a providential testing.

Moreover, we can see in Oliver's incorruptible goodness another important motif of the novel. For Oliver need not *do* anything to ensure his own ultimate salvation. He need only endure his suffering passively. The terms of his father's will are of great importance here. Oliver is to inherit his father's money on condition that "he should never have stained his name with any public act of dishonour, meanness, cowardice, or wrong." It might be possible to see a hint of religious allegory in the conditions of the will. Oliver has been cast by God the Father into this vale of tears, and will inherit a room in the mansions of heaven if he obeys God's will and keeps his soul pure. But the conditions of the will operate more importantly to give us a basis for judging Oliver's reactions. Oliver must not to the least degree become an accomplice of the thieves, not even by reacting to violence with violence. What might otherwise seem weakness is shown to be the only way to salvation. It might seem that Oliver's passivity is all we could expect from a child of his age. But the Artful Dodger, with his irrepressible energy, his resolute (and witty) defiance of all constituted authority, represents the other possibility. The Dodger is "about [Oliver's] own age." He has begun in Oliver's situation, but he has reacted in exactly the opposite way. He does not have the special grace and the "nature or inheritance" of good which guard Oliver and make him naturally a gentleman in speech and action. Without this grace and this inheritance the Dodger has become the natural child of the slums, the boy one might have expected Oliver to become. But this is inevitable if the Dodger acts at all. For in such an evil environment any act is "dishonorable." You cannot touch pitch without being defiled. The consequences of positive action in the London of *Oliver Twist* are shown in the Dodger, Sikes, Fagin, and the other thieves. Like Oliver they have been born good in an evil world, but unlike Oliver they have not been merely passive sufferers. They have taken matters into their own hands, have created their own hidden society in the slums, and have seized by force the goods of the world which have been denied to them. Their punishment for this is the end which shadows all the book: death by hanging. *Oliver Twist* expresses Dickens' fear that the orphan child, outcast and victim, will grow up to be the man of resentment, the outlaw whose hand is against everyone. It is probably not fanciful to associate Oliver's providential escape from what seems his inevitable fate with Dickens' feelings about his own plight when he worked in the blacking factory. "I know," Dickens writes, "that, but for the mercy of God, I might easily have been, for any care that was taken of me, a little robber or a little vagabond."[11] In the deaths of Fagin and Sikes we can see fulfilled the destiny that might, but for the grace of God, have been Dickens' own, and those deaths are also the fulfilment of the prophecy of the man in the white waistcoat who said Oliver would come to be hanged. In their deaths we can see enacted the fate which waits for Oliver if he lifts his finger in any positive action. In a way he is most in danger when he "asks for more," and when he fights Noah Claypole for having insulted his mother. These are his only aggressive acts, and society reacts by imprisoning him and labeling him gallows-bait. If he had continued in this direction he would indeed have come to be hanged, like Fagin and Sikes. His only hope is passivity.

The importance of Oliver's passivity may be seen if we compare *Oliver Twist* with *Tom Jones*. Both novels have the same basic plot: the illegitimate child recovers his inheritance after a prolonged period of testing. With Tom Jones, however, it is not a question of action versus passivity, but of the proper sort of action. Tom must learn to temper his natural impetuosity with prudence. But Oliver must refrain altogether from action, just as Dickens' later heroes tend not to be characterized by the strength of their wills or the efficacy of their actions. Even Pip waits passively for his great expectations to be bestowed from above.

And here too we can see the deeper significance of the unlikely coincidences which bring Oliver to be unwittingly involved in the robberies of his father's oldest friend and of the household of his aunt. These coincidences are of course part of the workings of Providence in the novel. A "stronger hand than chance" protects the principle of Good lost in an evil world, and leads Oliver to Mr Brownlow and to Rose Maylie. But the coincidences also dramatize further the disaster which lies in wait for Oliver if he takes positive action. If Oliver persists in his passive goodness he will somehow inherit, in this world or the next, the place which is rightfully his. If he seizes by force the goods of this world, he will in effect be robbing his own parents, and then can be justly deprived forever of the goods which ought to be his.

IV

Oliver's encounters with Mr Brownlow and the Maylies are of importance for him in another way. Through them he discovers that the malice and cruelty, which he has found everywhere else in the world, from the paupers' workhouse to the slums of London, are not universal. Within this world, but not part of the infernal labyrinth of London, lie areas which are as it were outposts of heaven, reminiscences and anticipations of that bliss Oliver lost when he was born and will apparently recover only after his death. Such outposts are the house of Mr Brownlow (to which Oliver is taken after he faints in Mr Fang's court), and the estate of the Maylies (where Oliver is received after the fiasco of the robbery). These places, little islands of goodness in a world of evil, are associated in Dickens' imagination with a consistent set of motifs. The Brownlows and Maylies of the world, like Oliver himself, are not part of the dog-eat-dog life of the city. As George Orwell has observed,[12] Dickens rarely shows his good people soiling their hands by the act of earning money. In one way or another, often unspecified, they are rich to start with, and thus avoid the curse which hangs, for Dickens, over any positive action. They need only spend money, not earn it, and they use their money to create for themselves a protected enclosure in the midst of the bad world.

This enclosure is associated by Dickens with three related motifs:

death, the past, and rural nature. All three suggest a separation from present-day life in the city. Oliver nearly dies when he is rescued by Mr Brownlow, and Brownlow himself is presented as a man whose dearest friends "lie deep in their graves." Oliver is dangerously ill again when he is taken in by the Maylies, and Rose Maylie, as we have seen, nearly dies of a fever. Some version of the motif of death appears whenever Oliver enters the good world.

But these islands of good are also associated by Dickens with the past. They hide the secrets of Oliver's birth and of the family he lost when he was born. On Mr Brownlow's wall is a portrait of a beautiful lady who turns out to be Oliver's own mother, and Rose Maylie turns out to be his closest living relative, his mother's sister. Everywhere in the good world Oliver finds hints and covert indications of past events, events which took place before his birth, and which he must rediscover in order to claim his rightful place in the world. The past which he must uncover lies now in the realm of death, and must be as it were resurrected into the present.

The areas of good are also associated with rural nature. If nature in London is bad, like the people who live there, nature in the country is beneficent and peaceful, a "foretaste of heaven." As in *The Old Curiosity Shop* and elsewhere, Dickens here reaffirms the contrast between country and city which is so important in eighteenth-century and romantic literature. As in *Tom Jones*, the city is a kind of earthly hell, and man's closest approach, on earth, to paradisiacal happiness is possible only in the country. As the place which is a kind of heaven on earth, the country in *Oliver Twist* is constantly associated with death. A whole chapter is given to Rose Maylie's sickness in the midst of idyllic rural scenery; there is a long paragraph about city-dwellers who go to the country to die, and a little churchyard is one of the chief items of scenery Oliver can see from his cottage window. Oliver often wanders there and thinks of his dead mother, and there he witnesses the funeral of a young girl who is buried while Rose Maylie lies so dangerously ill. So closely are the country scenes associated with death that it seems natural for them to be the place where it is possible to experience a direct remembrance and foretaste of heaven. Several times in the novel Dickens tells us that country scenes are a kind of stimulus to involuntary reminiscence, the affective memory of times long gone by. As for Proust, so for Dickens, something seen or heard in the present can bring back the past in all its immediacy. For Dickens, however, as sometimes for Wordsworth, it is reminiscence not of the earthly past, but of experiences we have never had in this world, and will never have again until we are out of it again:

> Thus, a strain of gentle music, or the rippling of water in a silent place, or the odour of a flower, or the mention of a familiar word, will

> sometimes call up sudden dim remembrances of scenes that never were, in this life; which vanish like a breath; which some brief memory of a happier existence, long gone by, would seem to have awakened; which no voluntary exertion of the mind can ever recall.

> The memories which peaceful country scenes call up, are not of this world, nor of its thoughts and hopes. Their gentle influence may teach us how to weave fresh garlands for the graves of those we loved . . . ; but beneath all this, there lingers, in the least reflective mind, a vague and half-formed consciousness of having held such feelings long before, in some remote and distant time, which calls up solemn thoughts of distant times to come, and bends down pride and worldliness beneath it.

But though heaven at first seems "a long way off" to Oliver, it is, in fact, represented on earth by certain select areas where God's grace and love seem to be directly present. And the dramatic action of the novel is made up of abrupt and unpredictable reversals, in which Oliver is suddenly rescued from the bad world, and then just as suddenly plunged back into it again. As Dickens himself said, the novel is based on a melodramatic principle of alternation, in which happiness and sadness follow one another "as the layers of red and white in a side of streaky bacon." Dickens claims, however, that such "violent transitions and abrupt impulses of passion or feeling" are true to life, and do not make the novel unrealistic.

The novel, however, is not simply made up of an aimless alternation between the good and bad worlds. Gradually, through this very alternation, Oliver finds that Providence has been working in his life all along. And gradually, through discoveries made in both worlds, Oliver comes to find out the secrets of his birth. He recovers his past, his inheritance, and his rightful place in society. In the end he escapes permanently from the world of Fagin and Sikes, is adopted by Mr Brownlow "as his own son," and becomes part of "a little society, whose condition approached as nearly to one of perfect happiness as can ever be known in this changing world." We leave Oliver living happily ever after a life entirely oriented toward the past, a life still passive rather than active, a life in which he is willing to be a mere repetition of his dead father rather than an independent person in his own right:

> Mr Brownlow went on, from day to day, filling the mind of his adopted child with stores of knowledge, and becoming attached to him more and more, as his nature developed itself, and showed the thriving seeds of all he wished him to become – [and] he traced in him new traits of his early friend, that awakened in his bosom old remembrances, melancholy and yet sweet and soothing –

In *Oliver Twist*, then, Dickens composed his version of a story traditional in fairy tale, in religious allegory, and in earlier fiction. He refitted this story to the conditions of life in industrialized England, and told it with a profusion of exact and circumstantial detail which assimilated it to its new environment. Oliver's sufferings in the labyrinthine city thereby became a notable expression of the spiritual anguish and sense of alienation generated by all the changes which have produced the modern world. Oliver's situation reappears in one form or another in most important fiction of the last hundred and fifty years, and there is, for example, a direct line from Dickens to Dostoevsky and Kafka, both of whom acknowledged their great debt to Dickens. But in adapting the traditional story to the new conditions Dickens changed it significantly. As we have seen, he must make his hero more acted on than acting, and there must be a breaking of the continuity between the evil world and the secluded spot where the hero lives happily ever after. Paradise Hall, in *Tom Jones*, is a recognizable and contemporary part of the same England that contains the dangerous city. But the cottages of the Maylies and Mr Brownlow hardly seem to exist in the same world as the dark dens of Fagin. There is something nostalgic about these rural nooks, something oriented, like Oliver himself, toward a past of settled values which is radically endangered by industrialization, and can exist only in sealed enclosures cut off from the forward-moving stream of history. Later on, the happiness proposed for Oliver was to seem less possible to attain, even to Dickens himself, not to speak of Hardy or Conrad or Kafka. *Oliver Twist* might be defined as one of the last expressions of a long tradition.

V

Anticipation of the later Dickens, the Dickens for whom the happy ending of *Oliver Twist* is impossible, can be seen in his attitude toward Fagin and Sikes. As other critics have noted, Dickens' treatment of the thieves, though it is melodramatic enough, is not marked by the sentimentality which damages the rest of the book. A modern reader finds it easier to believe in Fagin and Sikes than in Rose Maylie or Harry. And though Dickens in his prefaces speaks of the thieves objectively, as sociological facts which have nothing to do with his own life, in the novel his sympathy goes out to them. He identifies himself with them. In a way the most impressive parts of the book are the accounts of the wanderings of Sikes after the murder of Nancy, and of Fagin's sufferings in court and in the condemned cell. And in both cases the treatments are subjective. We are put within the minds of Sikes and Fagin, and suffer with them. And when Oliver visits Fagin just before he is hanged, and the old man cries, "He has been the – the – somehow the cause of all this," our sympathy is all with the condemned man. Oliver has won happiness with the good people, but only by betraying the hidden society of the thieves, the underworld which must be sacrificed to his happiness.

It would be easy to say that Dickens' sympathy for Fagin and Sikes, the vividness of their portraits, and Dickens' ability to present their experiences from the inside are merely the result of the normal power of the dramatic writer to enter into his imagined characters. And it is a cliché to say that it is easier to present bad characters than good. But I think there is more to the matter than this. Just as Shakespeare and Browning are to be found entire in no single one of their characters, but are present in all, even the villains, and just as Dostoevsky expressed himself as much in Kirillov, Stavrogin, or Ivan Karamazov as in Alyosha or Prince Myshkin, so Dickens was expressing part of himself in Sikes, or in Quilp in *The Old Curiosity Shop*, even though it may have been a part of himself he rejected and effaced in his own life.

When Dickens in 1869, many years after the writing of *Oliver Twist*, came to make a public reading out of the novel, it was not Oliver's happiness with Mr Brownlow or the Maylies which he chose to adapt. It was Sikes' murder of Nancy, and he turned this section of the novel into a terrific monologue, a monologue which he performed again and again in his readings, often four nights in a single week. The effect of these readings was tremendous. "We had a contagion of fainting," he wrote of one of them, "and yet the place was not hot. I should think we had from a dozen to twenty ladies taken out stiff and rigid at various times!" During these readings Dickens' pulse rose dangerously, and he was prostrate afterwards. The readings were in fact a major cause of his death in 1870. Dickens' compulsive re-enactment of the murder of Nancy is perhaps his most revealing comment on *Oliver Twist*. It leads us to see Fagin, Sikes, and the other thieves as victims of society, more sinned against than sinning. Our hearts should go out to them in pity and sympathy. Dickens as much identifies himself with them as with little Oliver, and in this sympathy for people who in the older versions of the story would have been seen as unequivocally evil there is an anticipation of Dickens' later sympathy for such characters as Magwitch in *Great Expectations* or John Jasper in *The Mystery of Edwin Drood*.

The best way, in fact, to see the relation of *Oliver Twist* to Dickens' later novels is to set it against *Great Expectations*. Pip too is an orphan, and like Oliver he passively awaits for the goods of the world to be given to him. He looks upon these goods as something he deserves for what he is rather than for what he does. Somewhere, he feels, there is a place waiting for him among the happy and secure. But all Pip's expectations are exploded. The actual source of his wealth and status as a gentleman turns out to be a strange permutation of Mr Brownlow – Magwitch, transported felon and "hunted dunghill dog," a man more like Fagin or Sikes than like any of the good characters in *Oliver Twist*. The secure seclusion of Mr Brownlow's "little society" exists nowhere in *Great Expectations*. Its closest parallel is the inturned solitude and spiritual imprisonment of Miss Havisham in Satis House. And Pip finds that he must accept responsibility for his own actions, make his own way amidst all the ambiguities and pitfalls of our industrial and commercial world. In his relations to other people he must initiate something novel rather than merely repeating the old. It is significant that Dickens uses the language of fairy tales to express the fatuity of Pip's expectations. Pip looks upon himself as the magic prince who is destined to set free the enchanted maiden and inherit the kingdom. In rejecting Pip's fantasies Dickens is also rejecting the tradition which lies behind *Oliver Twist*. He replaces the old idea of the acceptance of the given with the new morality of the creation of the new. Gradually, throughout his whole career as a novelist, Dickens puts in question, one by one, the assumptions of his early work, until finally his last masterpieces, *Great Expectations* and *Our Mutual Friend*, are categorical reversals of *Oliver Twist*. The early novel is the first act in a drama which includes all of Dickens' novels. This drama is made up of the gradual bringing to the surface of the ultimate implications, both social and existential, of the vision of the world so powerfully expressed in *Oliver Twist*.

Notes

1. See T. S. Eliot, *Selected Essays*, 1917–32 (New York, 1947), p. 173.
2. For a discussion of the relation between *Oliver Twist* and the *Sketches by Boz*, see Kathleen Tillotson, *"Oliver Twist," Essays and Studies by Members of the English Association*, XII (London, 1959), pp. 90, 91.
3. See Kathleen Tillotson, *Novels of the Eighteen-Forties* (London, 1954), Monroe Engel, "Dickens on Art," *Modern Philology*, LIII (1955), pp. 25–38, and Richard Stang, *The Theory of the Novel in England, 1850–1870* (New York, 1959) for discussions of the complexities of the Victorian theory of the novel.
4. See *The Dickens World* (London, 1941), and House's Introduction to *Oliver Twist* in the New Oxford Illustrated Dickens edition of the novel (London, 1949), pp. xii–xiv.
5. *The Rise of the Novel* (Berkeley and Los Angeles, 1957), pp. 9–34.
6. John Forster, *The Life of Charles Dickens* (Philadelphia, 1873), I, p. 53.
7. *ibid.*, p. 51.
8. See his essay on *Oliver Twist* in *The Lost Childhood and Other Essays* (London, 1951).
9. See Lauriat Lane, Jr, "The Devil in *Oliver Twist*," *The Dickensian*, LII (1956), pp. 132–36.
10. "*Oliver Twist*," *loc. cit.*, pp. 91, 92.
11. Forster, I, p. 57.
12. See his essay on Dickens in *Dickens, Dali, and Others* (New York, 1946).

4

The theme of the disappearance of God in Victorian poetry

Post-medieval literature records, among other things, the gradual withdrawal of God from the world.* This long process is nearly accomplished by the nineteenth century. Many Victorian writers find themselves in the situation of the characters in *Vanity Fair*. They are "a set of people living without God in the world."[1] This situation must not be misunderstood. It does not mean blank atheism (the "God is dead" of Nietzsche) as it is often interpreted. God, for such writers, still lives, but, as Hölderlin said, he lives "above our heads, up there in a different world."[2] Arthur Hugh Clough expresses perfectly this paradoxical belief in a God of whose existence there is no immediate evidence:

> That there are beings above us, I believe,
> And when we lift up holy hands of prayer,
> I will not say they will not give us aid.[3]

He will not say the gods do not care for man, but neither will he say they do. For such a man God exists, but is out of reach. The lines of connection between man and God have broken down, or God himself has slipped away from the places where he used to be.

How did this situation come about? In the Presocratic philosophers,[4] in the earliest books of the Old Testament,[5] perhaps even in archaic Egyptian sculpture,[6] we can see evidence that our culture, at its beginnings, experienced the divine power as immanent in nature, in society, and in each man's heart. So Moses saw God in the burning bush, and so Parmenides and Heraclitus are philosopher-poets of total immanence. And even though the central tradition of Western civilization, in later Judaism, in Platonism, and in Christianity, defines God as transcending his creation, the miracle of the Incarnation brought God back to earth, so that once more he walked among us as he had before the fall, when history had not yet begun. Christ was seen as the mediator joining a fallen world and a distant God, and the daily re-enactment of the Incarnation on all the altars of Christendom was the manifestation and guarantee of communion. Poetry in turn was, in one way or another,[7] modeled on sacramental or scriptural language. The words of the poems participated in the things they named, just as the words of the Mass shared in the transformation they evoked.

The history of modern literature is in part the history of the splitting apart of this communion which has been matched by a similar dispersal of the cultural unity of man. God, nature, and language. The transformations making up this dispersal can be identified easily enough, even though the question of which change causes the others can never be answered. In the social and material worlds there are those changes associated with the rise of science and technology: industrialization, the increasing predominance of the middle class, the gradual breakdown of the old hierarchical class structure, the building of great cities. In the modern world nature is slowly *humanized* until, finally, man is surrounded by things he has made over into their present form. The city is the objective manifestation of this humanization of the world. And where is there room for God in the city? Though it is impossible to tell whether man has excluded God by building his great cities, or whether the cities have been built because God has disappeared, in any case the two go together. Life in the city is the way in which many men have experienced most directly what it means to live without God in the world.

Paralleling the development of urban, technologized life there has been a gradual dissipation of the medieval symbolism of participation. Many scholars have studied the breaking of the circle, the untuning of the sky, the change from the closed world to the infinite universe which slowly destroys the old polyphonic harmony of microcosm and macrocosm.[8] During this process belief in the Incarnation begins gradually to die out of the European consciousness. The Reformation, if not immediately, certainly in its ultimate effects, means a weakening of belief in the sacrament of communion. The bread and wine come to be seen as mere signs commemorating the historical fact that Christ was once, long ago, present on earth: "This do in remembrance of me." And, as Claude Vigée has suggested, the Protestant reinterpretation of the Eucharist parallels exactly a similar transformation in literature (pp. 51–60). The old symbolism of analogical participation is gradually replaced by the modern poetic symbolism of reference at a distance. Just as the modern city is the social and material creation of a set of people living without God in the world, so modern literature betrays in its very form the absence of God. God has become a *Deus absconditus*, hidden somewhere behind the silence of infinite spaces, and our literary symbols can make only the most distant allusions to him, or to the natural world which used to be his abiding place and home.

When the old system of symbols binding man to God has finally evaporated, man finds himself alone and in spiritual poverty. Along with the development of modern science, the building of cities, and the destruction of the old forms of mediation goes the rise of subjectivistic philosophies. Modern thought has been increasingly dominated by the presupposition that each man is locked in the prison of his consciousness. From Montaigne to Descartes and Locke, on down through associationism, idealism, and romanticism, to the phenomenology and existentialism of today, the assumption has been that man must start with the inner experience of the isolated self. Whether this experience is thought of as consciousness (the *Cogito* of Descartes), or as feelings and sense impressions (the sensation of Locke), or as a living center (the *punctum saliens* of Jean Paul), or as the paradoxical freedom of Sartre, in all the stages of modern thought the interior states of the self are a beginning which in some sense can never be transcended.

Much modern writing has been a dramatization in existential terms of the consequences of this subjectivism. One great theme of modern literature is the sense of isolation, of alienation, of "world-alienation," in Hannah Arendt's phrase.[9] Most of the great works of nineteenth-century literature have at their centers a character who is in doubt about his own identity and asks, "How can I find something outside myself which will tell me who I am and give me a place in society and in the universe?" Subjectivism, like urbanization and the failure of medieval symbolism, leads man back to an experience of the absence of God.

The discovery or redefinition of the autonomy of consciousness is associated with one more all-important quality of modern times: the appearance of the historical sense. The central factor in historicism is an assumption of the relativity of any particular life or culture, its limitation and fragility. The attitude of historicism accompanies the failure of tradition, the failure of symbolic language, the failure of all the intermediaries between man and God. Historicism consequently can mean the anguish of feeling that one is forced to carry on one's life in terms of a mockery of masks and hollow gestures. To Matthew Arnold, for example, it seems that a sense of history undermines our culture and our life within that culture, until all seems artificial and sham. "Modern times," he says,

> find themselves with an immense system of institutions, established facts, accredited dogmas, rules, which have come to them from times not modern. In this system their life has to be carried forward; yet they have a sense that this system is not of their own creation, that it by no means corresponds exactly with the wants of their actual life, that, for them, it is customary, not rational. The awakening of this sense is the awakening of the modern spirit.[10]

Historicism and the rise of subjectivistic philosophies are intimately related. What once seemed objective fact, God and his angels, with all the harmonious structure depending therefrom, is now transformed into mere figments of man's imagination. This cultural change is once more mirrored in literature. As Ortega y Gasset has shown,[11] the change from traditional literature to a modern genre like the novel can be defined as a moving of the once objective worlds of myth and romance into the subjective consciousness of man. To Don Quixote the windmills are giants, to Emma Bovary, Rodolphe is the fulfilment of her romantic dreams, and for Henry James the novel presents not facts but someone's interpretation of them. The ideal world still exists, but only as a form of consciousness, not as an objective fact. Love, honor, God himself exist, but only because someone believes in them. Historicism, like all the other qualities of life in modern times, brings us back to the absence of God. Life in the city, the breakup of medieval symbolism, the imprisoning of man in his consciousness, the appearance of the historical sense – each of these is another way in which modern man has experienced the disappearance of God, and taken together they form the essential background against which much Victorian literature must be seen.

A number of possible responses to the disappearance of God have presented themselves since the early nineteenth century. Humanism, perspectivism, nihilism, pious acceptance – each of these has been a way to deal with the absence of God. But a group of important Victorian poets belong to another tradition: romanticism. The romantics still believe in God, and they find his absence intolerable. At all costs they must attempt to re-establish communication. Romanticism defines the artist as the creator or discoverer of new symbols, symbols which establish a new relation, across the gap, between man and God. The romantic artist, as Meyer Abrams has told us, is a lamp, not a mirror.[12] He is a maker or discoverer of the radically new, rather than the imitator of what is already known. The central assumption of romanticism is the idea that the isolated individual, through poetry, can accomplish the "unheard of work,"[13] that is, create through his own efforts a marvelous harmony of words which will reintegrate man, nature, and God.[14]

Many Victorian poets inherit this romantic conception of poetry, but such poets differ in one essential way from their predecessors. Almost all the romantic poets begin with the sense that there is a presence in nature, an immanent spiritual force. But many Victorians precisely do *not* possess this "sense sublime / Of something far more deeply interfused."[15] The spiritual power, for them, is altogether beyond the world. The literary strategy of the Victorian poets must therefore often be more extreme, more extravagant, as the gap between man and the divine power seems greater.

The initial situation of Arnold, Browning, Tennyson, and Hopkins is like that of many other modern men. For them too God is absent or unavailable. But unlike the novelists, who turned toward a purely human world, and unlike the nihilists, who turned toward a devouring emptiness as the true reality, these Victorian poets tried, each in his own way, to bring God back to earth as a benign power inherent in the self, in nature, and in the human community. Though their situations are more desperate than those of the romantics, their goals are similar. Their spiritual adventures might be defined as so many heroic attempts to recover immanence in a world of transcendence. Each of these attempts has its own special tone and atmosphere. Every poetic universe is unique and ultimately incommensurable with any other. The spiritual wrestling of Hopkins in "Carrion Comfort," for example, is quite unlike the passive resignation of Arnold. Nevertheless, the writings of Arnold, Browning, Tennyson, and Hopkins, in spite of all their differences, can be seen as responses to similar spiritual situations. For these four poets the absence of God is, in one way or another, the fundamental starting place and presupposition.

I

Matthew Arnold's special way of experiencing the disappearance of God is his inability to find any inner certitude or stability or permanence. Arnoldian man is bound to the law of succession in time and the law of limitation in place, for, as Arnold's Empedocles says, "Man's measures cannot mete the immeasurable All."[16] This means that there is no possibility of possessing a substantial and authentic self. Man, for Arnold, is merely a series of half selves, fragmentary and incomplete. As he says in "The Buried Life":

> we have been on many thousand lines,
> And we have shown, on each, spirit and power;
> But hardly have we, for one little hour,
> Been on our own line, have we been ourselves.
> (*Poetical Works*, 246)

Each man is forced to "fluctuate idly without term or scope," and, as a result, "half lives a hundred different lives" (260). Moreover, this series of half lives, each one truncated and momentary, is defined and redefined by whatever happens outside it in the aimless flux of events:

> Hither and thither spins
> The wind-borne, mirroring soul,
> A thousand glimpses wins,
> And never sees a whole. (415)

Caught up, willy-nilly, in the universal flux, and "whirl'd" "in action's dizzying eddy" (60), the mirror-soul is condemned to a fragmentation imposed by a triple motion. It is moving with an aimless spinning through a milieu which is itself in motion, swirling to and fro in aimless ebb and flow. The double eddying, an eddying within an eddying, determines the incoherent fluctuations within the soul, where "passions . . . for ever ebb and flow" (37), "linking in a mad succession / Fits of joy and fits of pain" (33). This vertiginous wavering within the soul is the result of its double submission to the motion of things outside itself and to its own crazy motion through that motion: "And on earth we wander, groping, reeling; / Powers stir in us, stir and disappear" (210).

Man has not always been in this intolerable situation. There was a time, near the green sources of history, when man possessed himself and at the same time possessed the whole world. Emanations and influences flowed back and forth between man and nature, and man and the gods. Man then had joy, and having joy possessed himself, the deep buried self making him one with the whole world. It was a time of pastoral immediacy, of the happy unselfconscious acceptance of a narrow, limited life. Such a time, when "the smallest thing could give us pleasure" (436), Arnold's Empedocles remembers from his youth. Arnold associates this joyful time with the early Greece of Homer, and with Wordsworth, Maurice de Guérin, and other romantic writers. The lost condition of joy is in fact man's proper state, and he seems to have been deprived of it by a mere superficial accident, the accident of a bad society, the "damned times" and damned place in which Arnold happens to live. Even now it would be better in France where they have the Academy and the *Revue des Deux Mondes*. "My dearest Clough," laments Arnold in a famous letter,

> these are damned times – everything is against one – the height to which knowledge is come, the spread of luxury, our physical enervation, the absence of great *natures*, the unavoidable contact with millions of small ones, newspapers, cities, light profligate friends, moral desperadoes like Carlyle, our own selves, and the sickening consciousness of our difficulties.[17]

But if man's present bad situation seems to have been so fortuitously produced, he should be able without too much difficulty to regain his primal state, and, in the phrase which Arnold quoted over and over again in his notebooks, fulfil his essential task, which is the establishment of the kingdom of God on earth.[18]

Arnold's first instinct is to turn outside himself, and to seek some still-living link between man and God, some power which will mediate between himself and the lost harmony. Man now is bare consciousness, the detached reflecting mirror. He must see if there is anything through which he can establish relationship again with the divine spirit. Arnold's early poetry and the letters to Clough are a record of the various means he tries. He tries the playing of a role, or the acceptance of a given law for his being. He tries the deliberate composition of poetry. He tries to believe that there is still some effective absolute law. He tries plunging himself into society. He tries, in the Marguerite poems, love. He tries to depend on the power of memory to form a link with the past. He tries to see nature as the romantic poets did. He even tries, in "The Strayed Reveller" and "The New Sirens," abandoning himself, in imagination, to passion and uncontrolled feeling. Each of these expedients leads, in one way or another, to further self-alienation. Through this repeated failure Arnold discovers for himself the truth expressed in Coleridge's "Dejection, an Ode": "we receive but what we give." Arnold cannot find joy in things outside himself unless he has joy already in his own heart.

So the poet turns within himself. "Resolve to be thyself," he cries (*Poetical Works*, 240). Withdraw from all false exterior forces, and seize the substantial inner core of self. Find your own *assiette*, Arnold advises Clough, and stick to it (*Letters to Clough*, 130). The movement of withdrawal means, in one direction, a complete rejection of the social world as it is. But this condemnation is undertaken in the hope that by a process of self-purification he will not only remove the inauthentic but will allow the deep buried self which is his real identity to rise up and fill his inner emptiness. At the same time this will be a possession of the "general life," the soul of the world, the All. But to possess the All is in the same moment to reach the divine. The spark from heaven will fall, and Arnold will be himself a source of a current of true and fresh ideas from God, a "bringer of heavenly light," as he puts it in "Westminster Abbey" (*Poetical Works*, 447). This light will illuminate and make authentic all human society.

But it is just through trying this strategy that Arnold makes his most frightening discovery, the discovery recorded in many poems, but most completely in "Empedocles on Etna." At this very moment, the thin strand connecting the self to the All is being cut, and the self is being transformed into sheer emptiness. Whether by going down toward the deep buried self and finding it infinitely distant, or by going up toward God, Arnold discovers that by separation of himself from everything limited he gets no possession of himself, but the final loss of all life and all joy. Though he gets higher and higher above the turmoil of contemporary life, he does not get one inch closer to the buried self or to the divine spark. No revelation, no intuition, no presence of God is possible. What happens is merely a progressive evacuation of the soul, a progressive appearance of the true emptiness of the self. This emptiness is defined by its infinite distance from the true buried self and from the divine transcendence. So Arnold writes of the tragic situation,

> When the soul, growing clearer,
> Sees God no nearer;
> When the soul, mounting higher,
> To God comes no nigher. (38)

Empedocles commits suicide just before this death of the soul, while a tiny strand of joy still connects him to nature, but after that darkness descends on the Arnoldian soul and isolation is his lot. He has become "Nothing but a devouring flame of thought – / But a naked, eternally restless mind!" (438). This mind transforms whatever it knows into itself, and therefore remains cut off from whatever it knows. Moreover, Arnold is now at last brought to recognize that this catastrophe is no accident. He sees that it is a true revolution or pivoting of history, the moment God withdraws completely from the world.

Arnold has now discovered the truth about man's present condition: emptiness and distance are what man really is, in these bad times. But he also learns that to know this and to suffer from it paradoxically bring man closest to the divine spirit and make him superior to forgetful, self-sufficient nature. So Arnold's last posture is that of the man "wandering between two worlds, one dead, / The other powerless to be born" (302). He is the man of the no longer and not yet, the man whose only honest way to testify God is negatively, by denying truth to whatever is now, and by formulas which are so general that, though they assert the existence of absolute values, they do not have enough real content to be false. This is the stance of Arnold the elegist, the mourner writing in sorrow for the death of Thyrsis, the dear friend whose death is a symbol of the death of a world, as are all the deaths in Arnold's poetry. For there are an extraordinary number of elegies among Arnold's poems. Arnold's notebooks, and his social, literary, and religious criticism are like the elegies in the sense that they too reject whatever exists in the present as inauthentic and hollow and, on the other hand, embalm an essentially dead wisdom: the best that is known and thought in the world, but is no longer current in society. Though the tone of Arnold's prose is so different from that of his poetry, this difference testifies not to Arnold's escape from his earlier situation, but to the resigned acquiescence in which he ultimately comes to poise. Arnold finds in the acceptance of the absence of God the *assiette* he has sought vainly in more positive strategies. Arnold the critic can only say:

> God exists, and I know it, but I don't know it directly, and I know too that He would be the only support of a true civilization, a civilization built

> on eternal truths. However, unfortunately, at this particular moment I cannot tell you, and no man can tell you, just what those truths are. Believe no man but him who tells you, like a prophet crying in the wilderness, that the truth is, but not here, not yet.

In the end, then, Arnold faces toward the future, not toward the past. Like the Scholar Gipsy he is waiting, in a purity and emptiness carefully preserved by criticism, for the return of God, for the "fugitive and gracious light . . . , shy to illumine" (268). Arnold's final orientation is toward the return of the divine spirit, a return which, as in "Obermann Once More," he can almost see, or can even see at a distance, as he waits in passive tension, rejecting everything here and now for the sake of something which is never, while he lives, quite actual and present.

II

The starting place for Robert Browning is a typically romantic one: a sense of the inexhaustible potentiality of his inner life, and of the way this potentiality cannot be fulfilled in any finite human existence. So, for example, the hero of *Pauline* finds in himself "a principle of restlessness / Which would be all, have, see, know, taste, feel, all."[19] Since the infinity of the actual outer world is an exact match for the infinity of the potential inner world, Browning wants to know all the universe at once, from an absolute point of view. But only God has this totality and simultaneity of experience. Browning's early Promethean heroes therefore try to identify themselves with God, to see things from God's point of view.

But when Browning's early heroes try to escape from the "clay prisons" of themselves, and reach divine knowledge and experience, they merely dissolve into a murky emptiness which is the absence of any experience at all. So Paracelsus "sickens" at last "on a dead gulf streaked with light / From its own putrefying depths alone" (*Works*, 21). The expansiveness of Browning's early heroes leads not to fulfillment of potentiality, but rather to just the opposite, a rarefaction, a volatilization, a dissipation of immense energies into the opaque inane, leaving the hero back where he started, still in a condition of unrealized potentiality.

This failure of romantic Prometheanism causes Browning to make a radical transformation in his poetry. After *Sordello*, instead of writing poetry which is disguised autobiography, the autobiography of Prometheus in search of the divine fire, Browning writes dramatic monologues, that is, as he said, "poetry always dramatic in principle, and so many utterances of so many imaginary persons, not mine" (1). The dramatic monologue presupposes a double awareness on the part of its author, an awareness which is the very essence of historicism. On the one hand the dramatic monologuist is aware of the relativity of any single life or way of looking at the world. He sees each one from the outside as merely one possible life, and yields himself with a certain irony or detachment to one after another of these imagined selves. But on the other hand the monologuist is also aware that reality, for us human beings, lies only in a life which is immersed in a material and social world, and living with all its energy the life appropriate to that situation. The only sin is the refusal to act or make choices, for "a crime will do / As well . . . to serve for a test, / As a virtue golden through and through," and man must above all avoid "the unlit lamp and the ungirt loin" (286). Reality for man is the inexhaustible multiplicity of all the lives which have ever been lived or could be lived, and it is these which the modern poet, the poet of historicism, must describe.

So we get the great gallery of idiosyncratic individuals in Browning's most famous poems: scoundrels, quacks, hypocrites, cowards, casuists, heroes, adulterers, artists, Bishop Blougram, Mr Sludge the Medium, the Bishop ordering his tomb. The reality of each of these lives lies in its limitation, its narrowness. It is one special way of living in the world chosen out of all the infinite possibilities. Browning seems to have committed himself wholeheartedly, like Nietzsche or Gide, to a life of perspectivism or role-playing.

This is not quite the case, however, for behind the great crowd of grotesques and idealists there lies one constant factor linking them all together: the consciousness of Browning himself. Browning has found in the poetry of the dramatic monologue a covert way to actualize all the infinite possibilities which at the time of *Pauline* lay dormant within him, each a "universe in germ" (991), potential, not actual, and seemingly with no way to be made real. In *Pauline* all these living germs existed simply as "impulses," "tendencies," "desires," which all bubbled together within his mind. There seemed no way "to trust / All feelings equally, to hear all sides" (7). But now, when Browning has accepted the perspectivism of the dramatic monologue, all these living forms, all these feelings, all these viewpoints, will be incarnated in the lives of the multitudinous variety of men and women who speak in his poems.

Browning carries his use of the dramatic monologue even further than this, however. In his masterpiece, *The Ring and the Book*, what appears at first an acceptance of perspectivism turns out to be a heroic attempt to escape the falsifications of point of view. The philosophical and aesthetic moral of *The Ring and the Book* is: "By multiplying points of view you may transcend point of view, and reach at last God's own infinite perspective." Slowly, bit by bit, the different versions of the story, like the distancing of the facts in the depths of the historical past, liberate the poem from being a "false show of things," and make of the eccentric interpretations an elaborate oblique incantation which evokes the truth, that divine truth at the center of each finite person or event which, in Browning's view, can never be faced directly or said directly. "Truth, nowhere," he says, "lies yet everywhere in these – / Not absolutely in a portion, yet / Evolvable from the whole" (555–6). All the retellings of the story, the multiplication of perspectives on it, the contradictory versions of what happened – all have as their goal by a kind of mutual negation to make something else appear, something which can never be said directly in words. The "something" is at once the central truth of this particular story, the central truth of the human condition, and the transcendental truth which underlies all the particular human facts that ever were or could be. So at the very end of *The Ring and the Book* Browning makes his great boast for the power of perspectivist art to go beyond the tragic situation of the unavailability of God:

> – Art may tell a truth
> Obliquely, do the thing shall breed the thought,
> Nor wrong the thought, missing the mediate word.
> So may you paint your picture, twice show truth,
> Beyond mere imagery on the wall, –
> So, note by note, bring music from your mind,
> Deeper than ever e'en Beethoven dived, –
> So write a book shall mean beyond the facts,
> Suffice the eye and save the soul beside. (601)

But this way of dealing with the absence of God ultimately fails. Even though we may agree that each finite human perspective is an authentic version of the world, even though we may agree that it contains one spark of the divine plenitude, nevertheless, however many of these fragmentary glimpses of God we may add up, we shall be no closer to the whole, or to a face to face confrontation with God. A very large number is not an infinite number, and only an infinite number would do. Browning's unconscious recognition of this may be revealed by the inclusion of the monologue of the Pope in *The Ring and the Book.* The Pope is somehow beyond the limitations and distortions of the other monologuists. He speaks for Browning. He speaks for God himself. To include such a character is to betray the aesthetic presuppositions of the poem, and implicitly to admit its failure to accomplish its end.

It turns out, however, that in this failure lies unsuspected success. For man's perpetual striving is his most God-like attribute. Only if Browning closes himself off is he finished for good, and excluded forever from God. As long as he keeps moving he is in God's grace, and imitates in little the very life of God. The uncouth, half-finished statues of Michelangelo are more in correspondence to the deity than any smooth perfection (333, 713, 771), and the form of Browning's poetry, in its internal contradictions, its rough-hewn quality, its openendedness, is the very image of infinity, and of the limitless perfection of God. God himself constantly transcends himself, and moves into ever-new spheres of being. On earth we are in a sense already in heaven, for in heaven we shall exist in the same dynamic motion as on earth, continually going beyond ourselves even as here. Though God is not temporal, the driving motion of time is a perfect image of his explosive eternity.

Browning always remains faithful to this intuition of the relation between the creator and the creation, and in "Fust and His Friends" he devises a brilliant and definitive metaphor to describe it. In this metaphor the creation is seen as one of those mathematical lines, like the tangent curve, which approaches always closer and closer to a straight line, its asymptote, which it will touch only at infinity. Though man can never, it may be, reach God's plenitude, he can maintain a "continual," however distant, "approximation to it" (1010), and in this approximation lies the fullness of life Browning has sought from the beginning:

> Why, onward through ignorance! Dare and deserve!
> As still to its asymptote speedeth the curve,
>
> So approximates Man – Thee, who, reachable not,
>   Hast formed him to yearningly follow Thy whole
> Sole and single omniscience! (985)

III

> All sense of Time
> And Being and Place was swallowed up and lost
> Within a victory of boundless thought.
> I was a part of the Unchangeable,
> A scintillation of Eternal Mind,
> Remix'd and burning with its parent fire.[20]

In these hyperbolic terms the young Tennyson describes his experience of union with God. All limitations of time, place, and finite selfhood are transcended in an expansion of the soul "even to Infinitude" (*Early Poems*, 12), and the self is melted in God's holy fire. To worship God is to worship the self, for the two are identical, and Tennyson can say: "Yea! in that hour I could have fallen down / Before my own strong soul and worshipp'd it" (*Early Poems*, 12). But though passages describing such experiences recur throughout Tennyson's work (as in "The Ancient Sage" and in the ninety-fifth lyric of *In Memoriam*) and may be said to form its center, nevertheless this ecstasy is always spoken of in the past tense. When it is present it cannot be described. To know it is to have lost it. For Tennyson the suffering caused by loss of an infinite plenitude determines the essential quality of the present, and the refrain of all his poetry is "Far – Far – Away."[21] Like other Victorian poets he believes in God, but his God too is "a Power / That is not seen and rules from far away,"[22] and for him we are all now in a situation of "believing where we cannot prove" (*Works*, 163). Loss of the intimate presence of God generates the anguish of "The Two Voices" and the "Supposed Confessions of a Second-Rate Sensitive Mind," and Tennyson's characteristic poetry expresses a sense of being "void, / Dark, formless, utterly destroyed" (*Works*, 6) because abandoned by the divine power.

What can the poet do in this state of abandonment? Two opposing motions of the spirit dominate Tennyson's poetry. One is a movement of withdrawal, circumscription, and concentration. As in Arnold's poetry this movement is justified by a sense that deep within itself the self is always flowing from fountains of divine being:

> If thou would'st hear the Nameless, and wilt dive
> Into the temple-cave of thine own self,
> There, brooding by the central altar, thou
> Mayst haply learn the Nameless hath a voice,
> By which thou wilt abide, if thou would be wise. (498)

There is an absolute incompatibility between this divine center of the self and the modern world of railroads and ugly cities. The deep fountains of being, which are also the fountains of poetic inspiration, must be carefully walled around and guarded from intrusion. In "The Poet's Mind" and, more successfully, in "The Hesperides," Tennyson expresses the effort of self-seclusion by which the poet can remain in ever-enduring possession of the sources of power deep within himself and within nature.

But inside the enclosure of the poet's carefully protected solitude the holy well gradually dries up, in spite of all his attempts to preserve it by the magic charm of verse. There is a progressive deadening, a withdrawal of the springs of being, and the poet finds himself at last in total isolation. Passivity and circumscription can then become the guilty self-enclosure in aesthetic beauty of "The Palace of Art," or the desire for complete relaxation and drifting of "The Lotos-Eaters," or the endless suffering of "Tithonus." Stagnant self-enclosure can generate that state of being so poignantly expressed in "Mariana" and in the fiftieth section of *In Memoriam* – a mere passive waiting for the return of the divine spirit, a waiting without hope, in utter desolation and dryness of soul. In this imprisonment of the self within itself life, deprived of all impetus, slows down almost to a stop, and the sufferer becomes painfully sensitive to the tiniest motions which remain. In this state "the blood creeps, and the nerves prick / And tingle; . . . / And all the wheels of being [are] slow" (175). Without being able to die the self hovers interminably at the very brink of death:

All day within the dreamy house,
The doors upon their hinges creak'd;
The blue fly sung in the pane; the mouse
Behind the mouldering wainscot shriek'd,
Or from the crevice peer'd about. . . .
She only said, "My life is dreary,
He cometh not," she said;
She said, "I am aweary, aweary,
I would that I were dead!" (8)

Centripetal withdrawal only leads Tennyson to a more exacerbated experience of the absence of God. The alternative motion of expansion begins with the poet's sense of his heaven-sent mission. Possessing unique access to the divine power, the poet should let his poems flow forth in all directions to vivify the world, as the "great vine of Fable," in "Timbuctoo," is filled with a "permeating life" and reaches "to every corner under heaven, / Deep-rooted in the living soil of truth" (780). If he deploys his energies in this way the poet will be a new mediator through whom God will once again become present in the world. Having access to the source of all truth and wisdom the poet can, as for Shelley, be a legislator, giving new authenticity to civilization. The poet is a fructifying river flowing from the fountains of being, or, in the metaphor of "The Poet," the bard is like a dandelion which showers forth seeds of wisdom until "truth [is] multiplied on truth, the world / Like one great garden show[s]" (14). This notion of the poet's mission leads Tennyson to write poems of action and social commitment. It is the source of the didactic side of his poetry, his urge to take part in the progress and amelioration of the world.

But ultimately expansion of the self works no better than contraction. Centrifugal diffusion coincides with progressive evaporation and thinning out of the self. It gets too far away from the fountains of being, and eventually all connection is lost. The poet enters the realm of the superficial and inauthentic: received opinions, false patriotism, sycophancy, jingoism, empty optimism, blind commitment to motion and action as escape from painful self-consciousness. Like Arnold, Tennyson cannot believe that the divine truth can be embodied in society without being gradually corrupted. The *Idylls of the King* is an elaborate expression of this view of history as the inevitable degradation of an original revelation.

Neither expansion nor contraction of the self will recover the lost immanence of God, and between these two sad alternatives Tennyson vibrates helplessly. Perhaps his deepest insight into the spiritual condition of his age, as well as his most successful poetry, is in those passages where, as in "Demeter and Persephone," "Tears, Idle Tears," and "The Ancient Sage," he uses oxymorons, transitional states, and images of broken, evanescent, or far-off things to express a peculiar apprehension of the totality of things as self-divided, and in despair over this self-division. In the end, for Tennyson, man, nature, and God himself are to be defined as transcending themselves, as riven by "a gulf that ever shuts and gapes" (179). Both man and God are essentially creatures of distance, "far off . . . but ever nigh" (196), and all things express the paradoxical combination of presence and absence which is at the heart of being:

> The first gray streak of earliest summer-dawn,
> The last long stripe of waning crimson gloom,
> As if the late and early were but one –
> A height, a broken grange, a grove, a flower
> Had murmurs, "Lost and gone, and lost and gone!"
> A breath, a whisper – some divine farewell –
> Desolate sweetness – far and far away – (500)

In this situation there is only one hope – the "far-off divine event" (198) which will reconcile height and depth, God and man, heaven and earth, until "all the Shadow die into the Light" (530). Or, it may be, we shall reach all we have lost only in death, and see our Pilot face to face, when we have crossed the bar. For these consummations the poet can only wait in patience.

IV

> God, though to Thee our psalm we raise
> No answering voice comes from the skies.[23]

Gerard Manley Hopkins' early poetry, the poetry he burned in the "slaughter of the innocents" after his conversion, is a consistent expression of the situation of a man who finds himself isolated in the midst of an alien universe, a universe which "rebuffs him with blank unlikeness."[24] Such a universe has a double emptiness. On the one hand there is nothing in it which shows any kinship to man himself. And on the other hand there is nothing in it which reveals any sign of its creator. It is "like a lighted empty hall / Where stands no host at door or hearth" (*Poems*, 43). Distance, vacancy, silence – these are the keynotes of Hopkins' early poetry. To read it is to enter a universe of "abysses infinite," where we gaze in vain "On being's dread and vacant maze," where "Vacant creation's lamps appal," and where "Our prayer seems lost in desert ways, / Our hymn in the vast silence dies" (*Poems*, 44, 43).

Within this vacant creation the self is imprisoned in its own immobile self-consciousness. The mind is "the unchanging register of change" (*Poems*, 147), and all things swirl in dynamic flux around it. Though Hopkins' tutor at Oxford, Walter Pater, could make a satisfactory philosophy out of such a situation, Hopkins found it intolerable, and all his career, as Jesuit and poet, might be defined as an attempt to escape from the prison to which Paterian phenomenalism had condemned him.

The escape takes place through an exploration of one of Hopkins' two definitions of the self. Both of these definitions are derived from the poet's sense that man is isolated from the rest of creation by his higher degree of particularization. "I find myself," he says, "both as a man and as myself something most determined and distinctive, at pitch, more distinctive and higher pitched than anything else I see" (*Sermons*, 122). This peculiar mode of isolation is the basis of Hopkins' proof of the existence of God. For him an individuated being "can have been developed, evolved, condensed, from the vastness of the world not anyhow or by the working of common powers but only by one of finer or higher pitch and determination than itself" (*Sermons*, 122–3). If man were one of the lesser creatures, a stone or a kingfisher, there would be no problem. He could see in the creation many things of higher determination than himself, and could thus imagine them to be his source. But man, the highest pitched of all, looks in vain throughout the creation for anything which could have made him. Therefore he must have been made by some being more highly pitched than himself – some being outside the creation, who exists as an "extrinsic power" (*Sermons*, 128). This being is God himself, the creator of all.

God is defined by Hopkins as a most "exquisite determining, self-making, power" (*Sermons*, 125). God's pattern is infinitely complex, and therefore he contains in himself the matrices for all possible and actual creatures, including man. God vibrates simultaneously at all possible pitches. But there is an apparent contradiction in Hopkins' thinking about the nature of selfhood. The contradiction about the self is also a contradiction about the nature of God. This contradiction lies at the heart of the poet's spiritual experience.

On the one hand individuality is a matter of complexity and fineness of pattern. If this is the case then the higher and more elaborate patterns as it were recapitulate all the lower ones, and God, the most complex pattern of all, contains in himself the archetypes of all things. God is the master key which opens all doors, and God the Son, Christ, is the model on which all things are created. Each thing repeats, not God's whole infinitely complex pattern, but some portion of it or simplified version of it. Man too, if we take this view of individuality, though he is not God, does contain in himself all the creatures lower than he in the scale of being. He too is created in the image of Christ. He need not feel alone in the universe, and can, if he is a poet, express his own inscape at the same time as he expresses the inscapes of nature. Beginning with the idea that "any two things however unlike are in something like" (*Sermons*, 123), Hopkins explores the realm of words and the realm of nature and finds everywhere proof that all things rhyme. The Parmenidean idea of the univocity of Being is fulfilled in the Scotist doctrine of Christ as the common nature on whom all the creation is modeled, and ultimately Hopkins sees the universe as a vast interlocking harmony, full of fraternal echoes and resonances. All things resemble one another because they resemble the God who has fathered them forth in pied beauty.

But on the other hand Hopkins thinks of individuality in another radically different way. Perfection of individuality is not complexity of pattern. It is a matter of pitch, of taste, something so highly tuned and idiosyncratic that it is like nothing else in the world. Hopkins' "selftaste" is what Scotus calls, in a striking phrase, the *ultima solitudo* of man. At the deepest center of selfhood each man is altogether alone. There are no resonances between men. God must now be defined as the most exquisitely tuned of all, the most isolated of all. God is now defined as unity, not as multiplicity. He is the key which fits no finite lock.

The first of these concepts of individuality provides Hopkins with the basis for his gradual integration of all things into one great chorus of creation. It allows him to transcend completely the isolation to which he seems at first condemned. All the positive side of Hopkins' poetry, the hopeful and "hurrahing" side, derives from this idea about selfhood. A man can be saved, so it seems from this point of view, by doing what comes naturally, because he is created naturally in the image of Christ. He can without qualms instress his own inscape.

The other definition of selfhood, however, is no less integral to Hopkins' thought. It leads to the idea that a man has no kinship with anything, not even with God. Man is "the one exception" (*Sermons*, 123) to the law that any two things are in something like. A man's selfhood, his stress of pitch, is like nothing else in the world, not even like God. And if this is the case then he can only hope for salvation if in some miraculous way he is transformed out of himself into the image of Christ. This side of Hopkins' thought leads to the analysis of grace in the commentary on the *Spiritual Exercises* and to the somber poetry of his last years. It means a total repudiation of the mood of "Hurrahing in Harvest."

In the end Hopkins feels himself to be utterly dependent on God's grace, for only grace can operate on the *ultima solitudo* and change a man from diabolical idiosyncrasy into a version of Christ, an "AfterChrist"

(*Sermons*, 100). He need only wait, in patience and hope, for grace to descend. But this is just what does *not* happen. Though Hopkins has isolated experiences of the descent of grace, such as those recorded in "The Wreck of the Deutschland" and "Carrion Comfort," the central religious experience of his last years is the prolonged anguish of spiritual paralysis, dryness of soul, the absence of God, and the failure of grace. It is as if God has withdrawn from the soul and from the world, leaving Hopkins in a situation strangely like that recorded in his early poems – a situation of abandonment and impotent suffering.

The final stance of Hopkins is rather like that of Matthew Arnold. Hopkins has given up everything positive, everything natural, and lives in complete deprivation of natural growth and productivity, except for brief spasms of poetic creation. He has emptied himself of his nature, and is waiting, so far fruitlessly, for the spark from heaven to fall. Though he seems so different from other nineteenth-century writers who suffered the absence of God, in reality he ends in a similar situation. Though he takes the most extreme measures he does not escape from their plight. The experience recorded in the "terrible sonnets," and in the late letters and retreat notes, is striking evidence that the nineteenth century was for many writers a time of the no longer and not yet, a time of the absence of God. Hopkins, it might be said, has, beyond all his contemporaries, the most shattering experience of the disappearance of God. He too believes in God, but is unable to reach him. And for him happiness can come only beyond the gates of death, just as Thomas De Quincey can rise from the depths of spiritual suffering only at the moment of death,[25] just as Arnold waits in the vacuum between two worlds, and just as Cathy and Heathcliff, in *Wuthering Heights*, must die to be reunited.

Only in Browning, of the poets discussed here, are there hints and anticipations of the recovery of immanence, beyond the dualism of earth and heaven, which was to be the inner drama of twentieth-century literature. Only Browning seems to have glimpsed the fact that the sad alternatives of nihilism, on the one hand, and escape beyond the world, on the other, could be evaded if man would only reject twenty-five hundred years of dualism. If man could do this, twentieth-century writers were to find, he might come to see that being and value lie in *this* world, in what is immediate, tangible, present to man, in earth, sun, sea, the stars in their courses, and in what Yeats was to call "the foul rag-and-bone shop of the heart." But Browning too, like Tennyson, Arnold, and Hopkins, was stretched on the rack of a dying transcendentalism, and could reach a precarious unity only by the most extravagant stratagems of the spirit.

Notes

⋆ Some of the material in this essay has been published in *The Disappearance of God* (copyright 1963 by the President and Fellows of Harvard College).

1. W. M. Thackeray, *Letters and Private Papers*, G. N. Ray, ed. (Cambridge, Mass., 1945), II, p. 309.
2. Friedrich Hölderlin, "Brod und Wein. An Heinze," *Sämtliche Werke* (Berlin, 1923), IV, p. 123: "Zwar leben die Götter, Aber über dem Haupt droben in anderer Welt."
3. *The Poems of Arthur Hugh Clough*, H. F. Lowry, A. L. P. Norrington, and F. L. Mulhauser, eds (London, 1951), p. 409.
4. Martin Heidegger is of course the champion of this interpretation of the Presocratics. See especially *Holzwege* (Frankfurt am Main, 1950), pp. 296–343, and *Vörtrage und Aufsätze* (Pfullingen, 1954), pp. 207–82. See also G. S. Kirk and J. E. Raven, *The Presocratic Philosophers* (Cambridge, 1957) for the best recent book in English on the Presocratics.
5. See Jacob Taubes, "From Cult to Culture," *Partisan Review*, XXI (1954), pp. 387–400. Oskar Goldberg, *Die Wirklichkeit der Hebraër* (Berlin, 1925), and Thomas Mann, *Doktor Faustus* (Stockholm, 1947), ch. xxviii.
6. See Claude Vigée, *Les Artistes de la faim* (Paris, 1960), pp. 40–42.
7. For varying interpretations see Erich Auerbach's two essays: *"Figura," Archivum Romanicum*, XXII (1938), pp. 436–89, and "Typological Symbolism in Mediaeval Literature," *Yale French Studies*, No. 9 (1952), pp. 5–8, and three papers by Charles S. Singleton: "Dante's Allegory," *Speculum*, XXV (1950), pp. 78–83, "The Other Journey," *Kenyon Review*, XIV (1952), pp. 189–206, "The Irreducible Dove," *Comparative Literature*, IX (1957), pp. 129–35; and see also Richard Hamilton Green, "Dante's 'Allegory of Poets' and the Mediaeval Theory of Poetic Fiction," *Comparative Literature*, IX (1957), pp. 118–28.
8. See A. O. Lovejoy, *The Great Chain of Being* (Cambridge, Mass., 1936), M. H. Nicolson, *The Breaking of the Circle* (rev. ed., New York, 1960), Alexandre Koyré, *From the Closed World to the Infinite Universe* (Baltimore, 1957), E. R. Wasserman, *The Subtler Language* (Baltimore, 1959), and John Hollander, *The Untuning of the Sky: Ideas of Music in English Poetry* (Princeton, 1961).
9. *The Human Condition* (Garden City, N. J., 1959), p. 6.
10. "Heinrich Heine," *Works* (London, 1903), III, p. 174.
11. José Ortega y Gasset, "The Nature of the Novel," tr. Evelyn Rugg and Diego Marin, *Hudson Review*, X (1957), pp. 11–42.
12. *The Mirror and the Lamp: Romantic Theory and the Critical Tradition* (New York, 1953).
13. Arthur Rimbaud, *Oeuvres complètes*, éd. de la Pléiade (Paris, 1946), p. 176: "l'oeuvre inouïe."
14. See the definition of the central project of romanticism at the end of Albert Béguin's *L'Ame romantique et le rêve* (Paris, 1956), pp. 393–404.
15. *The Poetical Works of William Wordsworth*, Ernest de Selincourt, ed. (Oxford, 1944), II, p. 262.
16. *The Poetical Works of Matthew Arnold*, C. B. Tinker and H. F. Lowry, eds (London, 1950), p. 423.
17. *The Letters of Matthew Arnold to Arthur Hugh Clough*, H. F. Lowry, ed. (London and New York, 1932), p. 111.

18. "Voilà le but présenté par le Christianisme à l'humanité tout entière comme son but dernier et définitif: le royaume de Dieu sur la terre" (That is the goal presented by Christianity to the whole of humanity as its final and definitive goal: the kingdom of God on earth). Édouard Reuss, *Histoire de la théologie chrétienne au siècle apostolique* (Strasbourg, 1860), II, p. 542, quoted in *The Notebooks of Matthew Arnold*, H. F. Lowry, Karl Young, and W. H. Dunn, eds (London, 1952), pp. 108, 141, 152, 176, 192, 229, 263, 366, 387, 544.
19. *The Complete Poetic and Dramatic Works of Robert Browning*, Horace E. Scudder, ed. (Boston, 1895), p. 5.
20. Alfred Tennyson, *Unpublished Early Poems*, Charles Tennyson, ed. (London, 1931), p. 12.
21. *The Poetic and Dramatic Works of Alfred Lord Tennyson*, W. J. Rolfe, ed. (Boston, 1898), p. 555.
22. *The Works of Alfred Lord Tennyson* (London, 1906), p. 882.
23. *Poems of Gerard Manley Hopkins*, W. H. Gardner, ed., 3rd ed. (New York, 1956), p. 43.
24. *The Sermons and Devotional Writings of Gerard Manley Hopkins*, Christopher Devlin, S. J. ed. (London, 1959), p. 123.
25. See "Levana and Our Ladies of Sorrow," in the "Suspiria de Profundis," *The Collected Writings of Thomas De Quincey*, David Masson, ed. (London, 1897), XIII, pp. 362–9.

5

Money in *Our Mutual Friend*

Our Mutual Friend is about "money, money, money, and what money can make of life." This theme plays an important part in Dickens' earlier fiction, too, but never does Dickens so concentrate his attention on the power of money as in this last of his completed novels. The central intrigue of the Harmon murder shows the inheritance of a great fortune apparently corrupting its inheritors, Noddy Boffin, and his ward, Bella Wilfer, just as the desire to "become respectable in the scale of society" corrupts Lizzie Hexam's brother, Charley. Money, one source of each character's station in life, separates Eugene Wrayburn and Lizzie Hexam. In this part of the story, as in others, Dickens is acutely conscious of the difference in people made by class distinctions. "How can I think of you as being on equal terms with me?" asks Lizzie of Eugene. "If my mind could put you on equal terms with me, you could not be yourself." Eugene's class status is an inextricable part of himself and stands between him and Lizzie as an almost palpable barrier. Class distinctions are shown in *Our Mutual Friend* to be closely intertwined with the power of money. The opposition of the "Voice of Society" to Eugene's marriage is as much based on the fact that Lizzie has no money as on the fact that she is "a female waterman, turned factory girl." In the England of *Our Mutual Friend* inherited rank is in the process of giving way to the universal solvent of money, and most of the characters set their hearts on "money, money, money."

Mr Podsnap's value in Mr Podsnap's eyes is exactly determined by the amount of money he has, just as his possessions are valuable to him only because they are worth so much cash. Greed motivates Silas Wegg and Rogue Riderhood, characters from the bottom of society, as much as it motivates the Veneerings, the Lammles, Fascination Fledgeby, and other characters near the top of society. A minor character like Twemlow has been rendered ineffectual for life by the gift of a small annuity from his cousin, Lord Snigsworth, and another character, Mortimer Lightwood, says, "My own small income . . . has been an effective Something, in the way of preventing me from turning to at Anything."

The good characters are obsessed with money, too. John Harmon's purpose in life is to find some way to take the curse from the Harmon fortune, and the same desire secretly motivates Mr Boffin. Old Riah suffers in the false position of being taken as the miserly head of Pubsey and Co. Even Betty Higden concentrates her waning energy on avoiding the workhouse and on protecting the burial money she has sewn in her dress. Her central aim is a desire for financial independence. From the top to the bottom of society most of the characters in *Our Mutual Friend* have their lives determined in one way or another by money, and think of little else.

What *is* money, for Dickens, and what has it "made of life"? Money, he sees, is the attribution of value to what is without value in itself: paper, gold, dust, earth, mud. The Harmon fortune has come from dust, the dust that rises in man-made geological formations around Boffin's Bower. Noddy Boffin is "the Golden Dustman." In one remarkable passage dust, the material source of money, is shown to be present everywhere in the city, along with a kindred mystery, the paper which is the basis of another form of currency:

> The grating wind sawed rather than blew; and as it sawed, the sawdust whirled about the sawpit. Every street was a sawpit, and there were no top-sawyers; every passenger was an under-sawyer, with the sawdust blinding him and choking him.
>
> That mysterious paper currency which circulates in London when the wind blows gyrated here and there and everywhere. Whence can it come, whither can it go? It hangs on every bush, flutters in every tree, is caught flying by the electric wires, haunts every enclosure, drinks at every pump, cowers at every grating, shudders upon every plot of grass, seeks rest in vain behind the legions of iron rails.

If money is the ascribing of value to valueless matter, the basis of its power for evil over man is his forgetting of this fact. *Our Mutual Friend* is about a whole society which has forgotten. Instead of seeing that man has made money of dust and is the source of its value, this society takes money as the ultimate value-in-itself, the measure and source of all other value. As one of the Voices of Society says, "A man may do anything lawful for money. But for no money! Bosh!" The novel is a brilliant revelation of the results of this false worship of money.

When money is detached both from its material basis and from its human origin, it takes on a power of infinite self-multiplication. Cut off from reality and yet treated by men as the final criterion of worth, its infinity is like that reached when any number is divided by zero. "Money makes money," says Mr Boffin, "as well as makes everything else." Such a false absolute are those "Shares," which, in their inexhaustible power to duplicate themselves and make everything of nothing, Dickens describes as the virtual god of a moneyed society. Like the mysterious paper currency blown everywhere in London, Shares pervade every corner of the nation's life and determine its nature:

> As is well known to the wise in their generation, traffic in Shares is the one thing to have to do with in this world. Have no antecedents, no established character, no cultivation, no ideas, no manners; have Shares. Have Shares enough to be on Boards of Direction in capital letters, oscillate on mysterious business between London and Paris, and be great. Where does he come from? Shares. Where is he going to? Shares. What are his tastes? Shares. Has he any principles? Shares. What squeezes him into Parliament? Shares. Perhaps he never of himself achieved success in anything, never originated anything, never produced anything! Sufficient answer to all; Shares. O mighty Shares!

Money in its proliferation is hopelessly separated from any authentic human value. Its infinity is nothingness. The human beings who measure themselves and one another by such a yardstick become nothing themselves.

This emptying out of human beings as they become more and more alienated from reality can be seen everywhere in *Our Mutual Friend.*

Most obvious is the hollowness of society people like the Veneerings, the Lammles, and their "friends" the "Fathers of the Scrip-Church." As the Veneerings' name suggests, such people are a false surface with nothing beneath it. If people in "Society" are worth exactly the amount of money (or Shares) they possess, and if money is a human fiction, then the appearance of money is as good as really possessing it, as long as one is not found out. The real possession of money is nothing in itself, and the pretended possession of money is a nothing to the second power, which is neither worse nor better. The Veneering dinner parties are an elaborate theatrical ceremony resting on nothing, and the people who come to these parties have been so dehumanized by their submission to money that they exist not as individuals, but as their abstract roles, "Boots," "Brewer," and so on.

In one sense it is true to say that Dickens shows people turned into objects by money. Instead of being a unique and therefore infinitely valuable individual, each person becomes his monetary worth, an object interchangeable with others. To Mr Podsnap it seems that his daughter can "be exactly put away like the plate, brought out like the plate, polished like the plate, counted, weighed, and valued like the plate." One of the potentates of Society describes Lizzie Hexam as a mere engine, fueled by so many pounds of beefsteak and so many pints of porter, and deriving therefrom power to row her boat. Bella Wilfer has been "willed away, like a horse, or a dog, or a bird," or "like a dozen of spoons." She suspects John Rokesmith of "speculating" in her. Her involvement in the Harmon mystery has alienated her from herself, and "made [her] the property of strangers."

Such objectifying is not the end of the malign magic performed on men by money. Money turns people into objects which are, like the Podsnap plate, valued only according to the money they are worth. This monetary measure of man might more properly be called a subjectifying. Money is an absolute value which has been generated by people in their living together. Another way to put this is to say that its value is entirely subjective. This value lies only in the collective hallucination of an existence where nothing exists, like the emperor's clothes. A piece of paper currency is worthless scrip. Its value is entirely *mediated*, that is, it is valued not for what it is in itself, but only as it is valued by others. In *Our Mutual Friend* all things and people have the mediated worth of a piece of paper money.

The title of the novel may be taken as an allusion to one form of this mediation. John Rokesmith exists not only for himself, but as he appears in the eyes of other people, and Bella Wilfer is guided at first in her response to him not by her own honest reaction, but by what other people think. Many characters in *Our Mutual Friend* are powerless to confront another person or thing directly. Like the unregenerate Bella, they can see others only through the haze which money casts over everything. This means that they value other people only as society values them, according to their worth in pounds, shillings, and pence. But money has reality only when it is based on some solid human or material reality. The characters in *Our Mutual Friend*, in their failure to see this and in their acceptance of money as intrinsically valuable, have come to live in a collective mirage. This mirage is a closed circuit in which nothing is reflected by nothing. Veneering's election to Parliament is a good example of this. The Veneerings, who are nothing in themselves, give value to the Lammles, Lady Tippins, and the rest, who are nothing in themselves, the Lammles give value to the Veneerings, and so back and forth, in a vain mirroring of nothing by nothing.

The motif of a literal mirroring occurs at crucial points in *Our Mutual Friend.* Poor little Miss Podsnap has derived her early views of life from "the reflections of it in her father's boots, and in the walnut and rosewood tables of the dim drawing-rooms, and in their swarthy giants of looking-glasses." She confronts life indirectly, as it is mediated by the massive presence of her father and his possessions. To see a Veneering dinner party reflected in "the great looking-glass above the sideboard," to see the vain Bella admiring herself in her mirror, or to see Fledgeby secretly watching Riah's reflection in the chimney-glass is to witness a concrete revelation of the way the lives of such people are self-mirroring. The reflection in the mirror is emptied of its solidity and presented as a thin surface of appearance hiding fathomless depths of nullity. Mirroring brings to light the vacuity of people whose lives are determined by money. Each such character is reflected in the blankness of the glass, and can see others only as they are mediated by a reflected image.

When this detachment from solidity is complete, human beings have only one opening for their energies: the attempt to dominate others by rising in the unreal scale which is generated in a society dominated by money. The image of a vertical scale permeates *Our Mutual Friend.* The characters feel themselves higher or lower on this scale as they possess more or less money, or as they can cheat others out of money in the perpetual poker game which society sustains. Mr Boffin invokes the primary law of an acquisitive society in his defense of miserliness: "Scrunch or be scrunched." The Lammles, when they find that each has married the other under the mistaken impression that he is rich, decide to cooperate in fleecing society. Fascination Fledgeby seeks the secret control of others money gives, and Silas Wegg, exulting in the power he thinks the Harmon will gives him, declares he is one hundred, no, five hundred times the man Noddy Boffin is. The unrecognized emptiness of money makes it an unlimited instrument of man's will to power.

A society in which personal relations reduce themselves to a struggle for dominance develops that drama of *looks* and *faces* which is so important in *Our Mutual Friend.* Scenes in the novel are frequently presented as a conflict of masks. Each person tries to hide his own secret and to probe behind a misleading surface and find the secrets of others. The prize of a successful uncovering is the power that goes with knowing and not being known. Bella Wilfer finds that the Boffin household has become a confrontation of stealthy faces: "What with taking heed of these two faces, and what with feeling conscious that the stealthy occupation must set some mark on her own, Bella soon began to think that there was not a candid or a natural face among them all but Mrs. Boffin's." In the same way the Lammles exchange hidden looks over the heads of their unconscious victim, Georgiana Podsnap, and Silas Wegg and Mr Venus trade glances as Wegg reads stories about misers to Mr Boffin. In this case, as in the others, the master of the situation is the man whose face is an opaque nonreflector and remains unread.

In *Our Mutual Friend* the unreality of money has spread out to define the lives of most of the characters and to dissolve them in its emptiness. Master or slave, high on the scale or low, such characters float free in an unsubstantial realm of subjective fantasy. This quality is the chief source of the comedy of the novel. As in Dickens' earlier fiction, this comedy has its source in the incongruity of a mind enclosed in its own grotesque vision of things. In *Our Mutual Friend* this detachment has a special linguistic expression, partly a matter of the language used by the characters themselves and partly a matter of the way the narrator describes them. Both narrator and characters speak in metaphors which have separated themselves from their material basis, and hover in a verbal realm, a realm which perfectly defines the deracinated existence of the characters. What begins as a *jeu d'esprit*, a vivid way of describing a character or event, undermines the human reality it names and infects it parasitically with its own inane unreality. The Veneerings' butler is first "*like* a gloomy Analytical Chemist," but the figure of speech soon displaces the reality, and the butler becomes simply "the Analytical." In the same way Mrs Podsnap is a rocking horse, Gaffer Hexam is a bird of prey, Mr Wilfer is a cherub, and so on. Sometimes a whole scene is pervaded by a figure of speech and is transformed into a surrealistic nightmare, as in the case of a Podsnap soirée which is described as a steam bath of dinner smells:

> And now the haunch of mutton vapour-bath, having received a gamey infusion and a few last touches of sweets and coffee, was quite ready, and the bathers came. . . . Bald bathers folded their arms and talked to Mr. Podsnap on the hearth-rug; sleek-whiskered bathers, with hats in their hands, lunged at Mrs. Podsnap and retreated; prowling bathers went about looking into ornamental boxes and bowls as if they had suspicions of larceny on the part of the Podsnaps and expected to find something they had lost at the bottom; bathers of the gentler sex sat silently comparing ivory shoulders.

In such passages Dickens admirably exposes the hollowness of his people by describing them in language which affirms that a fantastic metaphor is as real here as anything else. The characters themselves use language which is hilariously detached from reality, like the poetry Wegg ludicrously misapplies to any situation. Dickens' characters, even stupid ones, have an extraordinary gift of speech. The comic characters in *Our Mutual Friend* unwittingly use this power to reveal their own vacuity. The weird scenes between Wegg and Venus, or the gammon and spinach of the Voices of Society, or the gorgeous nonsense of the colloquies between Mrs Wilfer and Lavinia are triumphs of this mode of comedy. Such characters are cut off from any anchor of substantial feeling and release a splendid linguistic energy which expands inexhaustibly in the void. Speech, like money, has become in *Our Mutual Friend* a traffic in counterfeit coin.

If the novel demonstrates what money can make of life, it also shows what lies behind money, and it shows characters who escape from the collective dream it creates. If the personages are mostly bewitched by a false god, the novel as a whole is a work of demystification.

This is accomplished first through the language of the narrator. The voice the reader hears is cool and detached, very different, for example, from the emotionally involved voice of David Copperfield as he tells his own story. This is especially apparent in the scenes of the Veneering dinner parties. These are described in the present tense, in language that is cold and withdrawn, terse, with an elliptical economy new in Dickens.

Sometimes verbs and articles are omitted, and the reader confronts a series of nouns with modifiers which produces the scene before his mind's eye as if by magical incantation: "Dining-room no less magnificent than drawing-room; tables superb; all the camels out, and all laden. Splendid cake, covered with Cupids, silver, and true-lovers' knots. Splendid bracelet, produced by Veneering before going down, and clasped upon the arm of bride." The ironic detachment of such language makes the consciousness of the narrator (and of the reader) into a mirror uncovering the emptiness of the characters. The reader himself becomes the great looking-glass above the sideboard which shows what money has made of life. This mirrorlike detachment to a greater or lesser degree is the narrative perspective of the entire novel. It allows the reader to escape from the enchantment which holds the characters.

Escape to what? What waking reality, for Dickens, lies behind the dream? Dickens gives unusual attention in this novel to elemental matter. If money is in one sense unreal, in another sense the paper or metal of which it is made has a solidity which mediated subjectivities can never possess. Mr Podsnap's hideous epergne reflects no value on its owner, but his desire not to have beautiful things on his table has inadvertently made it possible to see in his silver and plate the sheer, massive inertia of matter – heavy, impenetrable, meaningless, alien to man:

> Hideous solidity was the characteristic of the Podsnap plate. Everything was made to look as heavy as it could and to take up as much room as possible. Everything said boastfully, "Here you have as much of me in my ugliness as if I were only lead; but I am so many ounces of precious metal worth so much an ounce – wouldn't you like to melt me down?" A corpulent straddling epergne, blotched all over as if it had broken out in an eruption rather than been ornamented, delivered this address from an unsightly silver platform in the centre of the table.

The otherness of elemental matter, brought to the surface in this passage, is kept constantly before the reader throughout *Our Mutual Friend*. It is the substance which lies behind or beneath the hollowness of an avaricious society. This substance is there on the literal level of the novel: in the fire where Lizzie Hexam sees pictures of her life, in the wind which blows the dust through the streets, creating a wild disorder in the clouds, and making the pitiful little tumults in the streets of no account. Elemental matter is present in the dust of the Harmon Mounds, in the mud of the river, in the dunghills where Noddy Boffin's misers hid their gold, in the gold itself in the Bank of England – in which Bella would like to have "an hour's gardening, with a bright copper shovel." Elemental matter is present in the river which flows through all the novel and is the scene of much of its action. All four elements are unobtrusively gathered together when Charley Hexam says of a glow in burning coal: "That's gas, that is, coming out of a bit of a forest that's been under the mud that was under the water in the days of Noah's Ark."

These material elements are not "symbols," if that means expressions of some reality which transcends them, and for which they stand. The river, the dust, the wind, and the fire are what they are: mere matter. *Our Mutual Friend* differs in this from Dickens' earlier novels. In *Dombey and Son* or *David Copperfield* the sea is a symbol of transcendent spiritual reality. The river of *Our Mutual Friend* is, in most of the passages describing it, only water, but, like the other material elements, it has a substantiality which the Voice of Society lacks. The narrator keeps this reality before the reader throughout the novel, not only in the literal scene, but in metaphors, overt and covert, in a thousand subtle linguistic touches which refer back to it, as the mutton vapor bath links the Podsnap drawing rooms to the Thames, or as Fascination Fledgeby, after his thrashing by Lammle, is shown "plunging and gambolling all over his bed, like a porpoise or dolphin in its native element."

The various dramatic actions of the novel show characters breaking through illusion to confront material reality. Such a confrontation takes two forms. There is first the literal descent into matter, Silas Wegg's plunge into a garbage cart, the drownings or near drownings of John Harmon, George Radfoot, Gaffer Hexam, Rogue Riderhood, Bradley Headstone, and Eugene Wrayburn. These entries into matter are also encounters with death, the dispersion into dust to which we shall all come at last. In addition, a human and inward form of substantial reality plays an important role in *Our Mutual Friend*: emotions, the affective depths of the self. Alienated, unreal people are incapable of authentic feeling. Their emotions are falsified or betrayed by their conscious behavior. The story of Bradley Headstone shows a man of strong repressed emotions destroyed when these feelings rise from his inner depths. Bradley's feelings are explicitly associated with the sea, those outer depths of water. "No man knows till the time comes, what depths are within him," Bradley tells Lizzie. "To me you brought it; on me, you forced it; and the bottom of this raging sea . . . has been heaved up ever since."

Only the characters who confront material and emotional depths, and then return to live their surface lives in terms of those depths can reconcile "Society" and reality. Eugene Wrayburn returns from his near death in the river to reject class distinctions, marry Lizzie Hexam, and conquer the boredom which has undermined his life, making him "like one cast away, for the want of something to trust in, and care for, and think well of." Bella Wilfer, who, like Eugene, has been "giddy for want of the weight of some sustaining purpose," renounces her desire for money and chooses to become the "Mendicant's Bride." This proves that "she's the true golden gold at heart." Gold does not measure the value of man. Man's heart, golden or empty, gives value to money and makes it a force for good or for evil. In the hands of Bella and John Harmon the Harmon fortune "turns bright again, after a long, long rust in the dark, and at last begins to sparkle in the sunlight." Just as Mr Boffin's change to a miser is only apparent, just as Rogue Riderhood is not changed by his near death in the Thames, and just as Eugene Wrayburn has been a good fellow all along, so Bella Wilfer does not really change. Her true nature is brought to the surface. Even in this last of his finished novels, a novel with so many apparent transformations of character, Dickens remains true to his feeling that each man or woman has a fixed nature, a selfhood which may be obscured or distorted but never essentially altered.

6

Some implications of form in Victorian fiction

The special place of Joseph Conrad in English literature lies in the fact that in his work a form of nihilism covert in modern culture is brought to the surface and shown for what it is. I am using the term "nihilism" here to describe two related forms of nothingness. First, nihilism is the emptiness left after what Nietzsche calls "the death of God." This emptiness is figured in the vacancy of astronomical space. It undermines man's values by depriving them of extra-human foundation. Second, nihilism is the hollowness of human consciousness itself. The second aspect of nihilism is associated with a tendency to define man in terms of his self-sustaining strength of will. The relation between these two aspects of nihilism is implicit in the speech of the madman in Nietzsche's *The Joyful Wisdom*. This text announces the death of God and defines it:

> "Where has God gone?" he called out. "I mean to tell you! *We have killed him*, – you and I! We are his murderers! But how have we done it? How were we able to drink up the sea? Who gave us the sponge to wipe away the whole horizon? What did we do when we loosened this earth from its sun? Whither does it now move? Whither do we move? Away from all suns? Do we not dash on unceasingly? Backwards, sideways, forwards, in all directions? Is there still an above and below? Do we not stray, as through infinite nothingness? Does not empty space breathe upon us?"

The death of God is not the same thing as the loss of faith in God's existence. Nor is it the same thing as a willing withdrawal of God from the world. God is dead because man has killed him. Man has killed God by dividing existence into two realms, subject and object, mind and world. This dualism, already implicit in Descartes' *Cogito ergo sum*, is present in many forms of modem thought and art, even in those forms which try to deny it or transcend it. It is, for example, the latent presupposition determining the forms of Victorian fiction, and it is these I shall discuss in this essay.

Descartes' hyperbolic doubt establishes the priority of consciousness over its objects. It leads to the notion that things exist, for man at least, only because he thinks them. When things exist only as represented or reflected in man's consciousness, then man has drunk up the sea and has become himself the measure of every coordinate of space. God was once seen as the power establishing the horizon which divides heaven from earth; but when man becomes the measure of all things, he drinks up the sea. In doing so he also drinks up God, the creator of the sea. God now becomes an object of thought like any other. It is in this sense that man, for Nietzsche, is the murderer of God. After this catastrophe, as the first sense of exhilarating freedom begins to wear off, man wanders "backwards, sideways, forwards, in all directions," through an "infinite nothingness" which is both within him and without. It remained for Conrad, in English literature, to bring to the surface in his own way these implications of modern subjectivism, but Conrad is the culmination of a development which can be traced through previous novelists.

This development is particularly well-marked in English fiction, though of course it is present in continental fiction too. Though it exists alongside the drama of the attempt to recover an absent God in mid-nineteenth-century poetry, Victorian fiction follows a different track. The novel shows man forgetting the death of God and attempting to establish a purely human world based on interpersonal relations. In the novel the secret nihilism accompanying man's new role as the source of all value is gradually revealed. Conrad is part of European literature and takes his place with Dostoevsky, Mann, Gide, Proust, and Camus as an explorer of modern forms of experience. Within the narrower limits of the English novel, however, he comes at the end of a native tradition leading from Dickens and George Eliot to Hardy and James.

Dickens begins his career as the inheritor of eighteenth-century conceptions of man and society. These assume that each man has a fixed nature, given to him by God. All men are naturally good, but the goodness in some men is invulnerable whereas in others it can be corrupted by the world. *Oliver Twist* takes up themes Dickens inherited from Fielding and Smollett. Oliver manages to protect his goodness from the stains of the world's evil and thereby earns the place which is waiting for him in the society of the good. His destiny is secretly manipulated by a Providence which is the presence of God in the world. But even as early as *Oliver Twist* Dickens sees the city as a place from which God is absent. Only in the country is God a sustaining presence in nature, the support of individual and social goodness. As Dickens' work progresses, there is a gradual widening of this split between the small communities where God is present and the vast city, teeming with people separated from God or touched by Him only intermittently. The central issue of *David Copperfield*, for example, is a metaphysical or even theological problem: What is the source of the pattern of David's life, as he presents it in retrospect? Is the structure a merely human one of memory, free choice, and linked associations, or has David's life been the gradual revelation of a destiny secretly prepared for him by a benign Providence? The old objective world, ordered by a living God, is delicately balanced against the new subjective one in which man gives pattern and value to the world by seeing it from a certain point of view and assimilating it into his mind, as all the world of *David Copperfield* exists in the reconstruction of David's first-person narration.

Dickens' last work moves toward a recognition of the hollowness which undermines a society constructed freely by men and women living together in the city. His last completed novel, *Our Mutual Friend* (1864–5), goes furthest toward recognizing the nihilism emergent in English culture. It is a novel about "money, money, money, and what money can make of life." Dickens sees that money is the collective ascription of value to what has no value in itself, but the "Society" of *Our Mutual Friend*, in forgetting this fact, has allowed itself more and more to be measured by the nullity of money. The result is a progressive emptying-out of the characters, as they are gradually more cut off from any extra-human reality. In the absence of any such reality, society becomes the scene of a spectral battle of vacuous wills struggling for dominance. In *Our Mutual Friend* Dickens sees that a human society cannot be self-generating. Values created entirely out of the interaction of one consciousness with another can have no authenticity. They are the reflection of nothing by nothing, as the Veneering dinner parties are reflected in the great looking glass over the sideboard and shown to be a vain pretense. Salvation is possible in *Our Mutual Friend* only for those characters who can break through the façade of mediated reflections and reach a reality, whether material or spiritual, beyond the human world.

If Dickens' last novel approaches a confrontation with nihilism which is something like Conrad's, the derivation of the formal conventions of Victorian fiction from an assumption of the separation of subject and object appears with great clarity in the work of George Eliot. The aesthetic and metaphysical presuppositions of the art form inherited by Conrad are already well developed in her novels. Her work is a deliberate attempt to construct a viable human world after the death of God. Following Feuerbach, she sees God as the projection of collective human values and tries to show that mankind can, as Barbara Hardy puts it, "be its own providence." George Eliot's novels are a full working-out of what follows from the assumption that each consciousness is a separate sphere, a "centre of self," as she puts it in *Middlemarch* (1871–2), "whence the lights and shadows must always fall with a certain difference." Everything exists as an appearance in some "centre of self." Nature, like God, is subjectivized and made over into a reflection of the qualities of human life. Each mind is cut off from other minds and has no natural access to them. The dramatic action of George Eliot's novels tends to develop from the obdurate opacity of minds to one another. Self-centered egotism is the great danger to man and the source of evil. Good follows from the enhancement of man's power of self-denying sympathy.

There is, however, an apparent contradiction in the form her novels take. They presuppose that every human being is imprisoned in his subjectivity, limited to his own perspective on the world. The lesson of life, even for so intelligent, so "ardent and theoretic" a person as Dorothea in *Middlemarch*, is a lesson of renunciation. Each man or woman must accept a narrow lot, both in power of vision and in range of effective action. But the narrator of the novels claims for herself precisely that all-embracing breadth of vision, that intimate access to the hearts of others, which is denied to the characters. If the acceptance of a separation of subject and object leads the novel inevitably to the technique of limited point of view as it is practiced by James or Conrad, George Eliot seems old-fashioned and naïve in her assumption of the possibility of angelic omniscience for the narrator. To borrow another phrase from *Middlemarch*, the narrator of her novels is related to the world of the novels in a way like that of "Uriel watching the progress of planetary history from the Sun."

Nevertheless, in spite of her appeals to a seemingly "realistic" theory of fiction, George Eliot is the most subjective of novelists. This can be seen in the fact that there is throughout *Middlemarch* a constant paralleling of the scientist's work and the novelist's. As the scientist investigates physical nature, so the novelist investigates society and human nature, and a good novel is an "experiment in life." A shift from one group of characters to another, for example, is justified by an appeal to scientific method: "In watching effects, if only of an electric battery, it is often necessary to change our place and examine a particular mixture or group at some distance from the point where the movement we are interested in was set up." The parallel between scientist and novelist would seem to make George Eliot an objective writer, effacing herself before external reality like a good scientist and discovering laws which are independent of her own mind. On the other hand, the characters in *Middlemarch* and all their world have no such objective existence as that of an electric battery. Even though the characters may be based in part on real people, these have been transposed into a purely fictive realm. George Eliot has invented all the novel, and the town of Middlemarch exists nowhere but in the words on the page. This seems to show her once more inconsistent. She claims scientific objectivity for what is in fact a fictitious invention.

Science, however, is not the effacement of the subjective before the objective. It is just the opposite: an assimilation of nature into an interior realm where everything can be manipulated as number and calculation and where the energies of nature can be "harnessed" to human ends. A remarkable passage in *Middlemarch* shows George Eliot's recognition of this, and gives, in a description of the subjectivity of correct scientific method, a covert description of her own method as a novelist. Proper imagination is no mere inventive fantasy, concocting ideal realms that never were. The imagination necessary for both scientist and novelist presupposes a turning inside-out of the objective world and its assimilation by the mind. When the world has been taken into the mind, then the scientist can follow sequences of causality otherwise hidden, just as the novelist can know the hearts of her characters in all their subtle interactions. The consciousness of the narrator is an all-embracing vessel which contains the characters and their world, bathing them in its permeating medium. George Eliot's description of the subjective realism of Lydgate the scientist is an exact description of her own "arduous invention" as a novelist:

> Many men have been praised as vividly imaginative on the strength of their profuseness in indifferent drawing or cheap narration: – reports of very poor talk going on in distant orbs; or portraits of Lucifer coming down on his bad errands as a large ugly man with bat's wings and spurts of phosphorescence; or exaggerations of wantonness that seem to reflect life in a diseased dream. But these kinds of inspiration Lydgate regarded as rather vulgar and vinous compared with the imagination that reveals subtle actions inaccessible by any sort of lens, but tracked in that outer darkness through long pathways of necessary sequence by the inward light which is the last refinement of Energy, capable of bathing even the ethereal atoms in its ideally illuminated space. He for his part had tossed away all cheap inventions where ignorance finds itself able and at ease: he was enamoured of that arduous invention which is the very eye of research, provisionally framing its object and correcting it to more and more exactness of relation. . . .

This admirable passage is a full statement of the aesthetics of that form of the novel which develops from modern subjectivism. The suprasensible world no longer exists. It is mere fantasy, product of a bad imagination diseased or drunken in its dreamings. The physical world is all that remains outside the mind. This world as it is in itself is an outer darkness, unknowable by any objective lens. Things can be known only as they are transformed into objects, that is, taken into the ideally illuminated space of the mind. When things have been absorbed into that inner space, their exact relations can be understood in finest detail and in necessary sequence. All things now are of the same nature as the mind and lie open to that searching inward light which is the substance of the mind's power piercing through every darkness to make its own contents transparent. The eye of research is turned inward, not outward, for nothing can be known which is not already inside the mind.

In *Middlemarch* or in *Daniel Deronda* (1876) the embracing consciousness of the narrator is the inner space in which all the characters dwell, as in a fluid, continuous, permeating medium. The minds of the characters are contained within the narrator's mind. That mind binds everything together in time and space and is the reader's guarantee that he can move freely from one mind to another, knowing them all completely. The narrator's mind is subtle, tactful, sensitive to delicate nuances, conscious that any process may be subdivided indefinitely into ever more minute parts. The greatness of a late novel like *Middlemarch*, as well as its advance over earlier works like *Adam Bede*, lies in the substitution of the image of an immense moving system, "a play of minute causes," for the simpler image of a chain of single causes used in the earlier novel. *Middlemarch* is an enormously complicated network of relations. On whatever moment in whatever mind the narrator focuses, the reader is constantly made aware of a multiple complexity: the complexity of the single mind in any moment, the complexity of that mind in relation to its own past and future, the complexity of the co-presence of all the minds, all misunderstanding one another, each living in its own world, and each with its own past and future – the whole making a dynamic web of interwoven influences. Any particular mental state participates in the "embroiled medium" of the whole and is inevitably "a part of that involuntary, palpitating life." This vision of society as a structure of reciprocal effects is achieved only through the subjectivizing of the world, its assimilation by the inward light of imagination. George Eliot's novels are the triumph of her will to understand the world. The ideally illuminated space we enter when we read one of her novels is sustained by nothing but her mind, just as her religion of humanity proposes that men in their living together can create their own God.

Like other mid-nineteenth-century writers, George Eliot was not fully aware of the implications of her humanism, and, as Nietzsche saw, attempted the difficult task of upholding the Christian morality of altruism without faith in the Christian God. "When one gives up the Christian faith," says Nietzsche in a paragraph on George Eliot in *Twilight of the Idols*,

> one pulls the right to Christian morality out from under one's feet. This morality is by no means self-evident: this point has to be exhibited again and again, despite the English flatheads. Christianity is a system, a *whole* view of things thought out together. By breaking one main concept out of it, the faith in God, one breaks the whole: nothing necessary remains in one's hands. Christianity presupposes that man does not know, *cannot*

> know, what is good for him, what evil: he believes in God, Who alone knows it. Christian morality is a command; its origin is transcendent; it is beyond all criticism, all right to criticism; it has truth only if God is the truth – it stands and falls with faith in God.

Another of the "English flatheads," Anthony Trollope, begins, like George Eliot, without full recognition of the implications of his vision, but his later work moves toward such recognition. Trollope's fanatical commitment to the writing of novels as a daily routine grew out of an early habit of daydreaming. His novels, like those of George Eliot, exist in a subjective inner space which is the consciousness of the omniscient narrator. Trollope's characters, however, unlike George Eliot's, are as transparent to one another as they are to the inward vision of the narrator. This transparency follows naturally from the fact that the characters live in a humanized world. In spite of the fact that many of Trollope's best novels are about clergymen and their wives and daughters, these novels do not center on religious themes. All ladies and gentlemen will go to heaven, but heaven is a long way off, beyond the barriers of death. It does not exist within the confines of the story, which are the confines of the narrator's mind. In the same way, nonhuman nature does not exist except as a sign of some subjective or social quality, as a man's estate signifies his wealth or as the rooms in *The Warden* are perfect expressions of the people who live in them. Trollope's novels concentrate on minds and their interactions; and since the characters share the assumptions and moral judgments which define their society, they can usually see perfectly into one another's hearts.

The dramatic action of a novel by Trollope can therefore rarely derive from that interplay of appearance and reality which arises when minds are opaque to one another and which is central in the work of a novelist like Jane Austen. The clarity with which the characters in Trollope's novels understand one another means that the drama often arises from a conflict of wills. His characters are distinguished by the strength and quality of their volition, and each novel is a kind of game in which each character plays with all his energy the role in which he finds himself cast. Trollope is a striking example of the way a definition of man as subjective ego leads to a definition of him as will. In Trollope's early fiction, however, there is no understanding of the autonomy of the will, or of the way society as a whole rests in consequence on nothing but human volition. This understanding is made impossible by the lack of abstract self-consciousness in the characters, the utter spontaneity with which they make the decisions which allow them to go on being themselves. They are able instinctively to decide to be true to themselves, and this keeps secret the fact that they could decide to be different. If their selfhoods are sustained only by acts of will, then those selves are in fact nothing but will. Continuity, self-consistency, is therefore the supreme virtue in Trollope's world. As long as the characters remain true to themselves, the fragility of their society will not appear. As long as the game does not appear as a game, its arbitrary quality will stay hidden. So Lily Dale sticks to the decision made in *The Small House at Allington* not to marry Johnny Eames and in *The Last Chronicle of Barset* writes herself down as "Lilian Dale, Old Maid." If she were to betray her earlier commitment and choose to marry Johnny, the earlier decision might appear to be gratuitous. If man is nothing but will, then he may change as often as he wills; and if a man recognizes this, he may become the shape-shifter of one form of twentieth-century existentialism.

The emptiness of a self-sustaining society never appeared in such stark terms to Trollope, partly because of his native English faith in the permanence of each man's character; but one of his last novels, *The Way We Live Now* (1874–5), moves toward an understanding of the latent implications of his earlier ones. *The Way We Live Now* denies all the laws of Trollope's earlier novels. It shows the new way of life in the city destroying the old provincial society. But in being the end of the apparently stable society of small communities, the new city life shows that society for what it secretly was all along: unstable because resting primarily on human wills. A community of such wills is a game held together by the fact that people go on obeying rules which are "absurd" in the sense that they might have been different, and they might be different now, if the characters should choose to play the game by different rules. Lack of detached self-awareness prevented the people in earlier novels from recognizing this, but many characters in *The Way We Live Now* have a new self-consciousness.

In place of the continuity usual in Trollope's fiction, *The Way We Live Now* shows sudden changes in society and in the individuals who make up society. The new men and women are radically different from Lily Dale. Instead of remaining true to themselves at all costs, they betray themselves and their allegiances to one another. They waver from moment to moment, make a decision and then reverse it. The novel's many plots are unified by the theme of betrayal. Society as a whole in *The Way We Live Now* is no longer moving in a gradual curve of change, the result of the tension of opposing forces. Now change comes suddenly and makes a radical break with the past. A fellow like Melmotte, who comes from nowhere, can get into Parliament and become a great power in the city.

The Way We Live Now also lacks the transparency normal in Trollope's novels. It is full of mysteries and opacities. The characters are again and again said not to be able to understand one another. Melmotte is the center of fascinated attention just because nobody knows whether he is a scoundrel or a great financier, as in *The Last Chronicle of Barset* the blank place of the Reverend Crawley's loss of memory is the center of concern for the community. In *The Last Chronicle* the blank place is opened at last to everybody's gaze, and what is revealed there sustains the homogeneity and safety of Trollope's world. In *The Way We Live Now* the opposite is the case. Melmotte is a great thief, as most people come to suspect, but in his suicide he takes his secrets to the grave and remains a mystery to the end.

As in *Our Mutual Friend*, money is the paradoxical agent of the degradation of society. Though it is in itself transparent, it is the source of secrecy. Since the appearance of money is as good as the real thing and since money is a zero which may through speculation multiply itself to infinity or disappear in a moment to nothing, it makes people opaque to one another and creates the possibility of discontinuity: Melmotte's rise to power or the marriage of aristocrats with parvenus. Money as an instrument of the will to power reveals in *The Way We Live Now* the ungrounded nature of the human will.

This is shown even more directly in the development of Marie Melmotte, the daughter of the central character. Marie is a Lily Dale brought into the full light of self-consciousness. As she gradually discovers the power of her own will, she finds at the same time its complete freedom. Instead of using her will to remain true to her original choice, as Lily Dale did, she takes possession of the freedom of her will and uses it to emancipate herself from all commitments. Like the fiery American Mrs Hurtle, she becomes a creature of dangerous strength of will. She decides to remain her own woman and to act only for herself. "Feeling conscious of her own power in regard to her own money, knowing that she [can] do as she [pleases] with her wealth," she tells the man she decides to marry that if she finds anything to induce her to change her mind, she will change it. She frees herself from all allegiances, even the allegiance to her own past self, and becomes, in her modest way, like her father before her, an embodiment of the will to power sustained by nothing but itself. In becoming so, she brings into the open latent implications of Trollope's earlier fiction.

George Meredith's characters, too, though they seem at first to be the offspring of an evolutionary naturalism, are ultimately dependent on only their own wills. The question in *The Ordeal of Richard Feverel* appears at first to be whether man's continuity with nature means that he must be thought of as a repeating mechanism or as a developing organism. Richard's original "choice" of Lucy is a spontaneous action of his nature and therefore not a free choice at all, but he discovers that he is free to remain true to Lucy or to betray her. The choice made spontaneously must be reaffirmed, consciously and deliberately. It is in this sense that "we make our own fates, and nature has nothing to do with it." *The Egoist* (1879) initiates that series of late novels in which Meredith takes full possession, in his own way, of the new novel, the novel which focuses exclusively on the conflict of consciousness with consciousness, will with will. Meredith has an extraordinary sensitivity to the pressure exerted on a mind by the mere presence of another person. In his fiction is already present that drama of mediated desire and that attempt of one consciousness to found itself on the enslavement of another person's freedom, which Sartre and others have explored in the twentieth century. Clara Middleton in *The Egoist* must discover that her "nature" is her freedom, the "whims, variations, inconsistencies, wiles" of her "currents of feeling." "Her needs [are] her nature, her moods, her mind." As a result, "her free will [must] decide her fate." In a proper relation between two minds, each person respects the freedom and individuality of the other, as Vernon Whitford says to Clara: "I wish you to have your free will." For Meredith, selfhood is freedom.

If Meredith believes that a happy love is possible because two people can sustain one another in their freedom, Hardy also begins with the notion that each human being is a freedom which must found itself on its relations to others; but he sees that if consciousness is defined as the will to possession of others, then that will can never be satisfied. Though Hardy and his characters try to place the blame for their sufferings on society, on man's biological nature, on the "crass casualty" of external nature, on absurd coincidence, or on the blind determinism of the immanent will, the secret source of pain in Hardy's intuition of existence is consciousness itself. Each man's mind is a hollow space between him and things, an annihilating power which nullifies whatever it touches. In *The Mayor of Casterbridge* (1886) Henchard hates and repudiates all those people and things he comes to possess. He repudiates them because he finds that he does not really possess them. His tragic grandeur is his persistence in the search for a happy possession of another person, but the climax of his story is his recognition that the "emotional void" in his heart can never be filled. When he sees this, his will turns in on itself, the only thing it truly possesses. The reflexive will in Hardy is not the will to will of Nietzsche. It is the suicidal will not to will. In Henchard's plea for annihilation in his testament ("& that no man remember me"), as in Jude's Jobian curse on himself in *Jude the Obscure* (1894–5) ("Let the day perish wherein I was born"), latent implications of the subjective bias of the novel come fully into the open. If man's thinking ego is the source of everything, then he can never encounter anything but his own mind and things which have been turned into objects by that mind. The isolated ego is nothing but an empty will, nothing, to borrow Matthew Arnold's words in "Empedocles on Etna," but "a devouring flame of thought," "a naked, eternally restless mind." If the subjective ego is for man the ground of all things, then all things are ultimately swallowed up in the ego's vacuity.

Henry James' fiction, to discuss briefly a final novelist, is continuous with Trollope's both in aesthetic presuppositions and in themes. James' novels, like Trollope's, limit themselves rigorously to encounters between one consciousness and another, and the theme of renunciation in James is, like similar themes in Trollope, a covert recognition that society is sustained in its continuity only by the free decisions of the characters to remain true to themselves. Catherine Sloper in *Washington Square* (1881) "sticks" to her love for Morris Townsend even when she discovers that Morris has betrayed her. Her allegiance is supported by nothing outside herself and preserves only the virtue of consistency. In the same way Isabel in *Portrait of a Lady* (1881) and Strether in *The Ambassadors* (1903) renounce new possibilities of life for the sake of remaining true to earlier choices made in ignorance. Human existence is necessarily tragic for James, since the good life can be discovered only by commitment to life. Initial commitments are always made in ignorance, therefore wrongly. Ultimately a person is faced with the choice either of betraying his first commitment in order to seize the good life or of renouncing happiness in order to remain true to an earlier self. That James' characters so often choose the second course shows that for him continuity in the self, the will willing to will itself as the same even in altered circumstances, is the supreme value. It is the supreme value because only through such consistency can a person avoid falling into that version of nihilism which is the evaporation of the self into an endless series of different selves, chosen arbitrarily, as a weather vane turns in response to the slightest shift in the wind. James' interest in the histrionic personality and his understanding of its dangers is shown in *The Tragic Muse*. For James, too, measuring man in terms of the strength of his will tends to lead to an evaporation of his substance.

From Dickens and George Eliot through Trollope, Meredith, Hardy, and James, the implications of subjectivism become more and more apparent. It remained for Conrad to explore these to their depths and, in doing so, to open the way for the transcendence of nihilism in the writers of the twentieth century. But the overtly "metaphysical" quality of Conrad's fiction, its grappling with experiences which take a man outside the safe bounds of civilized society, is, as I have tried to suggest in this essay, a development of themes and aesthetic conventions which were already present in Victorian fiction.[1]

Note

1. I have discussed Conrad's work in *Poets of Reality: Six Twentieth-Century Writers* (Cambridge, Mass., 1965). In this essay I have adapted a few sentences from the Introduction to that book.

7

Three problems of fictional form:

first-person narration in *David Copperfield* and *Huckleberry Finn*

Any work of literature, including any novel, is the verbal expression of a consciousness. The words on the page give the reader access to another mind, its feelings and thoughts, its way of encountering an imagined world. Criticism of fiction, like the criticism of other forms of literature, begins with an act of reading which may be defined as consciousness of the consciousness of another. The critic must, as far as possible, dispossess himself of his own mental structures and attempt to coincide, in an act of pure identification, with the mental structures of the novel. Criticism is a putting in words of the results of this approach toward identification.

A novel, however, has special structures of its own. To these pertain the special problems of the criticism of fiction. As critics like Georg Lukács, José Ortega y Gasset, Lionel Trilling, and Ian Watt have assumed,[1] the novel came into existence in a particular time in the history of Western man and therefore expresses the personal, social, and metaphysical experiences of man during that time. The rise of the novel is associated with a new discovery of the isolation and autonomy of the private mind, with a sense of the absence of any pre-established harmony between the mind and what is outside the mind, with a diminishing faith in the existence of any supernatural power giving order and meaning to this world, and with a turning to relations between persons as the chief, if not exclusive, source of authentic life for the individual. The novel is the form of literature developed to explore the various forms intersubjective relations may take. If reading a novel is consciousness of the consciousness of another, the novel itself is a structure of related minds. To read a novel is not to encounter a single mind but to take part in an interaction among several minds – the relation of the narrator to the protagonists, of the protagonists to one another. The narrator is one mind among others, and the question of point of view or narrative stance may be assimilated into the question of relations between minds. Intersubjectivity is an important dimension of fictional form, and a sensitive discrimination of the ways minds are related to one another in a given novel is a primary requirement in the interpretation of fiction.

A second aspect of fictional form is time. Time is constitutive for the novel in a way which makes it different from other forms of literature. Any work of literature has a temporal rather than a spatial form. It takes time to read it. The words follow one another in time and establish in their sequence a temporal rhythm of connections and relationships. In a short lyric poem, however, the beginning and ending are so close to one another that they appear to be virtually simultaneous. This generates the illusion of spatial form and gives rise to a whole critical vocabulary of spatial terms: "pattern of imagery," "ironic juxtaposition," "design of the whole," and so on. Moreover, our language and our imaginations are strongly spatialized, rich in spatial terms and poor in temporal terms. It is much easier to talk about a work of literature as if it were a spatial mosaic than to do justice in critical language to its temporality. Nevertheless, the fundamental dimension of literature is time.

This becomes especially important in a work of literature as long as a novel. A simultaneous possession by the reader of all the words and images of *Middlemarch, À la recherche du temps perdu*, or *Ulysses* may be posited as an ideal, but such an ideal manifestly cannot be realized. It is impossible to hold so many details in the mind at once. To point to the fact that all the words do exist side by side on the page and the pages side by side in the book is to commit the error of thinking of the work of literature as a physical object, like a stone or a tree, rather than as a structure of signs.[2] The novel exists, it is true, as black marks on the pages, but it exists as a work of literature only as it is read. As such, it is not a spatial structure of simultaneously related parts but an ever-changing rhythm of relationships. The passage being read at a given time constitutes itself as the momentary center of the work. The rest of the novel organizes itself with varying degrees of immediacy around that temporary center.

To think of a novel in this way is to confront what might be called the paradox of the first and second reading. Which is the proper reading of a novel, the first reading, when the outcome of the story is in doubt for the reader, so that he is experiencing the events as if they had an open future, like his own life as he lives it, or the second reading, when the future is known from the beginning and the full significance of all the passages understood as they are encountered? To meet this paradox is to glimpse the hidden connections among the several problems of fictional form. In most novels, as a matter of fact, the reader is put even in the first reading virtually in possession of the perspective allowed by the second reading, that perspective which no one in "reality" can have on himself while his life continues. The protagonists live their lives in ignorance of the future. The narrator speaks from the perspective of the end. The reader enjoys both these points of view at once. He experiences the novel as the reaching out of the protagonists' point of view toward the narrator's point of view, as if they might at some vanishing point coincide. This reaching out toward completeness, in which the circle of time will be drawn closed, is the essence of human temporality. It may therefore be said that a novel as it is read from passage to passage, brought into existence as a structure of meanings, expresses a distinctive form of lived human time.

The importance of human time as the constitutive dimension for the novel may be approached from another direction. Pre-modern forms of narrative literature, for example, the epic, were often structured around the relationship between human time and divine or eternal time. Many critics, notably Ortega y Gasset and Georg Lukács, have centered on a comparison with the epic their attempts to define the unique qualities of the novel. One difference between the epic and the novel is a difference in the kinds of time expressed in each. On the one hand, there is the mythical time of the epic, with its eternal repetition of celestial archetypes. These put human time in relation to the end of time or to an escape from time. Christian epics like *The Divine Comedy* or *Paradise Lost* are based on allegorical or anagogical conceptions of time which again put human time in close relationship to God's time. Human time, in Christian literature, is a moving image of eternity. The novel, however, tends to be a post-Christian form of literature, a form which assumes that God is distant or dead. In such a form the connection between human time and divine time is broken. Man's time is experienced as determined by its finitude. It becomes the dimension in which man experiences his lack of fullness of being, the impossibility of a permanent attainment of an ideal life. Though Lukács remains bound within a linear conception of human time,[3] he has nevertheless provided in *The Theory of the Novel* a striking formulation of the way time is essential to modern fiction:

> Time then can first become constitutive when the connection with the transcendent homeland is broken. . . . It is only in the novel, the content of which consists in a necessary quest for essence and in an inability to find it, that time is an inseparable part of the form. . . . In the epic, the immanence of meaning within life is strong enough to abolish time.[4] Life as such accedes to eternity. . . . In the novel, meaning and life separate and, with them, essence and time; one could almost say that the whole inner action of the novel is no more than a struggle against the power of time.[5]

If temporality is constitutive in new ways for the novel, so are there new structures in the relation of imaginary and real. The question of realism is a third problem of fictional form. Traditional theories of fictional realism are based on a representational dualism, often expressed in the image of a mirror, as in Stendhal's often-cited description of a novel as *un miroir qu'on promène le long d'un chemin* (a mirror that one carries along on a walk down a road). On one side there is reality, the solid substance of the social and physical world. On the other side there is the novel, which must mirror this reality as exactly as possible in words. George Eliot, in the seventeenth chapter of *Adam Bede* (1859), provides one of the best expressions of this mimetic theory of realism. "[M]y strongest effort," she says,

> is . . . to give a faithful account of men and things as they have mirrored themselves in my mind. The mirror is doubtless defective; the outlines will sometimes be disturbed, the reflection faint or confused; but I feel as much bound to tell you as precisely as I can what that reflection is, as if I were in the witness-box narrating my experience on oath.[6]

The connection of the question of realism with the question of intersubjectivity appears clearly in this text. The reflections in the mirror are not, in George Eliot's formulation, initially the words and images of the novel. They are the duplication in the mind of the beholding artist of "men and things" in the outside world. The novel springs from the response of the mind of the novelist to the minds of others as they are embodied in appearances. The novel itself is a representation of this representation, an "account" of it in words, the copy of a copy.

Georges Blin, in the introduction to *Stendhal et les problèmes du roman*,[7] has shown in masterly fashion the contradictions and paradoxes of this traditional theory of realism, and many recent critics have turned their attention to elements of the "anti-novel" present even in works of fiction addressed most unambiguously to the work of representational realism. One of these contradictions is brought into the open in the passage from *Adam Bede*. A novel is an objective imitation, a cunning model in words of a reality to which it should, like a photograph, correspond point for point. At the same time it is the account of someone's experience of reality. It has a mental, not a physical, existence, therefore is unable to escape the necessary defects, disturbances, indistinctions, and confusions of any subjective mirroring of reality.

More important still is the paradoxical fact that a novel is based on reality, impossible without it, constantly referring to it whether accurately or with subjective distortions, and at the same time is an autonomous structure of words creating its own independent reality, a world which may be encountered nowhere but in the pages of this particular book.

The anti-novelistic elements which creep into the most unequivocally mimetic fiction are those details in the language in which the novel turns back on itself. This reflexive movement reveals the fact that the novel is not the report of a witness of actual events, but something made up by its author, a lie, a fiction, the generator of its own reality rather than the reflection of a reality outside itself. An example of this is the contrast between those pages in Scott's novels, often given as footnotes, in which he calls attention to the historical accuracy of some event or of some detail of dress or custom, and those passages in which he asserts the fictive nature of his narrative, the fact that he has made the story up out of his imagination.

The structure of this conflict between the imaginary and the real is intrinsic to the novel. It perhaps finds its origin in the fading of faith in celestial models or archetypes which would give a narrative stability and ground it in the transcendently real. Such a supernatural ground would be the source and sanction both for works of art and for the objective world, that artwork of God's. In place of this secure structure of correspondences, the novel often puts an overlapping or interaction of real and imaginary which is like those optical illusions which may be seen as right-side-up or upside-down, inside-out or outside-in, depending on how they are looked at, and come, as one looks, to vibrate with dizzying rapidity between the first orientation and the second.

This alternation of true and false is easiest to see in the interpenetration of minds (and therefore of levels of reality) which makes up a novel. The narrator of a novel may sometimes seem to be the novelist himself, speaking in his own voice, as in many passages in *Tom Jones* (1749), or in *Vanity Fair* (1847–8), or as in those notorious interventions in Trollope's novels which Henry James deplored. At other times the narrator may exist entirely on the other side of the mirror. In this case he is a persona or invented voice of the author who speaks as if the events he retells had an historical existence. The narrative voice in many novels goes back and forth without warning from one side of the mirror to the other.

Another place to see this vibration is in the use of stories within stories, or narrators within narrators. These have been part of fictional technique from the Renaissance to the present and may be traced from the puppet-show of Master Pedro and the interpolated stories in *Don Quixote* (1605; 1615), through the interpolated stories and use of scenes in the theater in Fielding's novels to nineteenth-century works like *Pickwick Papers* (1836–7), *Wuthering Heights* (1847), *Bleak House* (1852–3), and *The Moonstone* (1868), and on to the complex use of multiple narrators by Conrad and others in the twentieth century. The effect of these reflections within reflections is curious. It parallels the effect of the play within the play in Renaissance drama.[8] The palpably fictive or subjective quality of the interpolated story tends to affirm the historical reality of the first level of the narration, but at the same time the reader may be led to see that he is himself hearing a story, like the characters on the first level of reality in the novel. The reader may then come to feel like the first participant in an echoing series of representations within representations, each equally real and equally imaginary, each affirming the reality of the preceding one and yet at the same time undermining it, like the endless sequence of images when two mirrors are held up to reflect one another's reflections. All the world's a novel, and the men and women merely characters in it, creating and sustaining their own illusory universes.

Intersubjectivity, time, and realism – each of these aspects of fiction has the same form. Each leads to the others and reveals its congruity with them. Each is so entangled with the others that it cannot be detached and investigated in isolation. All three have the form of an incomplete circle, a circle in which consciousness moves away from itself in order to move back to its ground.

Moving toward itself by moving away from itself, however, the mind never reaches its goal. Though human temporality is a reaching from the present toward the future to reappropriate the past, the circle of time is never complete. Past and future never come together in the present. Though art may be defined as a search for the real by way of the imaginary, the echoing sequence of reflections is never stilled in a coincidence of the fictive and the true. Though interpersonal relations may be defined as a search for the true self by way of other people, a man never fully possesses his buried self by means of his possession of another person.

To move toward these goals, nevertheless, is a momentary revelation of them, as well as a failure to reach them. As long as the fiction continues it holds in the open the incomplete structure of temporality, of the imaginary seeking to become the real, and of one mind trying to reach its hidden depths through others. Holding this never-finished structure in the open, the novel also holds in the open a glimpse of its ground, its secret origin and end.

When the fiction is over the revelation is over, over in open-ended fiction in the silence after the last page of a failure of the protagonist to coincide wholly with the narrator, over in closed forms of fiction in the disappearance of the protagonist's detached self-consciousness when he finds his true self and dissolves into the collective consciousness of the community. American novelists have tended to feel that authenticity lies in maintaining one's separate individuality. In English fiction, even in the twentieth century, the attainment of a proper self has often seemed to coincide with the discovery of a place in the community. For such novelists the goal for the individual is the assimilation of his private mind into that public mind for which the omniscient narrator is a spokesman.

David Copperfield (1849–50) and *Huckleberry Finn* (1884), among nineteenth-century English and American novels, are salient examples of masterworks of fiction written as first-person narratives. The first-person novel, in spite of Henry James' distaste for its baggy looseness, is not so much formless as a special case of fictional form. It provides a good example of the interaction of the three aspects of that form.

The distinguishing characteristic of the first-person novel is the fact that the narrator in most cases coincides with the protagonist. This does not mean, however, that in this coincidence the structure of intersubjective relations usual in the third-person novel is truncated or collapsed. Rather, it takes another form. In *David Copperfield* or *Huckleberry Finn* the author attempts to come to terms with his own life by playing the role of an imaginary character who in both cases has obvious similarities to the author himself. This imaginary character, in his turn, retraces from the point of view of a later time the earlier course of his life. The interpersonal texture of both novels is made up of the superimposition of two minds, the mind of the adult David reliving his experiences as a child, the mind of Huck after his adventures are over retelling them from the perspective of the wisdom, if wisdom it is, to which they have led. In both novels the older narrator, from the vantage of a later time, watches his younger self engage himself more or less naïvely in relations to other people. Behind this double consciousness may be glimpsed the mind of the author himself, the Charles Dickens who is reshaping the events of his life to make a novel out of them, the Mark Twain who is present in the irony which runs through *Huckleberry Finn* as a pervasive stylistic flavoring. This stylistic quality results from Huck's inability to understand his experiences, either while they are happening or as he retells them, as well as the reader and the author understand them.[9] From author to narrator to youthful protagonist to other characters – the structure of *David Copperfield* or *Huckleberry Finn* is no less than that of *Pride and Prejudice* (1813), *Middlemarch* (1871–2), or *The Golden Bowl* (1904), a pattern of related minds. In both first-person novels the author may be seen going away from himself into an imagined person living in an imagined world in order to return to himself and take possession by indirection of his own past self and his own past life.

If intersubjective relations and relations of the imaginary and the real are so closely intertwined in these two first-person novels, they both provide classic examples of the incomplete circle or spiral form taken by temporality in fiction. The autobiographical novel has exactly the structure of human temporality. It is a moving toward the future in order to come back to what one has already been, in an attempt to complete one's deepest possibility of being by drawing the circle of time closed and thereby becoming a whole. But the circle of time is complete only with my death. As long as I live I cannot reach that future moment when I shall understand myself completely, coincide completely with the hidden sources of my being. Going forward in time through a recapitulation in language of his experiences in the past, the narrator of a first-person novel returns eventually back through his past to himself in the present, but at a higher level of comprehension, it may be, than he had when he began to tell his story. The insight born of the act of retelling may lead the narrator to an authentic understanding of his life, a recognition of its hitherto hidden patterns. On the basis of this recognition he may then take hold of his past life, accept it in a new way in the present, and come to a resolute decision about the future. This revelation, however, is never complete as long as the narrator lives. The spiral is endless. Huck or David could go around and around the circle indefinitely, bringing their past lives up to the present in the light of the new insight gained by the act of retelling, recapitulating their lives over and over without exhausting them or finding that a new circling repetition had brought them back to exactly the same place.

Even so, the moment of return from a journey through the past to the present, when the two levels of the narrator's mind coincide, is the crucial instant in a first-person novel. It is the moment at the end of *Huckleberry Finn*, for example, when Huck speaks in the present tense of his present situation. Having gone through his life up to the present, he sees it whole and sums up what he sees in his decision to run away from civilization. Only in this way can he escape from another repetition of his repetitive adventures, adventures which have rhythmically alternated between solitude and disastrous involvement in society, and are about to culminate, as Daniel Hoffman and others have seen,[10] in a recurrence of the involvement most dangerous of all to his integrity: subjection to the loving-kindness of a well-meaning member of respectable society. "But I reckon I got to light out for the Territory ahead of the rest," says Huck, "because Aunt Sally she's going to adopt me and sivilize me and I can't stand it. I been there before" (226).[11]

At the end of *David Copperfield* David, like Huck, returns after a long looping circuit through his past to present-tense speech about the present. He too looks toward the future on the basis of a clear understanding of the past and makes a decision about that future. But how different is his state of mind! How different is his relation to other people, and how different the resolution he takes! David has experienced in childhood, like other Dickensian heroes or heroines, Oliver, Pip, Arthur Clennam, or Esther Summerson, solitude and deprivation, the lack of a satisfactory place within a family or within society. He has been "a somebody too many"[12] "cast away among creatures with whom [he has] had no community of nature" (105). His search through the adventures he retells is for something which will focus his life and give it substance. Throughout his experiences he is troubled by "a vague unhappy loss or want of something" (386). He seeks something to fill the void in his heart. The novel is his "written memory" (527), in which the adult David, as he says, "stand[s] aside, to see the phantoms of those days go by me, accompanying the shadow of myself, in dim procession" (479). *David Copperfield*, like Thackeray's *Henry Esmond* (1852), contains many references to time and memory. These call the reader's attention to the distance between the present condition of the narrator and that of his past self. They interpose between the one and the other "a softened glory of the Past, which nothing could [throw] upon the present time" (494). Retracing the journey which has led him step by step to the present, David seeks to find the source of the cohesive force which associates each detail with the others and gradually organizes them all, as he retells them, into the pattern which constitutes his destiny.

Is it a private power of feeling in David which does this, a subjective energy of association? The many references to the psychology of association suggest that this is the case. Agnes is "associated" in David's mind with "a stained glass window in a church" (176), just as the image of Ham's anguish after little Em'ly runs away "remain[s]," says David, "associated with that lonely waste, in my remembrance, to this hour" (347), or as David says of Steerforth's death: "I have an association between it and a stormy wind, or the lightest mention of a sea-shore, as strong as any of which my mind is conscious" (599). It may be such associations which gather all the events of David's life together and make them one.[13]

On the other hand, the source of the coherence of David's life may be a providential power which has been secretly working behind the scenes to give an objective design to his life. This is suggested by the way the sea, especially in the descriptions of little Em'ly walking on the causeway by the shore and of the storm in which Steerforth and Ham are drowned, becomes a mysterious supernatural reservoir, an external memory and prevision gathering the past and the future together in a time out of time sustained by God. "Is it possible," asks David as he remembers little Em'ly walking so dangerously close to the sea, "among the possibilities of hidden things, that in the sudden rashness of the child and her wild look so far off, there was any merciful attraction of her into danger, any tempting her towards him permitted on the part of her dead father, that her life might have a chance of ending that day?" (35). Later Ham says "the end of it like" seems to him to be coming from the sea (352). In Steerforth's drowning "the inexorable end [comes] at its appointed time"

(352). During the storm which is to wash the body of Steerforth up at his feet, David feels that "something within [him], faintly answering to the storm without, tosse[s] up the depths of [his] memory and [makes] a tumult in them" (603). The personal memory within is matched by a cosmic memory without.

The conflict between these two organizing powers is reconciled when David discovers that Agnes has been all along the secret center of his life, the pivot around which everything else will turn out to have been patterning itself as the circle of his life pervaded by her presence. Agnes is the rock on which he can base himself, the person who will fill the void of his old unhappy loss or want of something. "Clasped in my embrace," says David after his marriage to Agnes, "I held the source of every worthy aspiration I had ever had; the centre of myself, the circle of my life, my own, my wife; my love of whom was founded on a rock!" (659).

In the last chapter of *David Copperfield* the narrator returns, like the narrator of *Huckleberry Finn*, to the present. The young David and the grown-up David coincide, and the narrator speaks for his situation in the present. But far from choosing, like Huck, a solitude which is the only guarantee of an honest life, David has escaped from his solitude into society. He is surrounded by his family and his friends. Far from speaking, like Huck, in the voice of solitude on behalf of the values of solitude, he is now and has been throughout the novel as much the spokesman in the language of the middle-class community for the values of that community[14] as any of the omniscient narrators of Victorian novels told in the third person – the narrators, for example, of *Vanity Fair*, *Middlemarch*, or *The Last Chronicle of Barset* (1866–7). Though the first-person novel and the third-person novel seem so different, both can become instruments by which Victorian novelists express their sense that authentic life lies in assimilation of the individual mind into the collective mind of society. In marriage to one member of good middle-class society and in a successful career as a writer of novels, like Dickens himself, David has found a way into that society.

Agnes is also for him the mediator of a heavenly light and a promise of heaven. As such, she is the means by which he sees other things and people, judging them according to universal standards. She is the way in which he will rise through society beyond society, not into the solitude of Huck's "Territory," that lonesomeness lacking any vestige of a divine presence, but into the celestial society of Heaven where he can enjoy Agnes' companionship forever.

Huckleberry Finn is an open-ended fiction. Huck's life is not over on the last page of the novel, and his ability to free himself from Aunt Sally and other agents of "civilization" remains in doubt. Dickens, on the other hand, tries to give *David Copperfield* a closed form. He presents the final sentences of David's narrative as a rehearsal of the final moments of his life. The latter will repeat in structure and content the former, realities fading then as memories fade now. The end of the book is an anticipation of the end of David's life, when there will be no more earthly future left. Like Henry Esmond retelling his life as an old man in Virginia, David speaks as if he were writing from beyond time, as if he were writing from the perspective of death:

> And now, as I close my task, subduing my desire to linger yet, these faces fade away. But one face, shining on me like a Heavenly light by which I see all other objects, is above them and beyond them all. And that remains.
>
> I turn my head, and see it, in its beautiful serenity, beside me. My lamp burns low, and I have written far into the night; but the dear presence, without which I were nothing, bears me company.
>
> Oh Agnes, Oh my soul, so may thy face be by me when I close my life indeed; so may I, when realities are melting from me like the shadows which I now dismiss, still find thee near me, pointing upward! (668, 669)

A modern reader may find it difficult to take seriously the image of Agnes "pointing upward," and Dickens himself was in later novels, most subtly in *Our Mutual Friend* (1864–5), to put in question the strategy by which the conflict between two sources of order is resolved in *David Copperfield*. The contrast between Dickens' novel and *Huckleberry Finn*, however, is a striking example of the different cultural and personal meanings which may be expressed within the form of the first-person novel. In Twain's hands the form is used in a masterpiece in the American tradition of ambiguous personal experience which goes from Hawthorne and Melville through Twain to Faulkner, Hemingway, and Bellow.

As many critics have seen, Huck speaks not the language of the community but a pungent vernacular which can thrive only outside society and is the instrument of a devastating criticism of it. *Huckleberry Finn*, however, does more than juxtapose two ways of speaking, one good and one bad. There are three kinds of language in the novel. Each speaks for a different condition of life. Existence within society is again and again dramatized as speaking a false language, playing a role, wearing a disguise, either wittingly or unwittingly perpetrating a fraud. Honest directness of speech, on the other hand, is possible only between Huck and Jim in their ideal society of two on the raft. This openness and lack of guile is the basis of poignancy in the scene in which Huck feels guilty for having fooled Jim into believing he has dreamed events which have really happened during a foggy night on the river. "It was fifteen minutes," says Huck, "before I could work myself up to go and humble myself to a nigger – but I done it, and I warn't ever sorry for it afterwards, neither. I didn't do him no more mean tricks, and I wouldn't done that one if I'd knowed it would make him feel that way" (71, 72). Huck's sin is to have imported into the Eden-like honesty of social relations on the raft the propensity for lies which is characteristic of life on the shore and which is, moreover, Huck's only self-defense when he is there. The colloquial rhythm and idiom of his narrative of his life is speech of the raft society. He does his readers the great honor of speaking to them as if they were in collusion with him against the society of the shore and could share with him his true speech.

There is, however, a third language in the novel, a language belonging neither to good society nor to bad society, but to solitude. This language, and the condition belonging to it, are described in two crucial passages in the novel, one near the beginning, when Huck is still living with Miss Watson, and one just before Huck reaches the Phelps Farm and just after he has made his resolution to steal Jim out of slavery again. The same elements occur in both of these passages: an association of isolation with a state of such desolate "lonesomeness" that Huck wishes for death; so complete an openness to inhuman nature and to the presences of the dead within nature that it is as if Huck were already dead; a transformation of language from a means of communication into silence or into an inarticulate murmur, like the speech of elemental nature. The companionship of the dead is a companionship of mute and incommunicable secrets. These texts are of fundamental importance as clues to the quality of Huck's authenticity. They seem clearly related to Twain's deepest sense of his own existence:[15]

> I felt so lonesome [says Huck in the first such passage] I most wished I was dead. . . . [T]he wind was trying to whisper something to me and I couldn't make out what it was, and so it made the cold shivers run over me. Then away out in the woods I heard that kind of a sound that a ghost makes when it wants to tell about something that's on its mind and can't make itself understood, and so can't rest easy in its grave and has to go about that way every night grieving. I got so down-hearted and scared, I did wish I had some company. (8, 9)[16]

Richard Poirier, in *A World Elsewhere*, has noted how often Huck remains speechless when he is with other people on the shore. He is often a silent watcher and listener who effaces himself as much as possible.[17] This silence is an expression of the onlooking detachment from society which is his natural condition and which is affirmed in his resolution at the end to free himself from civilization. If Huck chooses for silence and solitude, the book allows the reader no illusion about what these mean.

They mean loss of language and a kinship with the dead. In solitude one becomes a kind of walking dead man, mute spectator of life. This, however, is preferable to the intolerable falsehood of existence within society.

This stark either / or replaces finally the choice between good society on the raft and bad society on the shore which has apparently structured Huck's narrative. Twain's hesitation before the darker implications of his story may explain that descent to the style of *The Adventures of Tom Sawyer* (1876) in the last episode, so troubling to critics. The Phelps Farm episode, however, plays a strategic role in the progress of the novel. It is the final stage in a gradual contamination of the honest language of the raft by the fraudulent language of the shore. In the end, Huck must choose not between true speech and false speech, but between speech and silence.

If the temporal structure of the novel brings Huck back to himself in the present and to the need for a decision there, the terms of this decision may be identified in its intersubjective structures. In *Huckleberry Finn* Twain plays the role of Huck in order to speak indirectly to the real society of his day, just as he took a pseudonym for his writing, so confronting his readers in disguise. In this novel he is Samuel Clemens pretending to be Mark Twain pretending to be Huckleberry Finn. This playing of roles is also fundamental to the inner structure of the novel, within the mirror-world its words create. Nothing is more natural to Huck, or more necessary, than lying. Repeatedly he leaves the "free and easy and comfortable" (95) life on the raft to involve himself in life on the shore. As soon as he meets someone there he spontaneously makes up a whole history for himself, a name, past life, present situation and intention. Only in this way can he protect Jim and that separate part of himself which can hear ghosts and understands what it would be like to be dead. When he enters society he must enter it in disguise, reborn as someone else. To be within the community is to be a fraud, to pretend to be another person, just as in writing the novel Clemens plays the role of Huck. Even the truth must be spoken by way of fiction. Significantly, Huck's final incarnation is as Tom Sawyer, for his greatest danger is that he will become, like Tom, someone who lives his life as a play and is entirely subjected to one form of fiction: the false idols of society and its romantic traditions.

This pattern of person within person, or of person confronting person by way of a disguise, is also a pattern of imaginary and real. If the novel is a fiction by which Twain attempted to approach his childhood and therefore to reach his own inmost reality, the story itself is constructed as a design of fictions within fictions – the fictions of Huck's lies and disguises, the fictional world taken from novels and historical romances within which Tom Sawyer lives, the no less fictional structures of religious and social beliefs which entrance the Mississippi communities, the frauds perpetrated by the duke and the king. In the travesties of *Hamlet* and *Romeo and Juliet* by the latter, they pretend to be a king and a duke pretending to be the famous actors Garrick and Kean pretending to be Shakespearean characters. These fictions within fictions keep before the reader a picture of interpersonal relations as a complex system of deceit within deceit in which every man lies to his neighbor.

The theme of lies leads back to the paradox of Huck's own language. As Ernest Hemingway, T. S. Eliot, and others have said, Huck's speech is the basis of the book's authenticity. He uses a rich vernacular idiom, couched in indigenous American rhythms, vocabulary, and syntax. His speech grows out of the way of life of a people in a place, and therefore is rooted in reality in a way no abstract language can be. At the same time the novel is full of demonstrations of the hollowness of the language spoken by people around Huck. This is most apparent in the vigorous satires of religious language, but it is also present in the satire of Southern romanticism in the references to Sir Walter Scott and *Lalla Rookh* (both names of steamboats in the novel). A similar theme is expressed in the imprisonment of the Grangerfords and Shepherdsons in linguistic molds which keep their absurd feud going from generation to generation. To belong to Mississippi Valley society is to be unable to speak the truth, to use one form or another of a fantasy language which justifies the greatest cruelties and injustices – slavery, economic exploitation, and the arrogant self-righteousness and psychological cruelties practiced, in Twain's view, in the name of Protestant Christianity.

Though Huck's language is a speech within the community speech, one based partly on the folklore and linguistic vigor of children and African Americans, nevertheless it has grown out of the community language and remains part of it. If it has drawn its strength from its source, it must share also the weaknesses of its origin. Huck's style comes from the popular culture of the Mississippi, but the novel is the exposure of that culture by way of its imitation in its own words. This use of the destructive power of imitative language reveals the silent presence of Twain behind Huck, of the lonesome and silent Huck behind his participation in his culture.

When Huck speaks he too gets caught in the speech patterns of his society. This is apparent in the irony of those many places where the reader can glimpse Twain judging Huck, deploring his enslavement to a false rhetoric. An example is the famous passage in which Huck, in response to a question about whether anyone was killed in a steamboat explosion, says, "No'm. Killed a nigger" (173). The poignant ambiguity of the crucial text in which Huck decides to rescue Jim from slavery lies in the fact that he is forced to express his decision in the language of the culture surrounding him. He must use religious and social terms which reverse Twain's judgment of good and bad in the situation. Worse yet, he is forced to experience the feelings appropriate to the rhetoric of the language he must use because he has no other. As long as he is within society he remains trapped in its language. However he acts, his actions are defined in the community's terms.

Twain and his readers may see in Huck's resolve a heroic act of moral improvisation, an intuition of the truth like that described in W. E. H. Lecky's *History of European Morals from Augustus to Charlemagne* (1869), a book Twain admired. Such a reading sees in Huck the courage to act in accordance with an intuitively perceived moral truth even though it goes counter to the rules of a bad society. Huck, however, does not see it that way at all. He sees his decision to free Jim as the victory of his innate evil over the good teaching of society. It is a conscious choice of damnation. To him it is not the creation of a just moral order in place of the evil one supported by society. His decision to "take up wickedness again" is reprehensible defiance of community laws defending religious right and the sanctity of private property. His act is not a "yes" in obedience to a higher ethical law but a "no" to the yes of a community which he continues to accept. "I was a trembling," says Huck, "because I'd got to decide, forever, betwixt two things, and I knowed it. I studied a minute, sort of holding my breath, and then says to myself: 'All right, then, I'll *go* to hell' " (168).

Even if Huck succeeds in freeing Jim, this freedom is still a social condition. As the concluding episode of Tom's "evasion" of Jim shows, Jim is as much subject to the sham of his society when he is free as when he is a slave. Only complete isolation is freedom. This is the meaning of the absurdity of Tom's freeing Jim when he is already legally free. Free man or slave, he is still enslaved, like Tom, Aunt Sally, and the rest, by the linguistic and cultural patterns of his society. To negate these is still to remain within them, and so to affirm them indirectly. Whenever Huck speaks he is necessarily subject to this inexorable law. To speak at all he must speak lies, not only because his situation forces him to deception, disguise, play-acting, but because the language of his community is inevitably the instrument of lies. The truth cannot be spoken directly in it, as Huck proves in the soliloquy of his decision to rescue Jim. The choice Huck faces is therefore between false language and no language at all. And this corresponds to the choice between participation in a false society and an isolation from other people which is like death.[18] Society is always imaginary. Solitude is the way to the real. Huck's final resolution, his final integrity, is a choice of lonesomeness and the silence which goes with it: "[S]o there ain't nothing more to write about, and I am rotten glad of it, because if I'd a knowed what a trouble it was to make a book I wouldn't a tackled it and ain't agoing to no more" (226). Then follows his decision to "light out for the Territory ahead of the rest."

To explore in a given novel temporal, interpersonal, and representational structures will lead to an identification of the specific shaping energy which generates form and meaning in the novel in question: the reaffirmation in *David Copperfield*, against alternative possibilities, of a traditional transcendentalism, or the rejection of society and its languages which in *Huckleberry Finn* prepares for the more overt nihilism of Satan's scorn for the "moral sense" in *The Mysterious Stranger* (1916).

Notes

1. See Georg Lukács, *Die Theorie des Romans* (Neuwied and Berlin, 1963; first published in 1914–15); José Ortega y Gasset, *The Dehumanization of Art and Other Writings on Art and Culture* (Garden City, N.Y., 1956); Lionel Trilling, *The Liberal Imagination: Essays on Literature and Society* (New York, 1950), and *Beyond Culture: Essays on Literature and Learning* (New York, 1965); Ian Watt, *The Rise of the Novel: Studies in Defoe, Richardson, and Fielding* (Berkeley and Los Angeles, 1957).
2. See Paul de Man, "New Criticism et nouvelle critique," *Preuves*, No. 188 (October, 1966), pp. 30–34, for a discussion of this distinction in terms of the concept of intentionality.
3. See Paul de Man, "Georg Lukács's *Theory of the Novel*," *Modern Language Notes*, LXXXI, No. 5 (December, 1966), pp. 533–4.
4. Lukács refers here to transcendent meaning, supernatural meaning.
5. Lukács, *Theorie*, pp. 125–6: "Die Zeit kann erst dann konstitutiv werden, wenn die Verbundenheit mit der transzendentalen Heimat aufgehört hat. . . . Nur im Roman, dessen Stoff das Suchen-müssen und das Nicht-finden-Können des Wesens ausmacht, ist die Zeit mit der Form mitgesetzt. . . . In der Epopöe ist die Lebensimmanenz des Sinnes so stark, dass die Zeit von ihr aufgehoben wird: das Leben zieht als Leben in die Ewigkeit ein. . . . Im Roman trennen sich Sinn und Leben und damit das Wesenhafte und Zeitliche; man kann fast sagen: die ganze innere Handlung des Romans ist nichts als ein Kampf gegen die Macht der Zeit."
6. *Adam Bede*, in *Works*, Cabinet Edition (Edinburgh and London [1877–80]), I, pp. 265–6.
7. (Paris, 1960), pp. 5–16.
8. See S. L. Bethell's discussion of this in *Shakespeare and the Popular Dramatic Tradition* (Durham, N.C., 1944), p. 39.
9. Examples of this are Huck's discussions of the efficacy of prayer: "[T]here's something in it when a body like the widow or the parson prays, but it don't work for me, and I reckon it don't work for only just the right kind," or the episode in which Huck, having been roundly defeated by the subtle enthymemes of Jim's rhetoric, says: "I see it warn't no use wasting words – you can't learn a nigger to argue. So I quit" (*Adventures of Huckleberry Finn*, Sculley Bradley, Richmond Croom Beatty, and E. Hudson Long, eds, Norton Critical Edition [New York, 1962], pp. 34, 67; further references to this novel will be by page numbers in this edition).

10. See Daniel G. Hoffman, *Form and Fable in American Fiction* (New York, 1961), p. 342.
11. See Roy Harvey Pearce, " 'The End. Yours Truly, Huck Finn': Postscript," *Modern Language Quarterly*, XXIV, No. 3 (September, 1963), pp. 253–6, for a discussion of the ironic historical actualities behind Huck's reference to the "Territory." The Territory is the Indian Territory, which was to become Oklahoma, and Huck's solitude if he were to go there would soon be invaded by the same "civilizing" people he has encountered along the Mississippi.
12. *David Copperfield*, George H. Ford, ed., Riverside Edition (Boston, 1958), p. 99. Further references will be to page numbers in this edition, which reprints the Charles Dickens Edition of 1868–70, the last to be revised by the author.
13. David's profession, which grows from the qualities which give him his power of fanciful association, reinforces this theme. His writing of fiction constitutes a realm of the imaginary within the imaginary. Dickens writes a novel about someone who writes novels. On this side of the mirror *David Copperfield* is a work by Dickens which transposes his life into a fiction. On the other side of the mirror it is the literal autobiography of David Copperfield, successful novelist.
14. As opposed to the false upper-class society he describes as "the Desert of Sahara" (667).
15. These passages were singled out for citation in the earliest recorded review of *Huckleberry Finn*, that by Brander Matthews in the *Saturday Review* [London], January 31, 1885, p. 153.
16. The second such passage reiterates the motifs of the first and expresses them with equal eloquence: "[T]here was them kind of faint dronings of bugs and flies in the air that makes it seem so lonesome and like everybody's dead and gone; and if a breeze fans along and quivers the leaves, it makes you feel mournful, because you feel like it's spirits whispering – spirits that's been dead ever so many years – and you always think they're talking about *you*. As a general thing it makes a body wish *he* was dead, too, and done with it all" (171).
17. (New York, 1966), pp. 183–4.
18. Kenneth S. Lynn, in *Mark Twain and Southwestern Humor* (Boston, 1959), p. 245, notes the relevance to this theme of the fact that one of the many sequels Twain contemplated for *Huckleberry Finn* "envisioned Huck as a broken, helplessly insane old man."

8

The sources of Dickens' comic art:

from *American Notes* to *Martin Chuzzlewit*

Dickens often emphasized the comic aspect of his work. "Oh! the sublimated essence of comicality that I *could* distil, from the materials I have!" he wrote of his first American journey.[1] To investigate the genesis of Dickens' comedy may help to identify its special qualities.

The comic view is in one way like the perspective of the outcast. Both see the world from the outside, from the point of view of someone who is not part of what he sees, who is ignored or "overlooked" by all the world. Such a man passively observes a world with which he is not involved. The chief difference is that someone like Dickens' first outcast hero, Oliver Twist, lives in fear for his life, in danger that the world of honest people may perform on his body the destruction it has already attempted to enact on his social existence by deciding that he is useless, a "burden on the parish." Oliver is "the victim of a systematic course of treachery and deception" (3). He is defined by society as naturally evil, as being destined for the gallows: " 'That boy will be hung,' said the gentleman in the white waistcoat. 'I know that boy will be hung' " (11). Such "abjection," Jean-Paul Sartre has argued, effects a "methodological conversion" of the world, a transformation which is parallel to those effected by the Cartesian doubt and the Husserlian "bracketing." Like the latter, social isolation "constitutes the world as a closed system which consciousness looks at from the outside in the mode of the divine understanding." Unlike the philosophical distancing of the world, however, abjection is a lived experience rather than a theoretical act. It leads to the discovery that one has a unique identity, an identity which can never be defined in terms of something outside itself.[2]

The comic attitude is a similar way of putting the world at arm's length. It too is lived. It too can lead to the discovery of subjectivity. It has this difference from abjection, however: it is chosen rather than imposed from the outside. The comic view is a voluntary transformation rather than, as in the case of abjection, a humiliating one to which the outcast submits whether he wishes to or not.

The change of the point of view of the outcast into the comic view made Dickens' fiction possible. From a safe position which saw things as comic, Dickens enjoyed the pleasure of making those whom he had once feared into a masquerade of innocuous puppets. It was a revenge on the world, but a revenge which did not transcend Dickens' initial isolation, the isolation he suffered during the blacking factory episode of his childhood.[3] The comic stance modulates this detachment into another form. Dickens the writer of comic novels chose to be what he already was. The underground terror of *Oliver Twist* became the "essence of comicality" of *Martin Chuzzlewit*, of *Pickwick Papers*, or of any of the comic parts of his novels. The alteration here, it will be seen, is not a chronological change, nor is it so much a deliberate spiritual act as it is an instinctive movement of liberation, a withdrawal which Dickens first performed, it seems likely, long before he began writing. This reversal is enacted again and again in his novels in the shift between melodrama and comedy, between the warmth of sympathetic feeling and the detachment of laughter.

Such a reversal can be detected in a context especially important for *Martin Chuzzlewit*, that is, in the letters written several years earlier when Dickens was having the experiences which gave him material for the American parts of the novel. In America Dickens was constantly exposed to the scrutiny of crowds of strangers. Scholars have noted how much Dickens disliked the lack of privacy in America.[4] "The people poured on board, in crowds, by six on Monday morning, to see me," he wrote to Forster, "and a party of 'gentlemen' actually planted themselves before our little cabin, and stared in at the door and windows *while I was washing, and Kate lay in bed*" (1,440, [Dickens' italics]). This so impressed Dickens that he described it again in a letter to Colden three days later. His hatred of being stared at by the Americans was more than a British love of privacy. He felt that the strangers' stares were in some way reaching his inner life and transforming it. "Imagine," he wrote in another letter, ". . . how now and then a republican boy, of surpassing and indescribable free and easiness comes in among the company, and keeping his cap upon his head, inspects me at his leisure" (1,419). Under the impersonal gaze of the republican boys Dickens felt his free inner life freezing into something which was himself and yet was not within his control. Beneath the American look Dickens felt himself turning into the "various impressions" he made on other people. He became what he looked like when "viewed from behind" (*American Notes*, 113). In helpless passivity he experienced the destruction of his sense of himself:

> We have been . . . so beset, waylaid, hustled, set upon, beaten about, trampled down, mashed, bruised and pounded by crowds, that I never knew less of myself in all my life, or had less time for those confidential

> interviews with myself whereby I earn my bread, than in these United States of America. (*Letters* 1,447)

Dickens felt himself turning into what the celebrity seekers saw, a kind of animated statue or photograph. "Whenever we come to a town station," he wrote, "the crowd surround it, let down all the windows, thrust in their heads, stare at me, and compare notes respecting my appearance, with as much coolness as if I were a marble image" (*Letters* 1,419).

If the anonymous look of the curious crowd destroyed Dickens' sense of himself, it also made it difficult for him to write. The look invaded that intimate area where his imagination performed its reshapings of his experience through "confidential interviews" with himself. He needed strict privacy, even at home, in order to write. Other people, those cool looks, had to be suspended. He had to put himself in an imaginative relation to the world in which he could see others without being seen.

Dickens saved himself from his objectification under the look of the Americans by an about-face which turned them into depersonalized objects, marionettes jerked by invisible wires. He saved his sense of himself by converting his experience into his consciousness of that experience. He saw the world now as though it were reflected in a mirror or projected in a "magic lantern" (*Letters* 1,782). He saw it as comedy, as emptied appearance. When this reversal had been performed, the people who had before endangered his sense of himself with their looks were now inanimate objects in human shape, mechanically endowed with motion, gesture, and speech. The America that Dickens now experienced existed for no one except himself. The shared social reality within which the Americans lived, a reality created by their acceptance of certain conventions and ways of speaking, was lightened, unsubstantiated, made into a kind of brittle façade by Dickens' oblique perception of it, by his continual transformation of it into something it was not. An old weazen-faced general, for example, with "the remains of a pigeon-breast in his military surtout," was transformed in Dickens' perception of him into a pigeon pie: "The breast has so subsided, and the face has become so strongly marked, that he seems, like a pigeon-pie, to show only the feet of the bird outside, and to keep the rest to himself." It is perhaps no accident that this man seemed to Dickens "perhaps *the* most horrible bore in this country" (*Letters* 1,426). The metamorphosis of the general into a pigeon pie depended on seeing him without sympathy, as comic appearance, not as a fellow human being whom he might understand or with whom he might communicate.

The same changes can be seen pervasively in the language of *American Notes*. A good part of this travel book is a direct transcription of Dickens' journal letters to Forster, Maclise, Beard, Mitton, and Fonblanque.[5]

The style of *American Notes* is the style of the letters: the transformation of a prosaic reality into an oblique poetic reality through the use of hyperbole, metaphor, the personification of inanimate objects, and the depersonification of human beings. Dickens described, for example, "a melancholy piece of waste ground with frouzy grass, which looks like a small piece of country that has taken to drinking, and has quite lost itself" (114–15). Boston, in his view of it, was metamorphosed into a comic stage set:

> When I got into the streets upon this Sunday morning, the air was so clear, the houses were so bright and gay; the signboards were painted in such gaudy colours; the gilded letters were so very golden; the bricks were so very red, the stone so very white, the blinds and area railings were so very green, the knobs and plates upon the street-doors so marvellously bright and twinkling; and all so slight and unsubstantial in appearance – that every thoroughfare in the city looked exactly like a scene in a pantomime. (24)

The American people, as Dickens saw them, were "all alike. . . . There is no diversity of character" (157). They were also less than human. A small boy, for example, looked like "a rather large fiddle in a brown bag" (141), and the entire male company on a river boat seemed "to be the melancholy ghosts of departed book-keepers, who had fallen dead at the desk" (157). After having "bolted his food in gloomy silence," each man "bolts himself, in the same state" (157), as though he were a strongbox or a door.

Martin Chuzzlewit is the culmination of the metamorphosis of people into mechanically animated objects which can be seen in Dickens' letters and in *American Notes*. Major Pawkins, for example, looks "very much like a stale weed himself: such as might be hoed out of the public garden, with great advantage to the decent growth of that preserve, and tossed on some congenial dunghill" (273), and the languid Elijah Pogram shakes hands with Martin "like a clock-work figure that [is] just running down" (537). The English characters are also depersonified. Old Chuffey, the Chuzzlewit clerk, is a piece of furniture, an old chair or table with "spindle legs" who can be stored away like any other inanimate object (182); or he is a "worn-out cask" (186): "He looked as if he had been put away and forgotten half a century before, and somebody had just found him in a lumber-closet" (182). Mrs Gamp's husband, in her fertile imagination, is changed into his wooden leg: "As to husbands, there's a wooden leg gone likeways home to its account, which in its constancy of walkin' into wine vaults, and never comin' out again 'till fetched by force, was quite as weak as flesh, if not weaker" (629). Or perhaps it would be better to say that the wooden leg appropriates the life of its owner, until the man lives in terms of the paradoxical vitality of the least-alive part of himself. A footman is described as so entangling his livery in the furniture that he is like "a blue-bottle in a world of cobwebs" (138), and Montague Tigg announces himself as "a premium tulip, of a very different growth and cultivation from the cabbage Slyme" (226). When these metaphors do not transform the character into a lifeless object which moves without consciousness according to the laws of inanimate nature, they may transmute him even more disquietingly into an organic being which grows or has grown without intention, without awareness, in the undirected proliferation of an insentient principle of life: "[H]e had such an obvious disposition to pimples, that the bright spots on his cravat, the rich pattern on his waistcoat, and even his glittering trinkets, seemed to have broken out upon him, and not to have come into existence comfortably" (55). This man shares his life with his clothes: if he is alive his clothes are alive too, as much alive as he is, and share his disposition to pimples; if they are inanimate objects, he is an object too.

Within a work of fiction, however, such depersonification of characters plays a different role from that played by it in the letters or in the travel book. In the fiction there is no longer a question of protecting oneself from an objectifying power in people by objectifying them in return. The relation between Dickens and his comic creations was internal. It existed in the realm of the "confidential interview" with himself. The invention of even comic characters was a means of self-creation rather than a means of self-defense. By playing a role a man becomes the self he imitates, as Dickens became the invented characters whose facial gestures he practiced before the mirror, or as he was addicted to theatrical performances and needed constantly the experience of "assuming" the life of another. Dickens' dependence on this form of "role-playing," both in the public form of actual theatricals and in the private "theatricals" or confidential interviews which gave birth to his novels, is suggested in a letter to Bulwer-Lytton: "Assumption has charms for me – I hardly know for how many wild reasons – so delightful that I feel a loss of, oh! I can't say what exquisite foolery, when I lose a chance of being someone in voice, etc. not at all like myself."[6]

In Dickens' fiction, however, this "assumption" at no point reached the intimacy and depth by which a great dramatic writer lives intensely the subjective life of his imaginary characters. To lose himself so would have been to lose that objectivity, that permanent detachment, which was for him an instinctive mode of self-defense as well as theoretically the best relation of the novelist to his imagined action. Again and again he advised novice writers to "let the story tell itself." The relation between Dickens and his invented characters was not the Stanislavskian merging of actor and role. It was the calculating and self-conscious taking of a part. The description of Dickens looking at himself in the mirror as he imitated one of his invented figures is a perfect image of his relation to his characters. He always watched himself become the imaginary personage. In the moment in which a character was brought into being by creative mimesis, he detached himself from it, drew back, and contemplated it from a distance performing its comical antics. Dickens wanted to be both actor and spectator, both character and witnessing narrator. Perhaps it is for this reason that he was primarily a novelist and not an actor, in spite of his abiding love for the theater. Dickens' great comic characters, Pecksniff or Sairey Gamp, to give examples in *Martin Chuzzlewit*, display themselves in a perpetual hyperbole. This exaggeration betrays the presence behind them of the actor in the costume, solemn behind the mask, deliberately driving the fictive personage through its stylized and unceasingly inventive repetitions of itself. Behind the verve of the comic characters of Dickens the reader can always observe the energy of Dickens himself, the energy of the great comic actor who continually and inexhaustibly improvised the role he played.

This structure is fundamental to Dickens' art. It was present not only in the genesis and mode of existence of the comic characters but in more pervasive thematic and formal structures in the fiction. Dickens' great comic characters were born out of a reaction to the "real" world, as a transformation of it or self-protection from it. They were, however, maintained within a reflexive relationship, in a "confidential interview" which was cut off from the world. Inside this relation of the self to itself Dickens created the comic character, played his role, and constituted himself as the audience of that performance. In an analogous way there is an oscillation between mimetic representation in the novels and self-creating, self-sustaining meaning. As many critics have demonstrated, Dickens' novels are rooted in history.[7] They closely follow, for example, London topography. Polemics against English institutions like the New Poor Law, the Court of Chancery, or the Civil Service constitute important thematic strands in his novels. Topical references abound, and there are even "real" models for many of the characters. On the other hand, each novel turns such external realities into language. Within the novel the meaning of a given motif is constituted by relations among linguistic elements rather than from reference to the external world. A "panoramic" novel like *Bleak House* offers itself to the reader's interpretation as a complex linguistic fabric which must be interpreted according to elaborate analogies among the characters, themes, symbolic scenes, and figures of speech which are woven within the text.

This self-generating web of meaning presupposes the absence or even the annihilation of the external world, as Dickens seems to have glimpsed in a curiously ironic passage in the preface of 1850 to the Cheap Edition of *Oliver Twist.* Ridiculing an alderman of Marylebone, Sir Peter Laurie, who had declared in a public meeting that Jacob's Island could not exist in reality because "it ONLY existed in a work of fiction, written by Mr. Charles Dickens ten years ago," Dickens was so taken by the idea of the incompatibility between fiction and reality that he concocted an outrageous series of examples of the power of fiction to destroy reality:

> remembering that when FIELDING described Newgate, the prison immediately ceased to exist; that when SMOLLETT took Roderick Random to Bath, that city instantly sank into the earth; that when SCOTT exercised his genius on Whitefriars, it incontinently glided into the Thames; that an ancient place called Windsor was entirely destroyed in the reign of Queen Elizabeth by two Merry Wives of that town, acting under the direction of a person by the name of SHAKESPEARE; and that Mr. POPE, after having at a great expense completed his grotto at Twickenham, incautiously reduced it to ashes by writing a poem upon it. (383–4)

The irony of this is obvious enough, as is its straightforward polemical intent. On the other hand, the irony cuts both ways, and the reader is left with a powerful series of images of the pen as a magic wand which destroys what it inscribes within the secondary existence of words. Jacob's Island existed, it is true, and yet the Jacob's Island of *Oliver Twist* exists only as language and can be encountered only in the novel.

Such an oscillation between realistic mimesis and self-generating meaning is fundamental thematically too in Dickens' fiction. An example is the question running through Dickens' novels of whether authentic selfhood is attained, as it seems to be for Oliver Twist, by accepting a source of meaning which comes from the outside, in his case by becoming a repetition of his father, or whether each man must reject such "great expectations" and take upon himself the responsibility of creating the meaning of his life through autonomous choices and commitments. This is Pip's discovery in *Great Expectations.*

Another example is the way the themes of fiction and of interpretation are important in *Bleak House.* This novel offers itself explicitly as a text to interpret in the sense that its fundamental strategy is to present people, actions, and scenes which are overtly "allegorical." They make evident the fact that they mean more than their surface sense. They refer to other parts of the book from which they draw their significance and to which they give significance. Krook, for example, is explicitly identified with the Lord Chancellor. The names of Miss Flite's birds are richly and ambiguously allegorical. Proper names throughout the novel are metaphorically significant. There is a "pointing allegory" on Mr Tulkinghorn's ceiling; it points at first "with no particular meaning" and then at last "with a deadly meaning" at Mr Tulkinghorn's corpse (503–4).

Moreover many of the characters in *Bleak House*, like the reader (or the author) of it, are involved in solving a mystery, in interpreting documents, or in turning factual reality into words. All the suitors in Chancery have their bundles of law papers (Gridley, Miss Flite, Richard Carstone). Inspector Bucket, Tulkinghorn, Guppy, Mrs Snagsby, and others are at work unraveling mysteries as much by interpreting documents as by tracking down people. Krook and the Smallweeds grub among old law documents seeking one which will make them rich. The scene in which the illiterate Krook is shown tracing laboriously the letters which spell "Jarndyce" is an emblem of the condition of many characters in the novel. Mrs Jellyby, on the other hand, is engaged, with Caddy's reluctant help, in turning Borrioboola-Gha and all its natives into an endless sequence of letters, just as the case of Jarndyce and Jarndyce is a "masterly fiction" (15) in which real lives have been changed into an interminable series of briefs, or rather into a series which can be terminated only by the "consumption" of both suit and suitors. The novel, however, is also a "masterly fiction." It exists as the transformation into language of everything it touches, and Dickens, like Mrs Jellyby, spent much of his time writing. Thematic strands within the novel function ironically to put in question the novel's own status as fiction and to call attention to the fact that it wavers between being an imitation of reality and being a self-enclosed integument of language.

Dickens, however, had no Mallarméan faith in the creation through fiction of a *spectacle de soi* (spectacle of the self), no Stevensian confidence that men could order their lives by a "supreme fiction," or that "the final belief is to believe in a fiction, which you know to be a fiction, there being nothing else."[8] One theme of *Martin Chuzzlewit* is a condemnation of poetry as lie. The "Literary Ladies" of America speak pure nonsense, and the constant return to the topic of poetry in connection with Tigg and the Anglo-Bengalee identifies poetry unequivocally with mendacity. But Dickens, like Tigg, also had "the gift of the gab." He created all the "light-hearted little fiction[s]" which make up the novel (434, 438), just as Tigg has made the Anglo-Bengalee out of nothing but words. Dickens as writer of comic fiction is in danger of ending in the same place as the transcendental ladies or as Tigg. Depending on a lie he may become a fiction himself, absorbed into and annihilated by his own invention.

To explore the mode of existence of Dickens' comic characters is to discover a problematic tension between realism and self-enclosed fiction which is fundamental to his work and which may also be identified in many other aspects of it.

Notes

1. *The Letters of Charles Dickens*, Walter Dexter, ed., Nonesuch Dickens ed., 3 vols (Bloomsbury [London], 1938), 1, p. 441. References in my text to *American Notes* and *Martin Chuzzlewit* are also by page numbers to the respective vols in the Nonesuch Dickens, ed. *Oliver Twist* is cited from the Clarendon Ed., Kathleen Tillotson, ed. (Oxford, 1966), and *Bleak House* from the Riverside Ed., Morton Dauwen Zabel, ed. (Boston, 1956).
2. *Saint Genêt, comédien et martyr* (Paris, 1952); 'L'*abjection* est une conversion méthodique comme le doute cartésien et l'epokhé husserlienne: elle constitue le monde comme un système clos que la conscience regarde du dehors, à la manière de l'entendement divin. La supériorité de cette méthode sur les autres, c'est quelle est vécue. . . . Aussi ne conduit-elle pas à la conscience transcendantal et universelle de Husserl, ni au cogito substantialiste de Descartes, mais à une existence singulière" (122) (*Abjection* is a methodological conversion like Cartesian doubt and the Husserlian epoché: it constitutes the world as a closed system that consciousness looks at from the outside, in the mode of divine understanding. The superiority of this method over the others is that it is experienced. . . . Also it does not lead to the transcendental and universal consciousness of Husserl, nor to the substantialist cogito of Descartes, but to a singular existence).
3. For Dickens' description of this see the autobiographical fragment written at the time of *David Copperfield* in John Forster, *The Life of Charles Dickens*, 3 vols (Philadelphia, 1873), 1, pp. 50–9.
4. E.g., Edgar Johnson, *Charles Dickens: His Tragedy and Triumph*, 2 vols (New York, 1952), 1, p. 383.
5. See *ibid.*, 1, p. 429.
6. Cited by E. D. H. Johnson in his admirable brief study, *Charles Dickens: An Introduction to His Novels* (New York, 1969), p. 21.
7. E.g., Humphry House, *The Dickens World* (London, 1941) and John Butt and Kathleen Tillotson, "The Topicality of *Bleak House*," *Dickens at Work* (London, 1957), pp. 177–200.
8. Wallace Stevens, *Opus Posthumous* (New York, 1957), p. 163.

9

The fiction of realism:

Sketches by Boz, *Oliver Twist*, and Cruikshank's illustrations

. . . the illusion was reality itself[1]

One important aspect of current literary criticism is the disintegration of the paradigms of realism under the impact of structural linguistics and the renewal of rhetoric.[2] If meaning in language rises not from the reference of signs to something outside words but from differential relations among the words themselves, if "referent" and "meaning" must always be distinguished, then the notion of a literary text which is validated by its one-to-one correspondence to some social, historical, or psychological reality can no longer be taken for granted. No language is purely mimetic or referential, not even the most utilitarian speech. The specifically literary form of language, however, may be defined as a structure of words which in one way or another calls attention to this fact, while at the same time allowing for its own inevitable misreading as a "mirroring of reality." "The set (*Einstellung*) toward the MESSAGE as such," says Roman Jakobson, "focus on the message for its own sake, is the POETIC function of language."[3] Realistic fiction is a special case of the poetic function of language. Its peculiarity may be defined as the reciprocal relation within it between the story narrated and the question of what it means to narrate a story. One may say of realistic fiction what Walter Benjamin says of Brecht's epic theater: its way of establishing the set toward the message as such is "to underline the relation of the represented action to the action signified by the fact itself of representation."[4] This essay will attempt to test these generalizations by a discussion of Dickens' *Sketches by Boz* and, more briefly, *Oliver Twist.* I shall also investigate the relevance to the issue of realism in these texts of the admirable illustrations for them by George Cruikshank.

At first sight the *Sketches by Boz* seem an unpromising text for such study. They seem still rooted in the journalistic mode which was Dickens' first way of writing as a parliamentary reporter.[5] The *Sketches* are a representation in words of scenes, people, and ways of living which really existed in London in the eighteen-thirties. Here, even if nowhere else, Dickens seems to have been practicing a straightforward mimetic realism, especially in the section of the collected sequence called "Scenes." Here the reader may find vivid descriptions of many aspects of London life at the period of Victoria's accession, descriptions which have great value as "social history." There are sketches of old Scotland Yard, of Seven Dials, of Astley's, of Greenwich Fair, of Vauxhall Gardens, of omnibuses, cabs, coaches, and the people who run them, of Newgate Prison, pawnbrokers' shops, old clothes shops in Monmouth Street, of gin shops, private theaters, first of May celebrations, and so on. No one can doubt the "photographic" accuracy of these descriptions. Dickens has obviously seen what he describes and reports it accurately with the good journalist's sharp eye for detail. Moreover, originals for many of the public figures alluded to in the *Sketches* or acquaintances used as models have been identified.[6]

The habitual narrative structure of the *Sketches* objectifies this journalistic model. The basic situation of the *Sketches* presents Boz as the "speculative pedestrian" (*SB*, 190) wandering the streets of London. Boz is, like a good reporter, detached from what he sees in the sense of not being caught up in the life he witnesses, but this lack of involvement liberates him to see with great clarity and to record exactly what he sees. There is a good description of this way of being related to the world in a passage in the periodical version of "The Prisoners' Van," a passage suppressed in the collected *Sketches*. "We have a most extraordinary partiality for lounging about the streets," says Boz. "Whenever we have an hour or two to spare, there is nothing we enjoy more than a little amateur vagrancy – walking up one street and down another, and staring into shop windows, and gazing about as if, instead of being on intimate terms with every shop and house in Holborn, the Strand, Fleet-street and Cheapside, the whole were an unknown region to our wandering mind."[7] Boz looks at London as if he were a stranger in his own city. He has no business to be where he is, and therefore he is a "wanderer," an "amateur vagrant." He refers to himself here, as throughout, with the journalistic "we," which depersonalizes him, reduces him from a private man to a function, and at the same time suggests that he is divided into two consciousnesses. One is the public role of journalistic recorder who speaks not for himself but for the collective experience of all the dwellers in the city, for the universal truth which all know but do not know they know until it has been articulated for them by Boz. Such a truth is shared by all but is visible only to those who are disengaged from immediate involvement in the life of the city. Behind this collective self is Boz's other self, the private man behind the public role, who watches the journalist at work, somewhat self-consciously.

This deeper self, it may be, expresses his private experience or private peculiarities covertly by way of the conventional mask.

Another text from the "Scenes" will show the characteristically exact notation of dress, behavior, time, and locale which Dickens' amateur vagrant makes of what he sees. Roland Barthes has called attention to the role of the "irrelevant detail" in fiction or in history as a device for establishing the authenticity of what is reported and for conveying "l'effet du réel."[8] In such passages as the following the distinction between "relevant" and "irrelevant" detail seems in principle impossible to make. The entire purpose of the passage is to tell the reader that such scenes do in fact exist in the London streets on a Sunday afternoon and that Boz has watched them with an eye on which nothing is lost, no detail "irrelevant." Each item is able by the fact of its existence to contribute to Boz's amusement and to ours:

> Can any one fail to have noticed them in the streets on Sunday? And were there ever such harmless efforts at the grand and magnificent as the young fellows display! We walked down the Strand, a Sunday or two ago, behind a little group; and they furnished food for our amusement the whole way. They had come out of some part of the city; it was between three and four o'clock in the afternoon; and they were on their way to the Park. There were four of them, all arm-in-arm, with white kid gloves like so many bridegrooms, light trousers of unprecedented patterns, and coats for which the English language has yet no name – a kind of cross between a great-coat and a surtout, with the collar of the one, the skirts of the other, and pockets peculiar to themselves.
>
> Each of the gentlemen carried a thick stick, with a large tassel at the top, which he occasionally twirled gracefully round; and the whole four, by way of looking easy and unconcerned, were walking with a paralytic swagger irresistibly ludicrous. One of the party had a watch about the size and shape of a reasonable Ribstone pippin, jammed into his waistcoat-pocket, which he carefully compared with the clocks of St. Clement's and the New Church, the illuminated clock at Exeter 'Change, the clock of St. Martin's Church, and the clock of the Horse Guards. When they at last arrived in St. James's Park, the member of the party who had the best-made boots on, hired a second chair expressly for his feet, and flung himself on this two-pennyworth of sylvan luxury with an air which levelled all distinctions between Brookes's and Snooks's, Crockford's and Bagnigge Wells. (*SB*, 218–19)

The *Sketches by Boz* seem firmly attached to the social facts of London in 1836. As such, they are apparently fully open to analysis according to a concept of interpretation which sets a solid reality on one hand and its mirroring in words on the other. The value of the *Sketches* is the exactness of the mirror's image. Such an analysis is confirmed by the rather slender tradition of critical comment on the *Sketches*. From the contemporary reviews down to the best recent essays they have been praised for their fidelity to the real. This critical line remains faithful to the linguistic doctrine of Plato's *Cratylus*, according to which "the correct name indicates the nature of the thing."[9] Things, in this case, as the critics note, are to be found especially in a region of lower middle class urban life which had not been much reflected before in fiction, in social history, or in journalism. This stratum of English life is that "Every-Day Life and Every-Day People" of which the *Sketches* are said in their subtitle to be "Illustrative." If there is a fallacy in the concept of realism, criticism of the *Sketches* from 1836 to the present provides an excellent example of the fallacy at its most straightforward. Here it affirms itself in the sunlight with a clear conscience. Nowhere is there evidence of an uneasy sense that something might be wrong with the formulas of realism.

Dickens himself may be said to have initiated this tradition of criticism, not only with the subtitle but also with his claim in the original preface of February, 1836, that "his object has been to present little pictures of life and manners as they really are." As Kathleen Tillotson has observed, the early reviewers picked up this note and praised the *Sketches* for their "startling fidelity," for their power of "bringing out the meaning and interest of objects which would altogether escape the observation of ordinary minds," for their discovery of "the romance, as it were, of real life."[10] "The *Sketches*," says Mrs Tillotson, "were acclaimed for their novelty and accuracy both in the kind of life observed, and the penetration of the observer accepting and transforming the commonplace. . . . Throughout the reviews there is gratitude for the discovery of 'every-day life' in neglected but immediately recognized pockets of urban and suburban society."[11] The fullest contemporary statement of this interpretation of the *Sketches* is that made by John Forster in his *Life*. "The observation shown throughout is nothing short of wonderful," says Forster.

> Things are painted literally as they are. . . . It is a book that might have stood its ground, even if it had stood alone, as containing unusually truthful observation of a sort of life between the middle class and the low, which, having few attractions for bookish observers, was quite unhacknied ground. . . . It was a picture of every-day London at its best and worst, in its humours and enjoyments as well as its sufferings and sins, pervaded everywhere . . . with the absolute reality of the things depicted.[12]

One might expect Victorian accounts of the *Sketches* to be caught within the Cratylean myth of representationalism. All Victorian criticism of fiction, for the most part, remains enclosed within the formulations and judgments of that myth. The only frequently expressed alternative was the other form of representationalism which values a text for its accurate mirroring of the feelings or subjective perspectives of its author.

Twentieth-century critics, however, might be expected to go beyond their predecessors. Nevertheless, praise of the *Sketches* for their "fidelity to reality" persists with little change in the relatively sparse commentary the book has received in our own day. Thea Holme, for example, in the introduction to the Oxford Illustrated Edition of the *Sketches*, commends Dickens for

> setting down . . . all the small events in the everyday life of common persons – bank clerks, shop assistants, omnibus drivers; laundresses, market women, and kidney-pie sellers: directing his powers of observation and description upon scenes and characters within the daily scope of any loiterer in London. . . . As an example of what is now called "documentary" the *Sketches* deserve a unique place in literature. It has been pointed out elsewhere that more than half this volume's contents are facts: facts observed with an astonishing precision and wealth of detail. (*SB*, vii, viii)

Mrs Tillotson uses the same kind of language as the nineteenth-century reviewers to identify the quality of the *Sketches*. "The tales and sketches themselves," she says, "without annotation, give us the world which the young Dickens saw."[13] Angus Wilson, in his recent lively study of Dickens, says of the *Sketches* that in them "we see how a brilliant young journalist's observation of London's movement is just on the point of taking wings into imaginative art."[14] An intelligent and sympathetic essay on the *Sketches* by Robert Browning, to give a final example, is constructed around the same assumptions. "The London of the *Sketches*," says Browning, "is not fictitious. . . . [Dickens] chronicles much that is small in scale and dull-toned with such fidelity, that it is the distinction of the *Sketches* as it is that of Joyce's *Dubliners*, that the reader senses the life of a whole city. . . . It is the first recommendation for this volume, that in it [Dickens] gave such a lively account of what he saw and heard in London. . . . Dickens . . . felt the artist's primary need, to record."[15]

The *Sketches by Boz*, in their apparent nature, in what Dickens said he intended them to be, and in the traditional interpretation of them, seem to offer little opportunity for a putting in question of realism. Moreover, the theoretical schemas of a critic like Jakobson allow for the existence of works of literature which refer outside themselves rather than remaining reflexive. In Jakobson's list of the six functions of language the "poetic" function, in which language is focused on itself, exists side by side with what Jakobson calls "a set (*Einstellung*) toward the referent, an orientation toward the CONTEXT – briefly the so-called REFERENTIAL, 'denotative,' 'cognitive function."[16] Elsewhere in the same essay and at greater length in the influential discussion of two types of aphasia in *Fundamentals of Language*, Jakobson implies that there is a connection between this opposition of poetic and referential functions of language, on the one hand, and the distinction between two figures of speech, on the other. Metaphor is based on similarity and metonymy on contiguity. Poetry proper depends on metaphor, but realistic fiction defines people in terms of their contiguous environment. It favors metonymy over metaphor and the referential function of language over the set of language toward itself. Jakobson, it should be noted, allows for a complex relation between metonymy and metaphor, and for the use of both in poetry: "Similarity superimposed on contiguity imparts to poetry its throughgoing [*sic*] symbolic, multiplex, polysemantic essence."[17] In spite of this insight into the relation between the two tropes, however, he sees a tendency for language to split into two distinct regions, each governed by one of the "gravitational poles" of these fundamental figures of speech:

> In manipulating these two kinds of connection (similarity and contiguity) in both their aspects (positional and semantic) – selecting, combining, and ranking them – an individual exhibits his personal style, his verbal predilections and preferences. . . . In poetry there are various motives which determine the choice between these alternants. The primacy of the metaphoric process in the literary schools of romanticism and symbolism has been repeatedly acknowledged, but it is still insufficiently realized that it is the predominance of metonymy which underlies and actually predetermines the so-called "realistic" trend, which belongs to an intermediary stage between the decline of romanticism and the rise of symbolism and is opposed to both. Following the path of contiguous relationships, the realistic author metonymically digresses from the plot to the atmosphere and from the characters to the setting in space and time. He is fond of synecdochic details.[18]

Here is a clue which, while granting the approximate correctness of the traditional interpretation of the *Sketches by Boz*, may allow criticism to proceed beyond general statements about their "faithful reproduction of the real." Following this clue, it may be possible to identify how this fidelity is expressed in certain habits of language. In any case, the *Sketches* offer an excellent opportunity to test the validity of Jakobson's historical and linguistic schematizations. They were written during the time which he says marks the ascendancy of "realism," and they seem on other grounds to belong unquestionably in that pigeon-hole.

In spite of some youthful crudities and some self-conscious awkwardness of style the *Sketches by Boz* are a characteristic expression of Dickens' genius. Moreover, they contain all of Dickens' later work in embryo – the comedy, the sentimentality, the respect for the vitality of his characters, however foolish or limited they are, the habit of hyperbole, the admirable gift for striking linguistic transformations, the notion of an irresistible social determinism in which the urban environment causes the sad fate of the unlucky people living within it. The *Sketches* provide an excellent opportunity to watch the development of a great writer and to see his characteristic ways with words at the level of emergence, where they may be more easily identified. The full implications of the *Sketches* are only visible in the light of their relations to the later work of Dickens. They inevitably derive some of their meaning for a twentieth-century reader from the fact that, for example, he may encounter in "The Hospital Patient" a preliminary sketch for the murder of Nancy in *Oliver Twist*. The *Sketches*, in spite of Dickens' well-known use of metaphor, are in fact based on a brilliant and consistent exploitation of what Jakobson calls "the metonymical texture of realistic prose."[19] Metonymy may be defined as a linguistic substitution in which a thing is named not directly but by way of something adjacent to it either temporally or spatially. Synecdoche, substituting part for whole, container for thing contained, attribute for substance, and so on, is an important subdivision of metonymy. In both cases the linguistic substitution is validated by an implied ontological link. Some relation of similarity or causality, it is suggested, actually exists in the real world between the thing and something adjacent to it.

If the *Sketches* are a work for the critic to explicate, searching for patterns dispersed in their multiplicity, London was for the young Dickens, in his disguise as Boz, also a set of signs, a text to interpret. The speculative pedestrian is faced at first not with a continuous narrative of the lives of London's people, not with the subjective state of these people at the present moment, and not even with people seen from the outside as appearance or spectacle. What he sees at first are things, human artifacts, streets, buildings, vehicles, objects in a pawnbroker's shop, old clothes in Monmouth Street. These objects are signs, present evidence of something absent. Boz sets himself the task of inferring from these things the life that is lived among them. Human beings are at first often seen as things among other things, more signs to decipher, present hints of that part of their lives which is past, future, or hidden.

The emblem for this confrontation of a collection of disconnected objects whose meaning is still to be discovered is the list. The many lists in the *Sketches* anticipate similar lists in Dickens' later novels, for example the description of the extraordinary things which tumble out of Mrs Jellyby's closet in *Bleak House*. In *Bleak House*, however, the contents of Mrs Jellyby's closet are immediately "readable" as evidence of her quality as a wife and mother. Her irresponsibility has already been encountered in other ways. In the *Sketches* the lists are often the starting point of an act of interpretation which moves beyond them to the hidden ways of life of which they are signs. The law of these lists is random juxtaposition. They are not so much metonymic in themselves as the raw material of metonymy, since there seems no meaningful connection between any one object and those next to it. Boz's task is to discover such connections, and at first the only metonymy involved seems to be the synecdoche whereby such lists stand for the apparent disorder of London as a whole. An admirable example of this motif is the description of a "broker's shop" in a slum neighborhood:

> Our readers must often have observed in some by-street, in a poor neighbourhood, a small dirty shop, exposing for sale the most extraordinary and confused jumble of old, worn-out, wretched articles, that can well be imagined. Our wonder at their ever having been bought, is only to be equalled by our astonishment at the idea of their ever being sold again. On a board, at the side of the door, are placed about twenty books – all odd volumes; and as many wine-glasses – all different patterns; several locks, an old earthen-ware pan, full of rusty keys; two or three gaudy chimney-ornaments – cracked, of course; the remains of a lustre, without any drops; a round frame like a capital O, which has once held a mirror; a flute, complete with the exception of the middle joint; a pair of curling-irons; and a tinder-box. In front of the shop window are ranged some half-dozen high-backed chairs, with spinal complaints and wasted legs; a corner cupboard; two or three very dark mahogany tables with flaps like mathematical problems; some pickle-jars, some surgeons' ditto, with gilt labels and without stoppers; an unframed portrait of some lady who flourished about the beginning of the thirteenth century, by an artist who never flourished at all; an incalculable host of miscellanies of every description, including bottles and cabinets, rags and bones, fenders and street-door knockers, fire-irons, wearing apparel and bedding, a hall-lamp, and a room-door. (*SB*, 178–9, and see also 189, 382–3 for additional lists)

Though these things were made by man and once expressed the quality of human life, they are now broken, incomplete, useless, detached from the environing context which gave them meaning, and thrown together in pell-mell confusion. From such unlikely material Boz must put together a coherent picture of London life. The Sketch from which the list above is quoted observes that the articles in such shops differ from place to place in the city and may be taken as trustworthy signs of the quality of life in that part of London. "Although the same heterogeneous mixture of things," says Boz, "will be found at all these places, it is curious to observe how truly and accurately some of the minor articles which are exposed for sale – articles of wearing apparel, for instance – mark the character of the neighbourhood" (*SB*, 179). He goes on to give as examples the theatrical character of the things for sale in such shops in Drury Lane and Covent Garden, the nautical character of the things for sale in the shops in Ratcliff Highway, and the way the shops near the King's Bench Prison are full of things sold by the debtors imprisoned there:

> Dressing-cases and writing-desks, too old to pawn but too good to keep; guns, fishing-rods, musical instruments, all in the same condition; have first been sold, and the sacrifice has been but slightly felt. But hunger must be allayed, and what has already become a habit is easily resorted to, when an emergency arises. Light articles of clothing, first of the ruined man, then of his wife, at last of their children, even of the youngest, have been parted with, piecemeal. There they are, thrown carelessly together until a purchaser presents himself, old, and patched and repaired, it is true; but the make and materials tell of better days; and the older they are, the greater the misery and destitution of those whom they once adorned. (*SB*, 181)

Here the literary strategy of the *Sketches* may be observed in little: first the scene, with its inanimate objects, then the people of whose lives these objects are the signs, and finally the continuous narrative of their lives which may be inferred from the traces of themselves they have left behind. Boz's work is analogous to that of a detective or archaeologist. From the bric-a-brac of a dead civilization he resurrects a whole culture, an unrecorded piece of history. This movement is recapitulated repeatedly. "The Streets – Morning" (*SB*, 47–52), for example, begins with the empty streets of London, an hour before sunrise, and as Boz watches they gradually fill with the life that is lived there. "Shops and Their Tenants" (*SB*, 59–63), to give another example, begins with the description of a certain shop and then follows the history of its successive tenants as they may be guessed from changes in the outer appearance of the shop.

Perhaps the most striking example of this characteristic imaginative progression in the *Sketches* is the admirable "Meditations in Monmouth Street" (*SB*, 74–80). This is one of the best of the Sketches, a text already marked by the special qualities present in Dickens' mature work. The organizing law of Boz's "meditations" is given early in the Sketch:

> We love to walk among these extensive groves of the illustrious dead, and to indulge in the speculations to which they give rise; now fitting a deceased coat, then a dead pair of trousers, and anon the mortal remains of a gaudy waistcoat, upon some being of our own conjuring up, and endeavouring, from the shape and fashion of the garment itself, to bring its former owner before our mind's eye. We have gone on speculating in this way, until whole rows of coats have started from their pegs, and buttoned up, of their own accord, round the waists of imaginary wearers; lines of trousers have jumped down to meet them; waistcoats have almost

> burst with anxiety to put themselves on; and half an acre of shoes have suddenly found feet to fit them, and gone stumping down the street with a noise which has fairly awakened us from our pleasant reverie, and driven us slowly away, with a bewildered stare, an object of astonishment to the good people of Monmouth Street, and of no slight suspicion to the policemen at the opposite street corner. (*SB*, 75)

Confronted with the clothes of the dead, Boz's speculations bring to life in an instant the personages who once wore these clothes. The clothes are metonymically equivalent to their absent wearers and give Boz access to them. The life which properly belonged to the wearers is transferred to the clothes. These leap up with an unnatural vitality to put themselves on the ghostly owners conjured up by Boz's speculative imagination. The fitting of the old clothes to mental images of their former owners begins as a voluntary act. It is soon described as proceeding without intervention by Boz. It becomes a spectacle rather than an act. The text moves toward that personification of the inanimate which has often been seen as one of the major sources of metaphor in Dickens' work: "waistcoats have almost burst with anxiety to put themselves on."[20] The metonymic reciprocity between a person and his surroundings, his clothes, furniture, house, and so on, is the basis for the metaphorical substitutions so frequent in Dickens' fiction. For Dickens, metonymy is the foundation and support of metaphor.[21] The passage quoted above from the "Meditations in Monmouth Street" moves not only to free Boz's speculations from their voluntary basis and to make them into a self-generating reverie. As speculation becomes vision, quaint fancy becomes grotesque hyperbole, and Boz witnesses the macabre ballet of whole rows of coats, lines of trousers, and half an acre of shoes stomping noisily off on their own accord. Finally the dream bursts of its own excess, and Boz finds himself back to himself, self-consciously aware that people are staring at his queer bewilderment. His return to himself gives him a guilty feeling that he must have committed some crime for which the policemen over the way may apprehend him as a danger to the community.

The initial description of the habitual progression of Boz's meditations in Monmouth Street is followed by a full-scale example of their operation on a particular occasion. From a row of old suits in a shop he identifies not only the person who must have worn them but his life story from his school-days to his death in banishment or on the gallows:

> We were occupied in this manner the other day, . . . when our eyes happened to alight on a few suits of clothes ranged outside a shop-window, which it immediately struck us, must at different periods have all belonged to, and been worn by, the same individual, and had now, by one of these strange conjunctions of circumstances which will occur

> sometimes, come to be exposed together for sale in the same shop. The idea seemed a fantastic one, and we looked at the clothes again with a firm determination not to be easily led away. No, we were right; the more we looked, the more we were convinced of the accuracy of our previous impression. There was the man's whole life written as legibly on those clothes, as if we had his autobiography engrossed on parchment before us. (*SB*, 75)

The row of old suits is a legible text. Its reader is led first to the person who owned them, in a metonymic progression, and then on to the narrative of the man's life, given in this case, as in other similar cases in the *Sketches*, as a connected *récit*.

If a movement from things to people to stories is the habitual structural principle of the *Sketches*, the law which validates this movement is the assumption of a necessary similarity between a man, his environment, and the life he is forced to lead within that environment. As a man's surroundings are, so will his life be. This metonymic law functions implicitly everywhere, but it is presented explicitly in several striking formulations early in the *Sketches*. In one place Boz tells his readers that there is no reason to provide an analysis of a certain character's personality. An objective description of what he looked like and how he dressed will convey immediately his inner spiritual nature:

> We needn't tell you all this, however, for if you have an atom of observation, one glance at his sleek, knowing-looking head and face – his prim white neckerchief, with the wooden tie into which it has been regularly folded for twenty years past, merging by imperceptible degrees into a small-plaited shirt-frill – and his comfortable-looking form encased in a well-brushed suit of black – would give you a better idea of his real character than a column of our poor description could convey. (*SB*, 158–9)

In another Sketch the three-stage process is entered at the second stage, and Boz's clairvoyant eye sees through to the life story of a solitary clerk he glimpses in St James's Park, "a tall, thin, pale person, in a black coat, scanty grey trousers, little pinched-up gaiters, and brown beaver gloves" (*SB*, 215). From the man's dress and behavior Boz can infer his whole way of existence. He states for the reader the close reciprocity which must exist between the two if his inferences are correct:

> There was something in the man's manner and appearance which told us, we fancied, his whole life, or rather his whole day, for a man of this sort has no variety of days. We thought we almost saw the dingy little back office into which he walks every morning. (*SB*, 216)

A detailed narration of this man's day follows, including what he eats for dinner and the amount he tips the waiter. In "The New Year" Boz presents an elaborate description of a party in the house opposite his own on the basis of the fact that the house has green blinds. He knows the profession of the master of the house by a glimpse of his clothes, by his way of talking, and by means of those same green blinds:

> We can fancy one of these parties, we think, as well as if we were duly dress-coated and pumped, and had just been announced at the drawing-room door. . . . The master of the house with the green blinds is in a public office; we know the fact by the cut of his coat, the tie of his neckcloth, and the self-satisfaction of his gait – the very green blinds themselves have a Somerset House air about them. (*SB*, 226)

A final succinct statement of the law of metonymy on which the *Sketches* are built is given in the seventh Sketch:

> The various expressions of the human countenance afford a beautiful and interesting study; but there is something in the physiognomy of street-door knockers, almost as characteristic, and nearly as infallible. Whenever we visit a man for the first time, we contemplate the features of his knocker with the greatest curiosity, for we well know, that between the man and his knocker, there will inevitably be a greater or less degree of resemblance and sympathy. (*SB*, 40)

Ex ungue lionem – as the whole beast may be conjured up from a single claw, or as an archaeologist reconstructs a vanished civilization from a few potsherds, so Boz can tell a man and all his life from even so small and peripheral a part of him as his door-knocker. The *Sketches* are constructed around Boz's exercise of this power.

This law of metonymic correspondence underlies many other characteristic linguistic procedures in the *Sketches*. Many begin with a generalization about a certain class of Londoners and then narrow down to a characteristic case. Mr John Dounce, for example, the hero of "The Misplaced Attachment of Mr. John Dounce" (*SB*, 244–9), is presented as one version of a whole class of Londoners, the "steady old boys." The part and the whole correspond, and John Dounce's nature and experiences seem determined by his membership in a class of which Boz could give many examples. Many of the characters in the *Sketches* are defined, in another form of metonymy, not as individual persons but as gestures, roles, or functions. One character says, "Yes, I am the upper-boots." He exists not as a man but as "a voice from inside a velveteen case, with mother-of-pearl buttons" (*SB*, 408). The guests at a benefit, in another Sketch, are described not as people but as the drinks they have ordered: "ninety-seven six-penn'orths of gin-and-water, thirty-two small glasses of brandy-and-water, five-and-twenty bottled ales, and forty-one neguses" (*SB*, 254). Here the part stands for the whole in a comic synecdoche which is a frequent stylistic resource in the later novels, as in the admirable metamorphosis of Sairey Gamp's husband, within her active imagination, into his wooden leg: "And as to husbands, there's a wooden leg gone likeways home to its account, which in its constancy of walkin' into wine vaults, and never comin' out again till fetched by force, was quite as weak as flesh, if not weaker."[22]

Metonymy provides a structuring principle for the *Sketches* in still another way. If each Sketch often recapitulates the progression from scene to person to narrative, the *Sketches* as a whole proceed through exactly this sequence. When Dickens collected the various texts from their random appearance over a period of three years in various periodicals, he rearranged the Sketches in a way which does not correspond to the chronological order of their original publication. The order finally adopted for the one-volume edition of 1839 and maintained in subsequent editions does match exactly, however, the sequence I have identified as appearing within the individual Sketches. First come a group of seven Sketches entitled "Our Parish," six of which had appeared originally as a connected series in a single periodical, the *Evening Chronicle*. The remaining Sketches are divided into three groups: "Scenes," "Characters," and 'Tales."[23] This grouping seems clear evidence that Dickens had become to some degree aware of the principle which had governed his imagination during the composition of the *Sketches*. From scene to character to tale – the metonymic chain of substitutions could not be more clearly named. The *Sketches* when they were first collected were set side by side like the heterogeneous objects in a junk shop, but the final ordering reveals a significant relationship among them which was at first hidden but which can be revealed by their proper juxtaposition.

The clue taken from Roman Jakobson has seemingly sustained a vindication of the traditional description of the *Sketches* as realistic copying and an identification of the basic trope whereby that *mimesis* is performed. Moreover, it is easy to see how, in the case of the *Sketches*, the predominance of metonymy reinforces that deterministic vision of man's life which is often said to be an essential aspect of realistic fiction. One narrative pattern recurring in the *Sketches* is an apparently inescapable progression of the city dwellers step by step toward starvation, sickness, degradation, crime, depravity, suicide, or execution. A character caught in this progression is "impelled by sheer necessity, down the precipice that [has] led him to a lingering death" (*SB*, 78). Such a sequence occurs in "Our Next-Door Neighbour," in "The Pawnbroker's Shop," in "The Hospital Patient," "The Prisoners' Van," and "The Black Veil," as the rather acerbic ending to a comic tale in "A Passage in the Life of Mr. Watkins Tottle," and with melodramatic emphasis in the last Sketch,

"The Drunkard's Death." There is a close relation between metonymy and this form of narrative. The story of a man's degeneration "impelled by sheer necessity" constitutes a spreading out on the diachronic scale of the determinism implied synchronically in saying that each man is defined by what is around him. The Tales are often the temporal unfolding of what is initially affirmed pictorially, in the instant of juxtaposition within a Sketch. Three examples of this will bring into the open the implicit relation between spatial and temporal contiguity in the *Sketches*. The law of metonymic correspondence is presupposed as much in the narrative sequence of the Tales as in the interpretation of the Scenes and Characters from which these tales emerge. The scenes may present as a simultaneous tableau a progression which is achieved by a single individual only through a long period of his life. The presence in a single instant of more than one stage of such a progression strongly persuades the reader of the inevitability of the sequence.

One such scene is Boz's glimpse of two young girls, sisters, the elder defiant, the younger weeping bitterly, being taken from the Bow Street police station to the prisoners' van which will convey them to jail:

> These two girls had been thrown upon London streets, their vices and debauchery, by a sordid and rapacious mother. What the younger girl was then, the elder sister had been once; and what the elder then was, the younger must soon become. A melancholy prospect, but how surely to be realised; a tragic drama, but how often acted! . . . The progress of these girls in crime will be as rapid as the flight of a pestilence. (*SB*, 274)

Another such text makes explicit once more the way the physical objects Boz encounters in London contain folded up in themselves a multitude of tales. Again there appears the motif of the "progress" frozen into a series of juxtaposed vignettes. The object contains, immobilized in an instant, the temporal history of the men and women who have used it:

> What an interesting book a hackney-coach might produce, if it could carry as much in its head as it does in its body! . . . How many stories might be related of the different people it had conveyed on matters of business or profit – pleasure or pain! And how many melancholy tales of the same people at different periods! The country-girl – the showy, over-dressed woman – the drunken prostitute! The raw apprentice – the dissipated spendthrift – the thief!. (*SB*, 84)

The final example appears in "The Pawnbroker's Shop." Three women side by side in the shop constitute three stages from shabby genteel respectability to destitution and misery:

> Who shall say how soon these women may change places? The last has but two more stages – the hospital and the grave. How many females

> situated as her two companions are, and as she may have been once, have terminated the same wretched course, in the same wretched manner! One is already tracing her footsteps with frightful rapidity. How soon may the other follow her example! How many have done the same! (*SB*, 195)

Here are three excellent demonstrations of the metonymic basis of realistic narrative. Such narrative places in temporal sequence what can also be seen as spatially contiguous. The diachronic sequence has the same irresistible coercion as the synchronic law which says that between a man and his door knocker there will inevitably be some degree of resemblance and sympathy.

Tales like "The Drunkard's Death," in the final ordering of the *Sketches*, seem to emerge as linear narrative out of the static poses of the earlier Scenes and Characters. They also anticipate the grimmer side of Dickens' later fiction, for example the slow deaths of those destroyed by the Court of Chancery in *Bleak House*. Stories in this mode, however, by no means make up the majority of the Tales, nor of the briefer narratives interpolated in the earlier Sketches. Most of the Tales are comic or farcical stories. They anticipate more Sairey Gamp or Mr Pecksniff than the career of Jonas Chuzzlewit. The comic Tales are also anticipated in the more journalistic Scenes, for example in the admirable account of "Aggerawatin Bill," the omnibus cad (*SB*, 146–51), or in the description of the visit of a bourgeois family to Astley's (*SB*, 104–6). What interpretation of the comedy of the *Sketches* can be made?

To account for the comic aspect of the *Sketches* is one path (there are others) which leads to a recognition that the analysis of them so far undertaken here has been a good example of the way a literary text may contain the invitation to its radical misreading. We have been inveigled into taking as *mimesis* solidly based on an extra-literary world a work which is in fact fiction and which contains the linguistic clues allowing the reader to recognize that it is fiction. Moreover, this accounting for its status as literature takes place in a way especially appropriate to narrative fiction, by a reciprocity between the Scenes, Characters, and Tales themselves, and the implications of Dickens' "representation" of them.

The theme of deception, play-acting, illusion, baseless convention pervades the *Sketches*, and Boz repeatedly performs what may be defined as an act of demystification. As a detached spectator he sees that the pretense is pretense and shows it as such to the reader, but for the most part the characters remain trapped in their illusions. This theme takes a number of different forms in the *Sketches*. One recurrent motif is the imitation of the upper class by the middle or lower class. Boz sees the speech, dress, and behavior of the aristocracy as conventions based on no substantial worth. They are justified by no supernatural models, no "divine right." The apprentices of London, however, in "Thoughts about People," or the *nouveaux riches* of "The Tuggses at Ramsgate," take the shadow for the substance. The four apprentices who go out for a Sunday stroll adorned "like so many bridegrooms" are said to be "the faint reflection of higher lights." In their good humor and innocent self-deception they seem to Boz "more tolerable" than the aristocracy they imitate, "precocious puppyism in the Quadrant, whiskered dandyism in Regent Street and Pall Mall, or gallantry in its dotage anywhere" (*SB*, 219). Mr Tuggs in "The Tuggses at Ramsgate" is a London grocer who inherits a fortune and straightway leaves for Ramsgate. The story which ensues is the traditional one of the social climbers who are in their naïveté defrauded by a dishonest couple whom they take to be authentic members of the social class they wish to join. Mr Frederick Malderton, in "Horatio Sparkins," was a young man "who always dressed according to the fashions of the months; who went up the water twice a week in the season; and who actually had an intimate friend who once knew a gentleman who formerly lived in the Albany" (*SB*, 358). His family "affected fashion, taste, and many other fooleries, in imitation of their betters, and had a very decided and becoming horror of anything which could, by possibility, be considered *low*" (*SB*, 356). The story turns on the way the Malderton family take Horatio Sparkins to be a nobleman in disguise and then discover that he is actually an assistant in a linen-draper's shop in the Tottenham Court Road.

If the theme of the inauthentic imitation by the lower middle class of an upper class without authenticity in itself runs through the *Sketches*, an even more pervasive theme is theatrical imitation as such. Critics from the earliest reviewers to present-day commentators have noted the importance of this in the *Sketches*. Dickens was already at this time of his life deeply involved in the theater, both as an amateur actor and as a novice playwright. During the period he was revising the *Sketches* he was at work on a burlesque, *O'Thello*, and on a farce, *The Strange Gentleman*, based on one of the Sketches, "The Great Winglebury Duel." The theater returns so often in the *Sketches* that London in this book comes to seem a place where everyone is in one way or another engaged not in productive work but in performing or witnessing scenic representations. They watch others pretend to be what they are not or play roles themselves. Certainly the attention paid to the theater and to musical performance is disproportionate. It constitutes a deformation in Boz's mirroring of the "real" London. In spite of the importance drama undoubtedly had in the culture of early Victorian London, it seems unlikely that quite so large a proportion of its people were obsessed with it, involved in it in one way or another, or allowed their life styles, attitudes, dress, speech, and gesture to be determined by it. The theatrical theme is also a good example of the way a topic frequently appears in the early journalistic Sketches and then is picked up as the background for a more frankly "fictional" treatment in the Characters or Tales.

Among the Scenes is the admirable sketch of "Astley's." This includes not only a description of the circus part of the performance but also a reference to the farces and melodramas which accompany the circus and a description of the hangers-on around the stage-doors of minor theaters. Central in "Greenwich Fair" is the description of "Richardson's," "where you have a melo-drama (with three murders and a ghost), a pantomime, a comic song, an overture, and some incidental music, all done in five-and-twenty minutes" (*SB*, 115). This is followed by an amusing paragraph describing the action of the melodrama. Next comes an important Sketch of "Private Theatres," then a description of "Vauxhall Gardens by Day." The theatrical or musical theme appears in several of the Characters: in "The Mistaken Milliner. A Tale of Ambition," which tells how a little milliner is persuaded to take voice lessons and then fails miserably at her first concert; in "The Dancing Academy"; in the visit to the theater in "Making a Night of It"; in the concert and vaudeville in the suburbs in "Miss Evans and the Eagle." Among the Tales there are musical performances aboard ship in "The Steam Excursion" and a return to the theme of private theatricals in "Mrs. Joseph Porter."

Throughout the *Sketches* characters are introduced whose lives are determined by the theater, for example a man seen "lounging up Drury Lane" in "Shabby-Genteel People": "The 'harmonic meetings' at some fourth-rate public-house, or the purlieus of a private theatre, are his chosen haunts; he entertains a rooted antipathy to any kind of work, and is on familiar terms with several pantomime men at the large houses" (*SB*, 262–3). Another example is prefatory to a description of the brokers' shops in the neighborhood of Drury Lane and Covent Garden:

> This is essentially a theatrical neighbourhood. There is not a potboy in the vicinity who is not, to a greater or less extent, a dramatic character. The errand-boys and chandler's-shop-keepers' sons are all stage-struck: they "gets up" plays in back kitchens hired for the purpose, and will stand before a shop-window for hours, contemplating a great staring portrait of Mr. Somebody or other, of the Royal Coburg Theatre, "as he appeared in the character of Tongo the Denounced." The consequence is, that there is not a marine-store shop in the neighbourhood, which does not exhibit for sale some faded articles of dramatic finery. (*SB*, 179)

"All the minor theatres in London," says Boz, "especially the lowest, constitute the centre of a little stage-struck neighbourhood" (*SB*, 120).

The two most extended treatments of this theme of fascination by the drama are the descriptions of amateur theatricals in "Private Theatres" and in the Tale called "Mrs. Joseph Porter." A passage in the last paragraph of the periodical version of "Astley's," later omitted, anticipates the topic which is treated with great circumstantiality and verve in "Private Theatres":

> It is to us matter of positive wonder and astonishment that the infectious disease commonly known by the name of "stage-struck," has never been eradicated, unless people really believe that the privilege of wearing velvet and feathers for an hour or two at night, is sufficient compensation for a life of wretchedness and misery. It is stranger still, that the denizens of attorneys' offices, merchants' counting-houses, haberdashers' shops, and coal sheds, should squander their own resources to enrich some wily vagabond by paying – actually paying, and dearly too – to make unmitigated and unqualified asses of themselves at a Private Theatre.[24]

"Mrs. Joseph Porter" is probably based on "Dickens's amateur production of *Clari* at Bentinck Street on 27 Apr. 1833; it may also bear some relation to his burlesque *O'Thello*, written about this time."[25] The Tale describes an amateur performance of *Othello* by a Clapham family all "infected with the mania for Private Theatricals" (*SB*, 421). From the near-slum areas where the private theaters flourish to the well-to-do suburbs like Clapham, from the edges of poverty to the upper middle class,[26] all Boz's London seems to have caught the disease of theatrical representation.

The theater permeates the *Sketches* in still another way, a way that will allow a more precise identification of its significance. If there are many characters in the *Sketches* who are actually involved in the theater, the theater is also one of Boz's major sources of metaphorical language. This language is used to describe even those characters who have no direct connection with the theater. Along with the people in Boz's London who either play a role or watch others play one there are many other characters who unwittingly behave, dress, or speak in ways that make them like characters in a melodrama or farce. A pretty young lady, for example, "[goes] through various . . . serio-pantomimic fascinations, which forcibly [remind] Mr. John Dounce of the first time he courted his first wife" (*SB*, 248). Another character is shown "standing up with his arms a-kimbo, expressing defiance melodramatically" (*SB*, 269). Another is "one of those young men, who are in society what walking gentlemen are on the stage, only infinitely worse skilled in his vocation than the most indifferent artist" (*SB*, 278). This man wears "a maroon-coloured dress-coat, with a velvet collar and cuffs of the same tint – very like that which usually invests the form of the distinguished unknown who condescends to play the 'swell' in the pantomime at 'Richardson's Show' " (*SB*, 281). Another person goes through "an admirable bit of serious pantomime" (*SB*, 279), speaks in "a stage whisper" (*SB*, 282), and appears later at a staircase window "like the ghost of Queen Anne in the tent scene in Richard" (*SB*, 306). Mr Septimus Hicks, in the same story, speaks "very tremulously, in a voice like a Punch with a cold" (*SB*, 285). A few moments later he has an "expression of countenance" more discomposed than "Hamlet's, when he sees his father's ghost" (*SB*, 285). A maid dresses "like a disguised Columbine" (*SB*, 295), and the "manners and appearance" of an Irishman "[remind] one of Orson" (*SB*, 298). Another character bursts out of a back drawing-room "like the dragon at Astley's" (*SB*, 309). A series of such metaphors punctuate the Tale called "Sentiment": a spoiled child is shown "looking like a robber in a melodrama, seen through a diminishing glass" (*SB*, 325), and his face looks "like a capital O in a red-lettered play-bill" (*SB*, 326). Boz makes self-conscious use in this story of the language of advertisements for dramatic performances: "Preparations, to make use of theoretical phraseology, 'on a scale of magnitude never before attempted,' were incessantly made" (*SB*, 327), and a group of "fat mammas" look "like the stout people who come on in pantomimes for the sole purpose of being knocked down" (*SB*, 329). In another story, "The Bloomsbury Christening," Mr Dumps speaks "in a voice like Desdemona with the pillow over her mouth" (*SB*, 478) and later rises from his chair "like the ghost in Don Juan" (*SB*, 481).

Whenever Boz wants to find a picturesque way to describe one of his characters he is apt to use some simile or metaphor drawn from a range of theatrical reference extending all the way from Punch to *Hamlet*. The characters are not aware of the similarity of their gestures to those of pantomime, melodrama, or farce, but Boz is aware and makes his readers share his insight. Such metaphors present the characters as unwittingly imitative of something which exists in the social world shared by Dickens and his readers. This social reality, however, is openly factitious, illusory. Unconsciously theatrical gestures or speech are the signs not of a plenitude but of an absence. They have the hollowness of a mask. They refer not to the solidity of physical reality but to the fictions of a highly stylized theater. Such reference is one of the chief sources of comedy in the *Sketches*. This comedy presents people not as victims of coercive social "forces," as seems the case in stories like "The Drunkard's Death," but as consciously or unconsciously frauds. Character after character in the *Sketches* is shown pretending to be what he is not. A man in one story displays ostentatiously "an immense key, which belonged to the street-door, but which, for the sake of appearances, occasionally did duty in an imaginary wine-cellar" (*SB*, 433). Another character looks like "a bad 'portrait of a gentleman' in the Somerset House exhibition" (*SB*, 369). Another person's face lights up with "something like a bad imitation of animation" (*SB*, 438). A coach in the same story draws up before "a cardboard-looking house with disguised chimneys, and a lawn like a large sheet of green letter-paper" (*SB*, 436). Everything in the *Sketches* seems to be what it is not, and Boz's chief work is not objective description but the uncovering of fraud.

The theme of disillusionment runs all through the *Sketches*, as in the description of the decay of May Day celebrations in "The First of May," or in Boz's confession that he is no longer enraptured by Astley's as he used to be and finds more interest in watching the audience than in watching the performance, or in that exercise in disenchantment, "Vauxhall Gardens by Day":

> We bent our steps to the firework-ground; there, at least, we should not be disappointed. We reached it, and stood rooted to the spot with mortification and astonishment. *That* the Moorish tower – that wooden shed with a door in the centre, and daubs of crimson and yellow all round, like a gigantic watch-case! *That* the place where night after night we had beheld the undaunted Mr. Blackmore make his terrific ascent, surrounded by flames of fire, and peals of artillery, and where the white garments of Madame Somebody (we forget even her name now), who nobly devoted her life to the manufacture of fireworks, had so often been seen fluttering in the wind, as she called up a red, blue, or parti-coloured light to illumine her temple! (*SB*, 127)

Such an uncovering of the sordid reality behind a beguiling surface is the essential movement of the *Sketches*. The drama is important to Boz not because he is taken in by the theatrical, as are his characters, but because the theatrical metaphor expresses perfectly the process whereby Boz sees behind the scenes and leads his readers to see behind them too. Boz is the man who knows that behind the stage set is the cobwebby disorder backstage. Behind each mask he sees the shabby performer.

In this context it is possible to identify the somewhat surprising function in the *Sketches* of a character who anticipates Scrooge in hating children and dogs, and in refusing to participate in the social fictions which make life bearable for others. This bachelor figure, "life-hater" as Robert Browning calls him,[27] is not so much rejected by Dickens in the two Sketches in which he appears ("Mr. Minns and His Cousin" and "The Bloomsbury Christening") as he is a surrogate for Boz himself. Like Boz he is a detached spectator able to see through the falseness of social life. Mr Minns is the point of view from which the reader sees the absurdity and vulgarity of the cousin's dinner party in his little cottage "in the vicinity of Stamford Hill" (*SB*, 312), and Mr Nicodemus

Dumps, who "adored King Herod for his massacre of the innocents; and if he hated one thing more than another, it was a child" (*SB*, 467), is the reader's perspective in "The Bloomsbury Christening." Mr Dumps is granted the honor of using a style of metaphor peculiarly Boz's own. He describes the baby about to be christened as looking "like one of those little carved representations that one sometimes sees blowing a trumpet on a tombstone" (*SB*, 476). When Boz himself describes the child's arm and fist as "about the size and shape of the leg of a fowl cleanly picked" (*SB*, 479), it is clear that Boz (and Dickens) shared some of Dumps' distaste for babies and for the fuss that is made over them.

Boz's uncovering of the fictive nature of society by way of the metaphorical use of other fictions is not performed in the name of some possible authentic way of living. Each way of living imitates another way which is itself not solid or authentic. Each character lives as a sign referring not to substance but to another sign. This emphasis on playacting and on the factitious calls the reader's attention to the fact that English society as a whole is based on arbitrary conventions, on the fictional ascription of value and significance to the stones, paper, glass, cloth of which the buildings, streets, clothes, and utensils of London are made. This giving of meaning is an act of interpretation creating a culture, generating those signs which Boz the speculative pedestrian must then interpret. Such ascription of meaning is not free. The imprisonment of the human spirit in its conferring of meaning is a fundamental theme of the *Sketches*. The collective creation of meaning and value is enclosed rigidly within conventions, modes of language, institutions, ways of behaving and judging, which have been inherited from the past. People in the *Sketches* are trapped not by social forces but by human fabrications already there within which they must live their lives. They live not in free creativity but as stale repetitions of what has gone before. The world of the *Sketches* is caught in the copying of what preceded it. Each new form is a paler imitation of the past. Each person is confined in the tawdry imitation of stale gestures. The reader of the *Sketches* receives a powerful sense not only of the comic vitality of Dickens' earliest creations, but of their enclosure, the narrowness of their lives, their spiritual poverty. They are pathetically without awareness that their cheapness is pathetic, hopelessly imprisoned within the cells of a fraudulent culture.

The comedy of the *Sketches* arises from the juxtaposition of Boz's knowledge of this situation against the blindness of the characters to it. They are blind either in the sense that they are not aware that their gestures have the stiff, conventional quality of pantomimic movements, or in the sense that they perform the imitation consciously but in the mistaken belief that what they are imitating has absolute value or substance, as the apprentices of London are beguiled by the dress and swagger of the Pall Mall dandies. The comedy of the *Sketches* depends on the innocence of the objects of our laughter and on the opposing presence of a spectator who sees the insubstantiality of the spectacle he beholds. At the same time Boz mimes the foolishness of the people he sees, creating it anew in a constant hyperbole which translates it into the linguistic acrobatics of his discourse. The pathos of Boz's characters lies in the fact that their spiritual energy is determined in its expressions by the objects within which they live, or rather by their acceptance of the meaning collectively ascribed by their culture to those objects. These objects are the residue of the culture they have inherited and have coercive force not as physical energies but as signs, habits of interpretation, forms. Such inherited forms constitute a world in which nothing is what it is, but everything is the arrow pointing towards something else. This world of the presence of an absence channels and confines the spirit in a metonymic determination of contained by container, vital energy by environment. In this sense the latter can indeed be taken by the attentive spectator as the index of the former.

The theme of inauthentic repetition persists in Dickens' later work and forms one of its most important continuities. Examples are the motif of theatricality in *Nicholas Nickleby* and the treatment in *Great Expectations* of Pip's snobbish imitation of the manners of the gentility when he is living in London. The use of the motif of repetition in *Oliver Twist* is of special interest here, however, not only because *Oliver Twist* is with *Sketches by Boz* one of the two works by Dickens illustrated by George Cruikshank, but also because *Oliver Twist* both in its comic and in its melodramatic aspects grows naturally out of the *Sketches*. The latter anticipate the former in so many stylistic and thematic motifs that *Oliver Twist* might almost be described as the last and longest of the Tales from the *Sketches*. The murder of Nancy, the last night in the condemned cell, the juxtaposition of the respectable girl and the prostitute, the description of a crowd of juvenile pickpockets, the labyrinthine disorder of London's streets, the contiguous presentation of comic and melodramatic stretches of narrative, the comic aspect of a parish beadle, the explicit references to stage melodrama – all are already present in the *Sketches* and are given what might be called their definitive form in *Oliver Twist*.

Oliver Twist dramatizes a covert struggle between two kinds of repetition, kinds which might be associated with two grand antagonists in the history of philosophy: Plato and Nietzsche. In Platonic imitation there exists a substantial model for the act of copying, and the imitation itself is spontaneous. In obedience to this paradigm of imitation, Oliver has no inkling of who he is and nevertheless behaves instinctively according to his God-given "nature." He is incorruptibly good, that is, modeled on his father. Ultimately Mr Brownlow adopts Oliver "as his own son"[28] and goes on,

> from day to day, filling the mind of his adopted child with stores of knowledge, and becoming attached to him, more and more, as his nature develop[s] itself, and [shows] the thriving seeds of all he wishe[s] him to become . . . He trace[s] in him new traits of his early friend, that awaken[s] in his own bosom old remembrances, melancholy and yet sweet and soothing." (*OT*, 367–8)

Oliver ends his life as a copy of his father.

Shadowily set against this, its mirror image and yet its deadly opposite, as the sophist in Plato is the dangerous simulacrum of the philosopher, is another kind of repetition. This other kind is present in *Oliver Twist* as a secret possibility which puts in question the credibility of the happy ending. It also puts in question the status of the novel as "realism" or as "history." This alternative form of copying brings into the open the inauthenticity of what is imitated. It is based on difference rather than on similarity. For it there is no eternal realm of archetypal models, no divine center.[29]

Dickens affirms the first kind of repetition and rejects the second, but the hidden energy behind the novel is the tension between the two. This tension is present in the opposition between those passages which confess that the model for the novel's structure is not the real world but popular melodrama, and those passages which affirm, perhaps a bit too emphatically, the historical verisimilitude of the novel. On the one hand, the narrator calls attention to the fact that *Oliver Twist* is structured according to stage conventions and, like "all good, murderous melodramas," "present[s] the tragic and the comic scenes, in as regular alternation, as the layers of red and white in a side of streaky, well-cured bacon" (*OT*, 105). On the other hand, Dickens, in the preface to the third edition of 1841, argues of his presentation of Nancy that "it is useless to discuss whether the conduct and character of the girl seems natural or unnatural, probable or improbable, right or wrong. IT IS TRUE" (*OT*, lxv). Dickens seems to have been at least partly aware of the similarity between the two forms of imitation in conflict here and of the threat that one poses to the other. Fagin's hidden society of thieves bears a sinister resemblance to the good bourgeois world of Mr Brownlow. The unsettling similarity of the community of outlaws to the community of the good puts the validity of the latter in question. The moment when this similarity is brought most dramatically into the open is the moment, it may be, when Oliver is in greatest danger of losing his birthright by betraying the conditions of his father's will. This moment comes in the scene in which Fagin enacts the role Mr Brownlow is going to play in the following chapter, the chapter in which Oliver is arrested for the supposed picking of Mr Brownlow's pocket as he stands at a bookstall:

> When the breakfast was cleared away, the merry old gentleman and the two boys played at a very curious and uncommon game, which was performed in this way: The merry old gentleman: placing a snuff-box in one pocket of his trousers, a note-case in the other, and a watch in his waist-coat-pocket: with a guard-chain round his neck: and sticking a mock diamond pin in his shirt: buttoned his coat tight round him, and putting his spectacle-case and handkerchief in his pockets, trotted up and down the room with a stick, in imitation of the manner in which old gentlemen walk about the streets any hour in the day. Sometimes he stopped at the fire-place, and sometimes at the door; making belief that he was staring with all his might into shop-windows. At such times, he would look constantly round him, for fear of thieves; and keep slapping all his pockets in turn, to see that he hadn't lost anything; in such a very funny and natural manner, that Oliver laughed till the tears ran down his face. (*OT*, 54)

As the reader laughs with Oliver at Fagin's performance of the role of the good man, he may realize that Mr Brownlow himself exists as Dickens' imitation of him. The act of role-playing, whether within the novel or as its generative source, comes to seem far from innocent. Its danger lies not so much in the way it is factitious in itself as in the way it leads the reader to suspect that what is imitated may be factitious too. This suspicion is reinforced a few paragraphs later when Fagin exhorts Oliver, apropos of the Dodger and his friend: "Make 'em your models, my dear. Make 'em your models. . . ; do everything they bid you, and take their advice in all matters; especially the Dodger's, my dear. He'll be a great man himself; and will make you one too, if you take pattern by him" (*OT*, 55). The Dodger, his dead father – these two models are presented to Oliver as patterns for his imitation. He must choose which to copy. What is the difference between imitating the one and imitating the other? Does it lie only in the fact that in one case the imitation is deliberate and in the other case spontaneous, based on what Oliver "naturally" is? Which form of imitation is *Oliver Twist* itself? The fundamental question in this novel is whether anyone can break the iron chain of metonymy whereby a person is inevitably like his environment. The determining pressure of what is around them dooms Fagin, Sikes, Nancy, and the Dodger. Oliver escapes this chain only to be bound by another, the form of copying which says, "like father, like son." The strength of *Oliver Twist* is its oblique suggestion that the two forms of imitation may be the same, though it is only in Dickens' much later novels, for example in *Great Expectations* or in *Our Mutual Friend*, that this dark truth is brought more clearly into the open.

My discussion of repetition in *Oliver Twist* has suggested that the thematic polarity of the represented action in this novel has the strange effect of raising questions about the status of the novel itself as a form of representation. Does this also happen in the *Sketches by Boz*, or should they be interpreted as a false society mirrored truly by an objective narrator? One way to see that the *Sketches* do put their own status in question is to return to the theatrical metaphors which appear in them so frequently. These work in a radically ambiguous way which contains in miniature the linguistic movement essential to the *Sketches*. This movement challenges the authenticity of what is represented while what is represented in its turn undermines the apparent solidity of the *Sketches* as an innocent act of representational mirroring. This reversal between two elements facing one another within the text is basic to the mode of existence of a work of literature and constitutes it as a literary use of language. In this fluctuation the figurative becomes the literal only to be transformed into the figurative again by a corresponding change of what it faces from the one into the other. In this subtle movement nothing moves but the interpretative act, but this movement may be stilled only at the peril of a necessary misreading. Such a hermeneutical wavering is like that egg mentioned by Yeats which turns inside out without breaking its shell, or it is like those Gestaltist diagrams which change configuration bewilderingly before the viewer's eyes. When Boz describes a character as having a "melodramatic expression of horror" (*SB*, 397), or another character as "going through a threatening piece of pantomime with [a] stick" (*SB*, 415), the first effect of this is to present a coolly analytical spectator confronting a real world whose factitiousness he uncovers by comparing it to the conventions of drama. In the second movement of the reader's interpretation, he recognizes that the characters have no existence outside the language Dickens has invented to describe them. Dickens has modeled them on the popular drama of his day. What had seemed "realistic" comes to be seen as figurative, and the radically fictive quality of the *Sketches* as a whole comes into the open. Back and forth between these two interpretations the reader oscillates. Neither takes precedence over the other, but the meaning of the text is generated by the mirage of alternation between them.

When the reader has broken through to seeing local fragments of the text inside out, as it were, as well as outside in, then he recognizes that the *Sketches* from beginning to end are open to being read in this way. The *Sketches* are not *mimesis* of an externally existing reality, but the interpretation of that reality according to highly artificial schemas inherited from the past. They came into existence through the imposition of fictitious patterns rather than through the discovery of patterns "really there." Though this double reading of the *Sketches* would be valid whether it was asserted explicitly or not in the text, it happens that there are abundant clues informing the reader that the *Sketches* are fiction rather than *mimesis*. These clues identify the main sources of the fictional patterns according to which Boz interprets the appearances he confronts when he walks through London. One of these is the drama, as I have shown. The other two are the conventions of previous fiction and the conventions of graphic representation. There are almost as many explicit references to these last as to the theater. If people in the *Sketches* are often seen as like characters in a pantomime or melodrama, they are also often presented as like characters in a novel or in a print. A "little coquette with a large bustle" looks "like a French lithograph" (*SB*, 480). Another character "with his white dress-stock, blue coat, bright buttons, and red watch-ribbon, strongly resemble[s] the portrait of that interesting but rash young gentleman, George Barnwell" (*SB*, 357), and a "young gentleman with . . . green spectacles, in nankeen inexplicables, with a ditto waistcoat and bright buttons" is dressed "like the pictures of Paul – not the saint, but he of Virginia notoriety" (*SB*, 392). The reference here is to the illustrations in *Paul et Virginie*. In another place a character is described as having "looked something like a vignette to one of Richardson's novels, and [having] had a clean-cravatish formality of manner, and kitchen-pokerness of carriage, which Sir Charles Grandison himself might have envied" (*SB*, 431). In another Sketch there is an explicit reference to Hogarth, whom Dickens much admired and who is mentioned again in the preface of 1841 to *Oliver Twist*. In the latter, Hogarth is invoked as an excuse for the presentation of "low" characters and is defined as "the moralist, and censor of his age – in whose great works the times in which he lived, and the characters of every time, will never cease to be reflected" (*OT*, lxiv). In the *Sketches* Boz abandons the attempt to describe in language what could only be represented by a great artist like Hogarth: "It would require the pencil of Hogarth to illustrate – our feeble pen is inadequate to describe – the expression which the countenances of Mr. Calton and Mr. Septimus Hicks respectively assumed, at this unexpected announcement" (*SB*, 289). The effect of this is to invite the reader to imagine the scene as if it were schematized according to the conventions of Hogarth's prints. If the reader has this reference in mind he may note, for example, that the juxtaposition of three women at different stages on the road to degradation in "The Pawnbroker's Shop" is as much modeled on the eighteenth-century pictorial convention of the "Progress" as it is on any observation of the real London of Dickens' day. The "real London," here, is presented according to forms borrowed from *A Harlot's Progress*.

In other Sketches Boz's imagination is controlled by literary rather than by theatrical or graphic conventions. In the examples already given of references to Richardson and to *Paul et Virginie* the allusion (significantly from the point of view of the interpretation I shall suggest of the relation between the *Sketches* and the illustrations for them by Cruikshank) is not to the texts of the novels but to their illustrations. These seem to have stuck in Dickens' mind as much as the stories themselves. There are, however, many explicit references to literary texts. The fare in a cab is "as carefully boxed up behind two glazed calico curtains as any mysterious picture in any one of Mrs. Radcliffe's castles" (*SB*, 471). There are several ironic references to the artificial conventions of fiction or journalism: "Like those paragons of perfection, advertising footmen out of place, he was always 'willing to make himself generally useful' " (*SB*, 382); "Then, as standard novelists expressively inform us – 'all was a blank!' " (*SB*, 270); "We are not about to adopt the licence of novel-writers, and to let 'years roll on' " (*SB*, 284); "A troublesome form, and an arbitrary custom, however, prescribe that a story should have a conclusion, in addition to a commencement; we have therefore no alternative" (*SB*, 354); " 'We will draw a veil,' as novel-writers say, over the scene that ensued" (*SB*, 369). Even the name Boz, as Dickens later revealed, was an allusion to *The Vicar of Wakefield*. It was a corruption of "Moses," a name in the novel, and was the nickname Dickens gave to one of his younger brothers.

Side by side with the realistic way of seeing the *Sketches* as the discovery by Boz of true stories hidden behind the objects he encounters in his walks through London, there is another way which involves the same elements but with reverse polarity, as the ghost of the other way, its "negative," in which black becomes white, white black. To see the *Sketches* in this new way is to recognize that metonymy is as much a fiction as metaphor. Both are the assertion of a false identity or of a false causal connection. The metonymic associations which Boz makes are fancies rather than facts, impositions on the signs he sees of stock conventions, not mirroring but interpretation, which is to say, lie. A man's doorknocker is no necessary indication of his personality. It only seems so to the imagining mind of the inimitable Boz. An excellent example of this importation of the fictive into the real is the "Meditations in Monmouth Street," which seemed, according to my first reading of it, such a perfect case of the linguistic act whereby metonymy is employed as a decoding of the hidden significance of the real. The row of old clothes which Boz sees in Monmouth Street gives rise, however, to a wholly conventional narrative, the story of the idle apprentice. This story has many antecedents in eighteenth-century fiction, drama, and graphic representation. To remember this is to see that the theme in the *Sketches* of the irresistible coercion of social forces, the motif which seemed to be a fundamental part of their representation of urban life, is not "truth" but literary fiction, perhaps no more than a sentimental lie. If the *Sketches* unmask their characters and show them to be living in terms of theatrical gestures, they also turn at crucial moments on their own conventions and expose these as fictions too. The stories which rise from the doorknockers, the old clothes, the objects in the pawnshop are Boz's inventions, not objective facts. Moreover, far from being the free creations of his imagination they are as much bound by forms inherited from the past as the gestures and speech of the characters within the *Sketches*. The movement from Scene to Character to Tale is not the metonymic process authenticating realistic representation but a movement deeper and deeper into the conventional, the concocted, the schematic.

Nor is Boz unaware of this. In several places he gives the reader the information he needs to free himself from a realistic interpretation of the *Sketches*. To be so freed is to perceive that throughout the *Sketches*, in the phrase I have taken from "The Drunkard's Death" as an epigraph for this essay, "the illusion [is] reality itself" (*SB*, 493). In "Meditations in Monmouth Street" Boz says, in a clause allowed to pass without question in my "realistic" reading of this Sketch, that he fits the old clothes "upon some being of [his] own conjuring up" (*SB*, 75). Later in the same Sketch, when Boz is in the midst of his invention of a new version of the story of the idle apprentice, he says, "we felt . . . much sorrow when we saw, or fancied we saw – it makes no difference which – the change that began to take place now" (*SB*, 76). It makes no difference which because the seeing of Boz is all imaginary rather than real, made out of the whole cloth of those old suits. In another Sketch Boz says that "the sudden moving of a taper" seen in the window of a hospital "is enough to awaken a whole crowd of reflections" (*SB*, 240). He then proceeds to narrate the story of a girl beaten to death by her ruffian lover which anticipates the murder of Nancy by Sikes in *Oliver Twist*. In another place Boz demystifies his childhood enslavement to literary convention when he says: "We remember, in our young days, a little sweep about our own age, with curly hair and white teeth, whom we devoutly and sincerely believed to be the lost son and heir of some illustrious personage" (*SB*, 171). To believe this was to be the victim of the fairy tale patterns of children's literature, but the adult Boz has been disillusioned, or, at any rate, one part of his mind has been disillusioned. The other part used this same story of the workhouse son of the "illustrious personage" as the basis of *Oliver Twist*. The *Sketches by Boz*, like *Oliver Twist*, express both the illusion and its deconstruction, just as the critic's interpretation of them must hover between realistic and figurative readings.

Perhaps the best example of a text explicitly calling attention to the fictive quality of the *Sketches* is a curious paragraph in which the failure of Boz's habitual processes of imagination brings into the open the laws by which it usually operates. Boz has been left alone in the parlor of "an old, quiet, decent public-house" (*SB*, 235) near the City Road in the east of London:

> If we had followed the established precedent in all such instances, we should have fallen into a fit of musing, without delay. The ancient appearance of the room – the old panelling of the wall – the chimney blackened with smoke and age – would have carried us back a hundred years at least, and we should have gone dreaming on, until the pewter-pot on the table, or the little beer-chiller on the fire, had started into life, and addressed to us a long story of days gone by. But, by some means or other, we were not in a romantic humour; and although we tried very hard to invest the furniture with vitality, it remained perfectly unmoved, obstinate, and sullen. (*SB*, 239)

Here the inability of Boz's romantic imagination to follow the established precedent brings to the surface the precariously fictive quality of that imagination. The pewter pot and the little beer-chiller are characteristic examples of utensils which in other Sketches are read as metonymic signs of the life which has been lived in their vicinity. In their failure to start into life there is a revelation of the fact that the vitality of such objects does not belong in reality to them. It is invested in them by Boz, and it is invested according to patterns of interpretation taken from traditional literary forms. In such moments the *Sketches* make problematical their mimetic function. In doing so they fulfill, in a way appropriate to narrative fiction, the definition of literature as a use of language which exposes its own rhetorical devices and assumptions.

This uncovering of the fictitiousness of the fictive is not performed, however, in the name of some "true" language for which a space is cleared through the rejection of the fictive. Behind each fiction there is another fiction, and this new fiction is sustained in its turn by the counterpart phantom of a beguiling literal reading. Once more this is easiest to see in its mirroring within the lives of the characters in the *Sketches*. This mirroring corresponds rigorously to the mode of existence of the *Sketches* themselves. In the *Sketches* the liberated characters are not those who escape from conventional behavior. No one can escape. Liberation is possible only to those who, like Aggerawatin Bill, the omnibus cad, play their roles to the hilt, perform their part with such abandon that this hyperbolic verve constitutes a kind of freedom. It is a paradoxical freedom which both accepts the role (any action in the world of the *Sketches* is a role of some sort) and, at the same time, reveals in the excess with which the part is played that it is a part, that it could be otherwise. Any behavior is incommensurate with the vitality which gives energy to it. The heroes of the *Sketches* are such characters as Bill Barker, the "cad," or his counterpart in the same Sketch, the red-cab-driver. The latter knocks down a gentleman who protests the way he is treated, and then "call[s] the police to take himself into custody, with all the civility in the world" (*SB*, 146).

Such admirable displays of deliberately outrageous behavior are exactly parallel to the function of hyperbole in Dickens' own playing of the role of Boz, the speculative pedestrian. In the incongruous metaphors, in the pervasive facetious irony, in a constant play of language which calls attention to its own clichés in ways which destroy their innocent existence as nominal turns of language, Boz liberates himself in the only way one can be liberated through language. He does not substitute true language for false, nor does he copy true models. Neither true language nor true models exist for Boz. Like Bill Barker, he must tell lies, employ fictions, in ways which expose the fact that they are lies. The use of clichés, in ways that reveal their reliance on metaphors which have come to be taken literally and which thereby have become the support of social fictions, contains this linguistic resource of the *Sketches* in miniature. An example is Boz's play with the phrase "coming out" in "The Mistaken Milliner. A Tale of Ambition":

> Now, "coming out," either in acting, or singing, or society, or facetiousness, or anything else, is all very well, and remarkably pleasant to the individual principally concerned, if he or she can but manage to come out with a burst, and being out to keep out, and not go in again; but it does unfortunately happen that both consummations are extremely difficult to accomplish, and that the difficulties of getting out at all in the first instance, and if you surmount them, of keeping out in the second, are pretty much on a par, and no slight ones either – and so Miss Amelia Martin shortly discovered. (*SB*, 254)

If the real world is a fiction and the reflection of it in literature a fiction too, what of the interpretation of the relation between them expressed by the critic? Can criticism formulate without equivocation the truth which the creative writer can only convey indirectly and in such a way that it will inevitably be misunderstood by his readers? No, the critic is caught in exactly the same predicament as the creative writer or as the man living in the real world. To formulate the relation between reader, text, and world assumed here will guard against misunderstanding what I have been saying as the return to a traditional polarity between seeing literature as realistic representation, on the one hand, and seeing it, on the other, as the creation of a self-contained subjective realm. The view of literary language I am presupposing would not see a work of literature as able ever to be self-contained, self-sustaining, hermetically sealed in its self-referential purity. A work of literature is rather a link in a chain of transformations and substitutions. To identify its ambiguous relation to the links in either direction is one way to articulate the incessant displacement of figurative by literal and of literal by figurative which takes place within a text in its transactions with the social world and with its readers. In one direction there is the social world which the *Sketches* "describe." This world is not a collection of hard facts. It is itself interpretation, based on other texts, of the matter of which London is made. In the other direction is the critic. His reading of the text, the connections he makes between one part of it and another, the pattern he establishes as his commentary on the whole, is interpretation in its turn. He asserts similarities and configurations which are not asserted as such in the text itself. He creates a pattern of meaning nowhere explicitly articulated. The fiction of the *Sketches* inserts itself as a text among other fictional texts, those within which the characters of the *Sketches* are shown to live. The critic's interpretation is fiction too. The *Sketches* are not a mirror of reality, but interpretation of interpretation, and the critic's discourse about the *Sketches* may be defined as interpretation of interpretation of interpretation. This chain of substitutions and transformations creates illusion out of illusion and the appearance of reality out of illusion, in a play of language without beginning, end, or extra-linguistic foundation.

A glimpse of this reciprocity is provided by the story of the young Dickens' visit in his capacity as journalist to review a new farce at the Adelphi Theater. The new play, he found, was a blatant plagiarism from one of his Sketches already published, "The Bloomsbury Christening." If his *Sketches* owed much to the theatrical part of the already existent culture, they entered themselves into that culture as one of its aspects. Dickens' interpretation of Victorian England is part of English history.

Now it is possible to see what is misleading in the formulation of Roman Jakobson which gave my interpretative journey its initial impetus. The distinction between romantic or symbolist poetry, based on metaphor, in which the set of language is toward itself, and "realistic" texts, based on metonymy, in which the set of language tends to be "primarily upon referent,"[30] cannot be made a diametrical opposition. Any literary text is both self-referential and extra-referential, or rather it is open to being not seen as the former and mistakenly taken as the latter. All language is figurative, displaced. All language is beside itself. There is no "true" sign for the thing. Even proper names, as linguists and ethnologists have come to see, are figurative.[31] The true word, the hidden Logos, always slips away, is always a matter of somewhere else or of some other time. Both metonymy and metaphor are versions of the same "fundamental of language," the fiction of identity. The lie which says A equals B (metaphor) is no more "poetic" than the lie which says A leads to B (metonymy). Both are naming one thing with the name of another, in a constant stepping aside which constitutes the life of language. Both metaphor and metonymy are open to a correct interpretation in which the figurative is seen as figurative. Both invite the misinterpretation which takes as substantial what are in fact only linguistic fictions. All poetry, however strongly based on metaphor, is liable to be read literally, and all realistic narrative, however metonymic in texture, is open to a correct figurative reading which sees it as fiction rather than *mimesis*. One might in fact argue that metonymic displacement, in its movement from presence to absence, is even more fundamental than metaphorical transference or superimposition. Metaphor could as easily be described as a special case of metonymy as metonymy a special case of metaphor. In any case, it is misleading to suggest that they are polar opposites, either as synchronic rhetorical fact giving rise to two distinct forms of literature or as the basis of literary history, for example the development from romanticism to realism to symbolism. All these historically located forms of literature are versions of the fundamental structure of a figurative language open to misreading as literal. All are open to similar procedures of correct interpretation.

In support of this view of language could be cited Nietzsche, Heidegger, Wittgenstein, Freud, or Jacques Lacan. Nietzsche in *The Will to Power* sees all cultural forms – art, science, metaphysics, religion – as "fictions," "lies," "interpretations." All are based on the mistake of "making similar, equal" what is "always something new"; "Form, species, law, idea, purpose – in all these cases the same error is made of giving false reality to a fiction, as if events were in some way obedient to something." "No, facts is precisely what there is not," says Nietzsche, "only interpretations." "We can comprehend only a world that we ourselves have made," and "*we cease to think when we refuse to do so under the constraint of language*," for "*rational thought is interpretation according to a scheme that we cannot throw off.*"[32] Heidegger in *Sein und Zeit* argues that naming something always means naming it *as* something. To do this assimilates the thing into the network of names and functions which incorporates it into the already existing human world. At the same time, this naming hides the thing by making it available only "as" something other than it is. Even the most authentic poetry is simultaneously revelation and covering up, disclosure and veiling.[33] In paragraphs 50 through 56 of *The Brown Book*, Wittgenstein assimilates the "narration of past events," that is, precisely the form of language which is the basis of realistic fiction, into the category of "language games." The telling of a story about the past becomes one more case in point in Wittgenstein's subtle demonstration of the impossibility of measuring the validity of any form of language by its one-to-one correspondence to some external structure of objects or events.[34] Freud identifies the two forms of dreamwork, condensation and displacement, in ways that Jacques Lacan, in his interpretation of Freud in the light of modern linguistics, can recognize as corresponding closely to metaphor and metonymy. Both figures are modes of that activity of naming which is always shifted aside and can never rest in a happy correspondence of name and thing.[35] This collective recognition of man's inescapable dependence on linguistic fictions constitutes a primary theme in recent developments in the arts of interpretation. Metaphor and metonymy are labels which may be given to two important categories of such fictions, but they are brothers rather than opposites, as Goethe recognized in a striking phrase cited by Jakobson: *Alles Vergängliche ist nur ein Gleichnis*. This Jakobson interprets as meaning that "anything sequent is a simile," so that "In poetry where similarity is superinduced upon contiguity, any metonymy is slightly metaphorical and any metaphor has a metonymical tint."[36] Jakobson here comes close to formulating the covert identity of metonymy and metaphor as two versions of the necessary displacement involved in language. This displacement is the basis of the interplay between literal and figurative understandings of language which is the foundation of literature.

So far in this essay I have concentrated on the language of the *Sketches by Boz* and on the way analysis of that language may help bring into the open what I have called "the fiction of realism." What role in the meaning of the *Sketches* and of *Oliver Twist* is played by the admirable illustrations for them by George Cruikshank? To ask this raises the complex aesthetic question of the meaning of the fact that novels have traditionally been illustrated, sometimes by crude woodcuts, sometimes by etchings or engravings, sometimes by sumptuous colored plates, sometimes, in more recent years, as in the case of James, Meredith, or Hardy, by photographs. What is the relation between text and illustration in a work of fiction? Both Flaubert and Mallarmé, for example, were hostile to the convention of illustrating works of literature. *Je suis pour – aucune illustration*, said Mallarmé in 1898, *tout ce qu'évoque un livre devant se passer dans l'esprit du lecteur* (I am for – no illustration, all that a book evokes needing to happen within the spirit of the reader).[37] Nevertheless, many novels (as well as other works) have been illustrated by distinguished artists, and the illustrations must be accepted as in some sense part of the texts they illustrate. Does the existence of illustrated books mean that there is something language cannot do or can only do imperfectly, so that in the picture we can see more exactly what a character or scene "really looked like"? To say this is to assume implicitly not that the illustration represents in pictorial terms something described in verbal terms in the text but that both text and illustration stand side by side as imitations in different media of a third entity, some "reality," whether ideal, psychological, or material, which exists independently outside both and needs neither words nor pictures to continue in existence. Certainly the first effect of illustrations in a work of fiction is to reinforce those mimetic assumptions which are, as I have shown, so problematical. To encounter, in a picture, people or scenes one has already encountered in the text is to be invited to assent to their authenticity and to say, "Ah, that's how he really looked at that moment, then!" The illustrations may take precedence over the text as affirmations of the presence and appearance of the characters. I have called attention to the fact that Dickens in the *Sketches by Boz* refers more to the illustrations of eighteenth-century novels than to their words, so that Sir Charles Grandison apparently existed for him as the pictures rather than as Richardson's text. Dickens was the victim of the same kind of response. For many readers Fagin, Sikes, Nancy, Oliver, Mr Brownlow, and Rose Maylie live even more in Cruikshank's etchings than in Dickens' words.

The most celebrated reader for whom this was so was, of course, Henry James. *Oliver Twist*, says James in *A Small Boy and Others*,

> perhaps even seemed to me more Cruikshank's than Dickens's; it was a thing of such vividly terrible images, and all marked with that peculiarity of Cruikshank that the offered flowers of goodnesses, the scenes and figures intended to comfort and cheer, present themselves under his hand as but more subtly sinister, or more suggestively queer, than the frank badnesses and horrors. The nice people and the happy moments, in the plates, frightened me almost as much as the low and the awkward.[38]

If the response to Dickens' language of a reader as sensitive to the power of words as James could be so overwhelmed and effaced by his response to the great Cruikshank illustrations, then the critic must be willing to consider those illustrations as perhaps an integral part of their texts.

To do this, however, creates a host of problems. What happens, for example, to the integrity of the literary text, its organic wholeness as an integument of words establishing its own meaning and the rules by which it is to be read? To allow a non-verbal element full rights within this structure of meaning is no longer to be able to maintain a now traditional view of the self-enclosed unity of the literary work. Moreover, if the illustrations are as much a part of the text as any of its verbal elements, which has priority over the other in the case of a discrepancy? Which is the "origin" of the other? Which illustrates which? There is more than paranoia, pathological lying, or professional jealousy in the claims the aged George Cruikshank made to have originated both the *Sketches* and *Oliver Twist.* As Jane R. Cohen shows in the most recent detailed study of the relation between the two,[39] there is little evidence to support Cruikshank's claim that he first drew pictures for which Dickens supplied the text, even though it is clear that Cruikshank made many suggestions to Dickens during the writing of *Oliver Twist.* Nevertheless, one might argue that within the atemporal realm of the finished works Cruikshank's drawings seem prior, originating. They appear to be the radiant source beside which Dickens' words are secondary, from which they appear to have derived. It will be remembered that *Pickwick Papers* was at first planned as pictures by a well-known artist, Robert Seymour, to be "illustrated" by Dickens' letter-press. I have shown that there are frequent references in the *Sketches* to the graphic arts or to pictorial effects. As their title after all suggests, the *Sketches* are often self-consciously visual. They strive for effects which have already been achieved in the other medium, or they are written so that they might be illustrated. The degree to which this is so is indicated by the correspondence between Dickens and Cruikshank.[40] It is true that Dickens kept the upper hand with his "illustrious" illustrator, rejected plates of which he disapproved, and often specified in detail what should be illustrated. At the same time, it is also evident that he wrote *Oliver Twist* in order that it might be illustrated by Cruikshank. He kept in mind as he wrote the necessity of having something suitable for illustration in each number, and, of course, he knew Cruikshank's earlier work just as he knew that of Hogarth. Cruikshank's work was part of that tradition of graphic illustration which is so important an ingredient in establishing the conventions of the *Sketches* and *Oliver Twist.*

The relation between text and illustration is clearly reciprocal. Each refers to the other. Each illustrates the other, in a continual back and forth movement which is incarnated in the experience of the reader as his eyes move from words to picture and back again, juxtaposing the two in a mutual establishment of meaning. Illustrations in a work of fiction displace the sign-referent relationship assumed in a mimetic reading and replace it by a complex and problematic reference between two radically different kinds of sign, the linguistic and the graphic. Illustrations establish a relation between elements within the work which short-circuits the apparent reference of the literary text to some real world outside. This is true even if the illustrations are photographs of the "original" scenes in the novel, as in the case of photographs in the Wessex and Anniversary editions of Thomas Hardy's novels. Such an

Plate I: Steam Excursion (I)

By permission of the Houghton Library, Harvard University

intrinsic relation between text and picture sets up an oscillation or shimmering of meaning in which neither element can be said to be prior. The pictures are about the text; the text is about the pictures, in another form of metaphoric superimposition or metonymic juxtaposition which may move in a spectrum all the way from the formal painting which is verbalized only with a descriptive title, through those intermediate cases, poised between *pictura* and *poesis*, like the paintings of Klee, which have their witty or inscrutable poetic titles as intrinsic parts of themselves, or the cartoons in *Punch*, which are meaningless without the lines of the dialogue pendant beneath. At the other extreme, a long novel may be "illustrated" only with a bare sketch for a frontispiece, as in the case of the Cheap Edition of Dickens' novels.

The *Sketches by Boz* and *Oliver Twist* are obviously nearer the equal balance between picture and text. A further understanding of the significance of Cruikshank's illustrations for these may come by investigating them as significances in themselves. Of what may they be said to be the signs, or the indications, or the images? There are four incompatible entities or regions to which Cruikshank's illustrations refer. Since my investigations so far have focused chiefly on the *Sketches by Boz*, I shall center my discussion on the forty splendid etchings Cruikshank produced for that text.

Just as critics from the publication of the first collected volumes of the *Sketches* until today have emphasized the representational accuracy of Dickens' description of London, so the Cruikshank illustrations are often valued for the authenticity of their mirroring of London in the thirties. It seems that Seven Dials did in fact look as it does in Cruikshank's etching. The apparatus for providing a street breakfast shown in the admirable illustration for "The Streets – Morning" has archaeological accuracy. The claustrophobic middle-class interiors, with somber carpets, heavy furniture, and dark curtains, with statues of Cupid under glass on little shelves on the wall, as in "Mr. Watkins Tottle and Miss Lillerton," show the way bourgeois drawing rooms did look at this time. The costumes of the ladies and gentlemen in "Steam Excursion (I)" (Plate I)[41] may be trusted as accurate copies of the fashions of the day. The fireplace and its equipment in an old-fashioned pub did look as Cruikshank shows them in "Scotland Yard." Portraits of Dickens himself are included in several of the illustrations (the Frontispiece, "Early Coaches," "Making a Night of It," "Public Dinners" [which also contains a picture of Cruikshank], and "A Pickpocket in Custody"). This reinforces the journalistic aspect of the illustrations. Cruikshank shows Boz, that is, a man recognizably Dickens himself, engaged in the activities described in the first person by the narrator of the *Sketches*.

Taken all together the forty illustrations for the *Sketches* constitute in another medium the same kind of authoritative representation of middle-class and lower-middle-class life in London in the eighteen-thirties as do Dickens' *Sketches* themselves. Ms Cohen asserts the validity of this aspect of Cruikshank's art:

> The artist's illustrations [for the *Sketches*] were also characteristic of [Cruikshank's] work in their accuracy. . . . Cruikshank, as Sacheverell Sitwell has observed, was among the first English artists "to attempt historical accuracy in their reconstruction of the past." He was so painstaking with certain fine points of his accessories that historians still find his plates authoritative. "The Last Cabdriver," for example, depicts an obsolete form of the cabriolet with the driver seated over the right wheel, while "The Parish Engine" commemorates the kind of fire-extinguisher then in use. His costumes were also meticulously accurate.[42]

If Cruikshank, like Dickens, was a man fascinated by the haunts and neighborhoods of London, if he was a man who, like Dickens, often stayed out all night walking the streets and visiting taverns, and if his illustrations for the *Sketches*, like the *Sketches* themselves, were based on first-hand experience, nevertheless it must be said that this representation of London was mediated rather than direct. It was mediated by the words of Dickens' texts. In the case of the *Sketches* the texts unequivocally precede their illustration, since almost all of them had been published in various periodicals before John Macrone, the publisher, suggested that they might be collected in a book and illustrated by Cruikshank. Thirteen of the illustrations were not completed until the publication in 1837–9 of the edition in twenty monthly parts by Chapman and Hall. Moreover, in spite of the trivial discrepancies noted by F. G. Kitton and Ms Cohen,[43] Cruikshank, for the most part, scrupulously follows Dickens' text. There is precedent in the words for everything, or almost everything, that appears in the pictures: gesture, furniture, clothes, décor. Here the verbal text has clear priority over its illustration in another medium. Cruikshank, it appears, created his etchings not by going directly to the London he knew so well, but by representing that London as it was already represented in Dickens' language. His images refer to that language rather than directly to the scenes and objects the language imitates.

Cruikshank's illustrations indicate, however, still another region, one perhaps more difficult to identify, but unmistakably present. I mean Cruikshank's unique sensibility or angle of vision on the world, what Charles Baudelaire, in his brief remarks on Cruikshank, calls *ce je ne sais quoi qui distingue toujours un artiste d'un autre, quelque intime que soit en apparence leur parenté* (this I know not what that always distinguishes one artist from another, however apparently intimate may be their relationship).[44] This *fugitive et impalpable* sentiment distinguishes Cruikshank from all other artists before and after him in his tradition. It may be partly a matter of habitual ways of composing a picture or of placing the figures against a background, and I shall try to identify these below. Or it may be a matter of the unifying mood which is communicated by the illustrations, that elusive quality which makes it possible to distinguish a Cruikshank from a Gillray or a "Phiz." It was this pervasive quality, peculiar to Cruikshank's pictures, which Henry James was describing in the passage quoted above. The same effect of frightening meanness and enclosure is described in another well-known passage, this one by G. K. Chesterton. The illustrations for *Oliver Twist* seemed to Chesterton "dark and detestable," the drawing "mean" and "morbid." "In the doubled-up figure and frightful eyes of Fagin in the condemned cell," said Chesterton, "there is not only a baseness of subject, but there is a kind of baseness in the very technique of it. It is not drawn with the free lines of a free man; it has the half-witted secrecies of a hunted thief. It does not look merely like a picture of Fagin; it looks like a picture by Fagin."[45] Here is one way to talk about the self-expressive aspect of Cruikshank's art. It imitates not the real London and not the imaginary world created by Dickens' words, but the special quality of Cruikshank's mind or vision of things. Chesterton, it happens, was intuitively right, for according to a well-known anecdote, Cruikshank is supposed to have told Henry Mayhew that Fagin was copied from a mirrored image of himself crouching in bed, with his hand to his mouth, meditating despairingly on the difficulty of drawing Fagin in the condemned cell. In his later years Cruikshank came increasingly to identify himself with Fagin and to like to play the role of his most famous illustration. In the same way, the preliminary sketches for his illustrations are often marginally decorated with miniature self-portraits. The narcissistic image of Cruikshank drawing his own mirrored face seems an appropriate emblem for the way his art is not copied from the external world or from the literary texts it is supposed to illustrate but is projected outward from his inner world.

To these three incompatible referents must be added a fourth. In spite of the undeniable existence of special qualities, both technical and more intangible, distinguishing Cruikshank's art from all other art, even so, Cruikshank's work is in many ways related to an elaborate tradition and may be fully understood only in terms of its references to the conventions of that tradition. The tradition in this case is that of caricature, whether political or comic, drawing, etching, or woodcut. Cruikshank's place in this tradition means that his work must be read in terms of its relationship to the work of his father, Isaac Cruikshank, to the work of

Seymour, Gillray, Rowlandson, and, of course, Hogarth, as well as to younger artists like Hablot K. Browne. E. H. Gombrich has shown how any tradition of graphic representation involves complex conventions whereby three-dimensional objects are signified by marks on a flat surface. These conventions are in no sense realistic but come to be taken for granted as adequate mirrorings of reality by artists and viewers of art who dwell within the conventions.[46] The system of conventions on which Cruikshank's art depends is only now beginning to be studied in detail. There is new work on Hogarth, Gillray, Rowlandson, and others, as well as on Cruikshank himself.[47] Much remains to be done along these lines, but one may expect that just as Richard A. Vogler can argue that all the figures in Cruikshank's illustrations for *Oliver Twist* (Fagin, Sikes, Nancy, Bumble, and the rest) are based on prototypes appearing in Cruikshank's earlier work,[48] so scarcely an aspect of a given picture by Cruikshank, figure, pose, background, composition, but will turn out to have antecedents within the tradition to which he belongs. Ms Cohen, for example, has observed a number of parallels between the illustrations for *Oliver Twist* and certain works by Hogarth.[49] Even Cruikshank's Fagin, in the etching showing Fagin welcoming Oliver back after he is recaptured ("Oliver's reception by Fagin and the boys"), matches almost exactly Hogarth's Jewish pedlar in the second plate of the "Election" series. Hogarth's Jew is in turn based on a specific tradition of representing Ashkenazic faces in this way.[50] Far from being a self-portrait, Cruikshank's Fagin is one of a long line of similar figures by various artists, each one referring back to earlier similar ones, and no one identifiable as the "archetype." Just as Dickens' *Sketches* contain many references to graphic, theatrical, and literary traditions, and just as they cannot be understood unless they are seen as repetitions with a difference of elements in those traditions, so Cruikshank's illustrations are based on complex conventions which include not only modes of graphic representation, but also the stereotyped poses of melodrama and pantomime, so clearly alluded to, for example, in the lively illustration for "The Tuggses at Ramsgate." Rather than imitating some extra-artistic realm, Cruikshank's pictures draw their meaning from their relation to other works of art to which they implicitly refer and on which they depend for the creation of their own significance.

To investigate a given illustration by Cruikshank on the assumption that it is a "sign" pointing to some reality outside itself is to discover that each illustration is the meeting point of a set of incompatible references – the "real" London, Dickens' text, Cruikshank's "sensibility," and the tradition of caricature. It is difficult to see how a single work could refer to all these realms at once, especially since each context makes claims not on a part of a picture but on its totality as a single complex emblem. Under the pressure of these mutually annihilating references the picture dissolves, explodes, and vanishes. It cannot mean, so it would seem, all these things at once. The multiple lines of reference tend to cancel one another out, and the beholder is left face to face with the bare ink marks on the page, marks which, it may be, constitute their own intrinsic meaning. They may establish such a self-sufficient meaning within the ruins left by the discovery of over-determination involved in any attempt at a complete "mimetic" reading. What may be said of the etchings when they are seen as if they had been cut free from their connections to the various entities outside themselves to which they seem so clearly to refer? Such intrinsic interpretation, it should be noted, does not mean reading each illustration separately. It means rather setting a group of plates, in this case the illustrations for the *Sketches by Boz*, side by side. The investigation moves back and forth from one plate to another in an attempt to identify the motifs and structuring forms which recur from one picture to another.

Almost all the illustrations for the *Sketches by Boz* have strongly centered, centripetal, circular compositions. They spiral inward toward a point. In this they may be opposed, for example, to Gillray's characteristic composition. Gillray's pictures are explosive, centrifugal, with objects or figures which seem about to fall off the edge of the page. In Cruikshank's case there is almost always something at the middle on which everything is focused and around which everything turns. Sometimes this is a vertical line, sometimes a spot. An example is "Horatio Sparkins," which is strongly centered on the hat of the lady in the middle whose back is to the viewer, or "Mr. Minns and His Cousin," which is organized around the urn in the middle of the table, or "The Boarding-House (II)," which is centered on the candle flame and on the point on the face of the organ from which lines in the woodwork radiate outward like rays from a sun, or "The Dancing Academy," in which all attention is drawn to the little boy dancing alone in the middle, or "Mr. John Dounce at the Oyster-Shop," in which the portly figure of John Dounce himself constitutes the central line. This kind of composition occurs so universally in these illustrations that it may be called one of their fundamental laws. It is varied only in those pictures which may have two circular forms, one a little behind the other and echoing it, as in "Theodosius Introduced to the New Pupil," or several compositional lines may move around the same center in the form of concentric circles.

Such a concentration of all energy on a central point is responsible in part for that sense of enclosure, even of suffocation, which critics have felt in looking at Cruikshank's plates. It seems as if everything were moving toward that point or were drawn toward it. This centripetal

Plate II: The Gin Shop

By permission of the Houghton Library, Harvard University

effect is reinforced by the fact that Cruikshank's plates are not only usually dark but are also overshadowed by ponderous architectural hangings – arches, pediments, or ceilings – or by somber, heavy curtains. Such weights impending from above occur again and again in the illustrations, sometimes in the form of external architectural elements, as in "The Election for Beadle," or in "Vauxhall Gardens by Day," or in the heavy overhanging outdoor lamps in "Seven Dials"[51] and "A Pickpocket in Custody," sometimes in the form of interior furnishings, perhaps most strikingly in the enormous barrels of gin which overshadow the patrons in "The Gin Shop" (Plate II). In some cases the effect of ominous overshadowing is achieved by the emphasis on heavy ceiling beams, as in "Private Theatres," or, more simply, on the corner of the ceiling in an interior scene, as in "The Tuggses at Ramsgate" or "Mr. Watkins Tottle and Miss Lillerton." In other plates, for example in "Under Restraint" or "The Boarding-House (I)," the sense of enclosure in interior scenes is emphasized by doors which are firmly closed. The doors and windows are almost always shut in these pictures. The curtains are always drawn. It seems that it might be impossible to escape or even to see beyond the confined place in which the inhabitants are trapped. Whatever the combination of these elements, each illustration contains some mixture of them. Their joint effect is to create a world in which even the outdoor scenes are enclosed, confined, hemmed in, and in which the human figures seem dwarfed and threatened by enormous masses of overhanging cloth or masonry poised above to close them in and imprison them tightly. The terrifying claustrophobia of "Fagin in the condemned Cell" is also characteristic to a lesser degree of the illustrations for *Sketches by Boz*.

Surrounded and belittled by these heavy pressures, driven in toward some focus of attention at the center, Cruikshank's oppressed human figures perform their little dramas. Charles Baudelaire has identified with great insight the form these dramas take. "Le mérite spécial de George Cruikshank," says Baudelaire ". . . est une abondance inépuisable dans le grotesque. . . . Le grotesque coule incessamment et inévitablement de la pointe de Cruikshank, comme les rimes riches de la plume des poëtes naturels. Le grotesque est son habitude" (The special merit of George Cruikshank . . . is an inexhaustible abundance in the grotesque. . . . The grotesque flows incessantly and inevitably from Cruikshank's etching-needle, like perfect rhymes from the pen of natural poets. The grotesque is his natural habit).[52] What characterizes Cruikshank's particular form of the grotesque? "Ce qui constitue surtout le grotesque de Cruikshank, c'est la violence extravagante du geste et du mouvement, et l'explosion dans l'expression. Tous ses petits personnages miment avec fureur et turbulence comme des acteurs de pantomime" (What above all constitutes

Plate III: Steam Excursion (II)

By permission of the Houghton Library, Harvard University

Cruikshank's grotesque is the extravagant violence of gesture and movement, and the explosion in the expression. All his little creatures mime with frenzy and turbulence like pantomime actors).[53] Baudelaire's analysis here is admirably exact. A grotesque comedy constituted by pantomimic violence of gesture, expression, and movement on the part of tiny figures each of whom "se culbute, s'agite et se mêle avec une pétulance indicible" (tumbles, rushes around, and mixes in with an indescribable petulance) in his "monde minuscule" (minuscule world)[54] – these are the essential characteristics of the actions performed in Cruikshank's pictures.

Each illustration takes a fleeting moment in the continuous action described in Dickens' text and concentrates on it to the exclusion of all else. The characters are represented in a moment of surprise in which they are so caught up in what is going on before their eyes that they forget past and future. They give themselves wholly to the excitement of the moment. Their responses to this moment are expressed in the gestures of open-mouthed, wide-eyed amazement which recur so often, as in "The Boarding-House (II)," "The Tuggses at Ramsgate," "Mr. Minns and His Cousin," and in many others, for example, in that queasy representation of universal seasickness, "Steam Excursion (II)," in which the decorum and elegance of "Steam Excursion (I)" has given way to swirling disorder (Plate III). Such absorption in the present moment is also imaged in the fact that the characters are often caught frozen in unstable gestures or in poses which could be held for only a fleeting second as a transition from one posture to another. Mr Minns, in "Mr. Minns and His Cousin," is halfway up from his chair. The outraged husband, in "The Tuggses at Ramsgate," balances on one leg with the other foot raised high in the air. Samuel Wilkins, in even so relatively calm an illustration as "Samuel Wilkins and the Evanses," is poised with his weight resting in unstable equilibrium on one elegantly shod toe. In each such picture Cruikshank catches a moment in which people are driven by the violence of their reactions to adopt without hindsight or foresight a gesture or pose that could last only an instant and then would pass, never to return. Everything is in lively motion, a motion which necessarily prefigures its own end. Sometimes this evanescence may be imaged in a gesture of eating or drinking, as in "Mr. John Dounce at the Oyster-Shop," "The Gin Shop," or "The Streets – Morning," or in the splendid illustration for "The Poor Clerk." The characters are stopped with the food or drink halfway to their mouths. Sometimes the fleeting instant may be given an emblem in the clouds of smoke, white places in the picture, areas on the etching plate not touched by the acid, as in "A Harmonic Meeting," in "London Recreations – The 'Tea-Gardens,' " or in "Greenwich Fair." The smoke will hold one shape for an instant only, an instant captured forever in the representation of it.

Plate IV: The First of May

By permission of the Houghton Library, Harvard University

If the pictures seem to dissolve under the pressure of the various incompatible realities they are meant to represent, or if Cruikshank's little people seem in danger of being overwhelmed by the weight of their surroundings, this vanishing away is pictured in the gestures and actions of the people themselves. The theme of Cruikshank's illustrations could without exaggeration be said to be time, or, better, the present instant in its fugacity. So great is the effect of various centripetal forces on the frail and over-sensitive figures at the center that freedom, it seems, could only be obtained by vanishing altogether – disappearing into a cloud of smoke, a burst of laughter, an exclamation of surprise. This vanishing seems about to occur. One is tempted to follow a given illustration not from preliminary sketch to finished etching, but backward, from complete etching, perhaps in the brightly watercolored form in which Cruikshank sometimes prepared them, back to the black and white etching, behind that to the careful tracing for transfer to the etching plate, back behind that to the finished pencil drawing, and behind that again, finally, to the initial sketch, mere ephemeral indications of the pencil on the paper, tentative, hesitant, experimental, an illustration more in possibility than in actuality, as in the preliminary drawing below the more finished sketch for "The First of May" (Plate IV). These preliminary drawings, it may be, are the most direct expressions of Cruikshank's genius at catching the elusive moment in its actuality. In their evanescence they are closest to the instant where presence becomes absence.

This aspect of Cruikshank's illustrations for the *Sketches* is countered by another motif which also occurs repeatedly. If the characters at the center are caught up in a moment so surprising, so violent, so all-absorbing that they live only in the vanishing present, such figures are overlooked by another sort of personage, a spectator who belongs to time and memory. This witness possesses a cool detachment, a power to see the moment in the perspective of what comes before and after. Such a figure corresponds to the viewer of the illustration. We see each plate in the light of the other illustrations, in the light of the tradition of caricature to which it belongs, and in the light of the diachronic text it illustrates. The spectator of "The Streets – Morning" or of "The Tuggses at Ramsgate" sees what is present there in the perspective of the series of events narrated in Dickens' description of the gradual awakening to life of London in the early morning or in relation to his story of the confidence trick played on the innocent Tuggses. This spectator also corresponds to the narrator of the *Sketches*, to Boz as the "amateur vagrant" wandering the streets and watching everything with a sharp eye. Such a figure appears in a number of illustrations, sometimes

Plate V: Theodosius Introduced to the New Pupil (Sentiment)

By permission of the Houghton Library, Harvard University

in the form of an actual portrait of Dickens as Boz, the "speculative pedestrian," as in "Making a Night of It" and "A Pickpocket in Custody." Sometimes this detached spectator is represented by someone on the sidelines who happens to be passing by and who is not caught up in the violent action which takes up the center of the picture. Examples are the figures on the edge of the scene watching the street fight in "Seven Dials."

The most important and pervasive versions of this motif are the portraits which hang on the walls of so many of Cruikshank's interiors. Variants of this are the busts or statues in a number of the interiors. There are portraits on the walls in "The Broker's Man," in "The Pawnbroker's Shop," in "Samuel Wilkins and the Evanses," in "The Boarding-House (II)," in "Mr. Minns and His Cousin," in "Theodosius Introduced to the New Pupil" (Plate V), in "The Tuggses at Ramsgate," in "Under Restraint," in "Mr. Watkins Tottle and Miss Lillerton," and in "The Bloomsbury Christening." No doubt, Victorian bourgeois households did in fact have portraits on their walls. This motif is part of the "realistic" texture of Cruikshank's recording of the London of his time. The function of these portraits, however, is more than mimetic. They are not allegorical or allusive. The allegorical use of pictures or other details appears more often in illustrations by Phiz, as Michael Steig has shown.[55] In Cruikshank's work such details appear occasionally, as in the picture of the Good Samaritan on the wall of Mr Brownlow's house in "Oliver recovering from the fever."[56] Such allegorical details never appear at all in the forty illustrations for the *Sketches by Boz*, except perhaps in attenuated form in the statue of Cupid under a glass bell in "Mr. Watkins Tottle and Miss Lillerton." (The pose of the statue echoes that of the coy Miss Lillerton.) The portraits on the walls in these plates are merely portraits. They do not allude to any iconographical tradition. They have no identifiable meaning as signs of something other than themselves. They are painted faces hung on the walls – impassive, serene, detached, dead. They are explicitly drawn in such a way that they appear to be paying no attention to the violent actions being performed by the "live" people in the center of the picture. Their expressions and gestures are exactly the opposite of the grotesque violence of the live figures. This contrast is emphasized by the striking similarity between the faces on the walls and the faces of the living actors. The two drawings on the wall in "Theodosius Introduced to the New Pupil" match exactly the faces of Theodosius and Miss Brook Dingwall, though one pair of faces is distorted with surprise and emotion, the other in static repose. The little bust on the mantelpiece in "Samuel Wilkins and the Evanses" echoes exactly the face of Samuel Wilkins himself, but one face is animated, the other has a marble fixity. Part of the comedy in the illustration for "The Bloomsbury Christening" lies in the fact that there is a portrait on the wall either of the cross-eyed father, Mr Kitterbell, or perhaps of *his* father. If the latter is the case, then there are, including the baby, three generations of cross-eyed Kitterbells in the illustration. Mr Dumps' mock horror as he exclaims, "Good God, how small he is! . . . *remarkably* small indeed" (*SB*, 475), is given a further twist by Cruikshank's illustration. In the plate, Dumps' horror appears to be his discovery that still another cross-eyed male has been added to the long line of Kitterbells. In "The Pawnbroker's Shop" Cruikshank has picked up Dickens' point by making the faces of the three women (the old prostitute, the young one in her finery, and the respectable girl who may be driven to the streets) all resemble one another closely. He has added, however, in the portrait on the wall in the background, a fourth woman who looks like the other three. This face is a figure from the past who has perhaps lived through the whole sequence represented in the living women and now has achieved the peace of death. All the portraits in this group of illustrations appear to be of ancestors, calm faces from the past looking down on the ephemeral violence of the present moment. "As we were once you are now," they seem to be saying, "and you too will someday be what we are now, only portraits on the wall."

The structure of the Cruikshank etchings for the *Sketches* is a double one. If the action at the center represents immediacy, life, self-forgetful engagement in the present moment, the portraits, like the spectator figures in other plates, represent time as duration, time as memory and anticipation, human temporality as detached self-possession. This double structure is exactly that ascribed by Baudelaire to the "absolute comic." For Baudelaire "le comique absolu" is comedy based on the grotesque, and in the passage cited earlier he describes Cruikshank as "un artiste doué de riches facultés comiques" (an artist endowed with rich comic faculties).[57] The comedy of Cruikshank's plates, however, lies not in the grotesque violence of gesture and expression of his "prestigieuses petites créatures" (enchanting little creatures) (751), but in the co-presence of that violence and the spectator of it. "Le comique, la puissance du rire," says Baudelaire in "De l'essence du rire," "est dans le rieur et nullement dans l'objet du rire" (The comic, the power of laughter, is in the laughter and not at all in the object of laughter) (717).[58] This means that "pour qu'il y ait comique, c'est-à-dire émanation, explosion, dégagement de comique, il faut qu'il ait deux êtres en présence" (in order for there to be the comic, that is to say emanation, explosion, release of the comic, there must be two beings in one another's presence) (727). An example of this is the absolute comic in Hoffmann's stories, *Daucus Carota, the King of the Carrots*, or in *The Princess Brambilla*. "Il est bien vrai qu'il le sait," says Baudelaire of Hoffmann, "mais il sait aussi que l'essence de ce comique est de paraître s'ignorer lui-même et de développer chez le spectateur, ou plutôt chez le lecteur, la joie de sa propre supériorité et la joie de la supériorité de l'homme sur la nature. Les artistes créent le comique; ayant étudié et rassemblé les éléments du comique, ils savent que tel être est comique, et qu'il ne l'est qu'à la condition d'ignorer sa nature" (It is perfectly true that he knows what he is doing, but he knows also that the essence of this type of the comic is to appear to be unaware of itself and to produce in the spectator, or rather in the reader, joy in his own superiority and joy in the superiority of man over nature. Artists create the comic, they know that a given being is comic, and that he is only so on condition of not knowing his nature) (728).

Baudelaire reserves his highest admiration for a comic structure which corresponds closely to the one I have identified in Cruikshank's illustrations. The perfection of the absolute comic is the combination in a single consciousness or structure of both the laugher and the object of his laughter. The personage so caught up in the moment that he has ceased to be fully human and has become the victim of a fall into nature is integrated into a single system of awareness with the laughing witness of this fall. "Ce ne'st point l'homme qui tombe qui rit de sa propre chute," says Baudelaire, "à moins qu'il ne soit un philosophe, un homme qui ait acquis, par habitude, la force de se dédoubler rapidement et d'assister comme spectateur désintéressé aux phénomènes de son *moi*. Mais le cas est rare" (It is not at all the man who falls who laughs at his own tumble, unless he happens to be a philosopher, a man who has acquired, by habit, the power to double himself rapidly and to be present as a disinterested spectator at the phenomena of his *ego*. But the case is rare) (717). To the rare self-doubling of the philosopher must be added the similar self-division of the great comic artists, "les hommes qui ont fait métier de développer en eux le sentiment du comique et de le tirer d'eux-mêmes pour le divertissement de leurs semblables" (the men who have made a business of developing in themselves the feeling for the comic and of drawing it from themselves for the amusement of their fellows) (727–8). The development of this feeling for the comic depends, argues Baudelaire, on a single all-important factor in man, "l'existence d'une dualité permanente, la puissance d'être à la fois soi et un autre" (the existence of a permanent duality, the power to be at once oneself and another) (728). Every great artist is only an artist "à la condition d'être double et de n'ignorer aucun phénomène de sa double nature" (on condition of being double and not of being ignorant of a single phenomenon of his double nature) (728). Baudelaire has here described exactly, though without specific reference to Cruikshank, the comic pattern in Cruikshank's illustrations for the *Sketches by Boz*. Their comedy depends on the co-presence, within the picture, of the comic personages and the witness of their comic antics. Cruikshank's etchings are divided within themselves. They contain both the moment and duration, both unself-conscious violence of engagement in action and the disinterested spectator of that violence, both the comic being and the detached witness in whom laughter resides.

There is more to be said about this double structure. This more will expose the homology between the pattern of meaning in Cruikshank's plates and the pattern I identified above in the text of the *Sketches*. The internal structure of the illustrations is a temporal pattern combining duration and the instant in an ambiguous tension. Such a doubling also constitutes a tension between *mimesis* and fiction. The portraits on the wall are mimetic, copies of faces which once existed in the real world. They are also pictures within pictures. As in all such cases, the picture within a picture calls the spectator's attention to the problem of representation. The action at the center of the picture is not "real life." It is, like the portraits themselves, a picture of real life, a representation. It is something derived and secondary, fixed and dead. To the doubling constituted by the presence of a picture within the picture could be applied the formula from Walter Benjamin used at the beginning of this essay to describe the doubling within the text of the *Sketches*. The portraits on the wall underline the relation of the represented action to the action signified by the fact itself of representation.

The play between the portraits and the foreground scene initiates an oscillation in which the location of authenticity changes place bewilderingly. The pictures on the wall are dead representations. As such they put the action at the center in question by reminding the viewer that however vital and explosive it seems it is only *mimesis* too. It is a picture of a moment of life and not that life itself. The "living" figures are as motionless, as mute and dead, as the figures in the portraits. Both exist as marks on the pages, scratches on the etcher's plate. The representative aspect, as in all great art, tends to dissolve before the spectator's recognition of the primacy of the medium in its meaninglessness. As a sculpture is stone, a painting paint, so an etching is ink on paper, or perhaps, as in the case of the clouds of smoke in several of the plates for the *Sketches*, the represented object exists not even as ink, but as a blank place on the paper.

On the other hand, the portraits in the illustrations represent, paradoxically, life as it is copied in art. The paradox lies in the fact that the central action is apparently life itself, though actually art masquerading as life, therefore deceptive. The portraits in their obvious stiffness and immobility are more honest. They openly reveal the inauthenticity of all art, its irremediable distance from life, the fact that it is the copy of the thing, not the thing itself. But, to turn to the other side of the coin once more, if the portraits exemplify the counterfeit quality of mimetic art, the grotesque comic figures, in their ephemeral violence, if they are seen as free from any mimetic relationships, manifest the authenticity of true art. This authenticity exists as the withdrawal from nature, as the transformation of natural objects, the paper, the ink, into signs. Such signs are freed from their inherence in the causal web of nature and have created a realm of fiction. This realm belongs neither to natural duration nor to the natural instant. It is the place of that time out of time created within art by the reference of each fiction to the near nothingness of other fictions. Such fictional representation of the moment remains, while the moment passes.

Here another hint in the brief passage by Baudelaire on Cruikshank may be followed as a clue to the fictional nature of his illustrations, "Tous ses petits personnages miment avec fureur et turbulence," says Baudelaire, "comme des acteurs de pantomime" (All these little personages mime with frenzy and turbulence, like pantomime actors). The allusion to pantomime is correct. Cruikshank, like Dickens, much admired the popular theater. Just as allusions to pantomimic gestures and theatrical expressions are fundamental in the text of the *Sketches*, so the poses of Cruikshank's figures are often borrowed from melodrama or pantomime. An example is the admirable tableau of "The Tuggses at Ramsgate." The English pantomime tradition also plays a fundamental role in Baudelaire's definition of the absolute comic in "De l'essence du rire." Central in that essay is Baudelaire's description of a performance he witnessed in Paris in 1842 of an English pantomime which probably included in the cast the famous English clown Tom Matthews. Baudelaire's description of this emphasizes, as does his commentary on Cruikshank, the violence of the performance. The pantomime actors seemed to be seized suddenly by a great wind of extravagant madness which carried them into that dizzy realm of hyperbole, the absolute comic. "Il m'a semblé que le signe distinctif de ce genre de comique était la violence. . . . Le Pierrot anglais arrivait comme la tempête, tombait comme un ballot, et quand il riait, son rire faisait trembler la salle; ce rire ressemblait à un joyeux tonnerre. . . . Et toutes choses s'exprimaient ainsi dans cette singulière pièce, avec emportement; c'était le vertige de l'hyperbole" (It has seemed to me that the distinctive sign of this type of the comic was violence. . . . The English Pierrot entered like a tempest, fell down like a sack of coals, and when he laughed, his laughter made the auditorium shake; this laugh was like a joyful thunderclap. . . . And all things in this singular work were expressed in the same way, with violence; it was the dizzyness of hyperbole) (723–4). The essence of comedy is this hyperbolic vertigo, an extravagance of gesture which transfigures the actors, puts them beyond what Baudelaire calls "la frontière du merveilleux" (the frontier of the marvelous) (725) and makes them into purely conventional figures. They are then no longer people playing the role of someone else, but men and women "introduits de force dans une existence nouvelle" (introduced by force into a new existence) (725). This existence is that realm of pure fiction which belongs neither to the moment nor to duration and which is not mimetic, for it imitates nothing, and yet not autonomous either. The more free, spontaneous, extravagant, hyperbolic the gestures or expression of pantomimic actors or of the figures of Cruikshank's plates become, the more conventional, melodramatic, repetitive, fictive they are. They allude not to anything outside art, but to other fictive entities, as Cruikshank's illustrations for the *Sketches* echo one another in faces, figures, gestures, and compositions, and then repeat earlier Cruikshanks, and behind that earlier figures in the pantomimic and graphic tradition.

Not Baudelaire, but Mallarmé, in a passage called "Mimique" in *Crayonné au théatre*,[59] identifies most exactly the power of the hyperbolic gestures of the mime to abolish both any representational element and any link to falsely naturalistic sense of the living present. Such abolition replaces representation and the presence of the present with a contradictory realm of fiction. This fictional space exists in the perpetual allusion of the present sign to a past and a future which it is both married to and separated from by an unbreakable glass. This glass is the "hymen" of the failure of the fictive gestures of pantomime, of literature, or of caricature to perform any action whatsoever in the real world. Mallarmé's text describes the performance of the mime Paul Margueritte of the pantomime "Pierrot Assassin de sa Femme." In this performance, of course, there is no wife, and she is not killed. "La scène n'illustre que l'idée, pas une action effective, dans un hymen (d'où procède le Rêve), vicieux mais sacré, entre le désir et l'accomplissement, la perpétration et son souvenir; ici devançant, là remémorant, au futur, au passé, *sous une apparence fausse de présent*" (The scene illustrates nothing but the idea, not an effective action, in a hymen [from which the Dream proceeds], vicious but sacred, between desire and fulfilment, perpetration and its memory; here anticipating, there remembering, in the future, in the past, *under a false appearance of the present*).[60] A false appearance of the present which establishes a realm of pure fiction, by its allusions to a past and to a future which never did and never will take place except as fictions in their turn – this describes perfectly the strange reality brought before our eyes by Cruikshank's best works. This reality is glimpsed at the vanishing point of that oscillation between mimetic and figurative readings of the illustrations which initiates the vibration leading to the "*vertige de l'hyperbole.*" In this oscillation, most easily identifiable in the interpretation the viewer makes of the portraits in their relation to the living figures, the values of each change place before his eyes. What seemed inauthentic, the portraits, becomes authentic. What seemed authentic becomes a fiction. The violent action the portrait figures so serenely behold seems at first to have the genuine quality of life in the immediate present. Then it comes to be seen as inauthentic, because these unself-conscious figures fail to see the instant in the perspective of its end, in the perspective of death. Then the central figures appear authentic again when they are recognized as constituting the fictive mobility and allusiveness of true art. Back and forth between representation and fiction the illustrations move, as does the text by Dickens which Cruikshank's pictures illustrate. In both cases this wavering is the life and meaning of the works and of our activity of interpreting them. For both Dickens' *Sketches* and Cruikshank's illustrations the validity of the fictive reading cannot be reached unless we are tempted into accepting and exploring the representational reading.

To raise the question of what it means to have an illustrated book, to set Cruikshank's etchings and Dickens' *Sketches* side by side,[61] or to investigate either separately, as I have done in this study, is to encounter a contradictory vibration between a mimetic reading sustained by reference to something extra-artistic and a reading which sees both the literary text and its illustrations as fictions. The meaning of such fictions is constituted and maintained only by their reference to other equally fictional entities. This reciprocally sustaining, reciprocally destroying vacillation between literal and figurative interpretations is crucial to the process of explicating both graphic and literary works.

Notes

1. Charles Dickens, *Sketches by Boz*, The Oxford Illustrated Dickens (London, 1966), p. 493. Further quotations from this text will be identified as *SB*, followed by the page number. I wish to thank Mr William E. Conway, Librarian of the Clark Library, and Mr William D. Schaefer, Chairman of the Department of English, University of California, Los Angeles, for their many courtesies when I delivered the second part of this essay at a Clark Library Seminar. I owe thanks to Mr Richard A. Vogler for valuable information and to Miss Ada Nisbet for her careful reading of my manuscript and for her expert advice on several important matters of detail. For all these helps and kindnesses I am extremely grateful, as well as for the pleasant opportunity provided by the Clark Seminars for the preparation of this paper.
2. Among the scholars representing this development in criticism are Georges Blin, Roland Barthes, Jacques Derrida, Gilles Deleuze, Gérard Genette, and Paul de Man. Derrida's "La double séance," *Tel Quel*, 41–42 (Printemps; Eté

1970), pp. 3–43, 4–45, and de Man's "The Rhetoric of Blindness," forthcoming in *Poétique* and in his volume of essays, are particularly valuable for their formulations of the theoretical bases of such inquiries. My *The Form of Victorian Fiction* (Notre Dame, Ind., 1968) is an attempt to make suggestions along these lines for nineteenth-century English novels.

3. "Closing Statement: Linguistics and Poetics," *Style in Language*, Thomas A. Sebeok, ed. (Cambridge, Mass., 1966), p. 356.
4. Cited by Jean-Michel Rey from the *Essays on B. Brecht*, in "La scène du texte," *Critique*, 271 (Décembre 1969), p. 1068.
5. See John Butt and Kathleen Tillotson, "*Sketches by Boz*: Collection and Revision," *Dickens at Work* (London, 1963), pp. 35–61; Philip Collins, "A Dickens Bibliography," *The New Cambridge Bibliography of English Literature*, George Watson, III, ed. (Cambridge, 1969), cols. 786–7; Appendix F, *The Pilgrim Edition of the Letters of Charles Dickens*, M. House and G. Storey, I, eds (Oxford, 1965), for detailed information about the writing of the *Sketches by Boz*, their publication in various periodicals, their revision and collection in 1836 in the two-volume *Sketches by Boz*, First and Second Series, published by Macrone, their further revision for the edition of 1839 in monthly parts published by Chapman and Hall and collected by them in the one-volume edition of 1839, and the final revision of 1850. Mrs Tillotson's essay (the preface of *Dickens at Work* says it is mainly hers) is especially valuable for its discussion of the process of revision which the *Sketches* underwent.
6. See *Dickens at Work*, pp. 46–8, 52–3, and the essays by W. J. Carlton in *The Dickensian*, cited in Collins, *Bibliography*, col. 787.
7. Cited in *Dickens at Work*, p. 44.
8. In the essay of this title in *Communications*. XI (1968), pp. 84–9.
9. *The Dialogues of Plato*, B. Jowett, third ed., I (New York, 1892), p. 374.
10. Quoted in *Dickens at Work*, p. 37, from *Metropolitan Magazine* (March 1836), p. 77; *Examiner* (28 February 1836), p. 133; *Spectator* (20 February 1836), p. 183. See Collins, *Bibliography*, cols. 786–7, for a fuller list of contemporary reviews, which were for the most part laudatory. Mrs Tillotson is right to say that the *Sketches by Boz* rather than *Pickwick Papers* were Dickens' first popular success as a writer.
11. *Dickens at Work*, p. 37.
12. *The Life of Charles Dickens*, Library Edition, revised, I (London, 1876), Book I, Section V. According to Collins, *Bibliography*, Forster is also the author of the review in the *Examiner* cited above.
13. *Dickens at Work*, p. 37.
14. *The World of Charles Dickens* (New York, 1970), p. 84.
15. *"Sketches by Boz," Dickens and the Twentieth Century*, John Gross and Gabriel Pearson, eds (Toronto, 1962), pp. 20, 21, 34.
16. *Style in Language*, p. 353.
17. *ibid.*, p. 370.
18. Roman Jakobson and Morris Halle, *Fundamentals of Language* (The Hague, 1956), pp. 77–8.
19. *Style in Language*, p. 375.
20. For the seminal description of this aspect of Dickens' imagination, see Dorothy Van Ghent, "The Dickens World: A View from Todgers's," *Sewanee Review*, LVIII (1950), pp. 419–38.
21. Gérard Genette, in an excellent article, "Métonymie chez Proust, ou la

naissance de Récit," *Poétique*, 2 (1970), pp. 156–73, published since I completed this study, has called attention to a similar founding of metaphor on metonymic assumptions in *À la recherche du temps perdu*.

22. *Martin Chuzzlewit*, chapter 40.
23. See *Dickens at Work*, pp. 41–3, 56–7, for a discussion of the ordering and re-ordering of the *Sketches* in the collected editions of 1836 and 1839.
24. Cited in *Dickens at Work*, p. 45.
25. *ibid.*, p. 47.
26. The head of the family in "Mrs. Joseph Porter" is "a stock-broker in especially comfortable circumstances" (*SB*, p. 421).
27. *Dickens and the Twentieth Century*, p. 28.
28. Charles Dickens, *Oliver Twist*, The Clarendon Dickens, Kathleen Tillotson, ed. (Oxford, 1966), p. 365. Further quotations from this text will be identified as *OT*, followed by the page number.
29. For a discussion of the opposition between these two kinds of copying, see Gilles Deleuze, "Platon et le simulacre," *Logique du sens* (Paris, 1969), pp. 292–307.
30. *Fundamentals of Language*, p. 81.
31. See Jacques Derrida's discussion of the problematic of proper names in Lévi-Strauss's *Tristes tropiques*: "La guerre des noms propres," *De la grammatologie* (Paris, 1967), pp. 157–73, and see also Roland Barthes, "Proust et les noms," *To Honor Roman Jakobson* (The Hague, 1967), pp. 150–58.
32. Friedrich Nietzsche, *The Will to Power*, paragraphs 515, 521, 481, 495, and 552. I have cited the translation by Walter Kaufmann and R. J. Hollingdale (New York, 1968).
33. See the crucial sections on language and the hermeneutical circle in Martin Heidegger, *Sein und Zeit*, eleventh ed. (Tübingen, 1967), sections 7, B, and 32–7, pp. 32–4, 148–75.
34. Ludwig Wittgenstein, *The Blue and Brown Books*, Harper Torchbooks (New York, 1965), pp. 104–9.
35. See Sigmund Freud, *Die Traumdeutung*, ninth ed. (Vienna, 1950), and Jacques Lacan, "L'instance de la lettre dans l'Inconscient," *Écrits* (Paris, 1966). A footnote in the French translation of Jakobson's "Two Aspects of Language and Two Types of Aphasic Disturbances," from *Fundamentals of Language*, notes a difference between Lacan and Jakobson in their interpretation of Freud. Jakobson identifies metonymy with both the "displacement" and the "condensation" of Freud, while he sees metaphor as the basis of Freud's "identification and symbolism" (*Fundamentals of Language*, p. 81). "On remarquera," says Jakobson's translator, Nicolas Ruwet, "que ce rapprochement ne coïncide pas avec celui fait par J. Lacan . . . ; celui-ci identifie, respectivement, condensation et métaphore, et deplacement et métonymie. Roman Jakobson, à qui nous en avons fait la remarque, pense que la divergence s'explique par l'imprécision du concept de condensation, qui, chez Freud, semble recouvrir à la fois des cas de métaphore et des cas de synecdoque" (One will notice that this bringing together does not coincide with that made by J. Lacan . . . ; the latter identifies, respectively, condensation and metaphor, and displacement and metonymy. Roman Jakobson, to whom we mentioned this, thinks that the divergence is to be explained by the imprecision of the concept of condensation, which, in Freud, seems to include at once cases of metaphor and cases of synecdoche) (Roman Jakobson, *Essais de linguistique générale*, tr. N. Ruwet [Paris, 1963], p. 66). It

would seem rather that Jakobson's exaggerated emphasis on the "polar" opposition between metaphor and metonymy has led him astray in his understanding of Freud. Lacan's interpretation is perhaps truer to Freud's insight into the dependence of both forms of dreamwork on the basic linguistic act of naming one thing with the name of another.

36. *Style in Language*, p. 370.
37. Stéphane Mallarmé, *Oeuvres complètes*, éd. de la Pléiade (Paris, 1965), p. 878.
38. Henry James, *Autobiography*, Frederick W. Dupee, ed. (New York, 1956), p. 169.
39. "'All-of-a-Twist': the Relationship of George Cruikshank and Charles Dickens," *Harvard Library Bulletin*, XVII, pp. 2, 3 (April, July 1969), pp. 169–94, 320–42.
40. This is recapitulated and commented on in detail by Ms Cohen.
41. The five plates accompanying this essay are reproductions of original drawings by Cruikshank of illustrations for the *Sketches by Boz*. They are in the Harry Elkins Widener Collection in the Harvard College Library, and I am most grateful for permission to reproduce them. I wish to thank especially Miss Caroline Jakeman for her many courtesies to me during my study of these and other drawings by Cruikshank from the Widener Collection. Three of the sketches reproduced here ("The Gin Shop," "Sentiment," and "The First of May") are original pencil drawings for these three etchings. The other two ("Steam Excursion [I]" and "Steam Excursion [II]") are original sketches, in color, with numerous studies in the margin, in Dickens' own copy of the 1839 edition of the *Sketches by Boz*. The five plates are versions of the illustrations for the *Sketches* which have not before, to my knowledge, been reproduced. In my discussion of Cruikshank's etchings I am assuming that readers will have available copies of the final plates as published in the edition of 1839. These are reproduced in the Oxford Illustrated *Sketches by Boz* or in the Nonesuch edition of the *Sketches*. The Oxford Illustrated edition omits the etching for "Making a Night of It," while it restores the plate called "A Harmonic Meeting" (originally "The Free and Easy") which was for some reason omitted from the parts edition of 1839. The titles given to the plates in the Oxford Illustrated edition differ in some cases from the titles in the early editions. I have used the Oxford Illustrated titles.
42. "All-of-a-Twist," p. 174. The quotation from Sacheverell Sitwell is from *Narrative Pictures: A Survey of English Genre and Its Painters* (London, 1937), p. 20. In her remarks about "The Last Cabdriver" and "The Parish Engine" Ms Cohen is following the notations of Frederic G. Kitton in *Dickens and His Illustrators* (London, 1899), p. 6.
43. *Dickens and His Illustrators*, pp. 7–8; "All-of-a-Twist," p. 175.
44. Charles Baudelaire, *Oeuvres complètes*, éd. de la Pléiade (Paris, 1958), p. 751.
45. G. K. Chesterton, *Charles Dickens: A Critical Study* (New York, 1935), p. 112.
46. See E. H. Gombrich, *Art and Illusion: A Study in the Psychology of Pictorial Representation* (Princeton, N. J., 1969); *Meditations on a Hobby Horse and Other Essays on the Theory of Art* (London, 1965); "The Evidence of Images," *Interpretation: Theory and Practice*, Charles S. Singleton, ed. (Baltimore, 1969), pp. 35–104.
47. In addition to the essays by Gombrich, "The Experiment of Caricature," *Art and Illusion*, pp. 330–58, and "The Cartoonist's Armoury," *Meditations*

on a Hobby Horse, pp. 127–42, there is the work by Robert Wark on Rowlandson, a comprehensive critical biography of Hogarth by Ronald Paulson, and John Harvey's book, *Victorian Novelists and Their Illustrators* (New York, 1970), as well as the essays by Robert Patten and Michael Steig cited below.

48. See his essay *An "Oliver Twist" Exhibition: A Memento for the Dickens Centennial 1970* (University Research Library, University of California, Los Angeles, 1970).
49. "All-of-a-Twist," p. 184.
50. See Israel Solomons, "Satirical and Political Prints on the Jews' Naturalisation Bill, 1753," *Transactions of the Jewish Historical Society of England*, VI (1908–10), pp. 205–33; Thomas Whipple Perry, *Public Opinion, Propaganda, and Politics in Eighteenth-Century England: a study of the Jew bill of 1753* (Cambridge, Mass., 1962); and Ronald Paulson's biography of Hogarth. According to Perry, Ashkenazic pedlars "spoke but little English, and that with an unfamiliar accent; in an age of clean shaving, they wore beards; their hair was worn long, and their dress was often both ragged and unorthodox" (p. 8). The Ashkenazic figure who is the prototype for Fagin also occurs in three Rowlandson etchings, *Jews at a Luncheon*, BM Sat. 8536; another called *Traffic* (evidently not in BM Sat.), which shows two Jewish pedlars trying to sell a pair of trousers with a huge hole in the seat; and as a detail in another Rowlandson, BM Sat. 9546. I owe thanks to Ronald Paulson for calling these to my attention.
51. These were real enough, as may be seen by their presence in another contemporary representation of Seven Dials, by Gustave Doré, reproduced from his *London* in Angus Wilson, *The World of Charles Dickens*, p. 88. Doré's plate, however, does not give the lamps the threatening weight and size, as if they were giant lamps or the people pigmies, which they have in Cruikshank's etching.
52. *Oeuvres complètes*, p. 751.
53. *ibid.*
54. *ibid.*, pp. 751–2.
55. "Dickens, Hablôt Browne, and the Tradition of English Caricature," *Criticism*, XI, 3 (Summer 1969), pp. 219–33. See also Robert L. Patten, "The Art of *Pickwick*'s Interpolated Tales," *ELH*, XXXIV (1967), pp. 349–66.
56. This has been noted by Robert L. Patten, review of the Clarendon edition of *Oliver Twist*, in *Dickens Studies*, III (1967), p. 165, by Jane R. Cohen, "All-of-a-Twist," p. 180, and by F. G. Kitton, *Dickens and His Illustrators*, p. ii.
57. *Oeuvres complètes*, pp. 721, 752. Further quotations from Baudelaire will be identified by page numbers from this edition in parentheses after the quotations.
58. See Paul de Man's discussion of *De l'essence du rire* in "The Rhetoric of Temporality," *Interpretation: Theory and Practice*, Charles S. Singleton, ed. (Baltimore, 1969), pp. 194–9.
59. See Jacques Derrida's subtle interpretation of this text in "La double séance," cited in footnote 2, above.
60. *Oeuvres complètes*, p. 310.
61. As Dickens did in one of his proposed titles for the first volume of the *Sketches*: "Sketches by Boz and Cuts by Cruikshank" (Letter to Macrone, Pilgrim edition of *The Letters of Charles Dickens*, I, p. 82).

10

Interpretation in Dickens' *Bleak House*

forcing, adjusting, abbreviating, omitting, padding, inventing, falsifying, and whatever else is of the *essence* of interpreting

Nietzsche, *On the Genealogy of Morals*, III: 24

Bleak House is a document about the interpretation of documents. Like many great works of literature it raises questions about its own status as a text. The novel doubles back on itself or turns itself inside out. The situation of characters within the novel corresponds to the situation of its reader or author.

In writing *Bleak House* Dickens constructed a model in little of English society in his time. In no other of his novels is the canvas broader, the sweep more inclusive, the linguistic and dramatic texture richer, the gallery of comic grotesques more extraordinary. As other critics have shown (most notably John Butt and Kathleen Tillotson in "The Topicality of *Bleak House*" and Humphry House in "*Bleak House*: The Time Scale"[1]), the novel accurately reflects the social reality of Dickens' day, in part of the time of publication in 1851–3, in part of the time of Dickens' youth, in the late twenties, when he was a reporter in the Lord Chancellor's court. The scandal of the Court of Chancery, sanitary reform, slum clearance, orphans' schools, the recently formed detective branch of the Metropolitan Police Force, Puseyite philanthropists, the Niger expedition, female emancipation, the self-perpetuating procrastinations of Parliament and Government – each is represented in some character or scene. Every detail of topography or custom has its journalistic correspondence to the reality of Dickens' time. Everything mirrors some fact – from the exact references to street names and localities – mostly, it has been noted, within half a mile of Chancery Lane – to the "copying" of Leigh Hunt and Walter Savage Landor in Skimpole and Boythorn, to such out-of-the-way details as the descriptions of a shooting gallery, a law stationer's shop, or the profession of "follower." Like Dickens' first book, *Sketches by Boz, Bleak House* is an imitation in words of the culture of a city.

The means of this mimesis is synecdoche. In *Bleak House* each character, scene, or situation stands for innumerable other examples of a given type. Mrs Pardiggle is the model of a Puseyite philanthropist; Mrs Jellyby of another sort of irresponsible do-gooder; Mr Vholes of the respectable solicitor battening on victims of Chancery; Tulkinghorn of the lawyer to great families; Gridley, Miss Flite, Ada and Richard of different sorts of Chancery suitors; Mr Chadband of the hypocritical Evangelical clergyman mouthing distorted Biblical language; Bucket of the detective policeman, one of the first great examples in literature; Jo of the homeless poor; Tom-all-Alone's of urban slums in general; Sir Leicester Dedlock of the conservative aristocracy; Chesney Wold of the country homes of such men. Nor is the reader left to identify the representative quality of these personages for himself. The narrator constantly calls the reader's attention to their generalizing role. For each Chadband, Mrs Pardiggle, Jo, Chesney Wold or Gridley there are many more similar cases. Each example has its idiosyncrasies (who but Chadband could be just like Chadband?), but the essence of the type remains the same.

Bleak House is a model of English society in yet another way. The network of relations among the various characters is a miniature version of the interconnectedness of people in all levels of society. From Jo the crossing-sweeper to Sir Leicester Dedlock in his country estate, all Englishmen, in Dickens' view, are members of one family. The Dedlock mystery and the case of Jarndyce and Jarndyce bring all the characters together in unforeseen ways. This bringing together creates a web of connection from which no character is free. The narrator formulates the law of this interdependence in two questions, the first in reference to this particular story and the second in reference to all the stories of which this story is representative:

> What connexion can there be, between the place in Lincolnshire, the house in town, the Mercury in powder, and the whereabout of Jo the outlaw with the broom, who had that distant ray of light upon him when he swept the churchyard-step? What connexion can there have been between many people in the innumerable histories of this world, who, from opposite sides of great gulfs, have, nevertheless, been very curiously brought together! (16)[2]

In the emblematic quality of the characters and of their "connexions" *Bleak House* is an interpretation of Victorian society. This is so in more than one sense. As a blueprint is an image in another form of the building for which it is the plan, so *Bleak House* transfers England into another realm, the realm of fictional language. This procedure of synecdochic transference, naming one thing in terms of another, is undertaken as a means of investigation. Dickens want to define England exactly and to identify exactly the causes of its present state. As everyone knows, he finds England in a bad way. It is in a state dangerously close to ultimate disorder or decay. The energy which gave the social system its initial impetus seems about to run down. Entropy approaches a maximum. Emblems of this perilous condition abound in *Bleak House* – the fog and mud of its admirable opening, the constant rain at Chesney Wold, the spontaneous combustion of Krook, the ultimate consumption in costs of the Jarndyce estate, the deaths of so many characters in the course of the novel (I count nine).

With description goes explanation. Dickens wants to tell how things got as they are, to indict someone for the crime. Surely it cannot be, in the phrase he considered as a title for *Little Dorrit*, "Nobody's Fault." Someone must be to blame. There must be steps to take to save England before it blows up, like the springing of a mine, or catches fire, like Krook, or falls in fragments, like the houses in Tom-all-Alone's, or resolves into dust, which awaits all men and all social systems. It is not easy, however, to formulate briefly the results of Dickens' interpretative act. His two spokesmen, the narrators, are engaged in a search. This search brings a revelation of secrets and leads the reader to expect an explanation of their meaning. The novel as a whole is the narrators' reports on what they have seen, but these can only be understood by means of a further interpretation – the reader's.

Bleak House does not easily yield its meaning. Its significance is by no means transparent. Both narrators hide as much as they reveal. The habitual method of the novel is to present persons and scenes which are conspicuously enigmatic. The reader is invited in various ways to read the signs, to decipher the mystery. This invitation is made openly by the anonymous, present-tense narrator through rhetorical questions and other devices of language. The invitation to interpret is performed more covertly by Esther Summerson in her past-tense narrative. Her pretence not to understand the dishonesty, hypocrisy or self-deception of the people she encounters, though she gives the reader the information necessary to understand them, is such an invitation, as is her coy withholding of information which she has at the time she writes, but did not have at the time she has reached in her story: "I did not understand it. Not for many and many a day" (17).

Moreover, the narrators offer here and there examples of the proper way to read the book. They encourage the reader to consider the names, gestures, and appearances of the characters as indications of some hidden truth about them. Esther, for example, in spite of her reluctance to read signs, says that Prince Turveydrop's "little innocent, feminine manner" "made this singular effect upon me: that I received the impression that he was like his mother, and that his mother had not been much considered or well used" (14). The anonymous narrator can tell from George Rouncewell's way of sitting, walking, and brushing his palm across his upper lip, as if there were a great moustache there, that he must "have been a trooper once upon a time" (21).

The reader of *Bleak House* is confronted with a document which he must piece together, scrutinize, interrogate, at every turn – in short, interpret – in order to understand. Perhaps the most obvious way in which he is led to do this is the presentation, at the beginning of the novel, of a series of disconnected places and personages – the Court of the Chancery, Chesney Wold, Esther Summerson as a child, the Jellyby household and so on. Though the relations among these are withheld from the reader, he assumes that they will turn out to be connected. He makes this assumption according to his acceptance of a figure close to synecdoche, metonymy. Metonymy presupposes a similarity or causality between things presented as contiguous and thereby makes story-telling possible. The reader is encouraged to consider these contiguous items to be in one way or another analogous and to interrogate them for such analogies. Metaphor and metonymy together make up the deep grammatical armature by which the reader of *Bleak House* is led to make a whole out of discontinuous parts. At the beginning of the second chapter, for example, when the narrator shifts "as the crow flies" from the Court of Chancery to Chesney Wold, he observes that both are alike in being "things of precedent and usage," and the similarity between Krook and the Lord Chancellor is affirmed in detail by Krook himself:

> You see I have so many things here . . . of so many kinds, and all, as the neighbours think (but *they* know nothing), wasting away and going to rack and ruin, that that's why they have given me and my place a christening. And I have so many old parchmentses and papers in my stock. And I have a liking for rust and must and cobwebs. And all's fish that comes to my net. And I can't abear to part with anything I once lay hold of . . . or to alter anything, or to have any sweeping, nor scouring, nor cleaning, nor repairing going on about me. That's the way I've got the ill name of Chancery. (5)

Such passages give the reader hints as to the right way to read *Bleak House*. The novel must be understood according to correspondences within the text between one character and another, one scene and another, one figurative expression and another. If Krook is like the Lord Chancellor, the various Chancery suitors – Miss Flite, Gridley, Tom Jarndyce and Richard Carstone – are all alike; there are similarities between Tulkinghorn, Conversation Kenge and Vholes; Tom-all-Alone's and Bleak House were both in Chancery; Esther's doll is duplicated with a difference by the brickmaker's baby, by the keeper's child at Chesney

Wold and by Esther herself. Once the reader has been alerted to look for such relationships she discovers that the novel is a complex fabric of recurrences. Characters, scenes, themes and metaphors return in proliferating resemblances. Each character serves as an emblem of other similar characters. Each is to be understood in terms of his reference to others like him. The reader is invited to perform a constant interpretative dance or lateral movement of cross-reference as she makes her way through the text. Each scene or character shimmers before her eyes as she makes these connections. Think, for example, how many orphans or neglected children there are in *Bleak House*, and how many bad parents. The Lord Chancellor himself may be included, figuratively, among the latter, since his court was charged in part to administer equity to widows and orphans, those especially unable to take care of themselves. The Chancellor stands *in loco parentis* to Ada and Richard, the "Wards in Chancery."

In this system of reference and counter-reference the differences are, it is important to see, as essential as the similarities. Each lawyer in the novel is different from all the others. Esther did not die, like the brickmaker's baby, though her mother was told that she was dead. The relation between George Rouncewell and his mother is an inverse variant of the theme of bad parents and neglected children. Krook is not the Lord Chancellor. He is only a sign for him. The man himself is kindly enough, though certainly a bit eccentric. The Lord Chancellor is a kindly man too, as he shows in his private interview with Ada and Richard. They are sinister only in their representative capacities, Krook as a symbol of the disorder, avarice and waste of Chancery, the Lord Chancellor as the sign of the authority of his court. An emblem is always to some extent incompatible with its referent. A sign with ominous or deadly meaning may be an innocent enough old weather-beaten board with marks on it when it is seen close up, or it may be the absurd painting of "one impossible Roman upside down," as in the case of the "pointing Allegory" on Mr Tulkinghorn's ceiling (16). The power of a sign lies not in itself but in what it indicates. *Bleak House* is made up of a multitude of such indications.

Though many of the connections in this elaborate structure of analogies are made explicitly in the text, many are left for the reader to see for himself. One valuable bit of evidence that Dickens took conscious pains to prepare these correspondences is given in his plan for Chapter 16.[3] In this chapter Lady Dedlock gets Jo to take her to see the paupers' graveyard where her lover lies buried. Jo points through the iron gate at the spot, and Lady Dedlock asks if it is "consecrated ground." Dickens' notes show that he was aware, and perhaps intended the reader to be aware, of the similarity between Jo's gesture of pointing and the gesture of the pointing Allegory on Mr Tulkinghorn's ceiling. The latter is mentioned in passing earlier in the chapter and of course is made much of at the time of Tulkinghorn's murder. "Jo – ," says the note for this chapter, "shadowing forth of Lady Dedlock in the churchyard. / Pointing hand of allegory – consecrated ground / 'Is it Blessed?' " The two gestures of pointing are alike, as is suggested by the similarity of pose in the illustrations of both by "Phiz" for the first edition: "Consecrated ground" and "A new meaning in the Roman." Both are examples of that procedure of indication which is the basic structural principle of *Bleak House*. This procedure is "allegorical" in the strict sense. It speaks of one thing by speaking of another, as Dickens defines the Court of Chancery by talking about a rag and bottle shop. Everywhere in *Bleak House* the reader encounters examples of this technique of "pointing" whereby one thing stands for another, is a sign for another, indicates another, can be understood only in terms of another, or named only by the name of another. The reader must thread her way through the labyrinth of such connections in order to succeed in her interpretation and solve the mystery of *Bleak House*.

The situation of many characters in the novel is exactly like that of its writer or reader. So many people in this novel are engaged in writing or in studying documents, in attempting to decipher what one chapter-title calls "Signs and Tokens," in learning to read or write, in hiding documents or in seeking them out, there are so many references to letters, wills, parchments and scraps of paper, that the interpretation of signs or of texts may be said to be the fundamental theme of the novel. Krook's shop is full of old law papers – one of them, it turns out, perhaps the authentic will for resolving the case of Jarndyce and Jarndyce. Krook is obsessed, rightly enough, with the idea that he possesses documents of value, but he does not trust anyone to read them or to teach him to read. He tries to teach himself, forming laboriously with chalk on his wall the letters that spell out "Jarndyce," rubbing out each letter in turn as he makes it. Miss Flite carries everywhere her reticule full of documents. Richard broods day and night over the papers in his case, as he is drawn deeper and deeper into Chancery. Gridley too pores over documents. Much essential business in this novel, as, to be sure, in many novels, is carried on by means of letters. Tulkinghorn finds out Lady Dedlock's secret by the law writing in her lover's hand which matches the note of instructions Trooper George has from his old officer, Captain Hawdon. Esther teaches her little maid, Charley, how to read and write. Mrs Jellyby's irresponsibility is signified in the way she sits all day writing or dictating letters about Borrioboola-Gha instead of caring for her family. Poor Caddy Jellyby, her mother's amanuensis, is bespattered with ink, and Lawyer Tulkinghorn is a fathomless repository of secrets, all inscribed on the family papers in his strong-boxes.

Some of the most dreamlike and grotesque episodes in the novel involve documents, for example, the chapter in which Grandfather Smallweed, after Krook's death, rummages among the possessions of the deceased, surrounded, in his chair, with great piles of paper, or the chilling scene of the end of Jarndyce and Jarndyce. The latter moves beyond "realism" in the usual sense toward what Baudelaire in "The Essence of Laughter" calls the "dizzy hyperbole" of the "absolute comic":

> It appeared to be something that made the professional gentlemen very merry, for there were several young counsellors in wigs and whiskers on the outside of the crowd, and when one of them told the others about it, they put their hands in their pockets, and quite doubled themselves up with laughter, and went stamping about the pavement of the Hall. . . . [P]resently great bundles of papers began to be carried out – bundles in bags, bundles too large to be got into any bags, immense masses of papers of all shapes and no shapes, which the bearers staggered under, and threw down for the time being, anyhow, on the Hall pavement, while they went back to bring out more. Even these clerks were laughing. (65)

Not to put too fine a point upon it, as Mr Snagsby would say, what is the meaning of all this hermeneutical and archival activity? The reader of the novel must go beyond surface appearances to the deeper coherence of which these surfaces are the dispersed signs. In the same way, many of the characters are cryptographers. They attempt to fit details together to make a pattern revealing some hidden secret. Like Krook they must put "J" and "a" and so on together to spell "Jarndyce." They want to identify the buried truth which is the substance behind all the shadowy signs with which they are surrounded, as Richard Carstone believes that there "is – is – must be somewhere" "truth and justice" in the case of Jarndyce and Jarndyce (37). Two motives impel these readers of signs. Like Richard, Gridley or even, in spite of herself, Esther, they may want to find out secrets about themselves. Each seeks his unrevealed place in the system of which he is a part. To find out how I am related to others will be to find out who I am, for I am defined by my connections, familial or legal. Esther *is* the illegitimate daughter of Lady Dedlock and Captain Hawdon. Richard *is*, or perhaps is not, a rightful heir to the Jarndyce fortune. Other characters – Mr Tulkinghorn, Guppy, Grandfather Smallweed, Hortense, Mrs Snagsby or Inspector Bucket – want to find out secrets about others. Their motive is the search for power. To find out the hidden place of another in the system is to be able to manipulate him, to dominate him, and of course to make money out of him.

These two versions of the theme of interpretation echo through the novel in melodramatic and parodic forms. Many characters find themselves surrounded by mysterious indications, sinister, threatening or soliciting. Poor Mr Snagsby says, "I find myself wrapped round with secrecy and mystery, till my life is a burden to me" (47). He is "a party to some dangerous secret, without knowing what it is. And it is the fearful peculiarity of this condition that, at any hour of his daily life, . . . the secret may take air and fire, explode, and blow up" (25). Most of the characters are more aggressive than Mr Snagsby in their relation to secrets. Mr Tulkinghorn's "calling is the acquisition of secrets, and the holding possession of such power as they give him, with no sharer or opponent in it" (36). Guppy slowly puts together the evidence of Lady Dedlock's guilt and Esther's parentage. "It's going on," he says of his "case," "and I shall gather it up closer and closer as it goes on" (29). In the same way, Hortense, Lady Dedlock's maid, is "maliciously watchful . . . of everyone and everything" (18), and the "one occupation" of Mrs Snagsby's jealous life "has been . . . to follow Mr Snagsby to and fro, and up and down, and to piece suspicious circumstances together" (54). She has, says Mr Bucket, "done a deal more harm in bringing odds and ends together than if she had meant it" (54). Just as Gridley, Richard and Miss Flite are obsessed with the documents in their "cases," so the Smallweeds carry on Krook's search for valuable papers after his death, "rummaging and searching, digging, delving, and diving among the treasures of the late lamented" (39). Tom Jarndyce, the original owner of Bleak House, who finally blew out his brains in despair, lived there, "shut up: day and night poring over the wicked heaps of papers in the suit, and hoping against hope to disentangle it from its mystification and bring it to a close" (8). Even Sir Leicester, when he hears the story of a noble lady unfaithful to her husband, "arranges a sequence of events on a plan of his own" (40), and Esther, though she makes no detective effort to uncover the facts about her birth, nevertheless finds Lady Dedlock's face, "in a confused way, like a broken glass to me, in which I saw scraps of old remembrances" (18). She is, in spite of herself, led to put these broken pieces together to mirror the truth about herself, just as, in relation to another secret, she says, "I observed it in many slight particulars, which were nothing in themselves, and only became something when they were pieced together" (50).

The remarkable fact is that these interpreters for the most part are failures. Sometimes their interpretations are false, fictional patterns thrown over the surface of things like a mirage without relation to any deeper truth. Sometimes authentic secrets are discovered but are found out too late or in the wrong way to be of any use to their discoverers. *Bleak House* is full of unsuccessful detectives. The "plan of his own" which Sir Leicester constructs does not save him from the revelation that will shatter his proud complacency. Mrs Snagsby is ludicrously mistaken in her idea that her husband has been unfaithful and is the father of Jo. Krook dies before he finds anything of value in his papers, and even Grandfather Smallweed makes little out of his discovery. Guppy finds out Lady Dedlock's secret, but it does not win him Esther's hand. Gridley dies without resolving his suit. The case of Jarndyce and Jarndyce is used up in costs before the revelation of the newly-discovered will which might have brought it to a close. Even Tulkinghorn and Bucket, the two most clairvoyant and persistent detectives in the novel, are failures. Tulkinghorn is murdered just before he is going to make use of the secret he has discovered about Lady Dedlock. Bucket, in spite of the fact that "the velocity and certainty of [his] interpretation . . . is little short of miraculous" (56), does not save Lady Dedlock. The masterly intuition which leads him to see that she has changed clothes with the brickmaker's wife (another lateral displacement) gets Esther to her mother just too late. They find her "cold and dead" on the steps of Nemo's graveyard. Moreover, the novel is deliberately constructed by Dickens in a way calculated to make the reader a bad detective. Carefully placed clues are designed to lead the reader to believe that either George Rouncewell or Lady Dedlock has murdered Tulkinghorn. Even now, when Dickens' strewing of false clues may seem amateur in comparison with the sophisticated puzzles in modern mystery stories, some readers, one may imagine, are inveigled into thinking that Lady Dedlock is a murderess.

A clue to the meaning of this emphasis on false or fruitless interpretation may be given by what appears to be a fault in the novel. The most salient case of an apparent loose end or inconsistency is the failure to integrate perfectly the two major plots. "[T]he plan, so logical and complete," says Angus Wilson in his recent lively study of Dickens,

> by which the Jarndyce lawsuit corrupts all who touch it (save Mr Jarndyce, a nonesuch) is quite upset when we discover that Lady Dedlock's fall from virtue has nothing to do with her being a claimant in the case. The fault is the more glaring because Miss Flite, the little, mad suitor at law, specifically tells how her own sister went to the bad as a result of the misery brought to the family by their legal involvement.[4]

This fissure in the novel, a conspicuous rift in its web, seems all the more inexplicable when we consider Dickens' obvious care in other parts of the book to tie together apparently unrelated details. This is done, for example, by the use of a pattern of figurative language which runs throughout the text. One case of this is the apparently trivial metaphor which Dickens uses in the second chapter to describe Lady Dedlock's icy boredom by saying that, unlike Alexander, "having conquered *her* world, [she] fell, not into the melting but rather into the freezing mood" (2). This is picked up in the climactic scenes of her death in the melting snow which lies everywhere and which matches the break in her frigid restraint leading to her death. Surely, the reader supposes, Dickens could have related Lady Dedlock's "crime" more closely to the corrupting effect of Chancery if he had wanted to do so. Perhaps he did not want to. Perhaps he wanted to mislead the reader into thinking that the revelation of Lady Dedlock's secret is at the same time an explanation of the real mystery in the novel – that is, the question of why English society is in such a sad state. At the same time he may have wanted, by leaving the loose end in the open, to invite the reader to investigate further before he takes the revelation of the one mystery as a sufficient explanation of the other. The larger mystery, the mystery of Chancery or of the degeneration of England, is in fact not explained, or if it is explained this is done in so obscure a manner as to leave things at the end of the novel almost as dark, as mud-soaked and fog-drenched, as they are in the opening pages.

The somber suggestion toward which many elements of the novel lead, like points converging from different directions on a single spot, is that the guilty party is not any person or persons, not correctable evil in any institution. The villain is the act of interpretation itself, the naming which assimilates the particular into a system, giving it a definition and a value, incorporating it into a whole. If this is the case, then in spite of Dickens' generous rage against injustice, selfishness and procrastination, the evil he so brilliantly identifies is irremediable. It is inseparable from language and from the organization of men into society. All proper names, as linguists and ethnologists have recognized, are metaphors. They alienate the person named from his unspeakable individuality and assimilate him into a system of language. They label him in terms of something other than himself, in one form of the differentiating or stepping aside which is the essence of language. To name someone is to alienate him from himself by making him part of a family. Even the orphans or the illegitimate characters in *Bleak House* – Jo, Guster or Esther Summerson – are not free from this alienation. Institutions like Chancery, the workhouse or the Tooting baby-farm where Guster "grew," or persons like Mrs Pardiggle and the Reverend Chadband, act in place of proper parents for such people and force them into social moulds. Everyone in *Bleak House* is, like Jo, made to "move on," in one form or another of the displacement which separates so many of the characters of *Bleak House* from themselves.

It is no accident that the names of so many characters in the novel are either openly metaphorical (Dedlock, Bucket, Guppy, Vholes, Smallweed, Summerson, Badger, Clare, Boythorn, Krook, Swills,

Flite, Volumnia) or seem tantalizingly to contain some covert metaphor lying almost on the surface of the word (Tulkinghorn, Turveydrop, Chadband, Pardiggle, Jellyby, Rouncewell, Squod, Bagnet, Snagsby, Skimpole). Each of these names, especially those in the last group, seems to shimmer with multiple meanings drawn from various contexts, like the portmanteau words of "Jabberwocky." They invite etymological interpretation or "explication" in the root sense of an unfolding. Turveydrop? Turf? Turd? Curve? Drop of turf? "Turvey, turvey, clothed in black," as in the children's singing game? An essay could be written exploring the implications of these names. The meaning of names and of naming is, as in Proust's *Remembrance of Things Past*, an important theme in *Bleak House*, though Dickens, unlike Proust, seems to remain in that realm of fiction where names truly correspond to the essence of what they name. He does not appear to move on to the stage of disillusion where the incommensurability of name and person or of name and place appears.[5] Dickens' version of this disillusionment, however, is the implicit recognition that the characters to which he gives such emblematic names are linguistic fictions. The metaphors in their names reveal the fact that they are not real people or even copies of real people. They exist only in language. This overt fictionality is Dickens' way of demystifying the belief, affirmed in Plato's *Cratylus*, that the right name gives the essence of the thing. Along with this goes the recognition throughout *Bleak House* that a man's name is a primary way in which he is separated from his privacy and incorporated into society. "Lady Dedlock," says Tulkinghorn in a reproachful reminder of her crime and of her responsibility to the name she has wrongly taken, "here is a family name compromised" (48). Just as Dickens names his characters and helps them do their duty as emblems by borrowing labels for them from other contexts, and just as Miss Flite gives her birds allegorical names which juxtapose the victims of Chancery (Hope, Joy, Youth and so on), its effects (Dust, Ashes, Waste, Want, Ruin, etc.), and its qualities or the instruments of its deadly fictions (Folly, Words, Wigs, Rags, Sheepskin, Plunder, Precedent, Jargon, Gammon and Spinach), so the characters have been appropriated by society, named members of it, and cannot escape its coercion.

If the metaphors in the names in *Bleak House* are functional, it is also significant that so many characters have more than one name – nick-names, aliases or occupational names. The effect of these nominal displacements, as the reader shifts from one to another, is to mime in the permutations of language that movement within the social system which prevents each person from being himself and puts him beside himself into some other role. Young Bartholomew Smallweed is "meta-phorically called Small and eke Chick Weed, as it were jocularly to express a fledgling" (20). Captain Hawdon takes the alias of "Nemo," "nobody," as if he were trying to escape the involvement in society inevitable if one has any name at all. Gridley is known in the court he haunts as "The man from Shropshire." Tony Jobling takes the alias of Mr Weevle. Jo is called "Toughey" or "the Tough Subject," names pathetically inappropriate. George Rouncewell is "Trooper George." Mr Bagnet is "Lignum Vitae," and Mr Kenge the lawyer has been given the splendid name of "Conversation Kenge." Ada and Richard are "the Wards in Jarndyce," and Miss Flite calls Esther "Fitz-Jarndyce," suggesting thereby not only her relationship to her guardian, John Jarndyce, but also the figurative similarity between her situation as an illegitimate child and the situation of Ada and Richard as wards of the court.

In the context of the sinister connotation of multiple naming in *Bleak House* there is something a little disquieting, in spite of its loving intent, in the way Mr Jarndyce gives Esther a multitude of nursery rhyme and legendary pseudonyms, including the name of a fifteenth-century witch: "Old Woman," "Little Old Woman," "Cobweb," "Mrs Shipton," "Mother Hubbard," "Dame Durden." To give someone a nickname is to force on her a metaphorical translation and to appropriate her especially to oneself. This is precisely Jarndyce's selfishness in planning to make Esther his wife, which after all would be another form of renaming. Nor can he protect Esther from her involvement in society by way of her birth. Perhaps her first experience of this is her receipt of a letter from Kenge and Carboy which takes her, as so many characters in the novel are taken, into the legal language which turns her into an object: "We have arrnged for your being forded, carriage free, p^r eight o'clock coach from Reading . . ." (3). A fit emblem for the violence exercised over the individual by language and other social institutions is that terrifying form of helplessness Esther endures when she lies ill with the smallpox caught from Jo, who caught it from Tom-all-Alone's, the Jarndyce property ruined because it is in Chancery, or perhaps from the place where her unknown father lies buried, "sown in corruption" (11). "Dare I hint," asks Esther, "at that worse time when, strung together somewhere in great black space, there was a flaming necklace, or ring, or starry circle of some kind, of which *I* was one of the beads! And when my only prayer was to be taken off from the rest, and when it was such inexplicable agony and misery to be a part of the dreadful thing?" (35).

Perfect image of the alienation the characters of *Bleak House* suffer by being named members of society! The figure of a moving ring of substitution, in which each person is not himself but part of a system or the sign for some other thing, is used throughout the novel to define those aspects of society Dickens attacks. The evil of Mrs Jellyby's "telescopic philanthropy" or of Mrs Pardiggle's "rapacious benevolence" is that they treat people not as individuals but as elements in a system of abstract do-gooding. Mrs Pardiggle has "a mechanical way of taking possession of people," "a show . . . of doing charity by wholesale, and of dealing in it to a large extent," and a voice "much too business-like and systematic" (8). The world of aristocratic fashion is a "brilliant and distinguished circle" (12), "tremendous orb, nearly five miles round" (48), just as London as a whole is a "great tee-totum . . . set up for its daily spin and whirl" (16). Within her circle Lady Dedlock lives imprisoned "in the desolation of Boredom and the clutch of Giant Despair": substituting one place for another in a perpetually unsuccessful attempt to escape from her consciousness of the false self she has assumed. "Weariness of soul lies before her, as it lies behind . . . but the imperfect remedy is always to fly, from the last place where it has been experienced" (12).

A similar metaphor is used in the satire of representative government. It underlies that brilliant chapter in which the ruling classes gather at Chesney Wold to discuss the dissolution of Parliament and the formation of a new Government. (John Butt and Kathleen Tillotson in the article cited above discuss the references here to Disraeli, Russell and the Parliamentary crises of the early fifties.) Representative government is another form of delegation. Each Member of Parliament acts as the synecdochic sign for his constituents. Dickens, as is well known, had little faith in this form of government. The relation between representative and represented is always indirect. Any authentic correspondence between sign and signified is lost in the process of mediation. When Sir Thomas Doodle undertakes to form a new ministry he "throw[s] himself upon the country," but this throwing is only figurative, "chiefly in the form of sovereigns and beer." This has the advantage over direct appeal to the voters that "in this metamorphosed state he is available in a good many places simultaneously, and can throw himself upon a considerable portion of the country at one time" (40). In the practice of Parliamentary government the People are no more than "a certain large number of supernumeraries, who are to be occasionally addressed, and relied upon for shouts and choruses, as on the theatrical stage" (12). The actual business of governing is carried on by a small group of leaders of the two parties, Lord Coodle, Sir Thomas Doodle and so on down to Poodle and Quoodle on one side, Buffy, Cuffy, Duffy, Fuffy, Guffy and so on on the other. The comic names admirably suggest not only the anonymity of these men but the fact that each may replace any of the others. They exist, like the letters of the alphabet which Krook or Charlie Neckett so painfully learn, as the possibility of an inexhaustible set of permutations and combinations in which Noodle would replace Moodle; Puffy, Muffy; Puffy, Poodle; or Nuffy, Noodle, and nothing would be changed at all. Government is a circular game of substitutions like the nursery rhyme based on the letters of the alphabet beginning "A was an apple-pie."

This nursery rhyme, incorporated into another reference to the basic elements of language and to naming as the absorption of the particular into a system, is referred to in John Jarndyce's analysis of the Court of Chancery. Chancery, he says, is a dance or round. It proceeds through interminable linguistic substitutions replacing one declaration by another and never getting closer to any end. People, once they are named parties to a suit, are swept into the ring, as Esther is caught in her dream necklace, and can never hope to escape. No other text identifies so well the structure of *Bleak House* as a work of literature and also the structure of the society it describes. "It's about a Will, and the trusts under a Will – or it was, once," says Jarndyce.

> It's about nothing but Costs, now. We are always appearing, and disappearing, and swearing, and interrogating, and filing, and cross-filing, and arguing, and sealing, and motioning, and referring, and reporting, and revolving about the Lord Chancellor and all his satellites, and equitably waltzing ourselves off to dusty death, about Costs. . . . Law finds it can't do this, Equity finds it can't do that; neither can so much as say it can't do anything, without this solicitor instructing and this counsel appearing for A, and that solicitor instructing and that counsel appearing for B; and so on through the whole alphabet, like the history of the Apple Pie. And thus, through years and years, and lives and lives, everything goes on, constantly beginning over and over again, and nothing ever ends. And we can't get out of the suit on any terms, for we are made parties to it, and *must be* parties to it, whether we like it or not. (8)

"Nothing ever ends" – an important thematic stand of the novel is the special mode of temporal existence in an unjust society, or perhaps under any social order. Such an order has replaced realities by signs, substances by shadows. Each sign, in such a "system," refers not to a reality but to another sign which precedes it and which is pure anteriority in the sense that it refers back in its turn to another sign. A sign by definition designates what is absent, something which may exist but which at present is not here, as the cross on the top of St Paul's Cathedral, "so golden, so high up, so far out of his reach," is a "sacred emblem" indicating the apparent absence of God from Jo's life (19). A sign which refers back to another sign designates what is in its turn another absence. Gridley, the "Man from Shropshire," protests against the explanation of his suffering that blames it all on that code of equity which Conversation Kenge calls "a very great system, a very great system" (62). "There again!" says Gridley.

> The system! I am told, on all hands, it's the system. I mustn't look to individuals. It's the system. I mustn't go into Court, and say, "My Lord, I beg to know this from you – is this right or wrong? Have you the face to tell me I have received justice, and therefore am dismissed?" My Lord knows nothing of it. He sits there, to administer the system. (15)

In spite of Dickens' sympathy for Gridley's indignant outrage, the whole bent of *Bleak House* is toward indicating that it is in fact the systematic quality of organized society which causes Gridley's suffering – not a bad system of law, but any system, not a bad representative government, but the institution itself, not the special evil of aristocratic family pride, but any social organization based on membership in a family. As soon as a man becomes in one way or another part of such a system, born into it or made a party to it, he enters into a strange kind of time. He loses any possibility of ever having a present self or a present satisfaction, loses any possibility of ever going back to find the origin of his present plight, loses the possibility of ever escaping from his present restless state or of making any end to it other than "dusty death." This intolerable experience of time is dramatized with admirable explicitness, not only in the Chancery suit which can never end except in its consumption in costs, but also in the unhappy life of Richard Carstone. If no proper "Will" or explicable origin of Jarndyce and Jarndyce can ever be found (there are in fact three wills in the case), Richard as a result lives in perpetual deferring or postponement, never able to settle down to a profession or to commit himself to a present project. He dwells in a continual expectation of a settlement which can never come: "Everything postponed to that imaginary time! Everything held in confusion and indecision until then!" (37). "The uncertainties and delays of the Chancery suit" have made him unlike his natural self and have "imparted to his nature something of the careless spirit of a gamester, who [feels] that he [is] part of a great gaming system" (17). "Now?" asks Richard. "There's no now for us suitors" (37). If there is no now there is also no past or future for people who have been forced to accept their membership in a pattern of signs without substance. Each element in such a game refers to other elements in it, in a perpetually frustrated movement which can hope for no end. The other nightmare of Esther's dream expresses this perfectly: "I laboured up colossal staircases, ever striving to reach the top, and ever turned, as I have seen a worm in a garden path, by some obstruction, and labouring again" (35).

Miss Flite, mad as she is, is close to the truth about Chancery when she says, "I expect a Judgment. On the day of Judgment. And shall then confer estates" (14). The only escape from the circle of signs would be the end of the world or death, that "beginning the world" which Richard undertakes at the moment he dies, but "Not this world, O not this! The world that sets this right" (65). Dickens here, as in his work throughout, suggests an absolute incompatibility between this world and the far-off supernatural world. The many deaths in *Bleak House* have a significance somewhat different from that in many novels. In fiction generally, according to Walter Benjamin, the reader enjoys vicariously a finality he can never experience directly in his own life, my death being on principle an end I shall never be able to view in retrospect. In a novel, says Benjamin, the "meaning" of each character's life "is revealed only in his death," and "what draws the reader to the novel is the hope of warming his shivering life with a death he reads about."[6] Certainly there are in *Bleak House* many deaths to read about. Their peculiarity is that they are not satisfactory ends for the lives of those who die. Each character who dies passes suddenly from one world to another, leaving his affairs in the world as unsettled and as unfinished as ever. Krook dies without discovering the secrets in his papers. Gridley dies without resolving his suit, as Richard is killed by the final frustration of his hopes for an end to his case. Tulkinghorn dies without being able to use the power he has gained over Lady Dedlock. Jo's death is elaborately portrayed as the final example of his "moving on." The deaths in *Bleak House* constitute only in a paradoxical way "ends" which establish the destinies of those who die. Their deaths define them once and for all as people whose lives were unfinished, as people who never achieved the peace of a settlement. Their lives had meaning only in reference to the perpetually unsettled system of which they were part.

Bleak House itself has exactly the same structure as the society it exposes. It too assimilates everything it touches into a system of meaning. In the novel each phrase is alienated from itself and made into a sign of some other phrase. If the case of Jarndyce and Jarndyce is a "masterly fiction" (3, 65), and if many characters in the novel spend their time reading or writing, *Bleak House* is a masterly fiction too, and Dickens too spent his time, like Mrs Jellyby, covering paper with ink, his eye fixed not on his immediate surroundings but on an imaginary world. The novel too has a temporal structure without proper origin, present, or end. It too is made up of an incessant movement of reference in which each element leads to other elements in a constant displacement of meaning. *Bleak House* is properly allegorical, according to a definition of allegory as a temporal system of cross references among signs rather than as a spatial pattern of correspondence between signs and referents. Most people in the novel live without understanding their plight. The novel, on the other hand, gives the reader the information necessary to understand why the characters suffer, and at the same time the power to understand that the novel is fiction rather than mimesis. The novel calls attention to its own procedures and confesses to its own rhetoric, not only, for example, in the onomastic system of metaphorical names already discussed, but also in the insistent metaphors employed throughout.

Each character in *Bleak House* is not only named in metaphor but speaks according to his own private system of metaphors. Moreover, he is spoken of by the narrators in metaphors which recur. Nor are these metaphors allowed to remain "buried." In one way or another they are brought into the open. Their figurative quality is insisted upon. In this way the reader has constantly before him one version of the interpretative act whereby nothing is separately itself, but can be named only in its relation to some other thing. Dickens is master of an artificial style which makes its artifice obvious. Among the innumerable examples of this the following contains the linguistic texture of the novel in miniature: "The Mercuries, exhausted by looking out of window, are reposing in the hall; and hang their heavy heads, the gorgeous creatures, like overblown sun-flowers. Like them too, they seem to run to a deal of seed in their tags and trimmings" (48). The nominal metaphor (Mercuries) has been used throughout to label the Dedlock footmen. To this is here added a second figure, a metaphor of a metaphor. These Mercuries are like gorgeous sunflowers. To name them in this way has a double effect. It invites the reader to think of real footmen being described by the narrator in ornately witty language. This language names them as something other than themselves, but it also calls attention to its own wit, uncovers it by playing with it and extending it. The reader knows it is "just a figure of speech." The footmen are not Mercuries, nor are they sunflowers. These are ways of talking about them which bring them vividly before the reader and express the narrator's ironic scorn for aristocratic display. At the same time, the figures and figures within figures remind the reader that there are no real footmen in the novel. The Mercuries have only a linguistic existence. They exist as metaphors, and the reader can reach them only through Dickens' figurative language. This is true for all the characters and events in the novel. The fabric of Dickens' style is woven of words in which each takes its meaning not from something outside words, but from other words. The footmen are to be understood only in terms of Mercury, Mercury only in terms of sunflowers. This way of establishing fictional reality matches the kind of existence the characters in the novel have. They too are helpless parts of a structure based on words.

Does the novel propose any escape from this situation, or is it a wholly negative work? How might one step outside the ring? Esther Summerson and John Jarndyce are the chief examples in *Bleak House* of Dickens' commitment to a Christian humanism compounded of belief in "the natural feelings of the heart" (55), in unselfish engagement in duty and industrious work, in spontaneous charity toward those immediately within one's circle, and of faith that Providence secretly governs all in this lower world. This Providence will reward the good with another existence not cursed by the shadow of indefinite postponement. John Jarndyce has "resolutely kept himself outside the circle" of Chancery (37), holding himself free of its false hopes in an heroic effort of detachment. "Trust in nothing but in Providence and your own efforts" (13), he tells Richard. He uses his apparently inexhaustible money to do good quietly to those around him, loving all, asking nothing in return, and purging himself ultimately from his one selfishness, the desire to take Esther as his wife. He is Dickens' most successful version of that recurrent personage in his fiction, the benevolent father-figure.

Esther has been much maligned by critics for her coy revelations of how good she is, how much she is loved, and for her incorrigible habit of crying for joy. Nevertheless, she is in fact a plausible characterization, more palatable perhaps if one recognizes the degree to which the other narrator is an ironic commentary on her language, her personality, and her way of seeing things. She has reacted to the harsh teaching of her godmother's "distorted religion" (17) ("It would have been far better, little Esther, that you had had no birthday; that you had never been born!" [3]) by resolving "to be industrious, contented and kind-hearted, and to do some good to some one, and win some love to myself" (3). The emotional logic of this reaction is well known by now, and it is acutely rendered by Dickens, though we would perhaps be less inclined than he to admire its indirections. As opposed to Mrs Pardiggle's abstract and wholesale philanthropy, Esther thinks it best "to be as useful as I [can], and to render what kind services I [can], to those immediately about me" (8). She is conspicuously unwilling to engage in that form of the will to power which infects so many others in the book, the desire to decipher signs and to ferret out secrets. "Duty, duty, Esther" (38) is her motto. She strikes out "a natural, wholesome, loving course of industry and perseverance" (38), ringing herself into her household tasks with a merry peal of her bundle of keys. These are the symbol of her power to "sweep the cobwebs out of the sky," like the little old woman in the nursery rhyme, and to bring order everywhere she goes.

Even so, the interpretation of Jarndyce and Esther cannot be so straightforward. Perplexing puzzles and inconsistencies remain. What *is* the source of Jarndyce's money? It must come by inheritance and through his membership in the Jarndyce family, since he is never shown lifting a finger to earn any of it. This kind of inheritance, however, is shown throughout the novel to involve a man, in spite of himself, in the evils of "system." Moreover, there are many ways to exercise power over others. Not the least effective of these is self-abnegation. There is a kind of coercion in Jarndyce's goodness. He gives Esther to Allan Woodcourt without consulting her in the matter, and there is something a little unsettling about the fact that the new Bleak House, exact duplicate of the old, built secretly by Jarndyce for Esther and Allan, is another example of that theme of doubling which has such dark implications elsewhere in the novel. The patterns created by the lives of the good characters correspond rigorously to the patterns in the lives of the bad. This is as true for Esther as for Jarndyce. If Chancery is a "system" which sweeps everything it encounters into its dance, Esther, in another disquieting detail, is said by Harold Skimpole to be "intent upon the perfect working of the whole little orderly system of which [she is] the centre" (37). If old Mr Turveydrop's falseness is expressed by the fact that he forms himself after the Prince Regent and is a "Model of Deportment," Bucket praises Esther's courage when they are tracking down her mother by saying, "You're a pattern, you know, that's what you are, . . . you're a pattern" (59).

Bleak House is a powerful book, an extraordinary work of Dickens' creative power. It is also to some degree a painful book. The pain lies partly in its prevailing darkness or bleakness, its presentation of so many admirably comic creations who are at the same time distorted, grotesque, twisted (Krook, Grandfather Smallweed, Mrs Jellyby, Chadband, Guppy, Miss Flite – what a crew!). It is painful also because of its self-contradictions. Like the case of Jarndyce and Jarndyce it remains unfinished at its end, a tissue of loose ends and questions rather than of neatly resolved patterns. As in all Dickens' work, there is at the center of *Bleak House* a tension between belief in some extra-human source of value, a stable center outside the shadows of the human game, and on the other hand the shade of a suspicion that there may be no such center, that all systems of interpretation may be fictions.

In *Bleak House* this tension is dramatized in a way appropriate for a novel which focuses on the theme of interpretation. It lies in the contrast between Esther's way of seeing the world and that of the anonymous narrator. Skimpole, Chadband, Mrs Jellyby and the rest each dwell hermetically sealed within an idiosyncratic system of language. In particular, Skimpole's light-hearted reading of the world as designed for his delectation and amusement, expressed with great verve by Dickens, is a frighteningly plausible reversal of Esther's commitment to duty and responsibility. Esther's language too is a special perspective, perhaps a distorting one, as is the view of the other narrator. Each has his characteristic rhetoric, a rhetoric which interprets the world along certain lines. To Esther the course of her life seems secretly governed by a divine Providence. She sees this most concretely in the benign presences she glimpses in the landscape around Chesney Wold: "O, the solemn woods over which the light and shadow travelled swiftly, as if Heavenly wings were sweeping on benignant errands through the summer air" (18). To the other narrator no such presences are visible. He sees a world darkening toward death, a world in which it is always foggy or raining. His vision, for example in the description of Tom-all-Alone's in Chapter 46, may be defined as nihilistic:

> Darkness rests upon Tom-all-Alone's. Dilating and dilating since the sun went down last night, it has gradually swelled until it fills every void in the place. . . . The blackest nightmare in the infernal stables grazes on Tom-all-Alone's, and Tom is fast asleep. (46)

Which of these is a misinterpretation? Perhaps both are? Though the happy ending of *Bleak House* may beguile the reader into accepting Esther's view as the true one, the novel does not resolve the incompatibility between her vision and what the other narrator sees. The meaning of the novel lies in this irresolution.

Like many other nineteenth-century writers Dickens was caught between his desire to reject what he found morally objectionable or false about Christianity, in particular its doctrine of original sin, and his desire to retain some form of Christian morality. This retention was for Dickens, as for others in his time, the only protection against nihilism. *Bleak House* presents the reader with a sick, decaying, moribund society. It locates with profound insight the causes of that sickness in the sign-making power, in the ineradicable human tendency to take the sign for the substance, and in the instinctive habit of interpretation, assimilating others into a private or collective system of meaning. At the same time the novel itself performs a large-scale act of interpretation. If there were no interpretation there would be no novel. It frees itself from the guilt of this only by giving the reader, not least in its inconsistencies, the evidence necessary to see that it *is* an interpretation.

On the one hand the distorted Christianity of Esther's aunt is firmly repudiated. Against her, "Watch ye therefore! lest coming suddenly he find you sleeping," is set Jesus' forgiveness of the woman caught in adultery: "He that is without sin among you, let him first cast a stone at her!" (3). On the other hand, the novel apparently sustains Lady Dedlock in her remorse, in her somewhat narrowly Christian interpretation of what from another point of view, abundantly suggested in the novel, is her natural and good love for Captain Hawdon. A later generation might see marriage as one of the perfidious legalities distorting the natural feelings of the heart. In fact in Dickens' own day Ludwig Feuerbach in *The Essence of Christianity*, George Eliot in her liaison with George Henry Lewes, perhaps even in her fiction, and Anthony Trollope in such a novel as *Dr Wortle's School* saw individual acts of love as sanctifying the legal institution of marriage rather than the other way around. Lady Dedlock's mystery and the mystery of Chancery are so closely intertwined that the reader may be enticed into thinking that the solution of the one is the solution of the other. Some "illicit" act like fornication must lie at the origin of Jarndyce and Jarndyce and be the explanation of the suffering it causes, visiting the sins of the fathers on the children, generation after generation. The novel persuasively shows, however, that nothing lies at the origin of Jarndyce and Jarndyce but man's ability to create and administer systems of law. Such systems give actions and documents a meaning. It would seem, nevertheless, that the Ten Commandments fit this definition of evil as well as the laws and precedents governing Chancery. Both the particular commandments against which Lady Dedlock has sinned and the system of Chancery have jurisdiction over the relations of man to woman, parent to child. Between its commitment to a traditional interpretation of these relations and a tendency to put all interpretation in question as the original evil *Bleak House* remains poised.

Notes

1. In *Dickens at Work* (1957), and *The Dickens World* (1941), respectively.
2. Numbers in parentheses after quotations refer to chapters in the novel.
3. See p. 940, Penguin edition.
4. *The World of Charles Dickens*, (1970), p. 234.
5. See Roland Barthes, "Proust et les noms," *To Honor Roman Jakobson* (The Hague, 1967), pp. 150–8.
6. *Illuminations* (New York, 1969), p. 101.

11

Nature and the linguistic moment

It may seem churlish, in a book that investigates so many aspects of the Victorian response to Nature, to argue that the Victorian imagination was almost always indirect in its response, at least in literature.* My hypothesis, nevertheless, is that for many of the most important Victorian writers, in spite of their apparent interest in observing Nature and in reproducing it exactly, Nature is not the primary interest. In some writers, concern for Nature is displaced by a concern for subjectivity as it may be described in metaphors drawn from the natural world[1] – since there is no literal language of consciousness, the self being itself a figure or an effect of language. In others, a direct confrontation with Nature is turned aside even more radically to a primary focus on language, to the words by which Nature is named and its "system" created or revealed.

In Victorian literature, alongside mimetic theories and practices, there exists a theory and practice more properly allegorical, intraliterary, or intralinguistic. The mimetic or "realistic" paradigm is well exemplified by a passage in Browning's "Fra Lippo Lippi":

> . . . Don't object [says Lippo], "His works
> Are here already; nature is complete:
> Suppose you reproduce her – (which you can't)
> There's no advantage! You must beat her, then."
> For, don't you mark? we're made so that we love
> First when we see them painted, things we have passed
> Perhaps a hundred times nor cared to see;
> And so they are better, painted – better to us,
> Which is the same thing. Art was given for that;
> God uses us to help each other so,
> Lending our minds out.[2] (II. 296–306)

A theory of art like that of Fra Lippo is of course pervasive in the Victorian period, as it is in Western tradition generally since Plato,

Aristotle, and before. It appears in the "realistic" theory of the novel that is standard for the Victorians, as well as in representational theories of poetry, for example in one dimension of Ruskin's aesthetics. The mimetic paradigm always involves, covertly or overtly, just those elements present in Fra Lippo Lippi's defense of realistic art: the goal (however unattainable) of an exact reproduction of the appearances of reality; an appeal to "truth" as the correspondence between things as they are and things as they are in their imitative copies; some reference to a transcendent deity or ideal spirit as the guarantee of that truth, the Truth behind all specific mimetic truths; an apparently contradictory, but actually consistent, introduction of the notion of art as revelation, *aletheia*, truth as uncovering rather than truth as adequation or as scrupulously accurate replica. Truth as reproduction leads to truth as revelation, for we see things in their imitations that we have passed in reality a hundred times without seeing. Mimetic art removes the veil of familiarity from the world.

Against such a paradigm and present as underthought or counter-thought to this more official thought, are all those modes of art among the Victorians that use the names of natural things figuratively to speak of some aspect of consciousness, or that focus on the words themselves in their interrelation. It is not possible here to give more than a few tentative examples as indications of a possible line of investigation that I intend to pursue in greater detail in a fuller study.

The notions of "example" and of "line of investigation," moreover, are not unequivocal or logically transparent concepts on which my enterprise can be solidly based. Both are, in fact, figures, with all the uncertainty or equivocation that always attends any effort of thought based on figure. The methodological problem is not unrelated to the topic of my essay. An "example" is a synecdoche, part for whole, and accompanied by the special ambiguities associated with synecdoche, as the range of meanings for "example" and "exemplary" in the *OED* will attest.[3] Synecdoche always hovers uneasily between metaphor, with its implications of substantial and intrinsic similarity, and metonymy, with its suggestions of mere contiguity or contingency. Is the example a fair sample of a homogeneous whole, containing all its elements and features, as each cell contains the genetic pattern of the whole organism? Or is the example only a part that happens to be there, perhaps an atypical part? How would one go about deciding, without analyzing all the parts in detail, that a given example is in fact typical? The problem is "exemplified" by the parable of Pooh and the honey pot:

> So he put his tongue in, and took a large lick. "Yes," he said, "it is. No doubt about that. And honey, I should say, right down to the bottom of

the jar. Unless, of course," he said, "somebody put cheese in at the bottom just for a joke. Perhaps I had better go a *little* further . . . just in case."[4]

In a work of literature every "example" is to some degree different from all the others, though how much this matters in a given case may be difficult to decide. Literary study is therefore based on the extremely problematic assumption of the validity of synecdoche. The problem is only made more difficult when the scope of interpretation is widened from a single long work like *Middlemarch* or *Idylls of the King* to the literature of a whole period, "Victorian fiction" or "Victorian poetry," or even, as in the title of this book, "the Victorian Imagination."

The notion of following a "line of investigation" also remains a figure, as dubious as that of the "example." The image of a "line" implies that writing a piece of critical discourse is like following a road already there, or perhaps like carving out a course or track in a pathless wilderness. In either case, the image evokes a linear sequence that has a beginning (some starting place or hypothesis), follows a continuous sequence of development, without gaps or illogical leaps, and reaches a definite goal. In fact, of course, matters are not so straightforward in most essays, certainly not with this one. The present essay (like the entire volume of which it is a part) might be better thought of as the bringing together, with some teasing out of implications, of a series of citations, passages, places of passage through which, in each case, the current of meaning found in longer works momentarily pauses or traverses. The work of several novelists, as well as of Gerard Manley Hopkins, will stand by synecdoche for many other possible illustrations.

Nature as such, in the Wordsworthian sense of trees, mountains, and daffodils, "one impulse from a vernal wood," does not count for much in nineteenth-century novels as a primary source of value and meaning. It may function, as in Jane Austen and Anthony Trollope, as a measure of the economic or social worth of the person who owns the fields, parks, and woodlands of an estate, or it may be present, as sometimes in George Eliot and Henry James, in an entirely negative way, as an expression of the impossibility of life in solitude, outside society. In *Adam Bede* (1859), in the climax of the extraordinary sequence describing Hetty Sorrel's wanderings, Hetty cannot bring herself to commit suicide. She looks across the cold waters of the pool toward her memories of community life with the Poysers. In spite of the strong Wordsworthian influence on Eliot, in *Adam Bede* especially, this passage at least, in its refusal to imagine any value in a direct relation to Nature, seems the antithesis of Wordsworth's rejection of human society for the greater authenticity of an unmediated relation, in solitude, to the things of Nature:

> Oh how long the time was in that darkness! The bright hearth and the warmth and the voices of home, – the secure uprising and lying down, – the familiar fields, the familiar people, the Sundays and holidays with their simple joys of dress and feasting, – all the sweets of her young life rushed before her now, and she seemed to be stretching her arms towards them across a great gulf. . . . The horror of this cold, and darkness, and solitude – out of all human reach – became greater every long minute: it was almost as if she were dead already, and knew that she was dead, and longed to get back to life again. But no: she was alive still; she had not taken the dreadful leap.[5]

Here the solitary relation to Nature is death. Life is belonging to a community. Society collectively humanizes Nature and gives it a meaning in shared social efforts, as the "familiar fields" are part of Hetty's memories of life at the Hall Farm.

A similar negative attitude toward Nature is expressed in a climactic scene of Henry James' *Washington Square* (1880). Dr Sloper takes his daughter Catherine to a desolate spot in the Alps to show her how forlorn she will be if she sticks to her lover Morris Townsend. The scene is a parody of the crossing of the Simplon Pass in Book VI of *The Prelude*. It contains many of the same elements, but with the values reversed, at least from the most usual reading of this episode in *The Prelude*. In *Washington Square* there is no Nature "like workings of one mind, the features / Of the same face, blossoms upon one tree / Characters of the great Apocalypse."[6] James' Nature expresses only the absence of human relationship in a negative wilderness, not even the positive discovery of the autonomous power of the human imagination that is the true theme of the Simplon passage in Wordsworth, as it is ultimately, in fact, of *Washington Square*:

> They followed this devious way, and finally lost the path; the valley proved very wild and rough, and their walk became rather a scramble. They were good walkers, however, and they took their adventure easily; from time to time they stopped, that Catherine might rest; and then she sat upon a stone and looked about her at the hard-featured rocks and the glowing sky. It was late in the afternoon, in the last of August; night was coming on, and as they had reached a great elevation, the air was cold and sharp. In the west there was a great suffusion of cold red light, which made the sides of the little valley look only more rugged and dusky. During one of their pauses her father left her and wandered away to some high place, at a distance, to get a view. He was out of sight; she sat there alone in the stillness, which was just touched by the vague murmur

somewhere of a mountain brook. She thought of Morris Townsend, and the place was so desolate and lonely that he seemed very far away. . . .

The Doctor looked round him too. "Should you like to be left in such a place as this, to starve?"

"What do you mean?" cried the girl.

"That will be your fate – that's how he will leave you."[7]

The great scene in the opening chapter of Book Third of *The Wings of the Dove* (1902) is a more complex permutation of the elements in the scene from *Washington Square.* The later scene echoes not only Wordsworth's crossing of the Simplon, but, behind Wordsworth, the temptation of Christ in *Paradise Regained.* To Mrs Stringham's sharp observation, Milly Theale poised on a rock at the edge of an Alpine abyss seems not to be contemplating suicide, and by no means to be enjoying "a sense sublime / Of something far more deeply interfused,"[8] but rather to be "looking down on the kingdoms of the earth, and though indeed that of itself might well go to the brain, it wouldn't be with a view of renouncing them. Was she choosing among them or did she want them at all?"[9] Once more, Nature has been transformed into a purely human sign, or even into a sign that draws its meaning from ironic or incongruous allusions to previous literary signs. For Milly there is to be no renunciation of the magnificence of worldly power, and her allegiance at this moment in her life seems to be to Satan rather than to Christ, which perhaps only measures the scope of her ultimate renunciation (or is it her ultimate affirmation of power?).

It might seem that *Wuthering Heights* (1847) is the great exception to my claim that Nature plays a neutral role in Victorian fiction, or a role merely as the sign of some human meaning, often a negative meaning at that. Surely, it might be argued, here is a Victorian novel in which vivid and circumstantial descriptions of natural features are incorporated for their own sake, as part of the primary material of the novel. In fact, however, Lord David Cecil, in his well-known essay on *Wuthering Heights* in *Early Victorian Novelists* (1934), has the priorities just backwards in arguing that the relations among Catherine, Heathcliff, and the rest dramatize a struggle between two great cosmic natural forces of storm and calm. The focus of *Wuthering Heights,* like that of other Victorian novels, is on relations between persons and on the problems of representing these verbally and interpreting them. Nature is no more than a major resource of figurative language by means of which the quality of the people and of their relations is defined. Nature is not confronted for itself but is transmuted into a set of figurative signs by means of which the narrators and the reader may interpret the characters and their enigmatic fates, as when Cathy says, "My love for Linton is like the foliage in the woods. Time will change it, I'm well aware, as winter changes the trees. My love for Heathcliff resembles the eternal rocks beneath – a source of little visible delight, but necessary." A full reading of the novel would be necessary to explore this emblematic use of Nature in *Wuthering Heights*, but one further striking example may be given. The second Catherine tells how she came near to quarreling with her cousin, Linton Heathcliff, on one of her visits to the Heights. Each preferred a different kind of weather, Linton a day without wind, "with the bees humming dreamily about among the bloom," Catherine a windy, cloudy day, "great swells of long grass undulating in waves to the breeze; and woods and sounding water, and the whole world awake and wild with joy."[10] This description of two kinds of Yorkshire weather functions entirely as a figurative means of describing the personalities of the two characters in their clashing incompatibility, outside serving splendidly, as it does throughout *Wuthering Heights*, as a means of naming the otherwise inaccessible inside.

George Meredith and Thomas Hardy are two other Victorian writers who might seem to treat Nature directly, for its own sake. Yet their work, too, displays a sublimation of Nature into signs for subjective states that could exist without Nature, though not without the figuratively used signs of things in Nature. Meredith and Hardy knew, each in his own way, that the self and its states are linguistically generated and sustained.

Meredith's admirably difficult "Nature" poetry moves toward the act of personification as its chief concern, and beyond that, through an elaborate interplay with earlier poetry, Romantic as well as classical, explores the function of figurative language as generating a mythological vision. Poems of this sort include "The South-Wester," "The Day of the Daughter of Hades," "Hard Weather," "Hymn to Colour" and "Night of Frost in May." In Meredith's novels the same operation occurs in reverse. In his fiction the names of things in Nature are borrowed to denote subtle and otherwise unnameable movements of the mind, as in chapter XXI of *The Egoist* (1887), "Clara's Meditations." Whereas, in the poetry, Nature is figured as a person, in Meredith's novels the person is figured by natural images. In either case, the exchanges of figuration are essential to his linguistic practices.

These figurative exchanges, and their base in a nonequivalence, are overtly commented on in crucial passages of interpretation proposed by the Meredithian narrator, as when he says, in chapter XVIII of *One of Our Conquerors* (1891), "It is the excelling merit of similes and metaphors to spring us to vault over gaps and thickets and dreary places. But, as with the visits of Immortals, we must be ready to receive them. Beware, moreover, of examining them too scrupulously: they have a trick of wearing to vapour if closely scanned."[11]

In Hardy's novels and even in his poetry, as in the work of George Eliot, Nature seldom is in itself a source of value or meaning. *Tess of the d'Urbervilles* (1891), for example, contains a running commentary that sardonically rejects what Hardy understands as Wordsworthian pantheism or spiritualization of Nature. "Some people," says the narrator, "would like to know whence the poet whose philosophy is in these days deemed as profound and trustworthy as his song is breezy and pure gets his authority for speaking of "Nature's holy plan.' " It seems to Tess, as she goes through the night toward the fatal convergence of the twain that will end poor Prince's life, that "the occasional heave of the wind" is "the sigh of some immense sad soul, coterminous with the universe in space, and with history in time." In a bitter parody of the Romantic union of subject and object, each of Tess's drunken companions, on the moonlit night of her violation, feels that he or she is the center of a harmonized universe:

> . . . as they went there moved onward with them, around the shadow of each one's head, a circle of opalized light, formed by the moon's rays upon the glistering sheet of dew. Each pedestrian could see no halo but his or her own, which never deserted the head-shadow, whatever its vulgar unsteadiness might be; but adhered to it, and persistently beautified it; till the erratic motions seemed an inherent part of the irradiation, and the fumes of their breathing a component of the night's mist; and the spirit of the scene, and of the moonlight, and of Nature, seemed harmoniously to mingle with the spirit of wine.[12]

In these passages, moonlight and the "correspondent breeze," two of the major Romantic symbols for the harmony of man and Nature, are mocked, ironically reduced to sleepy illusions or to drunken self-deceptions. Rather than being of value in itself, Nature for Hardy has meaning and use only when it has been marked by man's living in it and so has become a repository of signs preserving individual and collective history.[13] The shift from Nature to subjective or intersubjective life to language is enacted, for Hardy, not only in the concern with spoken or written language as such, but also in the shift of interest to the embodied signs of himself that man imprints on Nature in his passage through life. "An object or mark raised or made by man on a scene," says Hardy in his autobiography, "is worth ten times any such formed by unconscious Nature. Hence clouds, mists, and mountains are unimportant beside the wear on a threshold, or the print of a hand."[14]

In a letter to A. W. M. Baillie written January 14, 1883, Hopkins develops the theory that in classical literature, the overt narrative meaning may be matched by a covert sequence of figures and allusions constituting what he calls an "underthought," an "echo or shadow of the overthought, something like canons and repetitions in music," . . . "an undercurrent of thought governing the choice of images used." "My thought," Hopkins confides,

> is that in any lyric passage of the tragic poets . . . there are – usually; I will not say always, it is not likely – two strains of thought running together and like counterpointed; the overthought that which everybody, editors, see . . . and which might for instance [can] be abridged or paraphrased . . . ; the other, the underthought, conveyed chiefly in the choice of metaphors etc used and often only half realised by the poet himself.[15]

It might be possible to extend Hopkins' insight hypothetically to all literary texts, including his own poetry, and to suppose that each text may have its underthought, a submerged counterpoint to its manifest meaning.

The religious thought of Gerard Manley Hopkins is centered on an ultimately acentering analogy: the parallelism between the structure of language and the structure of the creation in relation to the creator. The most obvious way in which this analogy appears is in the systematic and wholly orthodox use of a metaphor drawn from language to describe the relation of the natural world to God. Christ, the second person of the Trinity, is the Logos, the word or utterance of God. The world of Nature with all its multitudes of creatures, including man, is created in the name of Christ, modeled on Christ, just as all the multiplicity of words in a language might be considered as the product of an increasingly elaborate differentiation of a primary word, an ur-word. The structure of language thus becomes the metaphoric vehicle, the irreplaceable means by which Hopkins expresses his conception of God's relation to the creation. If Hopkins' theological terminology is logocentric, it is also true that language itself is a primary theme in his writings. The theme of language is not only developed in the brilliant etymological speculations in the early diaries or in the early essay on words, but also in the mature poetry itself, for example, in "That Nature is a Heraclitean Fire and of the Comfort of the Resurrection" and in "I wake and feel the fell of dark, not day." The most elaborate treatment, however, occurs in Hopkins' masterpiece, "The Wreck of the Deutschland," where his concern with language displaces the focus of the poem from the relations among the self, Nature, and God to linguistic puzzles that become the indispensable yet ultimately subversive model by which these relations can be expressed.

If the overthought of "The Wreck" is the salvation of the tall nun and the poet's corresponding experience, in madrigal echo, of a renewed inspiration or awareness of God's grace breathing in the natural world, the underthought of the poem is language itself. Like so many Romantic and post-Romantic poems, "The Wreck" has as one of its themes its own possibility of being. The center around which Hopkins' linguistic speculations revolve, the unsettling intuition toward which they approach and withdraw is the exact opposite of his theological insight. It is the notion that there is no primal word, that the divisions of language have always already occurred as soon as there is language at all. If this is so, there is no word for the Word, only displaced metaphors of it.

In the word lists that Hopkins compiled at the time of his early onomatopoeic etymological speculations each list goes back to an ur-gesture, action, or sound. In each case this is an act of division, marking, striking, or cutting. Here are examples of these lists: "grind, gride, gird, grit, great, grate, greet"; "flick, fleck, flake"; "skim, scum, squama, scale, keel"; "shear, shred, potsherd, shard." Of the first list Hopkins says, "Original meaning to *strike, rub*, particularly *together*." Of the second list,

> *Flick* means to touch or strike lightly as with the end of a whip, a finger etc. To *fleck* is the next tone above flick, still meaning to touch or strike lightly (and leave a mark of the touch or stroke) but in a broader less slight manner. Hence substantively a *fleck* is a piece of light, colour, substance etc. looking as though shaped or produced by such touches. *Flake* is a broad and decided fleck, a thin plate of something, the tone above it. Their connection is more clearly seen in the applications of the words to natural objects than in explanations.

The third list involves the notion of "the topmost flake what [*sic*] may be skimmed from the surface of a thing," and the fourth list of words plays variations on the act of division, as "The *ploughshare* [is] that which divides the soil." For Hopkins, "the onomatopoetic theory has not had a fair chance," and all these word lists lead back to an original sound or sound-producing act of differentiation. For Hopkins, as for modern linguistics, the beginning is diacritical.

The dramatic climax of "The Wreck of the Deutschland" is also the climax of its treatment of the theme of language. Its dramatic climax is the tall nun's saying the name of Christ and thereby being saved, transformed into Christ at the moment of her death. The linguistic climax is the implicit recognition, in stanzas 22 and 28, that there is no way of speaking of this theological mystery except in a cascade of metaphors whose proliferation confesses to the fact that there is no literal word for the Word. Stanza 22 presents a chain of words for the act of sign-making, the marking of the nun with the stigma that signs her with the seal of sacrifice, of "resignation":

> Five! the finding and sake
> And cipher of suffering Christ.
> Mark, the mark is of man's make
> And the word of it Sacrificed.
> But he scores it in scarlet himself on his own bespoken,
> Before-time-taken, dearest prizèd and priced –
> Stigma, signal, cinquefoil token
> For lettering of the lamb's fleece, ruddying of the rose-flake.

In stanza 28 the poet's syntactical control breaks down, as well as his ability to find a single adequate literal name for "it," the apparition of Christ to the nun, walking towards her on the water in the moment of her salvation:

> But how shall I . . . make me room there:
> Reach me a . . . Fancy, come faster –
> Strike you the sight of it? look at it loom there
> Thing that she . . . there then! the Master
> *Ipse*, the only one, Christ, King, Head. . . .

Rather than being in happy correspondence, Hopkins' theological thought and its linguistic underthought are at cross-purposes. They have a structure of chiasmus. The theological thought depends on the notion of an initial unity that has been divided or fragmented and so could conceivably be reunified. The linguistic underthought depends on the notion of an initial bifurcation that could not by any conceivable series of linguistic transformations, such as those that make up the basic poetic strategies of Hopkins' verse, reach back to any primal word. There is no such word. Hopkins' linguistic underthought subverts his Catholic overthought. Though not published until 1889, Walter Pater's essay "Aesthetic Poetry" was written in 1868, six years before Hopkins composed "The Wreck of the Deutschland." In his essay, Pater argued that "Greek poetry, medieval or modern poetry, projects above the realities of its time, a world in which the forms of things are transfigured." For Pater, all poetry is an idealization, a transfiguration of the raw material of sensation: "Of that transfigured world this new poetry takes possession, and sublimates beyond it another still fainter or more spectral, which is literally an artificial or 'earthly paradise.' "[16]

Although Pater's remarks are meant to describe Pre-Raphaelite poetry, or, more narrowly, the poetry of William Morris, they apply also to the "examples" cited above in this essay. The Victorian writers tended to be strongly committed to one version or other of a mimetic doctrine of literature, whether the imitation in question involved a copying of Nature or a copying of subjective "realities." Yet despite this commitment, their works also tend to contain a version of what might be called the linguistic moment: the moment when language as such, the means of representation in literature, becomes problematic, something to be interrogated, explored, or thematized in itself. In the work of many prominent Victorian writers, for example, in Ruskin, in Meredith, in Hopkins, or in Pater, this linguistic moment becomes explicit enough and prolonged enough so that it can displace Nature or human nature as the primary focus of imaginative activity.

The linguistic moment tends to involve a recognition of the irreducibly figurative nature of language, a seeing of language not as a mere instrument for expressing something that could exist without it – a state of mind or an element of Nature – but as in one way or another creative, inaugurating, constitutive (but constitutive of what?). Also of moment in the linguistic moment is a more or less explicit rejection of unitary origin. Single sources are replaced by some self-generating diacritical structure of repetition with a difference. This mode of repetition exists in three planes or dimensions. Nature or "reality" itself is seen, as by Ruskin, according to the principle of the identity of indiscernibles. Each leaf, wave, stone, flower, or bird is different from all others. Their similarity to one another arises against the ground of this basic dissimilarity. In a similar way, language is related to what it names across the gap of its incorrigible difference from its referent. Within language itself, the relation of sign to sign, of a literary work to the precursor work that it brings to a strange new flowering after date, is, once again, a similarity based on discontinuity and difference.

The appearance in the Victorian writers of a momentum toward concern with the medium of literature rather than with its subject matter suggests that for the Victorians too, as for all writers generally in the Western tradition, literature is distinguished from other uses of language by the explicitness of its orientation toward language rather than by thematic concerns for Nature or for selfhood. This orientation, however, can only be expressed in language that invites its thematic misreading. The shift from Nature and self to language can only be expressed in terms drawn figuratively from Nature and the self, therefore always liable to be taken literally. The study of literature should certainly cease to take the mimetic referentiality of literature for granted. Such a properly literary discipline would cease to be exclusively a repertoire of ideas, of themes, and of the varieties of human psychology. It would become once more philology, rhetoric, an investigation of the epistemology of tropes. This shift, however, would not lead to some happy purification making the study of literature a branch of "the human sciences" without tears. It would only put the philologist, lover of words, more painfully within the baffling shifts between referentiality and the refusals of referentiality that make up the intimate life of any literary text.

Notes

* This essay first appeared in a collection of essays by various authors entitled *Nature and the Victorian Imagination*. The paragraphs on Gerard Manley Hopkins are incorporated in revised form here and there in the extended chapter on Hopkins in *The Linguistic Moment* (Princeton, N.J.: Princeton University Press, 1985).

1. See, in this connection, John Paterson's description of Hardy's characterization of persons through natural images in "Lawrence's Vital Source: Nature and Character in Thomas Hardy," *Nature and the Victorian Imagination*, U.C. Knoepflmacher and G.B. Tennyson, eds (Berkeley: University of California Press, 1977), pp. 455–69.
2. Robert Browning, "Fra Lippo Lippi," *The Works of Robert Browning*, F. G. Kenyon, ed., 10 vols. (London, 1912), IV, p. 113.
3. Glenn Most, in an unpublished paper on George Eliot, has called my attention to the problems of exemplification.
4. A. A. Milne, *Winnie-the-Pooh* (New York, 1950), p. 60.
5. George Eliot, *Adam Bede, Works of George Eliot*, Cabinet Edition (Edinburgh and London, n.d.), pp. 147–8.
6. William Wordsworth, *The Prelude*, Ernest de Selincourt, ed., 2nd ed. revised by Helen Darbishire (Oxford, 1959), p. 211.
7. Henry James, *Washington Square* (New York, 1950), pp. 193, 195.
8. William Wordsworth, "Tintern Abbey," *The Poetical Works*, Ernest de Selincourt, ed., (Oxford, 1944), II, pp. 262.
9. Henry James, *The Wings of the Dove, The Novels and Tales of Henry James*, New York Edition (New York, 1909), XIX, p. 124.
10. The quotations from *Wuthering Heights* are from the Norton Critical Edition, William M. Sale, Jr., ed. (New York, 1972), pp. 74, 198–9.
11. George Meredith, *Works*, Memorial Edition (London, 1910), XVII, p. 189.
12. Thomas Hardy, *Tess of the d'Urbervilles, Writings of Thomas Hardy*, Anniversary Edition (New York and London, [1920]), I, pp. 24, 34, 84. "Nature's holy plan" is from Wordsworth's "Lines Written in Early Spring," line 22.
13. See Bruce Johnson's discussion of *Tess* in chapter fifteen of *Nature and the Victorian Imagination*, pp. 259–77.
14. Florence Emily Hardy, *The Life of Thomas Hardy: 1840–1928* (London and New York, 1965), p. 116.
15. *Further Letters of Gerard Manley Hopkins*, Claude Colleer Abbott, ed. (London, 1956), pp. 253, 252.
16. Walter Pater, *Appreciations* (London, 1889), pp. 213–14.

12

Béguin, Balzac, Trollope and the double double analogy

Albert Thibaudet a dit un jour – en passant, et comme s'il ne se doutait pas des prolongements possibles de son idée – que *la Comédie humaine* était "l'imitation de Dieu le Père." C'était mettre le doigt sur l'origine profonde du génie de Balzac, sur le sens de son angoisse, de sa souffrance, et sur la relation qui le lie à ses personnages.
(Albert Thibaudet said one day – in passing, and as if he did not doubt that his idea had possible extensions – that *The Human Comedy* was "the imitation of God the Father." To say that was to put the finger on the profound origin of Balzac's genius, on the meaning of his anguish, of his suffering, and on the relation that linked that to his personages.)

(Albert Béguin, *Balzac lu et relu*)[1]

Then he thought of the pelican feeding its young with blood from its own breast, but he gave no utterance to that either . . .

(Anthony Trollope, *The Warden*)[2]

In the beginning was the Word, and the Word was with God, and the Word was God. The same was in the beginning with God. All things were made by him; and without him was not any thing made that was made.

(John 1:1–3)

Quand j'étais petit et qu'il me vint une soeur, la bonne me dit ce qu'on dit aux enfants: – *Votre soeur a été trouvée sous un chou pendant la nuit.* J'allai voir sous les choux chaque matin avec une persévérance inoüie au jeune âge, et je n'y trouvai rien que des herbes. Quand je devins grand, et que je demandai, lors de ma première communion, au bon vieillard qui nous catéchisait, où Dieu avait pris le monde, il ne me dit pas précisément *sous un chou*, mais il me dit ces belles paroles de saint Jean: – *Au commencement était le Verbe, et le Verbe était en Dieu*. Personne à mon âge n'aurait pu comprendre le sens de cette phrase, sur laquelle sont basées toutes les philosophies, et qui peut-être les résume. Aussi voulais-je, comme tous les incrédules, *du positif*, non pas des idées,

> mais des faits. Je lui demandai donc d'où venait ce Verbe. – De Dieu, me dit-il.
>
> (When I was little and a sister arrived for me, the nurse said to me what one says to children: – *Your sister was found under a cabbage during the night.* I went to look under the cabbages each morning with a perseverance unheard of in one so young, and I did not find anything there but weeds. When I grew up, and when I asked, at the time of my first communion, of the good old man who catechized us, where God had taken the world from, he did not exactly say to me *under a cabbage*, but he said to me Saint John's beautiful words: – *In the beginning was the Word, and the Word was with God, and the Word was God.* Nobody of my age would have been able to understand the meaning of that sentence, on which all philosophies are based, and which perhaps summarizes them. I also wanted, like all disbelievers, *something positive*, not ideas, but facts. I therefore asked him where this Word came from. – From God, he answered.)
>
> (Honoré de Balzac, Preface to *Ecce Homo*)[3]

My aim is to explore briefly the meaning of two analogies and the relation between them. The first analogy is that borrowed by Albert Béguin from Albert Thibaudet comparing Balzac to God the Father. The second is that mute comparison Mr Harding makes, in Anthony Trollope's *The Warden*, between his own act of sacrifice and the sacrifice of God the Son. God the Father, God the Son – what is the difference between comparing the act of literary creation, the act of story-telling, the act of moral choice, or the act of literary criticism to the act of one of these or to the act of the other? Since the theological figures in question are both familial and linguistic, in fact what is in question here is a double double analogy.

Before trying to answer this question, however, let me propose two analogies of my own. When I think of the effect on my conception of what literary criticism might be of my reading, around 1953, first of Marcel Raymond, and then, soon after, of Georges Poulet, Albert Béguin, Jean Rousset, Jean-Pierre Richard, Jean Starobinski, and Gaston Bachelard, I am reminded of a passage in George Eliot's *Middlemarch*. Marcel Raymond I read first in the English translation, published in 1950, of *De Baudelaire au surréalisme*. It became immediately a precious book for me, both as an evidence of the power of poetry and as evidence of a power in criticism I had not before encountered. The reading of this book and then of Georges Poulet's first volume of the *Études sur le temps humain* as much marked an epoch in my life as did Dorothea's first encounter with Rome, in George Eliot's novel, mark an epoch in *her* life:

> To those who have looked at Rome with the quickening power of a

> knowledge which breathes a growing soul into all historic shapes, and traces out the suppressed transitions which unite all contrasts, Rome may still be the spiritual centre and interpreter of the world. But let them conceive one more historical contrast: the gigantic broken revelations of that Imperial and Papal city thrust abruptly on the notions of a girl who had been brought up in English and Swiss Puritanism, fed on meagre Protestant histories and on art chiefly of the hand-screen sort. . . . Forms both pale and glowing took possession of her young sense, and fixed themselves in her memory even when she was not thinking of them, preparing strange associations which remained through her after-years.[4]

The fit is not perfect. The analogy is not exact. One of the issues here, in fact, is the question of what one might mean by an "exact analogy." Nevertheless, I can say that the work of the Geneva critics took possession of my imagination as decisively as Rome did of the imagination of Dorothea. As the experience of Rome altered forever Dorothea's way of seeing, so Geneva criticism has determined, often probably in strange fashions, the ways I read English and American literature and write about them. As Rome for George Eliot is not so much a thing in itself as a power of interpretation, "the spiritual centre and interpreter of the world," so Geneva criticism has been for me a means of access to a whole world of French and German literature. It was a world which my own education had given only in imperfect glimpses, by way of "meagre histories." No doubt also that mediation depended on my own power to "breathe a growing soul into all historic shapes," since the reading of criticism, like the reading of literature proper, requires an act of imaginative adherence, of identification, on the part of the reader. This is that transmission from consciousness to consciousness to consciousness about which Georges Poulet has written so eloquently. This transmission depends at every stage on the reader's power to "breathe a soul" into those dead letters on the page, traces left by the "soul" who wrote them. Moreover, as Dorothea did not come to Rome without some culture of her own, that English Protestant culture of which George Eliot speaks so disparagingly, so I had been formed, at the time I first read the Geneva critics, by the not inglorious Anglo–American tradition of the New Criticism, chiefly, in my case, by Kenneth Burke, I. A. Richards, William Empson, and G. Wilson Knight. This was my first filiation in criticism, my primary sonship. The encounter with Geneva criticism was a new fathering and a second birth, so that my work, to extrapolate this second analogy a little further, has been the product of a genetic crossing, more recently crossed again by other forms of European and American criticism, to create, no doubt, something odd enough. It might even be like a *lusus naturae* generated by recombinant-DNA molecules made by procedures of gene-splicing. I suspect, however, that anyone who wished to do so could trace out the suppressed transitions which unite these contrasts among ways of doing criticism.

The relation between these two analogies – the linguistic one which sees Rome or Geneva criticism as the "interpreter of the world," and the genetic one which thinks in terms of paternal power and the father–son relation – are in fact at issue in the comparison between Balzac and Trollope I want to explore. I must first here testify, however, to the way Geneva criticism has determined once and for all my sense of what literary criticism can do in the way of providing intimate access to the thought of others and thereby serving as the interpreter of the world. Here and now, then, in the context of this celebration of the work of Marcel Raymond and Albert Béguin, I express my profound homage to the Geneva critics, the homage of one who dares to call himself at least in part a son, at any rate a foster-son.

To return to the two analogies comparing Balzac to God the Father and and Trollope's character Septimus Harding to God the Son – it is easy to see that they form part of a complex hierarchical system which might be the basis of a full interpretation of Balzac, of Trollope, and of the relations between them. Only the barest sketch or groundplan of this can be made here. It will be a preliminary tracing out or a cutting of a *Grundriss*.

The theological metaphor comparing Balzac's creativity and that of his characters, those vicarious self-representations, to the divine creativity is the basis of Albert Béguin's interpretation of Balzac in *Balzac lu et relu*. In fact, it can be said to be the basis of all his criticism, from *L'âme romantique et le rêve* on. This analogy could even, without too much exaggeration, be said to be in one way or another the basis of all the work of the Geneva critics. If consciousness is, in that criticism, seen as a *point de départ* from which all in literature springs, which sustains it, and to which it returns, that concept of consciousness as a performative voice, as a creative power, is in its turn modeled on the Biblical concept of an omnipotent God who creates all things by the fiat of his Word. Or is it the other way around, the human conception of God modeled analogically on man's sense of himself and of the powers of his mind? In any case, the theological analogy is the indispensable means of thinking about literature as the product of a consciousness. One of the strengths of Béguin's book on Balzac, as of Geneva criticism generally, is to have recognized this and to have explored the manifold implications of the theological analogy. If Balzac's own creativity is like that of God the Father, his characters in turn – misers, lovers, artists, politicians, courtesans, great ladies, men and women all hungry for power – reflect or express his own creativity, just as the narrator of his novels, different from himself in speaking of those characters as if they were real, is his vicar, sharing and projecting his creative voice, serving as its indispensable instrument. Balzac's critic in turn, the Béguin of *Balzac lu et relu*, renews Balzac's own creative power. The critic repeats in his turn the imperative which brings the heterocosm of Balzac's vast literary universe into being. From God to the author to the narrator to the characters to the critic there may at every level and between every term be drawn an analogy which could be explored in detail.

The same thing might be said for Trollope, his narrator, his characters, and his critic, except that here the appropriate theological analogy is with the sacrificial "Thy will be done" of Christ. Between Trollope and Balzac, moreover, at every point of each sequence of analogies, there would be a further analogy to explore, an analogy in difference, as Christ repeats God the Father with a difference. An example would be that strange parallel between the hyperbolic self-assertive will of Balzac's characters and the quiet obstinacy which is nevertheless an act of irresistibly efficacious willing on the part of Trollope's characters.

The exploration of such a ramifying network of analogies is especially appropriate for this colloquium, not only because the forty-four novels of Anthony Trollope are the closest thing in English literature to *la Comédie humaine*, analogous to it in abundance and scope, and in the creation of a whole world with its own laws and with characters who recur from novel to novel. Such an exploration is also appropriate because my understanding of our English Balzac, Anthony Trollope, owes so much to conversations over the years with Georges Poulet. It is also appropriate because several among the Geneva critics besides Béguin – Poulet himself and Jean-Pierre Richard especially – have written admirably about Balzac. They have presented me with models of how one might write in small compass and yet comprehensively about authors like Balzac and Trollope. The works of such authors fill many volumes in which the same themes and motifs are presented over and over and yet with subtle variations which make accurate generalization by synecdoche a critical act of extreme difficulty. Here I shall avoid that difficulty rather than solving it by taking as my focus, my part for whole, the novels by Balzac and Trollope which serve as genuine *points de départ* in each case. Each is a point of departure in the sense of being the first novel which represents the characteristic genius of its author and which presents, for the first time, his characteristic themes and strategies of narration. In each case the novel in question functions as the germ for the vast multitude of novels to come from each pen. What *La peau de chagrin* is for Balzac, *The Warden* is for Trollope.

Balzac first, then. What does it mean when Béguin, following Thibaudet, says Balzac's creativity is "like" that of God the Father? It means that

Balzac has the power to create an alternate world to that of the creation, with its own laws, its own time, its own characteristic population, its own atmosphere of a distinctive color and texture. Though this alternate world is brought into existence by language, the words on the pages of Balzac's novels, or the words spoken by Balzac himself through the mouth of his narrators, this language is the instrument of a hyperbolic will, a will to create, to dominate, and to know. This will is seen by Balzac as a kind of material energy, an electric fluid which tends to expand, to transform everything after its own measure, and to move toward limitless command. If *la Comédie humaine* is the triumphant product of such a will, all the characters within the vast globe of the *Comédie* – artists, lovers, criminals, usurers, financiers, politicians, harlots, fine ladies – are in their turn so many incarnations of a similar will to power.

What then of God's own creation, the physical and social worlds which are already there? What of Balzac's famous "realism," his desire to copy exactly all the multitudinous details of French life during the Restoration? Béguin pays full homage to this submission to the real, as indeed one would expect in someone with his recognition of the substantial "thereness" of the cultural world and of the incarnated condition of terrestrial man. How does he reconcile Balzac the realist with Balzac the "visionary"? It would seem that Béguin's interpretation of Balzac is caught in the irreconcilable contradiction between two notions of imitation, the imitation by a man with God-given genius and volition of the manner of production whereby God fathered forth the world and, on the other hand, that servile imitation which takes the form of an exact copy, the work mirroring the world. This is what George Eliot in *Adam Bede* called the "faithful representating of commonplace things."

Here the principle of analogy comes to Béguin's rescue. It is in fact a system of analogies which has as its head or as its ground the *Logos* of God. That *Logos* is the principle of the principle of analogy. To imitate God the Father in his manner of production is to imitate the real world too, natural and social, since material reality also has God as its source, and "like father, like son." Moreover, those Balzacian characters, children of his radiantly productive imagination and inhabitants of the second universe of literature he has created, will at the same time, by a happy resemblance, a parallelism at once natural and divine, correspond rigorously to the nature of real people in the real world. They thereby fulfill simultaneously the requirements of both kinds of mimesis:

> Les créatures de Balzac . . . confondent avec de pauvres désirs matériels l'élan qui les jette à la possession de l'absolu ou à la connaissance illimitée. Balzac les regarde se tromper ainsi sur leurs vraies espérances, et il les aime

> dans leur erreur, dans leur aveuglement, parce qu'il est le dieu qui les a créées à son image et qui les connaît mieux qu'elles ne se connaissent. Il devine surtout, – lui qui tend toujours à déceler les grandes ressemblances et à découvrir l'unité cachée sous les multiples apparences, – que chacun des êtres qui habitent son univers est, comme lui-même, un chercheur d'absolu et un assoiffé d'éternité. Et puisque les créatures de son imagination sont ainsi, il en conclut, – pour lui la conclusion de l'un à l'autre est logique et impérative, – que les créatures de Dieu, les simples créatures vivantes, leur resemblent, ressemblent à Balzac.
>
> (Balzac's creatures . . . confuse with poor material desires the elan that drives them toward the possession of the absolute or toward limitless knowledge. Balzac watches them fool themselves in this way about their true hopes, and he loves them in their error, in their blindness, because he is the god who has created them in his own image and who knows them better than they know themselves. He divines above all – that each of the beings who inhabit his universe is, like Balzac himself, a seeker after the absolute and someone thirsty for eternity. And since the creatures of his imagination are like this, he concludes from that – for him the conclusion of the one from the other is imperative – that God's creatures, simple living creatures, resemble them, resemble Balzac.)[5]

One knows already the reasons why this immense effort to achieve dominion by means of the creative will is doomed to defeat, both for all Balzac's characters, and for Balzac himself. It is a defeat admirably symbolized by the fatal shrinking of Raphaël Valentin's wild ass's skin. This shrinking may be stopped by no means, spiritual or material. If the creative power of willing is a material energy, a kind of reservoir of the fluid of volition given to each man and woman, but especially to the artistic genius, by God, then that reservoir is finite. It has been loaned to the son by the father. What the son has comes only from his father, by genetic inheritance. What comes from the father must return to him. To be human is to wish, to will, to have desires. These desires are in fact absolute, a thirst for eternity. This thirst must, however, express itself as a desire for this or that earthly cup. By an inevitable law, each wish, each act of will, uses up some fraction of the treasury of volition-fluid. Ultimately the accumulation of wishes exhausts that treasury, the man or woman dies, and the portion of energy, down to the last drop, returns to its source. It returns with the plus value or interest for God the Father of his pleasure in witnessing the display of productive activity by his creatures as they use themselves up. Bit by bit the wild ass's skin inexorably shrinks, bringing Valentin closer and closer to death. He exerts his will in spite of himself, since for Balzac to live is to will. In the end, Balzac, like all his creatures, is brought to that place where Georges Poulet, in his essay on Balzac in *La distance intérieure*, chooses to leave him:

> Et la dernière attitude, dans laquelle nous devons laisser Balzac, est encore une fois celle de l'homme de désir; c'est-à-dire de l'être que, éternellement, se projette au-delà de son être:
>
> Je vis une grande ombre. Debout et dans une attitude ardente, cette âme *dévorait les espaces du regard, ses pieds restaient attachés par le pouvoir de Dieu sur le dernier point de cette ligne où elle accomplissait sans cesse la tension pénible par laquelle nous projetons nos forces* lorsque nous voulons prendre notre élan, comme des oiseaux prêts à s'envoler. Je reconnus un homme . . . Par chaque *parcelle de temps*, il semblait éprouver sans faire un seul pas la fatigue de traverser *l'infini qui le séparait* du paradis où sa vue plongeait sans cesse.
>
> (And the final attitude, in which we must leave Balzac, is once more that of the man of desire; that is to say the being who, perpetually, projects himself beyond his own being:
>
> I saw a great shadow. Upright and in an ardent attitude, that soul *devoured space with his look, his feet remained attached by God's power on the last point of that line where it exercised unceasingly the painful tension by which we project our forces* whenever we want to fulfil our elan, like birds ready to fly. I recognized a man . . . in each *fragment of time*, he seemed to experience without taking a single step the fatigue of traversing *the infinity that separated him* from that paradise into which his vision ceaselessly plunged.)[6]

"Par le pouvoir de Dieu" – no finite power can ultimately be other than impotent if it pits itself against an infinite potency. Moreover, as Béguin demonstrates, that power of willing in Balzac, which seems at first, especially in Balzac himself and in the artist-characters in his work, so God-given and spiritual, becomes finally, when it attempts to reach absolute autonomous dominion, angelism, a refusal of incarnation and creaturely dependence. It becomes a Promethean or diabolical defiance of God which will receive the punishment it deserves. Satan too is an imitator or ape of God. All Balzac's work is haunted by a fear of the ambiguity or double-nature of spiritual power as it exerts its dominion over nature. "Mais l'esprit," says Béguin, "a d'inquiétantes ressemblances avec les puissances infernales. Une peur règne sur toute l'oeuvre de Balzac, qui est la peur du surnaturel, de son intrusion dans le monde de la nature." (But the spirit has disquieting resemblances to the infernal powers. A fear reigns over all the work of Balzac, which is the fear of the supernatural, of its intrusion into the world of nature.)[7]

What of Balzac's critic, the last mode of willing in the sequence, the last link in the chain of analogies leading down from God? Is there anything in the act of criticism as conceived by the Geneva critics which corresponds to the *échec* of Balzac himself and to the *échec* of the creatures of his imagination? Here the interpreter enters a shadowy realm of speculation, where he feels on uncertain ground, but it may be said that a mode of criticism which defines itself as functioning through the identification of one consciousness with another and which defines consciousness as power, energy, or élan, should in principle add nothing to the consciousness with which it identifies itself. It is therefore apparently caught between the bad alternatives of being an exact doubling of what already exists or of falsifying it by adding something of itself to it. It owes its power, in both senses of "owe," to the power of the work, as Balzac owes his power, in both senses, to God. At best, so it seems, such criticism can concentrate the power of the work criticized by distilling it so that a single essay may contain all the potency of many volumes. Moreover, if the work itself culminates in defeat, the critic must, in his reliving of that work, suffer again the same defeat. He must be led again to that moment in which the great artistic creator, by the power of God, remains poised, paralyzed, face to face with a great gulf, measuring all the infinite distance between himself and the infinite energy he would possess. This may be the case, but to suffer or resuffer to its bitter end such a defeat is a great victory, perhaps the only sort of victory which literature or criticism may achieve.

If this is where the analogy between Balzac and God the Father finally leads, what alternative journey is initiated by the counter analogy between Trollopian man and God the Son? It would seem at first that the two journeys would be so different as to be in no way analogous. The world of Trollope does not seem except in superficial ways at all like that of Balzac. Far from being men and women hungry for absolute power, his characters, at least the good ones, are English ladies and gentlemen, models of rectitude, only quietly self-assertive. Their self-assertion, moreover, characteristically takes the form of resignation or of self-sacrifice, as Septimus Harding, in *The Warden*, resigns his wardenship in his soft-spoken way (" 'But I shall resign,' said the warden, very, very meekly."),[8] or as Trollope's heroines give themselves to the men they love. Nor is there in Trollope's narration anything like the vigorous, ostentatious analysis of Balzac's narrator, an open expression of the will to dominion over the imagined characters and their world, an opaque screen of language which mediates between the reader and that world, through which the reader must penetrate to reach the characters. Trollope's narrator quietly submits himself to his characters. He allows them to speak for themselves, or speaks for them in that indirect discourse of which Trollope is so great a master. The Trollopian narrator makes himself a medium so transparent that his language and the language of the character cannot be distinguished. Trollope, like Balzac, is a realist. He is anxious to represent comprehensively the manners, values, and ways of life of the Victorian middle and upper classes. His procedures of realism, however, do not involve a violent taking possession, or an exhaustive inventory and analysis. Rather, he is content to let these things be and, so it seems, to transpose them within his fiction without transforming them, as in that description of his work by Nathaniel Hawthorne which Trollope so proudly quotes in *An Autobiography*. Trollope's novels, wrote Hawthorne in 1860, are "just as real as if some giant had hewn a great lump out of the earth and put it under a glass case, with all its inhabitants going about their daily business, and not suspecting that they were being made a show of."[9]

In spite of these qualities of passivity, self-effacing transparency, and abnegation, however, Trollope and his characters are men and women of power. Their power is modeled more on that of Christ the Logos than on that of God the infinite paternal power, as the parallel Trollope draws between Mr Harding and the pelican who feeds its young with blood from its own breast makes explicit. What is the difference between the two models? The difference between overt self-assertion and quiet self-denial is clear enough, but exactly what kind of exercise of power is self-denial?

The Christ-like act of power differs fundamentally in two ways from the God-like act of power. If human will-power is for Balzac a finite reservoir of energy, hence inevitably used up in being used, the exercise of will for Trollope is a matter of performative language, as its analogy with Christ the Word might suggest. The warden's meek "But I shall resign," makes something happen. It turns him from being the Warden of Hiram's Hospital back into being the mere Precentor of the Cathedral. It also heals, as no other act could do, the fissure which threatens to destroy the happy clerical community of Barchester. Such a linguistic act of will does not use up any energy and so is infinitely repeatable in different forms. It draws on an inexhaustible resource. Such an act of power leaves the one who exercises it still with as much vitality as he had before, or perhaps with even more.

The second difference is in the mode of repetition. Since the volitional fluid of Balzac or of his characters is of the same substance as the infinite reservoir of God's will-power, in fact part of that divine will, and since that will intends to dominate things by possessing them, transposing them, and so repeating them (in love, in art, or in worldly power), the repetition, like the repetitive power, is of the same substance as what it repeats and so submissive to it. On the other hand, Harding's act of resignation, in its repetition of Hiram's foundation of the Hospital of which he is warden, and in the repetition by both of Christ's charity, like the falling in love of Trollope's heroines, and in fact like Trollope's creation of his novels, repeats its models with a difference. It thereby brings absolute novelty into the world. Moreover, it is autonomous, founded only on an act of "conscience" whereby the self serves as a ground for itself in a tautological or circular will to will, as in the title of one of the greatest of Trollope's novels: *He Knew He Was Right.* "I have very little but an inward and an unguided conviction of my own to bring me to this step," says Mr Harding in his letter of resignation.[10] Three times he uses the word "conscience" to name the basis of his decision to resign, just as Trollope himself, in his autobiography, says that to the good novelist it is "a matter of deep conscience how he shall handle those characters by whose words and doings he hopes to interest his readers,"[11] and just as Archdeacon Grantley was not modeled on any living clergymen, even though readers found him a marvel of verisimilitude. The archdeacon was, says Trollope,

> the simple result of an effort of my moral consciousness. It was such as that, in my opinion, that an archdeacon should be, – or, at any rate, would be with such advantages as an archdeacon might have; and lo! an archdeacon was produced, who has been declared by competent authorities to be a real archdeacon down to the very ground.[12]

"And lo! an archdeacon was produced"! – Trollope's creativity, though it seems, like the moral decisions of his characters, so meek, so subservient to the already existing world it apparently copies, is like the creativity of Balzacian genius as interpreted by Béguin in at least one way. It is an imitation of the divine creativity rather in renewing in its own way the divine mode of production than in being a slavish copy of something already existing. The difference is that the productive acts of Trollope and of his characters are freer than Balzac's, more autonomous, more self-generating, since they are performed by language rather than by any more substantial instrument.

The familial metaphor appears in Trollope alongside the linguistic one affirming the power of the pen to create *ex nihilo.* That familial metaphor, however, is the figure of auto-fecundation and spontaneous self-generation, rather than an image of subservience to the father. An extraordinary passage in *An Autobiography* mingles the two metaphors to describe Trollope's intense joy in the exercise of a generative power based on nothing but his own say-so. It is a creation of the self by itself which goes by way of the detour of the creation of imaginary characters who then become the support of that self, the self and its creatures creating one another. Here is Trollope's description of the writing he has done "at some quiet spot in the mountains":

> At such times I have been able to imbue myself thoroughly with the characters I have had in hand. I have wandered alone among the rocks and woods, crying at their grief, laughing at their absurdities, and thoroughly enjoying their joy. I have been impregnated with my own creations till it

> has been my only excitement to sit with the pen in my hand, and drive my team before me at as quick a pace as I could make them travel.[13]

Against the sovereign pen with which Trollope drives his horses in the irresistible momentum of his creativity (it is a pen which is also a self-impregnating organ of generation), one may put that walking-stick of Balzac which was inscribed, "I smash every obstacle," or its ironic counterpart in Franz Kafka, "Every obstacle smashes me,"[14] or that cane of Laurence Sterne's Corporal Trim with which he executes the flourish in the air that furnishes Balzac with the epigraph for *La peau de chagrin*. The latter is a zig-zag wandering vertical line which parodies the Hogarthian line of beauty, but which gradually becomes, in successive editions of Balzac's novel, a horizontal snake with head and tail – origin, end, and orientation – matching the concentrated élan of the Balzacian will.

In place of Balzac's world of a gradual and inexorable using up, a using up which is made unavoidable by the unbroken continuities and firm causal bindings which tie every part of Balzac's universe to every other part, Trollope's world (both the realm of his own literary creativity and the social world of love, marriage, the redistribution of property and social roles which that literature presents), is a place of continuous and inexhaustible novelty. It is therefore the place of unpredictable discontinuities. It is the place of the perpetual introduction of new commitments of the self, new creations of the imagination. These are based on ungrounded and unpredictable acts of language, incommensurate with any model. ("But I shall resign"; "and lo! an archdeacon was produced.") In the same way there was no model for Christ's unparalleled act of taking the sins of the world upon himself with his, "nevertheless, not as I will, but as thou wilt" (Matthew 26: 39).

Could there be, one may finally ask, with the utmost of tentative caution, a mode of literary criticism which would be analogous to Trollope's creativity and to that of his characters? Such criticism would repeat the work with a difference rather than exactly. It would repeat in its own way the productive power of the language of the work. It would thereby see the work as an inexhaustible resource of further acts of production rather than as something that can be worked through only once, imitated as exactly as possible, and then dismissed.

It would seem that I have established a firm barrier between my two analogies, that defining power as material will and that defining power as performative language. It might even seem that I have calculated my analysis so as to seem to favor my English novelist over the French one. Of course this is not the case. The means of God's creation is, was, and always will be the Word. God's *Fiat Lux*, moreover, is the archetype of efficacious performative language. Christ the Word has always coexisted with God the Father, "from the beginning," "with" him and at the same time the "same" as him, as the opening of *The Gospel According to St. John* says. All analogy is of the Word and by the Word. To imitate God is to imitate Christ, without whom "was not any thing made that was made." Christ is therefore the principle or voice by means of which things may be said to be analogous, named according to the same *logos*. Even Raphaël Valentin, in *La peau de chagrin*, who seems to want, perhaps diabolically to want, God's omnipotence, is said in the end to suffer "la passion de Dieu" (the passion of God) and to be "un agneau pascal" (a paschal lamb).[15] In the other direction, to imitate Christ is to imitate God, for Christ's self-sacrifice in his "Thy will be done" was after all the act of God, of one member of that Trinity which is three in one, in which what one does all three do. Like all God's acts, Christ's self-sacrifice was free, not grounded in anything outside itself, as much so as the original performative "Let there be light." The original double doubling of the analogy I am exploring is in God or in the language by which Christian theology speaks of God. It is there in the elliptical relation between God and Christ and there in the interference or non-symmetry of the two basic metaphors by which that relation must be thought.

Both these metaphors or analogies are absolutely necessary to thinking about that relation, and yet the relation between the two metaphors is a-logical. It cannot be thought without an inhibiting torsion of the mind which leaves it baffled. In the familial metaphor the Son is generated by the Father in an autonomous act of paternity. The Son owes all to the Father and, as in Milton's *Paradise Lost*, Christ speaks and acts only in the name of the Father, as his supplement or vicar. On the other hand is the linguistic image of God as creating by means of speech acts. According to this image, God is dependent on Christ for his power of creation, for he creates by means of the Word. "Without him was not any thing made that was made," and the Word must therefore pre-exist God's use of it in his thunderous "Fiat!" The mind cannot logically think according to both of these analogies at once, and yet it must, if the relation between God and Christ is to be conceived by the mind, in both the genetic and linguistic sense of "conceived." The mystery of human thinking repeats the mystery of the Trinity and cannot be separated from it.

If one thinks in terms of the family metaphor one can follow a regular and continuous series of emanations from Father to Son and then out to all parts of that creation God makes in the image of the Son. If one thinks in terms of the linguistic metaphor, the original performative Word of the Logos both governs all analogies and at the same time is free of them itself. It is not itself analogous. It is outside the system of analogies as their head word which makes it possible that analogies can exist. Insofar as that original Word is repeated in the lesser speech acts which are analogous to it, each of them is outside any system of analogies too, unlike the paternal–filial Logos in every way except in being unlike. This paradox of thinking by analogy governs all such thought, or, rather, undermines it. It forces the analogical to be illogical. This dismantling of the pyramid of orderly thought would extend also to my attempts here to use analogies to think through the problems of analogy in relation to Béguin, Balzac, and Trollope. I cannot speak in analogy of that which makes analogy possible, and yet I cannot speak of it except in analogies, analogies which are, after all, prescriptive rather than descriptive.

What does this mean for literature, for moral action, and for criticism? It means that there is no consciousness without language, in any of these realms, and vice versa, in a perpetual crisscross in which each defines and is the ground of the other, its absent center. It means a concept of language which is performative rather than referential. Such language serves as the ultimate principle of all analogies while at the same time untying the close correspondences among all the elements in the system of analogies I have described. Each is therefore analogous, has the same voice, word, or mind, as the other, rather in bringing into existence something unique, unheard of, impossible to measure by any common ratio, than in actually being in resonance. All analogies are analogical in both senses of the double antithetical prefix, *ana*, which means "upward," "according to," "back," "backward," "reversed," "again," "anew," all at once.

Insofar as literary creation, whether Balzacian or Trollopean – insofar as moral action, whether of the overtly willing kind of Balzac's characters (which finds its archetype in Raphaël Valentin), or of the quietly obstinate kind of Trollope's heroes and heroines (which finds its type in Septimus Harding) – insofar as literary criticism, whether modeled, as Albert Béguin's seems to be, on the affirmations of a Balzac, a Novalis, or a Bernanos, or modeled, as another kind of criticism might be, on the more indirect Trollopean affirmations – insofar as all three of these are acts of consciousness which are simultaneously speech acts, they imitate God's autonomous performatives not by copying their results but by renewing their mode of generation. They thereby bring into the world the incommensurate, the unmeasured, the immeasurable, something which is inassimilable and has no analogy. In this the diabolical and the Christlike are strangely alike, opposite poles which mirror one another, as Béguin, Balzac, and Trollope in their different ways all knew, and as Gerard Manley Hopkins also knew and affirmed in "The Wreck of the Deutschland," where Christ is a "double-naturèd name" and so the basis of puns and double meanings in language, while puns are at the same time Satanic, as "Deutschland" is "double a desperate name":

> But Gertrude, lily, and Luther, are two of a town,
> Christ's lily and beast of the waste wood:
> From life's dawn it is drawn down,
> Abel is Cain's brother and breasts they have sucked the same.[16]

Insofar, finally, as consciousness or conscience (*conscience* in both its senses in French), whether in the criticism of the Geneva School or in any other uses of the concept, is theological in origin and cannot be detached from its place within the complex metaphysical system I have sketched, mind and word are at every point enigmatically and elliptically intertwined. Consciousness can be a *point de départ* only in the equivocal sense I have described. Consciousness is the constant renewal of an act of the mind which is also a speech act. It is dangerous, double-natured, as all speech acts are. An example is the way Septimus Harding's benign firmness in taking the decision to resign upon himself may become, in Louis Trevelyan, the hero of Trollope's *He Knew He Was Right*, the possibility of an infinite detour away from the human community.

Balzac as interpreted in Albert Béguin's admirable book, and Anthony Trollope, the English Balzac, are not the same, nor are the same modes of criticism quite appropriate to each. The differences between Trollope and Balzac are essential, but these differences are a different ratio or proportion of the same elements, a different *logos* within the *logos*. They represent different balances of the same elements rather than opposite poles. The title of Béguin's book is *Balzac lu et relu*. It contains the set of prefatory essays to individual novels by Balzac as well as *Balzac visionnaire*, just as the work of others of the Geneva critics, the work of Georges Poulet conspicuously, for example in his two essays on Balzac, is characterized by a freedom to return again and again to the same author and never to exhaust that author or the essays which may be written on his work. There is no doubt that Béguin's criticism of Balzac is a perpetually renewable creative act in its own right. Rather than being a mere copy of the Balzacian texts, it adds something new to them, a plus value or accrued interest of inestimable worth achieved by a submission to the work which is more like Harding's resignation than like Raphaël's will to power.

For both Balzac and Trollope, finally, and for the criticism appropriate to each, in different ways, there is no consciousness without the performative word, and no performative word without an "I" to perform. Neither can be said to be prior to the other, though exactly who this "I" is or exactly what happens when that "I" says, "But I shall resign," remains forever undecidable and unsayable, a vanishing point where subjectivity and word would coincide. The analogical relation between the two continues in a movement of literature, of moral action, and of criticism that may not be stilled in any fixed thought or in any fixed language.

Notes

1. (Paris, 1965), p. 65.
2. Oxford Classics Edition (London, 1963), p. 227.
3. *La Comédie humaine*, Collection l'Intégrale, vol. VI (Paris, 1966), p. 706.
4. Cabinet Edition (Edinburgh and London, n.d.), vol. I, ch. 20, pp. 295–7.
5. *Balzac lu et relu*, pp. 50–51.
6. (Paris, 1952), p. 193. The passage by Balzac is from *Les proscrits*.
7. *Balzac lu et relu*, p. 67.
8. *The Warden*, p. 227.
9. Oxford Classics Edition (London, 1961), p. 125.
10. *The Warden*, p. 236.
11. *An Autobiography*, pp. 189–90.
12. *ibid*., p. 80.
13. *ibid*,. pp. 151–2.
14. Quoted from Kafka by Philip Rahv in the "Introduction" to Franz Kafka, *Selected Short Stories*, tr. Willa and Edwin Muir (New York, 1952), p. xxi.
15. Collection l'Intégrale, Vol. VI, p. 516.
16. *Poems*, 4th ed. (London, 1967), p. 58.

13

Middlemarch, chapter 85

These things are a parable . . .

George Eliot, *Middlemarch*

All things in parables despise not we,
Lest things most hurtful lightly we receive;
And things that good are, of our souls bereave.

John Bunyan, *The Pilgrim's Progress*

Like more or less any passage or episode in *Middlemarch*, chapter 85 can be shown to exemplify most of the novel's themes and issues. It can stand by synecdoche for the whole. This, however, is not so much because it contains the whole novel in reduced similitude, like a little wave within a big wave, repeating the structure of the big one, to use one of George Eliot's own figures, but because it raises questions about the adequacy of similitude and synecdoche. As George Eliot says in the "Finale" of *Middlemarch*, employing once more one of the grand organizing metaphors of the novel, "the fragment of life, however typical, is not the sample of an even web." How can a fragment be typical, when it is not a valid sample? The answer lies in George Eliot's technique of "parable," to use her word for it, and on this I shall concentrate here.

Chapter 85 might be taken as a typical example of George Eliot's realism, the exact recording of speech and social fact along with that grave compassionate inwardness mixed with ironical judgment which characterizes her use of indirect discourse: "Some time, perhaps – when he was dying – he would tell her all: in the deep shadow of that time, when she held his hand in the gathering darkness, she might listen without recoiling from his touch. Perhaps. . . ." The chapter just before this one ends with Dorothea's refusal to tell her sister Celia how it came about that she and Will Ladislaw are to marry: "No, dear, you would have to feel with me, else you would never know." George Eliot's realism operates on the principle that knowledge of other human beings is only possible through sympathy or "feeling with." Chapter 85 has as a chief goal leading us to understand Bulstrode and his wife by making it possible for us to feel with them, even though sympathy, in Bulstrode's case, is combined with implacable judgment. Though Harriet Bulstrode does not know it, the man is a murderer as well as a thief.

Harriet Bulstrode's "duteous merciful constancy" is shown in this chapter, as well as earlier, in chapter 74, in the admirable episode in which she comes to her fallen husband and bids him, "Look up, Nicholas," to bring good out of evil. This happens despite that irrevocability of evil-doing on which George Eliot always insists. Good comes of evil in chapter 85 because Harriet's faithfulness to her husband leads him to do the one thing he can do to make amends to her and to her family. He enables Fred Vincy to find his vocation at last as the farmer-manager of Stone Court, which has of course become Bulstrode's property. To what degree does this depend on her ignorance of the right name by which her husband should be called? She renames his evil good, in part through her ignorance, and this enables him to do good. This question implicitly motivates the self-referential rhetoric of chapter 85. By "self-referential rhetoric" I mean the way the chapter accounts both for its own mode of narration and for the ethical judgments this mode supports. This occurs primarily in the epigraph and in the first two paragraphs. These set the stage for the narration proper of the conversation between Bulstrode and his wife.

It would seem that George Eliot builds the affirmations of chapter 85 on a straightforward deconstruction of both the narrative mode and the value judgments of *The Pilgrim's Progress*. George Eliot is among the most subtle of epigraph makers. Among the many ways in which she uses chapter epigraphs is as a demonstration of how not to do it. This makes an ironic clashing between epigraph and text. The juxtaposition of her chapter and a fragment from the trial of Faithful in the Vanity Fair section of *The Pilgrim's Progress* sets the abstractions of allegory against the minute psychological and social particulars of Victorian realism. These are two modes of faithfulness, faithfulness to spiritual realities as they were seen by Bunyan as against what George Eliot in *Adam Bede* calls "the faithful representing of commonplace things." Epigraph and text also oppose the basing of ethical judgments on God's all-seeing eye to the Feuerbachian basing of such judgments on interpersonal relations in society. In *The Pilgrim's Progress* the jury of what George Eliot calls "the persecuting passions," "Mr No-good, Mr Love-lust, Mr Live-loose," and the rest, brings in its verdict of guilty, but God sees and judges Faithful as faithful. After his martyrdom he ascends to heaven: "Now, I saw that there stood behind the multitude a chariot and a couple of horses, waiting for Faithful, who (so soon as his adversaries had dispatched him) was taken up into it, and straightway was carried up through the clouds, with sound of trumpet, the nearest way to the Celestial Gate" (Penguin, 1978, 134). "Now, I saw. . . .": the authority of *The Pilgrim's Progress* is that of the dream vision, or at any rate of what the title page calls "the similitude of a dream." This means, ultimately, the authority of God's clear-seeing and all-seeing eye, granted for the moment, in the dream, at least in similitude, to John Bunyan. What is the source of George Eliot's judicial authority? Presumably it is the human authority of sympathy or penetrating "feeling with." George Eliot as narrator exemplifies this in relation to her imaginary personages, and she exhorts her readers to share it if they are to understand and to judge correctly the imaginary characters of the novel or their own real neighbors.

In the first paragraph of the chapter proper George Eliot opposes her procedure to Bunyan's. This happens not, as the reader might expect, by distinguishing the mode of realistic fiction from that of religious allegory, but by opposing the pity we should feel for Bulstrode to the lack of pity we feel for the triumphant Faithful. Faithful, who is after all an allegorical "abstraction," is spoken of as if he were as much a real person as Nicholas Bulstrode: "When immortal Bunyan makes his picture of the persecuting passions bringing in their verdict of guilty, who pities Faithful?" Faithful knows he is denounced solely for the good in him, while Bulstrode is pitiable because he knows he is justifiably stoned for hypocrisy, "not for professing the Right, but for not being the man he professed to be." We feel admiration for Faithful but not pity, and in that sense *Middlemarch* is superior to *The Pilgrim's Progress*. The former enhances, as the latter does not, that sympathy for our erring and imperfect neighbors which is the basis of all right-doing and of all community cohesion.

The ground of the comparison between Faithful and Bulstrode, and the basic figure underlying the whole chapter, is the "real-life" situation of a man on trial, confronting a jury of his peers. This may occur either in an actual courtroom or in that more informal but no less implacably judicial situation of man surrounded, as Bulstrode is, by his neighbors in a closed community. Chapter 85 opposes not just two but several different ways of being on trial. It seeks, on this basis, to identify the grounds of right ethical judgment or the right naming of human acts. Who has the right to judge and to name, and how would we know the correct judgment has been made? Correct judgment is defined as correct denomination, naming the person and his deeds correctly as what they are. To call a person or a deed by its right name is proper realism or faithfulness in narration. The question of ethical judgment is, it can be seen, intimately associated with the question of the proper narrative mode.

The condemnation of Faithful in the courtroom of Vanity Fair by Mr No-good, Mr Malice, Mr Blindman, and the rest is parallel to the condemnation of Bulstrode by his neighbors. Faithful is named faithless, a heretic ("Mr Blindman, the foreman, said, I see clearly that this man is a heretic"), while Bulstrode is named thief, liar, hypocrite, if not murderer. The difference is that Faithful is not what he is named by his neighbors. He is renamed Faithful by God and by the visionary narrator. He is therefore not by any means pitiable. Bulstrode is what he is named by his peers. Therefore he is pitiable. The double structure of *The Pilgrim's Progress* sets God's true judgment against the false judgment of sinful man or "the persecuting passions." This construction, however, is dismantled. It is "deconstructed" by what George Eliot says of Bulstrode's ability to exonerate himself before the imaginary bar of the God to whom he prays. For George Eliot, God does not exist except as an individual or collective projection. It is therefore possible, in a false imaginary transaction with this nonexistent deity, to rename any bad act a good one by a species of metaphor or metamorphosis, as stolen money is "laundered" in another country, the black made white. The tendency in religious belief to baseless self-justification and hypocritical false renaming is the basis of George Eliot's repudiation of Christianity throughout her work: for example, in her early reviews, "Evangelical Teaching: Dr. Cumming" and "Worldliness and Other-Worldliness: The Poet Young." Of this false renaming the religious hypocrite Bulstrode is the most celebrated incarnation in the novels. Bulstrode's wife, on the other hand, is a real person, not an imaginary deity. Before her potential condemnation of him, Bulstrode shrinks into his usual secrecy. He "takes the fifth," so to speak, refuses to incriminate himself, and cries out for a lawyer:

> The duteous merciful constancy of his wife had delivered him from one dread, but it could not hinder her presence from being still a tribunal before which he shrank from confession and desired advocacy. His equivocations with himself about the death of Raffles had sustained the conception of an Omniscience whom he prayed to, yet he had a terror upon him which would not let him expose them to judgment by a full confession to his wife: the acts which he had washed and diluted with inward argument and motive, and for which it seemed comparatively easy to win invisible pardon – what name would she call them by? That she should ever silently call his acts Murder was what he could not bear. He felt shrouded by her doubt: he got strength to face her from the sense that she could not yet feel warranted in pronouncing that worst condemnation on him.

This admirably eloquent passage is the core of chapter 85. It is implicitly a devastating rejection of Bunyan's religious allegory. Bunyan's naming of Faithful as faithful in the name of his imaginary deity must be as unreal as Bulstrode's naming of his evil as good in the name of *his* invisible Omniscience. When one goes by the detour of a nonentity, one can turn anything into anything else. At the same time, the passage replaces the unreal religious tribunal with the real one of those direct I–thou relations which are the basis of right action and of community solidarity in George Eliot's Feuerbachian view of man. Allegory is set against realism. A false mode of ethical judgment and a false mode of literature are opposed to the right ground of ethics and the right kind of literature.

A moment's reflection, however, will show that things are not so simple here. George Eliot undermines her own affirmations at the same time as she dismantles those of Bunyan. For one thing, Bunyan is as much a realistic novelist as George Eliot is. To put this another way, she is as much an allegorist as he is. To call the jury which condemns Faithful a list of "persecuting passions" is clearly reductive. The allegorical names ("Mr Blindman, Mr No-good, Mr Malice, Mr Love-lust, Mr Live-loose, Mr Heady, Mr High-mind, Mr Enmity, Mr Liar, Mr Cruelty, Mr Hate-light, Mr Implacable") are as much kinds of persons as they are denominations of faculties or passions. The list is heterogeneous. It cannot be subsumed under a single conceptual type. The names of the jury exceed abstract allegory, as *The Pilgrim's Progress* does throughout. The names verge on becoming a list of metaphorical proper names such as people in the real world or in a realistic novel might have. In the same way, the power of Faithful, as of *The Pilgrim's Progress* as a whole, lies in the way he ceases to be an abstraction and comes to be taken as a real person by the reader. "Who pities Faithful?" We forget that the truthfulness of *The Pilgrim's Progress* lies not in its novelistic realism but in what these stand for, according to the law of language formulated in the epigraph from Hosea 12:10 on the title page: "I have used similitudes." Allegory as a mode is by no means incompatible with realism in the sense of psychological and social verisimilitude. Far from it. Allegory in fact is a name for literature in general in its uneasy combination of a referential dimension which supports and contradicts an abstract, conceptual, or linguistic dimension. The latter both is based on the referential dimension and denies it. Ethical judgment, which belongs simultaneously to the referential and to the conceptual dimension of literature, is caught between the two.

If *The Pilgrim's Progress* is both realistic and allegorical, the same thing may be said of *Middlemarch*. "Bulstrode," like the other names in *Middlemarch* or in any other realistic novel, or like the proper names of real people, shimmers with possible metaphorical meanings. Dorothea is not given her name for nothing, nor is Casaubon, nor Ladislaw, nor Lydgate. Bulstrode: strode like a bull? Bull-lode? Is Bulstrode not bulldung, according to a twentieth-century meaning of a more vulgar word signifying empty language, or is he not a "bull' in the good nineteenth-century sense of an Irish bull, a living contradiction or linguistic aporia? Bulstrode, heavy and lumpish, the Merdle of Middlemarch, blindly justifies his wrong exercise of power. If the jury in *The Pilgrim's Progress* incarnates "the ugly passions," Bulstrode, as I have said, "incarnates" George Eliot's theory of religious hypocrisy. He is an allegory or parable of that theory, just as George Eliot's scrupulously realistic description of a pier glass, in a famous passage at the opening of chapter 27 of *Middlemarch*, is a parable of the egoism of Rosamond or of all mankind. "These things are a parable. The scratches are events, and the candle is the egoism of any person now absent – of Miss Vincy, for example." *Middlemarch*, like *The Pilgrim's Progress*, is simultaneously realistic and parabolic throughout. The difference is in the mode of allegory. George Eliot does not replace allegory by realism but one kind of allegory by another.

However, George Eliot's condemnation of the false denominations of Bunyan's allegory also implicitly condemns her own procedure. Bunyan names Faithful Faithful on the basis of a nonexistent God. George Eliot names Bulstrode Pitiable. She makes that the basis of Harriet's sympathy for him, model of the sympathy we should all have for our erring neighbors. On the other hand, she shows us that his true name is Murderer. The chapter implies that if Harriet knew what we know of him she would be unable to maintain that sympathy for him which is the basis of her ability to draw good out of evil. The ethical and the epistemological dimensions of George Eliot's humanist allegory contradict one another. The ability to do good in George Eliot's novels always in one way or another depends on ignorance, while the novels themselves show over and over the terrible dangers of ignorance (for example, Dorothea's illusions about Casaubon in *Middlemarch*). The novels exhort the reader to clear-seeing knowledge and imperturbably provide him with the sort of knowledge which, if taken seriously, would inhibit or thwart the doing good she praises in her characters. How can we help taking it seriously? Once we know, we know. While persuading the reader to have sympathy, she gives that knowledge which shows the reader that the sympathy which finds one's neighbors pitiable is as epistemologically groundless as the religious naming which calls Faithful worthy of salvation. Ethical good for George Eliot is based not on sound judicial verdict but on a performative fiat. It is an act of arbitrary renaming which has no more solid base than the religious denominations it replaces. It therefore is precariously balanced in the air, vulnerable to the knowledge which would make it impossible. It is always endangered by just that insight her dismantling of religious naming gives.

The unreadability of chapter 85 of *Middlemarch*, as of the novel as a whole, lies in the way it simultaneously shows the reader he can and must know, and shows him he cannot and must not know. The "can" and "must" here are both an ethical and a linguistic imperative. We should know and not know, and we cannot help both knowing and not knowing, both reading and failing to read. To return to my epigraph from Bunyan's "Apology for His Book," it is indeed the case that parables should not be despised, since they have the power both to hurt and to do good. The problem is that we can never know, even on George Eliot's own terms, which of these is happening with a given parable. We cannot know whether it is better to read *The Pilgrim's Progress* or to read *Middlemarch*.

14

The ethics of reading: vast gaps and parting hours

A wicked book they seized; the very Turk
Could not have read a more pernicious work . . .

George Crabbe, "The Parting Hour"[1]

A distinctive feature of literary study in America at the present time is its internationalization. The result has been a fissuring of what not too long ago seemed perhaps about to become a seamless whole, whether under the aegis of literary history and the history of ideas, or under the aegis of the New Criticism, or under the aegis of the archetypal criticism of Northrop Frye. The diffusion in America of new linguistic theories of various sorts, of Slavic formalism, of phenomenology, of structuralism, of continental Marxism and Freudianism, and of so-called "deconstruction" has put an end, for the moment at least, to any dreams of unification. Nor can the various invading theories be reconciled among themselves. This penetration, fracturing, or "crazing" has made the institution of literary studies in America a house divided against itself, its domestic economy invaded by alien hosts or guests from abroad. These foreign imports have been around long enough now for their disruptive implications to be at least partly understood, and we are in the midst of the predictable negative reaction against them.

My purpose here is to investigate the question of the ethics of reading in the context of this situation. The phrase "the ethics of reading" might seem to be an oxymoron. The obligation of the reader, the teacher, and the critic would seem to be exclusively epistemological. The reader must see clearly what the work in question says and repeat that meaning in his commentary or teaching. He functions thereby, modestly, as an intermediary, as a midwife or catalyst. He transmits meanings which are objectively there but which might not otherwise have reached readers or students. He brings the meaning to birth again as illumination and insight in their minds, making the interaction take place without himself entering into it or altering it. It would seem that the field covered by reading involves exclusively the epistemological categories of truth and falsehood, insight and blindness. The teacher is a revealer, not a creator.

Nevertheless, ethical issues arise in all sorts of ways, both practical and theoretical, in the act of reading. Men and women have given up their lives over questions of interpretation, the reading of a phrase of scripture, for example. One expects reading in one way or another to have moral effects, for good or for ill. To the couplets, truth and falsehood, insight and blindness, themselves not quite congruent, must be added the pair good and bad, both in the sense of aesthetic judgment and in the sense of ethical judgment, and the pair speech and silence. These pairs cross the others widdershins, and no one of them may be easily twisted to superimpose exactly on the others in a single act of critical judgment. It is impossible to divide, discriminate, sift, or winnow the wheat from the chaff, true from false, good from bad, in a single moment of parting.

As a result, difficult questions arise in the attempt to adjudicate between epistemological and ethical responsibilities. Does a teacher or critic have an obligation to choose only certain works to teach or write about? Who has the right to set the canon and to establish the Index? Should "the state see to it," as Matthew Arnold thought? Is a good work always moral? Should a teacher or a critic keep silent if he is led, perhaps unexpectedly, to ethically negative conclusions about a given work? Should certain aspects of a given work be suppressed at a preliminary level of teaching, or should there perhaps be a hierarchy of works of increasing ethical complexity in a given curriculum? How is the need for a firm ethical commitment in the teacher-critic compatible with that openness or "pluralism" often said to be necessary to the sympathetic understanding of works from different periods and cultures? The commitment of both the scientific and religious strands of our American heritage to seeing and saying the truth fearlessly (*veritas vos liberabit; lux et veritas*) can easily, in a given teaching or writing situation, come to collide with concrete ethical responsibilities towards students and colleagues, no less a part of our heritage. Nor is this conflict external, between one critic and another, one teacher and another, one mode of criticism and another. The most intense conflict is likely to take place within the mind and feelings of a single person, in his or her attempt to fulfill incompatible responsibilities.

This problem is a universal one in humanistic studies. It arises in one way or another in any time, place, or culture, even in pre-literate cultures. Oral song or narrative, ritual performances, need interpretation too. Their interpretation may be problematic from the point of view of practical ethics in its relation to cognitive truth. The written text of *Beowulf* may be seen as a Christian interpretation which is also a distortion of the pagan oral poem on which it is based. Was that reinterpretation ethically justified?

The problem I am attempting to focus has, however, a particular context in the present state of humanistic studies in America. The concrete situation of teachers of the humanities is changing at the moment with unusual rapidity. More even than usual it seems as if we stand within the instant of a crisis, a dividing point, a "parting hour." Aspects of the change include the increasing emphasis on the teaching of writing (which may be all to the good if it does not involve the imposition of narrow notions of clarity and logic), the decline of enrollments in traditional courses in literature and other humanities, the catastrophic reduction of the number of positions open to younger humanists, and a conservative reaction in the universities. This tends to declare certain kinds of speculative questioning anathema. Perhaps this reaction is confined within the universities and colleges, a response in the seventies to the sixties. Perhaps it is part of much larger political shifts in our society as a whole.

One form of the closing of ranks is a return to basics in the name of a reaffirmation of traditional humanistic values, perhaps in the name of a reaffirmation of the faith in reason of the enlightenment. This tends to be accompanied by a rejection of "theory" as such and in particular by a strong hostility to certain fairly recent methodological developments in Europe and America. The latter have converged to put in question the most cherished stabilities of traditional humanistic studies in the United States: the stability of the self, the coherence of story-telling, the possibility of straightforward referential language, the possibility of a definitive, unified reading of a given work, the traditional schemas of history and of literary history which have formed the bases for the structuring of curricula in the humanities, for example the objective and definable existence of literary "periods."

Some of the methodological innovations which have challenged the traditional bases of literary study in America are scientific or claim to be part of the so-called "human sciences." These would include insights about the way language works from modern linguistics, from psychology, from psychoanalysis, from anthropology, from semiotics, and from common language philosophy, Wittgenstein and his progeny. Some of these methodological innovations are ideological or have developed from recent historical pressures. An example would be the newer forms of Marxist literary criticism which are beginning to be institutionalized in America and to exert force, particularly over younger teachers. A curious and I think important fact should be noted, however. Marxist literary criticism, both in its somewhat more naïve traditional American forms and in the more sophisticated (sophisticated perhaps in the sense of "adulterated" as well as "wiser") newer forms influenced by semiotics, structuralism, Lacanian psychoanalysis, and so on, tends, strangely enough, to join forces with that conservative reaction to affirm more or less traditional notions of history, of selfhood, of the moral function of literature, and, most of all, of its mimetic or referential status. For Marxism, literature cannot help but reflect social and historical conditions and the superstructure of ideology these have created. Marxism here joins forces with the most traditional "humanism" against those methodological innovations I am describing.

Many of these have been imported from abroad, for example, phenomenology, structuralism, semiotics, and so-called "deconstruction." This is often held against them on the argument that methods brought in from old Europe cannot thrive in New World soil. Nevertheless, an internationalization in literary study is one of its most obvious features today, and this has concrete effects, for example in a tendency to weaken the departmental boundaries of the curricula devoted to national literatures. The transnational diffusion of literary theory and literary methodology occurs now more rapidly than ever before, in part because of technological developments: the rapidity of global transportation which can bring people together from all over the world for a conference anywhere in the world, electronic communication, the increased speed of translation, publication, and distribution, the improved teaching of foreign languages, at least in some schools and programs,[2] the development of international journals in the various branches of humanistic study. One example among many would be *Poetics Today*, published in Tel Aviv, but drawing together essays by scholars from all over America and Europe.

The internationalization of literary study has, as I have said, generated attacks from various directions in defense of those stabilities which seem endangered. These attacks are more or less reasoned or cogent, but their existence is itself an important symptom of our current version of the problem of the ethics of reading. Whether a given anathematizing of these new developments as immoral, nihilistic, or unAmerican is based on an understanding of them and is a genuine going beyond the challenges they offer, or is only a coverup, a repression, can only be told by a careful study of each case. It can be said, however, that the excommunications, extraditions, or convictions of heresy seem often to take place without a careful reading of the documents involved. At least so it seems on the evidence of the inadequacy of what is often said of them: "A wicked book they seized." The texts of the new methodologies must be mastered before they can be discussed, no easy task, since in part they have to do with the impossibility of mastery. Most of all, the readings of particular works which are derived from these theories or from which the theories derive need to be confronted in detail. The efficacy of a theory is to be measured by its results in interpretations. A theory as such cannot be confuted in isolation, for example by deploring its presumed destructive consequences, but only by showing in detail that the readings to which it leads are inadequate or wrong, untrue to the texts. It can also be supposed that young teachers and critics are more likely to have taken genuine stock of the new methodological developments before trying to go beyond them or to return in a new way to the old verities of literary study. For better or for worse literary study in America can never be quite the same again. A difference, perhaps even a "vast gap" has been introduced. This separates us from the days of the New Criticism, Yvor Winters, R. P. Blackmur, and R. S. Crane. Any reconstruction is going to have to be reconstruction with a difference.

I propose to investigate the problem of ethics of reading in this moment of our history a little more closely. I shall do so by way of an example, though with an awareness that my example, like any other, raises the question of exemplarity or of synecdoche. Is this part an adequate sample of such a vast whole? That issue is in fact exemplified and thematized within the poem I shall discuss as well as in my use of it.

Suppose there should fall into my hands "The Parting Hour," a poem by George Crabbe (1754–1832) published in *Tales* (1812). Should I teach it or write about it? What will happen when I do so?

It might be said that this poem is a marginal part of the canon of English literature, even more marginal a part of Western literature as a whole. No one and no institution or curriculum force me to teach or to write about this particular poem. There may be something willful or perverse in my choice of this example. This is to some degree true of any choice of an item for a syllabus, however, and this particular poem may in fact be a good choice. If even Crabbe offers support to those who challenge the assumptions of traditional humanistic study in America, then there may be some force in the challenges.

Crabbe's place in English literary history is an honorable but relatively small one. He is seen as a writer of narratives in verse of idiosyncratic distinction. His work moves across the transition in modes from eighteenth-century styles to verse stories by Wordsworth such as "The Ruined Cottage." There is a general sense that Crabbe's poems are of great interest and that he has perhaps not yet received his due. The debt of criticism to Crabbe will soon be at least partially paid off by Gavin Edwards of Saint Davids College, University of Wales. Edwards has a book on Crabbe in preparation, and my obligation to him is considerable. "The Parting Hour," in any case, is an admirable poem. It raises just those questions about the ethics of reading which are most my interest here and which, as I hope to indicate, are always present in literature and literary criticism in the West, for example in Aristotle's *Poetics* and Sophocles' *Oedipus the King*. Crabbe's poem is a good example of the way an apparently peripheral and unproblematic example in literary studies, taken more or less at random, always turns out to raise again all the most difficult questions about literature and about literary criticism.

"The Parting Hour" opens with no less than five epigraphs from Shakespeare, about each of which there would be much to say, as well as about the fact itself of the multiplication of epigraphs. It is as though Crabbe must try over and over to find a precursor fragment which will be a solid foundation allowing him to begin telling the story he has to tell. The text proper begins with a double claim: the claim that any human life, however strange, hangs together, and the claim that any human life is therefore narratable. It can be retraced later on as a continuous story which makes sense, has a beginning, middle, and end:

> Minutely traces man's life; year after year,
> Through all his days let all his deeds appear,
> And then, though some may in that life be strange,
> Yet there appears no vast nor sudden change:
> The links that bind those various deeds are seen.
> And no mysterious void is left between.
>
> (ll. 1–6)

The opposition here is between strangeness and mystery; minutely traced causal continuity on the one hand, and sudden discontinuous change on the other, across the "void" or "vast gap." Though a given life may in one way or another be odd, if it is narrated with an absolute fidelity to detail it will hang together like the unbroken links of a chain. "Minutely traced": the figure is of one image superimposed on an earlier image and following it over again, like marked tracing paper over a previously made design, tracking it again with the utmost care as one follows the spoor of a beast. This is the image latently present in the Greek word for narrative or history: *diegesis*. On the other hand, if there is any failure at all in this tracing, the life will appear not strange but utterly mysterious, unfathomable. It will be broken by the abyss of a blank. Crabbe's image for this is what happens if one juxtaposes a vignette from the early life of a person with one from his old age without tracing minutely every event between. The opposition is between a continuous temporal line and the placing side by side of two spatial images separated by an unfilled temporal gap, like two portraits beside one another, in a diptych of "before" and "after." This graphic figure of the picture or of two pictures side by side Crabbe himself uses more than once during the course of the poem:

> But let these binding links be all destroy'd,
> All that through years he suffer'd or enjoy'd;
> Let that vast gap be made, and then behold –
> This was the youth, and he is thus when old;

Then we at once the work of Time survey,
And in an instant see a life's decay;
Pain mix'd with pity in our bosoms rise,
And sorrow takes new sadness from surprise.

(ll. 7–14)

This passage is curious in a number of ways. It opposes the line of the temporal continuity, within which binding links may be minutely traced, to the spatial juxtaposition, within a single instant, of two images from different times of a man's life. The two are separated by the blank of the temporal gap. The continuous narrative is by implication appeasing to the mind. It gives calm understanding, since the rationale of the movement of the person from here to there, from youth to old age, is all exposed. No gap for surprise and shock is left. On the other hand, the sudden exposure, across the gap, of the difference between youth and old age produces pain, pity, sorrow, a sadness generated by surprise. The terminology closely approximates that of Aristotle in the *Poetics* if we can understand "pain" to involve some fear for ourselves as well as pity for the degradation exposed in the juxtaposition of the two pictures: "This was the youth, and he is thus when old." The same elements as those in Aristotle are present but apparently in a crisscross relationship, a chiasmus. In Aristotle's theory of tragedy it is the blinding revelation, the recognition (*anagnorisis*) of the links of connection binding apparently dispersed data together which produces the pity and fear appropriate to tragedy, for example in Oedipus' discovery that he has fulfilled the oracles, killed his father, and married his mother. For Crabbe, it is the vision of a non-connection, the confrontation of an unbridgeable gap, which produces these emotions, while the demonstration, by a careful retracing, of all the links of connection is appeasing. It abolishes mystery and satisfies the mind's need for rational understanding.

The chiasmus, however, is only apparent. After all, the Aristotelean recognition and reversal, showing how everything fatally hangs together and bringing the tragic hero down, not only produces pity and fear but also effects the catharsis of these emotions. This catharsis is a transformation or transport turning the painful emotions of pity and fear into the pleasure appropriate to a successful *mimesis*. This transport, as S. H. Butcher long ago recognized in his brilliant essay on the *Poetics*,[3] is in effect a metaphor turning this into that or carrying this over to that, renaming pain as pleasure. The image of the ship is of course one of Aristotle's basic metaphors in the *Poetics*. It serves not only as an example of metaphor but implicitly as a metaphor of metaphor. The same metaphor is woven into the text of his prime example of tragedy, *Oedipus the King*. It appears in the recurrent image of all the citizens of Thebes as frightened passengers on a ship steered, for better or for worse, by Oedipus. The chorus of Theban priests and citizens, all the citizens of Thebes, the actual audience in Athens watching Sophocles' play, all those who have read it or seen it or tried to translate it, down through Hölderlin and Freud to readers and interpreters of today, are carried by the ship, the vehicle Oedipus steers. We are taken where he takes us, in the tragic transport of our witness of the self-blinded hero at the end. We are, strangely, the tenor of that vehicle, the subject of the metaphor. We are what is carried over by it.

Where we are carried we know: "How can we ever find the track of ancient guilt now hard to read?" (*Oedipus the King*, ll. 108–9).[4] Oedipus is the type of the successful interpreter. He reads the various riddles and oracles right, puts two and two together to make a coherent story, the continuous track of a *diegesis*. He is so strongly motivated to obtain at any expense a rational understanding, an absolutely perspicuous vision of the whole line from here to there, that he is willing (or forced by his interpreter's zeal) to convict himself of the most terrible of crimes, parricide and incest, in order to preserve the values of clear and complete seeing through. These are just the values Aristotle says a good tragedy offers its spectators. The beast whose spoor he follows is himself, but only if he follows the track wherever it leads can full enlightenment take place, the audience be purged of pity and fear, the land of Thebes be freed from Apollo's plague.

In Aristotle's theory of tragedy, in *Oedipus the King* itself, and in the narrative theory proposed by Crabbe at the beginning of "The Parting Hour," the unbroken causal continuity of the plot is the necessary means of a transport which transforms pain into pleasure by giving full knowledge. The pleasure of *mimesis*, or what Crabbe calls minute tracing, is both for Aristotle and for Crabbe the pleasure of learning the truth about what is imitated. It is also the pleasure of rhythm or of the harmonious hanging together of the elements of the work. Crabbe in the opening lines of "The Parting Hour" implicitly affirms all Aristotle says in Section VII of the *Poetics* (1450 b 22–1451 a 15) about the primacy of plot. Plot is the soul of the work. For both, a good work should be like a living organism, with no discontinuities and nothing present which does not form part of an unbroken whole. It should have a beginning, a causally linked middle, an end, and an underlying ground or unifying soul binding all together and making it live. It should have a sufficient magnitude, "a length," as Aristotle says, "which can be easily embraced by the memory," so that it is "perspicuous."[5] The efficacy of a *mimesis* depends on our being able to see through it, to hold it all in our memory, or to "embrace [it] in one view" (33): "the beginning and the end must be capable of being brought within a single view" (91). This is just what Crabbe says in his emphasis on the need to see all the links that bind the various deeds of a man's life.

Crabbe's poem, Aristotle's *Poetics*, and Sophocles' *Oedipus the King* as interpreted by Aristotle are all versions of a certain system of concepts, figures, and narratives which have recurred in different ways throughout our history. That system includes just those assumptions about the continuity of selfhood, determinate univocal meaning in literary works, the sovereignty of reason, and the coherence of the march of history which, as I began by saying, seem most endangered by those methodologies imported from abroad. Crabbe's "The Parting Hour" states those assumptions with elegant economy in its opening lines. It presents itself as a promise to fulfill once more these millennial claims for the possibility of a narrative coherence. These are based on the necessary though sometimes hidden coherence of each man's or woman's life from one end of it to the other.

Are the claims paid off, the promise fulfilled, the debt discharged, by the story Crabbe then tells? By no means. What happens, rather, is that the more the story-teller or his protagonist try to fill in all the gaps by a careful retracing, the more they discover that inexplicable gaps remain. The continuity of the story line and of the life is suspended, the line pulverized into static moments which do not hang together, like a rope of sand. Once the apparently innocent fissure of a parting hour has been inserted, the continuity can never be re-established.

About the details of Crabbe's poem there would be much to say. Only an opening toward a full interpretation can be made here. Like others of Crabbe's narratives, "The Parting Hour" is a poem about thwarted or inhibited sexual desire. It is almost, one might say, the Oedipus story in reverse. It is the story of a man who does not marry the woman he loves because of a bar which is, metaphorically at least, that of consanguinity. Though Allen Booth and Judith Flemming are of different families in their village, they have loved one another almost like brother and sister as children and, as Gavin Edwards says, there is some vaguely Oedipal taboo opposed by the parents on either side against their marriage. In their old age they live together in a relation shown as entirely innocent sexually. She cherishes him in his feeble state as mother, sister, wife, though she is none of these. She is connected even more closely to him, in a nameless proximity or alliance, across the gap of their permanent difference and distance from one another: "No wife, nor sister she, nor is the name / Nor kindred of this friendly pair the same; / Yet so allied are they, that few can feel / Her constant, warm, unwearied, anxious zeal" (ll. 18–21). "Few can feel her . . . zeal" – this seems to mean both that few people can experience anything like the strength of her feelings for him and that few people are so lucky as he in being the recipient of such zealous care.

"The Parting Hour" begins its narration proper with a reverse diptych. Not "This was the youth, and he is thus when old," but first Allen Booth in old age, cared for by Judith ("Beneath yon tree, observe an ancient pair –" [l. 15]), and then, in abrupt juxtaposition, Allen Booth as a child ("To David Booth, his fourth and last-born boy,/Allen his name, was more than common joy" [ll. 32–3]). The rest of the poem then attempts to fill in the void between the two pictures by showing the binding links joining the deeds between.

This attempt conspicuously fails. The way it fails turns on just that opposition, so important already in Aristotle, between what is conspicuous or perspicuous, what is theatrical, what can be seen or seen through, so that time becomes space, the diachronic synchronic, and, on the other hand, what can be told or narrated in a minute tracing which retains its diachronic sequentiality, like the links of a chain, one following another. Such a claim may be seen or seen through only metaphorically, as when one says, "I see it all now." The words "prospect," "prospects," "picture," "feature," and "scene" echo through the poem. These words keep before the reader the visual image for understanding. To understand is to read a picture. The poem demonstrates, however, that all the attempts by the poet–narrator and by the hero to bring into the light of clear-seeing the continuity of his life only makes more evident the gaps within it. These make his life not like a picture but like a sentence of faulty grammar, an anacoluthon beginning with one person or tense and shifting suddenly and unaccountably to another. The hour during which Allen Booth parts from his beloved on the beach and fares forth by ship to seek his fortune so that he may marry her inserts a void between them and within his life which can never be filled by any retrospective narration. His subsequent betrayal of Judith and of his community by marrying a Spanish Catholic maiden, fathering Catholic children, and converting to Catholicism only reaffirms the betrayal which occurred when he parted from Judith in the first place. Once he has left her he can never return to her and never return to himself, nor can he explain how he came to differ from himself, how he came to betray both Judith and himself;

> They parted, thus by hope and fortune led,
> And Judith's hours in pensive pleasure fled;
> But when return'd the youth? – the youth no more
> Return'd exulting to his native shore;
> But forty years were past, and then there came
> A worn-out man with wither'd limbs and lame . . .
>
> (ll. 181–6)

Two of Crabbe's four epigraphs from Shakespeare, chosen with admirable insight, provide models for this discontinuity. The first is from Imogen's speech in *Cymbeline*, I: 3. It opposes a "parting kiss" as the jointure between two words to the abrupt intervention of her father: "ere I could / Give him that parting kiss, which I had set / Betwixt two charming words – comes in my father." A "parting kiss" is an oxymoron combining joining and separation. The entrance of the father only anticipates the separation the kiss would have signalled, just as the loving separation of Allen and Judith is imposed by their parents' disapproval. They cannot marry until he has a fortune. Once something which does not fit the sequence has been inserted between two words, even a parting kiss, the grammar of the sentence of which they are part can never be satisfactorily completed. The sentence becomes a failure in following, which is the etymological meaning of the word anacoluthon.

In the second epigraph, from *Comedy of Errors*, V: 1, Aegeon tells how "careful hours with Time's deformed hand / Have written strange defeatures in my face," just as time changes Allen Booth from hopeful youth of fair prospects into an old man in no recognizable way like his former self. Far from being that principle of irresistible force making for form, for continuity, and guaranteeing them, as Crabbe's opening lines promise, time is for Crabbe, as for Shakespeare, a deforming power making things differ from themselves. The figure for this is the changes in a face, its "defeaturing," in Shakespeare's use of a word of which this is the first example in the *OED*. The word shifts the understanding of a face from a visual image to an image of reading. This parallels the clash between picture and story, scene and narrative, theater and discourse, in Crabbe's poem. The face is not an image to see but a set of signs or features, a written text to decipher. The distinctive feature of the text written by time on a face is its unreadability, its disconnection from itself, its discontinuity with itself, its defeaturing. Allen Booth tries in vain, when he returns to his native shore after forty years' exile, "to trace / Some youthful features in some aged face" (ll. 221–2).

Time for man is not a natural or organic continuity, nor is it ever a picture which can be seen at a single glance. Time for man is always experienced as some kind of sign, as a track to be followed, a line to be retraced, a face with features to be read. This means that time is always experienced as an incongruous repetition. It is experienced as a picture with gaps or as two pictures side by side which cannot be reconciled. This means also, as Crabbe's story-teller and his protagonist find out, discovering those gaps, discontinuities, incongruities, and incoherences which are intrinsic to any repetitive structure of signs. When one tries to retrace the line it never can be made to hang together. Far from doing what he promises at the beginning, showing the continuity of a life, all Crabbe's story-teller's efforts only make the "mysterious void[s] . . . between" more evident. His narration presents discontinuous vignettes rather than a continuous chain of events. There is no way to explain how or why Allen Booth came to differ from himself, why he married someone else, abjured his faith, failed to come back sooner, postponing from day to day and year to year the reunion that would heal the gap opened by the parting hour.

The temporal structure of 'The Parting Hour" is strange enough. First the narrator presents the "ancient pair" beneath the tree. Next he leaps back to Allen Booth's childhood and the events leading up to his parting from Judith Flemming. Then he leaps forward forty years to Allen's return and to his attempt to pick up again the continuity of his life by returning to Judith. This he can do only if he can satisfactorily account for the intervening years and bring the past up to the present.

The narrative responsibility at this point shifts to Allen himself. He is shown compulsively telling his story over and over to Judith, "running it through" in the phrase from Othello's narration of his life to Desdemona Crabbe uses as his fourth epigraph (*Othello*, I: 3). Allen tells his story repeatedly in a hopeless attempt to get it right, to justify himself in his eyes and hers. The key term for this narration is the word "relate." It is a word for connection, for telling, and for family tie. The signal of the temporal incoherence of his "relation" is the shift back and forth between the past tense and the historical present. Only if his narrative can turn the past sequence of events into a present simultaneous possession can the relation succeed, but this can never happen, and so his relation vibrates between the two tenses, and must be repeated over and over without any hope of ever succeeding: "To her, to her alone, his various fate, / At various times, 'tis comfort to relate" (ll. 309–10); "First he related . . ." (1. 313); "He next related . . ." (l. 372); "Here his relation closes . . ." (l. 434). Far from connecting the past to the present by a minute tracing of the intervening events, Allen only succeeds in bringing himself back to a present in which he is two persons, the faithful husband of his Spanish wife Isabel, father of her children, and at the same time the faithful fiancé of Judith. Whichever way he turns he must betray one or the other of them. Each is the dream which makes the other impossible as waking reality, and so his selfhood, his "life," is irrevocably divided, parted from itself. With that parting goes any hope of a coherent narrative with beginning, middle, and end:

> . . . how confused and troubled all appear'd;
> His thoughts in past and present scenes employ'd,
> All views in future blighted and destroy'd:
> His were a medley of bewild'ring themes,
> Sad as realities, and wild as dreams.
>
> (ll. 429–33)

Separated from his origin by his betrayal of his childhood love, Allen has no certain prospects or views toward the future. He can only hope for the "little earth" Cardinal Wolsey asks for in the passage from *Henry VIII* (IV, 2) Crabbe uses as his fifth epigraph to the poem. Allen Booth returns to "his native bay / Willing his breathless form should blend with kindred clay" (ll. 189–90). The old folk of his native village say, "The man is Allen Booth, and it appears / He dwelt among us in his early years; / We see the name engraved upon the stones, / Where this poor wanderer means to lay his bones" (ll. 279–82). Only when Allen Booth is a dead body buried in a little plot of earth, a tombstone over his head with a single name engraved on it joining him to his family already buried there, can he be related enough to himself to be joined to anything or to anyone else without danger of parting from it or from her. He can be indissolubly wedded only to the "kindred clay."

"The Parting Hour" ends where it began, with the aged Allen Booth sleeping under a tree watched over by the unwearied care of his beloved Judith. Far from being an unequivocal ending tying Allen Booth's life together, this picture, the reader now knows, is the image of Allen Booth's disconnection from himself, as he dreams of his Spanish wife and children in the presence of the loving Judith whom he cannot help but betray as long as he is still alive. The poem ends with his waking from his dreams of Isabel to face Judith and cry, "My God! 'twas but a dream" (l. 473).

"The Parting Hour" provides one striking image for this failure of narrative continuity. Allen is exiled for heresy from the Spanish colony where he has married and prospered. While he is poor no one pays any attention to him, but when he is wealthy they notice him and single him out for punishment:

> Alas! poor Allen, through his wealth was seen
> Crimes that by poverty conceal'd had been;
> Faults that in dusty pictures rest unknown
> Are in an instant through the varnish shown.
>
> (ll. 361–4)

It was lack of money which drove Allen away from England in the first place. If he had had enough of it he could have married Judith and maintained his continuity with himself and with his sworn fidelity to Judith. Money in the first life of Allen Booth stands for the missing principle of coherence. In his second life, however, when money is obtained it becomes the instrument of discontinuity, separating him forever from Isabel, from his children, and from his second self. The figure Crabbe uses seems an especially striking one when the use of the image of the "picture" elsewhere in the poem as a metaphor of a given state of a man's life is remembered. The attempt to varnish over a dirty picture only brings out its "faults." 'Faults" – the word recalls "gaps" and "void" in the opening of the poem. Varnish may be taken as a figure for narrative, for the attempt to relate one thing to another in a sequential discourse. This attempt at varnishing over only brings out its impossibility. It reveals unbridgeable gaps, like geological faults in a terrain. Crabbe's "The Parting Hour," in its attempt to fulfill its promise of being able to show how a life hangs together, reveals the impossibility of fulfilling this promise. Any attempt to do so is a coverup, a varnishing over. This infallibly betrays the hiatuses it tries to obscure.

"The Parting Hour," almost in spite of itself, deconstructs two of those cherished certainties of humanist literary study, the continuity of the self and the organic continuity of narrative from beginning to middle to end. It might be claimed that the poem is an aberration among those by its author or among those of its period, but this could be shown not to be the case. One need only think of the doubts raised about the unity of the self and about the cohesion of time by Locke, Diderot, or Hume, or in their different ways, by Rousseau and Wordsworth, to recognize that Crabbe's poem is a miniature version of one of the distinctive features of Pre-romanticism and Romanticism. This feature is the co-presence of a powerful affirmation of the system of metaphysical assumptions of which Greek thought was one version, along with an equally powerful disarticulation of that system. This double affirmation and denial, tying and untying, in fact characterizes our own moment as I began by describing it. Without denying that there have been vast gaps and new beginnings both in linguistic history and in cultural history, this affirmation and denial may by hypothesis be said to form the unity in disunity of any "period" in Western intellectual and literary history, even that of the Greeks. The distinctiveness of any historical period, "the Renaissance," "Romanticism," "Modernism," or whatever, lies in its special combination of certain recurring elements rather than in its introduction of anything unheard of before. The gaps and discontinuities making linguistic and cultural history a vast anacoluthon are within each synchronic expression, making it heterogeneous, as well as in the diachronic movement from one expression to another.

I said this was true even of the Greeks. If one turns back to Aristotle and Sophocles and reads them more narrowly, in the light of what has been found in "The Parting Hour," in order to test the "sources" against their modern apparently subversive counterpart, one finds that Aristotle's *Poetics* and Sophocles' *Oedipus the King* are also coverups which reveal, in spite of themselves, what they mean to obscure. Far from subverting something unequivocal and whole earlier present in our culture, far from unravelling a seamless fabric, Crabbe does no more than repeat in his own way a gesture of unsuccessful varnishing over performed already by Sophocles and Aristotle in their own ways.

As a long modern tradition of the interpretation of *Oedipus the King* has recognized, the guilt of Oedipus may be a sin of interpretation. In order to bring everything out in the open, or to persuade himself that he has done so, he is willing, on not entirely convincing evidence, to convict himself of parricide and incest. The self-condemnation depends on a certain way of reading the various oracles, prophecies, and reports he is given. It is a way based on just that logocentric assumption of beginning, middle, and end which the Sphynx's riddle embodies and which Aristotle makes the logical or reasonable basis of a good plot. The fault in Oedipus' interpretation, revealed by the bringing to light, is there, for example, in the famous discrepancy between the two versions of the Phocal massacre. According to one version, Laius' murderers were many. According to the other version, there was but one murderer. As Oedipus himself says, "One man and many men just do not jibe" (l. 845). This discrepancy is never cleared up in the play. Oedipus' self-condemnation is a glossing over of the contradictory evidence. It is an interpretation in excess of the facts he has. It is a varnishing over which reveals the fault in his story and his fault as a too arrogant interpreter. From Hölderlin through Freud to such diverse modern critics as William Empson, Thomas Gould, William Chase Greene, Karl Harshbarger, René Girard, Sandor Goodheart, Philippe Lacoue-Labarthe, and, most recently, Cynthia Chase in a brilliant article,[6] Romantic and Post-Romantic interpreters have in one way or another confronted the fact that Oedipus may not have had an Oedipus complex, that he may not have killed his father, and that his crime may be an error of misreading. For Hölderlin in "Remarks on *Oedipus*," "The *intelligibility* of the whole [play] rests primarily upon one's keeping before one's eyes the scene, in which Oedipus interprets in *too transcendent* [or *too infinite*] *a way* the word of the oracle and in which he is tempted to an act of *sacrilege* (Die *Verständlichkeit* des Ganzen beruhet vorzüglich darauf, dass man die Szene ins Auge fasst, wo Oedipus den Orakelspruch *zu unendlich deutet, zum nefas* versucht wird)."[7] As Philippe Lacoue-Labarthe comments, "The transgression, the sacrilege, would then be the excess of interpretation" (*ibid.*, p. 81). The intelligibility of the whole rests on keeping before one's eyes Oedipus' blind spot, the moment of his failure in intelligence, reason, and perspicuity, the moment when he commits the sacrilege of seeing himself as the sacred sinner who stands between men and the gods and who can, in expiating his crime, reconcile heaven and earth once more, appease the gods and cure Thebes of its plague.

For Cynthia Chase, following Freud, to leap all the way to the end of my line of commentators, the crime of Oedipus lies not in something he originally did, nor in its later repetition in his self-condemnation and self-blinding, but in between, in the interpretative connection of one with the other:

> Like "Emma''s typical 'psychoneurosis'" [in Freud's *Project* of 1895], "Oedipal" sexuality concerns a certain lag or limp of the subject in relation to structures of meaning. . . . An initial recollection of Sophocles' play gives us a "first scene" in the murder of Laius, the Phocal crime, and a "second scene" precisely in the drama itself, the moment of the legendary story chosen by Sophocles for representation on the stage; the quest for and recognition of the deed's agent and meaning. The accession to sexual awareness that converts an indifferent episode into a seduction in "Emma''s" case is paralleled in Oedipus' "case" by an accession to genealogical awareness that converts an accidental manslaughter into patricide.[8]

If Oedipus was the first misreader of his own story, even when he apparently had come to see it most clearly, in his blindness, all the readers who come after, including those I have just been discussing, can do no more than repeat his gesture of a coverup which gives itself away through its own excess of repressive coherence, like a man who confesses to a crime by compulsively denying that he has committed it.

The first and most spectacular example of this was Aristotle when he chose *Oedipus the King* as the archetype of the perfect tragedy in the *Poetics*. The key word in the *Poetics* is *logos* in its various forms. The whole effort of the *Poetics* might be defined either as the banishing of the alogical or irrational from tragedy or as the argument that it is the function of tragedy to make the alogical logical, to bring into the light of reason what is dark, unreasonable, monstrous, incommensurate with the *logos*. The theatrical, what can be seen or seen through perspicuously, is implicitly identified by Aristotle with the reasonable or logical. In taking on *Oedipus the King*, with its play on blindness and insight and with its plot of the monstrous crimes of parricide and incest, with its one which is also more than one, with its dark illogic of family relationships in which a man's wife is also his mother, his children his siblings, Aristotle undertook to reduce a great deal of unreason to reason. In fact the remorselessly clear logic of Aristotle's exposition ("Aristotle is a skeleton," said Wallace Stevens[9]), is everywhere threatened by a dark fringe of the alogical which is exposed, even by Aristotle, in the act of its coverup.

The alogical is dealt with in two ways by Aristotle, neither of which works as a successful varnishing over. One way is to banish it altogether, as when he says, categorically, that nothing irrational or that does not square with the reason should be presented directly on the stage: "The tragic plot must not be composed of irrational parts. Everything irrational (*alogon*) should, if possible, be excluded; or, at all events, it should lie outside the action of the play (as, in the Oedipus, the hero's ignorance as to the manner of Laius' death)."[10] Of course the whole theatrical force of *Oedipus the King* focuses on this irrational fact. The plot exists not to exclude it but to bring it into the light, not outside but inside the words and actions of the play.

The other way in which the irrational is dealt with in poetry, according to Aristotle, is by transforming it into something else through two puissant forms of metamorphosis or metaphor (which are really the same form). These are forms of change appropriate to poetry. They are performatives, ways of doing things with words which turn the alogical into the logical, the monstrous into the human, the pain of pity and fear into the aesthetic pleasure of a satisfactory denouement. These two forms of transforming are of course *mimesis* and *catharsis*. The remarkable thing about *mimesis* or imitation is that the pleasure of learning it provides is strong enough to counteract even the horrible or monstrous in the objects imitated: "Objects which in themselves we view with pain, we delight to contemplate when reproduced with minute fidelity: such as the forms of the most ignoble animals and of dead bodies. The cause of this again is," says Aristotle in his imperturbable way, "that to learn gives the liveliest pleasure."[11] In a tragedy, it is the *catharsis* which performs this transmogrification. "Even without the aid of the eye," says Aristotle, "he who hears the tale told will thrill with horror and melt to pity at what takes place. This is the impression we should receive from hearing the story of the Oedipus."[12] This pity and fear, however, are changed to pleasure as we learn, with Oedipus, the facts, tie them together rationally, and accept, in their *mimesis*, the reason even of such terrifying unreason as Apollo has imposed on Oedipus. We go forth in calm of mind, all passion spent.

Catharsis, however, as commentators on Aristotle have long recognized, is a homeopathic medicine. It cures by administering a small dose of the disease of unreasonable passion it would free us from. How can one be sure the dose is not excessive? The alogic of the theory of *catharsis* is like that of the killed virus as a vaccine. If the virus is truly dead it will have no effect. If it is alive it will cause the disease it is meant to cure. It must be both dead and alive, absurdly or in contradiction to logic.

Everywhere in Aristotle's *Poetics* one finds the contradiction or alogic of an exclusion of the alogical which is at the same time an accommodation of it to reason. The pattern is there not only in the theories of *mimesis* and *catharsis*, but also in the historical sketch of the development of poetry and meter. This must show, and yet cannot show, how the natural became the cultural, just as *mimesis* itself is both natural to man, therefore part of nature, and at the same time reasonable and cultural, special to man alone, above brute nature. The same pattern is there in the aporias of beginning and ending which Aristotle's formulas encounter, as for example in the way the beginning must be both outside the play as its presupposed base and at the same time inside it, presented as part of the play. Aristotle is even led to recognize, absurdly, the possibility and even the existence, in the *Lynceus* of Theodectes, of a play which is all end or unraveling, since the beginning and the complication are presupposed as having happened before the play begins.[13]

The pattern of something alogical which is unsuccessfully covered over by logical reasoning is present, finally, in Aristotle's theory of metaphor. Here the neat logic of proportional or analogical metaphor (A is to B as C is to D) is undone by Aristotle's own recognition of the possibility of catachresis. This is the figure of speech in which one of the four terms is missing from the language and from our experience: "For some of the terms of the proportion there is at times no word in existence; still the metaphor may be used. For instance, to scatter seed is called sowing; but the action of the sun in scattering his rays is nameless. Still this process bears to the sun the same relation as sowing to the seed. Hence the expression of the poet 'sowing the god-created light.'"[14] Aristotle's theory of metaphor depends on a firm distinction between literal and figurative. The theory is subverted when Aristotle recognizes the existence of words which are neither literal nor figurative. In the example Aristotle gives, "sowing" is not literal, since there is no literal word for the sun's shedding its rays, and not figurative, since the definition of a figure is that it is a metaphorical substitution for a literal word.

Aristotle's *Poetics* is not only surrounded by a fringe or margin of the irrational. It is invaded and its rationality everywhere undermined by various forms of unreason which it does not by any means wholly succeed in reducing to reason. Even Aristotle's logic cannot expunge or cover up the alogical in literature.

Beginning with an apparently marginal or innocuous example, Crabbe's "The Parting Hour," I have been led to recognize that not only in this poem but also in two grand precursor texts, the system of assumptions about selfhood, history, and literary form I began by describing is both affirmed and dismantled. If one should dare to extrapolate from these three examples, one might formulate this hypothetically as a general law for all texts in our tradition. If this law holds, then the conflict at this moment in American literary study between conservatives and deconstructers is only the latest example of a recurrent pattern in Western literature and literary criticism. If this should be the case, what then follows for "the ethics of reading"?

Two related provisional hypotheses about this may be briefly made in conclusion. The first is that neither the challenges to traditional humanistic certainties in contemporary American criticism nor the defensively aggressive reaffirmation of those certainties is willful, malicious, or blindly ignorant, nor is either something unique to our epoch, some unheard of nihilism, the "end of man," in one case, or a "new humanism" special to these far Western shores, in the other. Each position repeats operations of writing and reading which have recurred throughout our history. The perhaps necessary error or blindness of either is not to recognize the necessity of the other.

The second conclusion is embodied in that word "necessity." Both sorts of reading are necessitated by the words of the texts they treat. This means that reading is always an epistemological necessity before it is a matter of ethical choice or evaluation. More radically, it means that the ethics of reading is subject to a categorical imperative which is linguistic rather than transcendent or a matter of subjective will. Epistemology must take precedence over ethics in reading. One cannot make ethical judgments, perform ethical actions, such as teaching a poem, without first subjecting oneself to the words on the page, but once that has happened, the ethical operation will already necessarily have taken place. As Hölderlin says, in a phrase quoted by Paul de Man in a recent essay, *Es ereignet sich aber das Wahre.* As de Man says, this can be freely translated, "What is true is what is bound to take place," which means that "reading . . . has to go against the grain of what one would want to happen in the name of what has to happen."[15] A reading is true as an acute angle is true to its model, or as one voice or word is true to another voice or word. The ethics of reading is not some act of the human will to interpretation which extracts moral themes from a work, or uses it to reaffirm what the reader already knows, or imposes a meaning freely in some process of reader response or perspectivist criticism, seeing the text in a certain way. The ethics of reading is the power of the words of the text over the mind and words of the reader. This is an irresistible coercion which shapes what the reader or teacher says about the text, even when what he says is most reductive or evasive. *Es ereignet sich aber das Wahre.* The ethics of reading is the moral necessity to submit in one way or another, whatever one says, to the truth of this linguistic imperative.

Notes

1. Ll. 355–6, *The Poetical Works*, A. J. Carlyle and R. M. Carlyle, eds (London, 1932), p. 229. Further citations from Crabbe's poem will be by line numbers from this edition. [William E. Cain uses the phrase "the ethics of reading," in an essay on my work first published in *College English* in 1979, then in *The Crisis in Criticism* (Baltimore, 1984). Cain's essay no doubt put the idea in my mind as a topic to investigate, as I have since done at length in *The Ethics of Reading* (New York, 1987), and *Versions of Pygmalion* (Cambridge, Mass., 1990). Note added 1990.]
2. The recent statistics are appalling enough. In 1964 only one high school student in four studied a foreign language. Now the ratio has dropped to one in seven. In 1966, thirty-four per cent of American colleges required a foreign language for admission. Now only eight per cent do. (*The New York Times*, Saturday, November 10, 1979.) Nevertheless, the techniques of teaching foreign languages have greatly improved in America, and some students, in public as well as in private high schools, are given excellent foreign language training.
3. S. H. Butcher, *Aristotle's Theory of Poetry and Fine Art; With a Critical Text and Translation of The Poetics* (New York, 1951), pp. 113–407; see especially "The Function of Tragedy," pp. 240–73.
4. I am using the translation by Thomas Gould (Englewood Cliffs, N.J., 1970), p. 29. Further citations from *Oedipus the King* will be by line numbers from this translation.
5. Butcher, *op. cit.*, p. 33. Further quotations from Aristotle's *Poetics* will be identified by page numbers in this translation.
6. "Oedipal Textuality: Reading Freud's Reading of Oedipus," *Diacritics*, IX, No. 1 (Spring 1979), pp. 54–68; see also Sandor Goodheart, "Oedipus and Laius' Many Murderers," *Diacritics*, VIII, No. 1 (Spring 1978), pp. 55–71. Chase and Goodheart include references to the work of the other critics in their essays. Empson somewhere observes that Oedipus did not have an Oedipus complex, since he did not know it was his mother he married or his father he murdered.
7. Quoted and discussed by Philippe Lacoue-Labarthe, "The Caesura of the Speculative," *Glyph: 4* (Baltimore and London, 1978), pp. 81–2.
8. Chase, *op. cit.*, pp. 57–8.
9. *Opus Posthumous* (New York, 1957), p. 168.
10. Butcher, *op. cit.*, pp. 95–7.
11. *ibid.*, p. 15.
12. *ibid.*, p. 49.
13. *ibid.*, p. 65.
14. *ibid.*, p. 79.
15. In Carol Jacobs, *The Dissimulating Harmony* (Baltimore and London, 1978), p. xi.

15

The truth will out:

Anthony Trollope's *Cousin Henry*

Cousin Henry was written near the end of Anthony Trollope's life, when he had given up fox hunting and was about to get rid of his house at 39 Montagu Square in London in order to move to a country house at Harting in West Sussex, his last home. Like *Mr. Scarborough's Family* and *An Old Man's Love*, *Cousin Henry*, though its hero is not old, is shadowed by the aging author's sense of being out of life, of being unloved and unlovable. It is one of his most concentrated studies of an isolated and neurotic personality. The novel was published in two slender volumes by Chapman and Hall in October 1879, having been published in weekly installments in the *Manchester Weekly Times* (Supplement) from March 8 to May 24, 1879, and simultaneously in the *North British Weekly Mail*.

Though every novel by Anthony Trollope uses themes and techniques which are also exploited in many other of his novels, there is no novel by him which does not contain something unique and thereby add to the reader's understanding of what is at stake in his work. *Cousin Henry* is no exception. There is no novel by Trollope which more strikingly dramatizes his conviction that in human affairs the truth will eventually out, whatever efforts are made to keep it hidden.

Why is this? Why is it that for Trollope the truth will always out? Why cannot some subjective secret, good or bad, be kept locked permanently in the heart of the one who harbors it? Why is the world of Anthony Trollope's fiction always a realm of transparency, of openness? In order to answer these questions it will be necessary to identify the salient presuppositions of Trollope's storytelling.

Like so many other novels by Trollope, *Cousin Henry* focuses on a double question, the question of marriage and the question of inheritance. Who will marry Isabel Brodrick and who will inherit Uncle Indefer Jones' estate, "a country house which looked down from the cliffs over the sea on the coast of Carmarthenshire." To put this in the terms provided by anthropologists in their studies of more "primitive" societies, the basic problems, in the models in miniature of English society Trollope provides, are the distribution of women and the distribution of property. The property in question is both real estate and money. With it goes a name or a title. Who will marry the girl; who will inherit the estate?

Women, property, money and title – these are the four things of value in Trollope's world, at least from the point of view of the men in it. The women are necessary to produce children to whom, if they are male, will eventually once more be passed on the money, the title, the estate, or who, if they are female, will once more be the means by which this process occurs, as generation follows generation. In a society like Trollope's, which is ruled by primogeniture, the estate, and all that goes with it, remains in principle intact. If all works smoothly, the process of birth, marriage and death is a perfect machine for ensuring the preservation of the estate, the title, and the money through the generations. Both men and women, in their bodily and psychological individualities, are no more than functionaries in this process of preservation and temporal succession. The men are the temporary embodiments of names, titles, and prerogatives which transcend them and are passed on from father to son. The women are the necessary means whereby that transmission is made possible.

Each individual, for Trollope, is like a word in a text, the locus of a meaning which arises from its differential interplay with the other words in that text. Or, it would be more accurate to say, each man or woman, in his or her bodily existence and in his or her consciousness, the presence of the self to itself, is like the momentary incarnation of the meaning of this or that word in one or another example of it. Each person is like this particular bit of ink making up a certain configuration on this bit of paper spelling the name Isabel Brodrick. Such words may be repeated from copy to copy, in all the copies of Trollope's novel, *Cousin Henry*, just as a name may be held by more than one person; but in each particular case there must be some material embodiment. Trollope's novels, particularly short single-plotted ones like *Cousin Henry*, are extraordinary in the concentration and economy with which they present simplified models of a human society which is structured in this way. They are extraordinary also in showing what it feels like to find oneself assigned a particular part to play in such a society.

Trollope's novels are more than this, however. Each novel by Trollope, in one way or another, in an admirable series of fine variations, focuses on the moment of transition, that crucial moment when the exact way in which the line of succession will be maintained remains in doubt. At this moment the tension is particularly evident between the synchronic aspect of the structure as something eternally fixed like a spatial design, and its diachronic nature as something that must necessarily change through time. By focusing on the moment when the roles of various characters are in doubt, when there are various candidates for the vacant places in the social structure, Trollope is able with great brilliance and tact to show regions where there are inherent contradictions, latent flaws within the system. These flaws invoke, always, contradictions between values which are each absolute, each equally compelling, but which may, in certain circumstances, be unable to be secured simultaneously.

One of the ways in which this is conspicuously the case is Trollope's tendency to focus, in his actual presentation of the social structure and its change, on the interior states of mind of characters within that structure. He focuses especially on the states of mind of female characters. As Henry James long ago observed, Trollope made the English girl especially his subject. The description I have so far given of Trollope's world intentionally emphasizes the "male chauvinist" aspect of it, the way women are viewed as "objects" of value to be "distributed," given by father to son-in-law, rather than as persons conscious of themselves and of their situations. Indeed, from the point of view of the self-sustaining and self-perpetuating social system, both men and women are irrelevant. What matters is their placement and function within the system. This fact, however, is experienced more by women than by men as a form of alienation, as when Isabel Brodrick is described in *Cousin Henry* as "speaking of herself as though she were altogether at the disposal of her uncle," or when Anna, in *Lady Anna*, feels that the lawyers who want her to marry Earl Lovel, "look upon her as an instrument, as a piece of goods that might now, from the accident of her ascertained birth, be made of great service to the Lovel family."

Nevertheless, each person in a novel by Trollope, even though he or she, from the point of view of the social structure as a whole, is no more than a locus or a function, has also an intense self-consciousness. It is a consciousness of the self as being in a certain social position. For Trollope, it is not, "I think, therefore I am," but, "I am aware of myself in relation to others, therefore I am. I *am* my relations to others." Basic to Trollope's representation of a model of social relations in each of his novels is the focusing one by one, in a rotating sequence, on the states of mind of the main characters, as each meditates on his or her situation and on the decisions he or she must make. The method of this presentation is most often what is called "free indirect discourse." The narrator speaks for the state of mind of the character in the third person, presenting it from within and from without at once, as in all that part of *Cousin Henry* which concentrates with great brilliance on Henry's knowledge, with an intense anguish of awareness, that there is another will, a will disinheriting him, and that he is living a lie before the world.

This awareness is embodied in his fascinated gaze, however hard he tries to resist, toward the book on the library shelf that hides the will, as in the following passage, one among many:

> Soon after two he left the room, and at the moment was unable not to turn a rapid glance upon the book. There it was, safe in its place. How well he knew the appearance of the volume! On the back near the bottom was a small speck, a spot on the binding, which had been so far disfigured by some accident in use. This seemed to his eyes to make it marked and separate among a thousand. To him it was almost wonderful that a stain so peculiar should not at once betray the volume to the eyes of all. But there it was, such as it was, and he left it amidst its perils. Should they pounce upon it the moment that he had left the room, they could not say that he was guilty because it contained the will.

Trollope's method as a novelist, in *Cousin Henry* as in all of his novels, is to establish a group of personages constituting a society in miniature which is in some state of unresolved tension. The story moves forward through a series of confrontations among these characters, and through a rotating series of scenes in which the narrator focuses in free indirect discourse on the state of mind of each one of the characters in turn, as he or she meditates on his or her situation. This is a method of great economy and elegance, almost musical in its formal purity and in its dependence on a method of repetition with variation as a means of advancing through time toward a conclusion. Each time the reader is returned by the narrator into the mind of Isabel or into the mind of Henry he finds the character still the same person, still in the same situation in relation to other people, but slightly further along in time toward the ultimate resolution that will remove the tension among the characters and end the novel.

In *Cousin Henry* the characters who are treated this way are five. There is the old man, Indefer Jones, who must decide whether to leave his estate to Isabel Brodrick, whom he loves, or to Henry Jones, whom he loves not, but who is apparently the more appropriate heir, since he is the nearest male who actually carries the name Jones. The second personage is Isabel Brodrick. She must decide whether or not to marry Henry and whether or not to marry William Owen, a minor canon attached to the Cathedral of Hereford. Henry Jones, the apparent heir, must decide whether or not to reveal the existence of the will which will disinherit him. William Owen, Isabel's true love, is hardly treated with much inwardness in the novel, but he must be shown remaining true to Isabel in spite of the "stubborn pride" which leads her to refuse him when she is too rich and then to refuse him again when she is too poor, though she loves him with all her heart. Mr. Apjohn, finally, is the lawyer who triumphs over the detestable Henry Jones by "seeing it all" in his mind and locating in a triumph of detective intuition the missing will, even identifying the very volume of sermons in which it is hidden.

It will be seen from Trollope's focus on the interior states of mind of his characters that the social role each plays is in fact not an abstract function in a disembodied network of signs. It is forcefully incarnated in the mind, the will, the feelings, the consciousness, and the conscience of the person, and in the bodily energy each is given to play the role he or she is assigned, to play it well or ill. The social role is also incarnated, as the admirable passage quoted above about Cousin Henry's anguished obsession with the book hiding the will shows, in the physical objects which form the environment of the characters. The physical world for Trollope is never something merely neutral, "out there," and there is certainly no Wordsworthian drama of the interaction of "subject," "object," and some nature spirit, "something far more deeply interfused." Physical objects which appear in Trollope's novels have always already been made over into signs of some social meaning, as that book hiding the will is the volume of sermons from which old Indefer Jones reads every Sunday as part of the ritual propriety of his life:

> On Sunday he read two sermons through, having been forbidden by the doctor to take his place in the church because of the draughts, and thinking, apparently, that it would be mean and wrong to make that an excuse for shirking an onerous duty.

Though that book, like other socialized objects in Trollope's world, exists as its human meaning, nevertheless its particular material nature is necessary to that meaning, as Cousin Henry's fascinated attention to that "small speck," the "spot on the binding," indicates. In this, physical objects are for Trollope like persons. The latter are wholly absorbed into their social roles but must give their minds and wills, and their bodily energies as well, to the performance of those roles. Each role depends on being incarnated in this way. Trollope's novels therefore tend to draw their dramatic tension from questions of conscience in which men and women must decide whether or not to give themselves to this role or that. To put this another way, Trollope's novels always focus not only on questions of conscience, and on the fine points of moral casuistry in the sense of special cases which cannot easily be subsumed under obvious moral laws, but also on questions of will. The question for Trollope's women, for Isabel Brodrick for example, is whether they will with their whole hearts and minds and bodies to give themselves to this or that person or whether they cannot in conscience will to do so. Trollope's love stories are strictly analogous to his stories of the inheritance of an estate, though the two things are sometimes opposed by critics. The documentary wills, such as that series of wills Indefer Jones makes and keeps neatly piled in chronological order, are a physical incarnation or emblem of this psychosocial theme of the relations of individual will to community role.

The person must fit the role. *Cousin Henry* is a novel about someone who is conspicuously unfit for his role. Old Indefer Jones agonizes over and vacillates between his sense that Henry Jones, as the nearest male heir, ought to inherit his estate, and his recognition that Henry is wholly unfit for that role, whereas Isabel Brodrick, though she is a woman and only a Jones on the female side of her family, is wholly fit to inherit the estate and to fulfill all the responsibilities which go with it.

If Isabel were to marry Henry, then all would be well; but it goes against her conscience to do so, since he is no more fit to be her husband than he is to inherit the estate – and in any case she loves William Owen. Shortly before his death Indefer Jones makes the correct will. *Cousin Henry* remains focused on the question of whether his will will or will not be done. The reader may be left to find out for himself or herself how this happens, but an anticipatory answer to the question initially posed may now be suggested. Nothing can remain permanently hidden in Trollope's world because everything human, however much it may seem to be private to one person, buried away in the secret recesses of that person's mind, is in fact embodied in the public realm of gesture, facial expression, and behavior. It is embodied also in the shared physical world, out there in the open for all to see. Sooner or later the signs will be interpreted correctly, as lawyer Apjohn correctly reads the signs that tell him there is another will and that it is hidden in that volume of sermons. The will safely preserves Indefer Jones' final intention beyond the grave. The preservation of the will triumphantly vindicates Trollope's conviction that the truth will always out.

16

The values of obduracy in Trollope's *Lady Anna*

Lady Anna was written on shipboard, in the early summer of 1871, during the long voyage taken by Anthony Trollope and his wife to visit their son Fred, who had emigrated to Australia. The circumstances of this novel's composition provide a good example of Trollope's extraordinary ability to create an entirely separate imaginary world and to dwell within it during the writing of a novel. *Lady Anna* has scarcely anything to do with the sea or with Australia. The hero and heroine at the very end of the novel sail to Australia to begin their married life there, where the union of a rich noblewoman and a journeyman tailor will not seem so strange. The novel's connections with Trollope's own life, if there are any, are obscure and roundabout. He located, for example, the apartment in London of Lady Anna's mother, the Countess Lovel, on Keppel Street in Bloomsbury. This happens to be the street where Anthony Trollope was born, on April 24, 1815. *Lady Anna* in fact is set in the reign of William IV, in the coaching days before the railroad. The fictional Lady Anna was born more or less at the same time as Anthony Trollope himself, though her time in Keppel Street comes when she is of marriageable age.

Lady Anna is also a good example of Trollope's well-known fanaticism of regularity in writing. As Trollope tells the reader in *An Autobiography*, when he embarked on *The Great Britain* for Melbourne on May 24, 1871, *Ralph the Heir* was appearing in installments in *St. Paul's Magazine*, and he left no less than three other completed novels behind in manuscript: *The Eustace Diamonds, Phineas Redux*, and *An Eye for an Eye*. Nevertheless, he had a desk set up in his cabin and went straight to work on another novel, *Lady Anna*, the day after the ship left Liverpool. He wrote away at it with admirable persistence day after day during the long voyage. *An Autobiography* gives the details of this: "Before I reached Melbourne," he says,

> I had finished a story called *Lady Anna*. Every word of this was written at sea, during the two months required for our voyage, and was done day by day – with the intermission of one day's illness – for eight weeks, at

the rate of 66 pages of manuscript in each week, every page of manuscript containing 250 words. Every word was counted.

Anyone who has seen the little handmade notebooks, now in the Bodleian Library at Oxford, in which Trollope recorded day by day the exact number of pages he had written on the novel currently going forward, with occasional notations of "Alas" or "Eheu" when a day was missed for some reason, will know that there was something more than merely practical and businesslike in Trollope's habits of writing. Trollope had to have his daily ration of novel writing, his daily period of inhabitation within the minds of a group of imaginary persons. Trollope was addicted to novel writing, as another man might be addicted to strong drink or to gambling. The daily writing served a deep existential need for him. It was a main principle of continuity in his sense of himself, parallel in this to the sometimes apparently Quixotic and self-harming persistence of fidelity to promises once made, commitments affirmed, on the part of the characters in Trollope's novels – for example, Lady Anna. The continuity of the self is for Trollope the highest value, that to which everything else must, if need be, be sacrificed. In Trollope's own case the writing of novels was the diurnally renewed act of will which assured his own persistence as himself. The writing of novels made him and kept him what he was. It even gave him a proleptic experience of his persistence beyond the grave, as in that ruefully ironic passage in *An Autobiography* in which he imagines his posthumously published works appearing in parts for an indefinite period after his death, as if he were still alive and writing them. "If therefore," he wrote, "the Great Britain, in which we sailed for Melbourne, had gone to the bottom, I had so provided that there would be new novels ready to come out under my name for some years to come," and then he added some sentences that were omitted in the first edition of *An Autobiography* in 1883, which is of course after Trollope's death, when he did indeed speak to his readers from beyond the grave. "I fear," he said in the omitted passage, "that the numbers appearing month after month, year after year, with persistent regularity – when the man who wrote them was all but forgotten, – would weary the British public." That may be so, but it is clear that the anticipation of that posthumous publication gave Anthony Trollope the sense of a strange kind of immortality.

Lady Anna first appeared in installments in the *Fortnightly Review* from April 1, 1873 until April 1874. It was published in book form in two small red-brown cloth-bound volumes by Chapman and Hall in March of 1874, though the Tauchnitz edition had already been published in two volumes in 1873, thus predating English publication. As Trollope might have expected, the main plot of *Lady Anna*, in which a rich and noble heiress marries a working tailor, did not please his English readers.

Trollope's own account in *An Autobiography* of *Lady Anna* and of the response to it is the best indication of what is at stake in the novel:

> In it a young girl, who is really a lady of high rank and great wealth, though in her youth she enjoyed none of the privileges of wealth or rank, marries a tailor who has been good to her, and whom she had loved when she was poor and neglected. A fine young noble lover is provided for her, and all the charms of sweet living with nice people are thrown in her way, in order that she may be made to give up the tailor. And the charms are very powerful with her. But the feeling that she is bound by her troth to the man who had always been true to her overcomes everything, – and she marries the tailor. It was my wish of course to justify her in doing so, and to carry my readers along with me in my sympathy with her. But everybody found fault with me for marrying her to the tailor. What would they have said if I had allowed her to jilt the tailor and marry the good-looking young lord? How much louder, then, would have been the censure! The book was read, and I was satisfied. If I had not told my story well, there would have been no feeling in favour of the young lord. The horror which was expressed to me at the evil thing I had done, in giving the girl to the tailor, was the strongest testimony I could receive of the merits of the story.

Horror was indeed expressed. Though the unsigned notice in *The Times* for July 24, 1874, was generally favorable and in support of Lady Anna's obstinacy in sticking to her tailor, the unsigned notice in the *Saturday Review*, May 9, 1874, was violent in its denunciation. "This is the sort of thing," the reviewer wrote,

> the reading public will never stand, except in a period of political storm and ferment. There are Radicals in the abstract, but a man must be embittered by some violent exasperation who can like such disruptions of social order as this. . . . In the interest of both male and female novel-readers we protest against Lady Anna's match; for their sensibility's sake, we expose at once the main feature of the story, that they may not be betrayed unawares into reading what will probably leave a disagreeable impression.

Two of Trollope's women friends, Lady Wood and Miss Mary Holmes, wrote strong letters of protest which the author answered with an obstinate defense of Lady Anna's obstinacy. "Of course the girl has to marry the tailor," he wrote to Lady Wood, and to Miss Holmes he vehemently defended the novel:

> *Lady Anna* is the best novel I ever wrote! Very much! Quite far away above all the others!!! – A lady ought to marry a tailor – if she chanced to fall in love with such a creature, and to promise him, & take his goodness, when she was not a bad lady. That is all! Will you deny it?

Though there is surely some intentional ironic hyperbole in Trollope's claim that *Lady Anna* is far and away his best novel, nevertheless it is clear that matters of great social and ethical importance are at stake here. They are at stake for Trollope himself, for Victorian readers, and perhaps even for readers today. *Lady Anna*, among all of Trollope's many novels, presents the most violent conflict between two equally compelling moral imperatives. Moreover, it dramatizes this conflict in a poignant opposition between Lady Anna and her mother, two persons bound by the strongest ties of family love and obligation. The scenes in which Lady Anna and her mother confront one another – each loving the other with deep affection, each denying what the other wants, each knowing exactly what is passing in the other's mind, each violently opposing the other's will and decision – are excellent examples of the way, in Trollope's novels, characters within the same family may see with entire clarity into one another's minds, share the same values and criteria of moral judgment, and yet come to be unalterably opposed to one another.

Lady Anna is also an excellent example of the way, in Trollope's novels, a small fissure between parent and child may develop by gradual degrees into a violent and painful opposition. In this case the opposition is between the value of degree, the rule in a class society that says people should always marry within their class, and the value of keeping one's word when one has given it. A gentleman should marry a lady, a lady a gentleman. Tailors should marry the daughters of tradesmen or artisans. On the other hand, the continuity of the self, the highest value for Trollope, the chief sign of being a gentleman or a lady, depends on remaining faithful to a promise once made. Each of these moral imperatives is equally binding. The losses are grievous if either of these social rules is not obeyed. The Countess Lovel has centered her whole life on winning recognition of her rank and that of her daughter. If her daughter marries a tailor, not only will the general rule that rank should marry rank be broken, but the whole project of her life, or so it seems to her, will have failed. On the other hand, Anna has promised herself to Daniel Thwaite.

Trollope is most eloquent in presenting, at each stage of the action, the arguments which seem absolutely compelling on both sides. He is a master advocate or casuist, able, like a great lawyer (in fact like Sir William Patterson, the silver-tongued Solicitor General in *Lady Anna*), to "make himself understood when he speaks," to argue a case persuasively. Sometimes this arguing is put in the mouths of the characters themselves, but often it is presented by the narrator in free indirect discourse. The narrator speaks in the third person for the minds, hearts, and feelings of each of the characters in turn. In either case, the argument for each of the opposing views is not presented abstractly but is embodied in the life of one of the characters. The argument for the priority of rank and name over every other value is incarnated with great passion and force in Lady Anna's mother, the Countess Lovel. The argument against rank and in favor of egalitarianism is embodied in Daniel Thwaite, not only in his radical views, his admiration for honest work, his disdain for the silken idleness of the aristocracy (these views are presented by the narrator as excessive), but, more forcefully, in his own innate nobility and manliness. Daniel Thwaite, is, after all, the reader comes to see, in every way more fit to be the husband of Lady Anna than is Earl Lovel.

Lady Anna herself is one of Trollope's most attractive incarnations of his conviction that faithfulness to one's word, to one's conscience, to the deepest commitment of the self to another, is the highest value of all, taking priority over all others. It even takes precedence over that responsibility, which Anna also recognizes, to maintain rank and class difference. "I am ashamed to marry Mr. Thwaite, –" Lady Anna tells her friend Alice Bluestone,

> not for myself, but because I am Lord Lovel's cousin and mamma's daughter. And I should be ashamed to marry Lord Lovel . . . Because I should be false and ungrateful. I should be afraid to stand before him [Daniel Thwaite] if he looked at me. You do not know how he can look. He, too, can command. He, too, is noble.

Later on the narrator puts Lady Anna's case eloquently, speaking on her behalf for her response to Mrs Bluestone's exhortation to Lady Anna to remember "that we should all do our duties in that state of life to which it has pleased Him to call us." The narrator speaks for Lady Anna in that indirect discourse which is perhaps Trollope's most important tool as a novelist: "The nobly born young lady did not in her heart deny the truth of the lesson; – but she had learned another lesson and did not know how to make the two compatible. That other lesson taught her to believe that she ought to be true to her word; – that she specially ought to be true to one who had ever been specially true to her."

Anna's best friend, Alice Bluestone, "the young female Conservative," makes the most eloquent speech in defense of degree, comically garbling a Biblical passage in support of the position which all Lady Anna's family and friends take against her engagement to the tailor. "I think that a girl who is a lady," says Alice,

> should never marry a man who is not a gentleman. You know the story of the rich man who could not get to Abraham's bosom because there was a gulf fixed. That is how it should be; – just as there is with royal people as to marrying royalty. Otherwise everything would get mingled, and there would soon be no difference. If there are to be differences, there

should be differences. That is the meaning of being a gentleman, – or a lady.

The words "gulf" and "difference" here covertly name not just the separation between members of different classes, but sexual difference itself. *Lady Anna* powerfully, if covertly, dramatizes the association between class distinctions, distinctions of sex, and even the distinctions between races. It seems "horrid" to Alice Bluestone's "mind that a tailor should be kissed by a Lady Anna Lovel," and words like "pollution," "degradation," and "base love" echo through Countess Lovel's attempts to dissuade her daughter from marrying the tailor: "Then go from me, thou ungrateful one, hard of heart, unnatural child, base, cruel, and polluted. Go from me, if it be possible, for ever!"

Daniel Thwaite is shown to be "manly" in every sense of the word, "a very man," and his power over Anna is shown, unmistakably, to be in part a strong sexual attraction. The taboo against their marriage is in part a taboo against sexuality itself. To marry within one's class, where there is no difference of rank, somehow allows a forgetting of sexual difference and of the facts of sexuality, whereas Daniel Thwaite seems to the Countess Lovel "a foul, sweltering tailor." She and all the Lovels hold in abhorrence the idea of Daniel Thwaite touching Lady Anna, kissing her, embracing her. It is like the horror of miscegenation, the horror at the marriage, for example, of Desdemona and the Moor, which underlies *Othello*. Daniel Thwaite is in fact once spoken of as a "negro," when Aunt Julia tells Earl Lovel, Lady Anna's unsuccessful high-born suitor, that "you can never wash a blackamoor white," and "mutter[s] to herself some further remark about negroes" in response to the Earl's insistence that the Lovel family must accept the tailor. So violent is the Countess Lovel's "infinite disgust" for the idea that the tailor might embrace her daughter that she – but I leave to the reader to find out what she does. No other novel by Trollope contains a more shocking act of physical violence, or more openly dramatizes the deep association of psychological with class prohibitions in a parent's jealous care for the social and sexual purity of a daughter.

The fundamental paradox of *Lady Anna* is the following: the qualities that mark her as noble, as the daughter of her father, the wicked Earl Lovel, and of her mother, the strong-minded, even fanatical, Countess, are the very features of her character that lead her to defy her mother and all her friends in order to remain true to the promise she made to Daniel Thwaite. She has promised herself to him and she will remain true to her promise. She loves the tailor, she has given her heart to him, and she will stubbornly remain faithful to that love. Her love for Daniel makes her what she is. If she were to betray that love she would not be worthy to be the Lady Anna Lovel. It is only by betraying her rank and caste that she can demonstrate to the world that she belongs to that rank and caste. As Mrs Bluestone says of her, "She looks as soft as butter . . . but she is obstinate as a pig all the time." Her obstinacy is the mark of her distinction. Through Lady Anna Trollope once more enjoys and lets his readers enjoy what is for him one of the highest pleasures of life, the pleasure of justified obduracy. In that obduracy the weak become strong, cause immense trouble to all those around and much suffering to themselves, and yet they know that they are doing what is right. They are doing what they must do. As the narrator says of Anna's harsh treatment by her mother and by all around her:

> She was being persecuted; and as the step of the wayfarer brings out the sweet scent of the herb which he crushes with his heel, so did persecution with her extract from her heart that strength of character which had hitherto been latent.

It would seem that the conflict between these opposing values and opposing persons could in no way be appeased. Nor, it seems, can peace ever be brought back to the family and to the community the novel describes. In Trollope's novels, however, a happy ending is almost always possible. The character who obstinately defies parents, relatives, and the whole community is in the end reassimilated into that community. The wound is healed, the fissures closed. Even Daniel Thwaite the tailor is accepted by the Lovels. In *Lady Anna* the reconciliation is based on a general and implicit recognition that in fact Anna's obdurate keeping of her word is admirable. Her highest value does in fact for the community as a whole take precedence over the value of keeping the gulf fixed between ranks. It might be said that Trollope in *Lady Anna* is dramatizing for the English aristocracy a theme studied by anthropologists in more "primitive" societies: the need for a certain amount of exogamy if the tribe is to be kept strong. How this is worked out in *Lady Anna* the reader must discover for himself or herself. It can be said, however, that *Lady Anna* is a splendid example of one of the primary pleasures of reading Trollope: the pleasure of the happy ending reached against seemingly impossible odds.

17

Trollope's Thackeray

Trollope's *Thackeray*, first published in 1879, in the English Men of Letters series, like Henry James' *Hawthorne* in the same series, is a biographical and critical assessment of one major nineteenth-century novelist by another major contemporary novelist. This means that there are four different ways to read this book: (1) for what it still has to tell the reader about Thackeray's life and works; (2) as one of the best expressions of Victorian presuppositions about the nature and function of the novel, as well as one of the best descriptions of the sociological conditions under which Victorian novels were written and read; (3) for what it tells the reader indirectly about Trollope himself, about his ideas and attitudes, and about his stance toward his fellow men; (4) as a work in the Trollope canon, a work which, like his books on Caesar and Cicero, turns a historical personage into someone recognizably like the protagonist of a novel by Trollope. I shall say a word about each of these in turn.

Like most of the volumes in the English Men of Letters series, Trollope's *Thackeray* is still valuable as an introduction to Thackeray's life and works. It is a little humiliating to discover how little, on the whole, has been added to our conception of Thackeray and of his works in the intervening century. On the biographical side, Gordon Ray's monumental edition of Thackeray's letters and private papers, his investigation of Thackeray's relation to Mrs Brookfield, in *The Buried Life*, as well as his authoritative critical biography, have added much to our knowledge of Thackeray, but the main outlines are already firmly sketched in Trollope's long opening biographical chapter. Trollope no doubt knew all about Mrs Brookfield, but could not, in 1879, say one word about Thackeray's hopeless passion for a married woman. Trollope speaks of the "two skeletons" in Thackeray's cupboard: "His home had been broken up by his wife's malady, and his own health was shattered,"[1] but of that third skeleton not a word can be written. A reticent paragraph is given to a description of the mental illness of Thackeray's wife and her permanent confinement. Thackeray is said to be a man who "became, as it were, a widower till the end of his days" (20), and that is all.

On the other hand, Trollope knew Thackeray fairly well at the end of his life. The Victorian reticence of his account of Thackeray's life is compensated for by a series of intimate anecdotes and descriptions which give the reader a vivid sense of what Thackeray must have been like when Trollope knew him, with "his six feet four in height, with his flowing hair, already nearly gray, and his broken nose, his broad forehead and ample chest" (39). Trollope's anecdotes are the primary source for certain important bits of information about Thackeray and his work. An example is the story Trollope tells of a conversation with Thackeray in which the latter said the hero of *Henry Esmond* was "a prig" (121). This is a precious clue and counterargument against those critics who think Thackeray wanted Esmond to be thought of as wholly admirable. The anecdotes Trollope tells are of course essential to that portrait of Thackeray which makes him into something like the protagonist of a novel by Trollope. About this I shall say something later.

What about Trollope as a critic of Thackeray? No doubt in the twentieth century the big guns of various sorts of criticism – semiotic, structuralist, "New Critical," and so on – have been turned on Thackeray's novels. In spite of that, the outlines of the interpretation of Thackeray's work still for the most part current today are already clear in Trollope's readings. Like Trollope, critics today still tend to value Thackeray chiefly for his "realism," his pictures of men and women as conditioned by society and history. Like Trollope, critics today tend to see *Barry Lyndon, Vanity Fair*, and *Henry Esmond* as Thackeray's most important works. Like Trollope, twentieth-century critics have tended to think one of their main responsibilities must be to defend Thackeray against the charge that he was a cynic, a "barking dog" of a satirist who dwelt only on the bad side of human nature. Trollope has already worked out the main strategy for making this defense, namely by showing that Thackeray was in fact kind-hearted and that his satire came from a moral hatred of hypocrisy, self-deception, and snobbism. Thackeray's so-called cynicism has the highly ethical aim of making the reader love the good and hate evil. "Thackeray," says Trollope,

> had no idea of giving pain, but when he saw a foible he put his foot upon it, and tried to stamp it out. Such is my idea of the man whom many call a cynic, but whom I regard as one of the most soft-hearted of human beings, sweet as Charity itself, who went about the world dropping pearls, doing good, and never wilfully inflicting a wound. (60)

Trollope anticipates a recent trend in Thackeray criticism, present conspicuously, for example, in John Carey's *Thackeray*,[2] in giving much attention to Thackeray's burlesques, parodies, verses, and drawings. Like Carey, Trollope understands that these constitute a major part of

Thackeray's work. Trollope's Thackeray, like Carey's, is a man who had a prodigal genius for catching and imitating absurdities of style in language and in life. Though Trollope admires *Barry Lyndon* and *Vanity Fair*, though he admires *Henry Esmond* most of all as Thackeray's one perfect work, he enjoys the burlesques, parodies and comic verses immensely, as any reader should. It is these which Trollope is most moved to quote in his book, for example that hilarious parody of Bulwer-Lytton (under the name of "Sawedwadgeorgeearllittnbulwig") from the early *Yellowplush Papers* in *Fraser's Magazine*. Trollope's Thackeray is the master of the impromptu comic, and he rightly emphasizes this as an essential aspect of Thackeray's genius:

> In inquiring about him from those who survive him, and knew him well in those days, I always hear the same account. "If I could only tell you the impromptu lines which fell from him!" "If I had only kept the drawings from his pen, which used to be chucked about as though they were worth nothing!" "If I could only remember the drolleries!". . . Though he so rarely talked, as good talkers do, and was averse to sit down to work, there were always falling from his mouth and pen those little pearls. . . . After so many years his old friends remember the fag-ends of the doggerel lines which used to drop from him without any effort on all occasions of jollity. And though he could be very sad – laden with melancholy, as I think must have been the case with him always – the feeling of fun would quickly come to him, and the queer rhymes would be poured out as plentifully as the sketches were made. (30, 31)

I have said that Trollope's *Thackeray* is one of the best expressions of the system of assumptions about novels held by most Victorian novelists, readers, and critics. The book is also one of the best descriptions of the conditions under which a man made a living as a professional writer in England during the Victorian period. Both these aspects of the book emerge incidentally in the course of Trollope's account of Thackeray's life and works, but the account is generalized to indicate how precarious and difficult the life of a journeyman writer was in Trollope's day and Thackeray's, how "nine must fail where one will make his running good" (12–13). Much circumstantial information is given, for example about *Fraser's Magazine* and *Punch*, for both of which Thackeray wrote, and about the *Cornhill Magazine*, of which Thackeray was the first editor and for which Trollope was commissioned to write *Framley Parsonage*, his first great public success, because "Thackeray had himself intended to begin with one of his own great novels, but had put it off till it was too late" (52).

The system of presuppositions about novels in Trollope's book is a Victorian version of assumptions about "realism" which are as old as

Aristotle in one historical direction, and still of great force today in the other. A novel, for Trollope in this book as well as in his *Autobiography*, draws its validity from being a faithful picture of men and manners in the middle level of society and from its reflection of the psychological idiosyncrasies of its author. We need novels to find out about people like ourselves and to enjoy the special flavor of the author's personality, his unique way of looking at things, as it expresses itself in his presentation of character in society. In style a novel should be midway between the sublime and the ludicrous or burlesque. Thackeray's *Vanity Fair* and *Henry Esmond* are novels. His *Rowena and Rebecca* is a comic parody of *Ivanhoe*. Its style calls attention to itself and calls attention to the absurdities of Scott's style too, so it is not really a novel. The chief stylistic requirement of a novel proper is to be perspicuous, so that the reader is not aware of its language except as a transparent medium of the story the novelist has to tell. The purpose of a novel is to amuse and to instruct.

To be realistic, to be formally unified, to stick to the middle level in style and subject matter, to give pleasure and to teach sound morals – these are the desiderata of a good novel. I have said they form a system. The reader will see how. If the function of a novel is to mirror reality, its style must not call attention to itself. The middle level must be held because, for middle-class readers, neither the sublime nor the ludicrous forms part of social and psychological reality. Real people do not talk in those ways. Morality is ultimately justified by an appeal to the nature of things as they are. Those who follow evil come to no good in the end, while those who love the good come to good. In order to show this, a novel must be formally unified. A good novel can give pleasure as well as teach its readers to love the good, as Aristotle said in the *Poetics*, because it is human nature to take pleasure in learning the nature of things as they are. As Trollope puts this: "Without the lesson the amusement will not be there. There are novels which certainly can teach nothing; but then neither can they amuse any one" (199).

This intertwined set of ideas makes up what is on the whole still the reigning group of assumptions about prose fiction today, though each assumption is open to question. Each has in one mode or another of countercriticism been put in question in our day. Part of the value of Trollope's *Thackeray*, even for those who want to do that sort of questioning, is the way it presents so clear and cogent an expression of the system. The system is presented from the inside, so to speak, by someone, himself a distinguished novelist, to whom it seems the most natural thing in the world, part of nature and part of human nature, not, as in fact it is, part of our "white mythology," that part of the ideology of the West which defines and defends mimetic realism. Measured by this yardstick, Thackeray, in Trollope's view, comes off well. All the elements in the system I have identified are there in the measurement:

> So much I have said of the manner in which Thackeray did his work, endeavouring to represent human nature as he saw it, so that his readers should learn to love what is good, and to hate what is evil. As to the merits of his style, it will be necessary to insist on them the less, because it has been generally admitted to be easy, lucid, and grammatical. . . . I hold that gentleman to be the best dressed whose dress no one observes. I am not sure but that the same may be said of an author's written language. . . . Thackeray's style is excellent. . . . [T]he reader always understands his words without an effort, and receives all that the author has to give. . . . I have said previously that it is the business of a novel to instruct in morals and to amuse. . . . Now let the reader ask himself what are the lessons which Thackeray has taught. Let him send his memory running back over all those characters of whom we have just been speaking, and ask himself whether any girl has been taught to be immodest, or any man unmanly, by what Thackeray has written. . . . I say that with Thackeray the physic is always curative and never poisonous. He may be admitted safely into that close fellowship, and be allowed to accompany the dear ones to their retreats. The girl will never become bold under his preaching, or taught to throw herself at men's heads. Nor will the lad receive a false flashy idea of what becomes a youth, when he is first about to take his place among men. (192–202)

All this sounds old-fashioned today, but it has a bracing directness and plausibility about it, nor does there seem to be a trace of hypocrisy in Trollope's defense of Thackeray or in his defense of the sort of novel both he and Thackeray wrote. I said initially that one value of Trollope's *Thackeray* is what it tells the reader of the ideas and attitudes of Anthony Trollope himself. In one of its aspects the book is a forceful apology for Trollope's own theory of the novel and practice of it. One of the pleasures of the book is to hear Trollope's manly voice speak out in support of his profession. After having said that it is the business of a novel to instruct in morals and to amuse, Trollope continues:

> I will go further, and will add, having been for many years a most prolific writer of novels myself, that I regard him who can put himself into close communication with young people year after year without making some attempt to do them good as a very sorry fellow indeed. However poor your matter may be, however near you may come to that "foolishest of existing mortals," as Carlyle presumes some unfortunate novelist to be, still, if there be those who read your works, they will undoubtedly be more or less influenced by what they find there. And it is because the novelist amuses that he is thus influential. (119)

If Trollope's *Thackeray* has great value for what it tells the reader of Trollope's theory of the novel, Trollope is present throughout in another way. This is in the balanced and thoroughly Trollopian judgment he makes of Thackeray. His goal is to bring Thackeray before the reader's eyes and to make him, with his strengths and weaknesses, transparent to the reader, just as the heroes and heroines of Trollope's novels are made transparent. This clear-sighted and clearheaded perception of another person is quintessentially Trollopian. It is admirably applied, in this case, to a real person whom the author has known and not to an invented figure of Trollope's imagination.

In this "introspection of another person," to borrow a splendid phrase from Charles Du Bos,[3] Trollope's *Thackeray* offers itself for that fourth kind of reading I mentioned. The book creates a character and a story for him like those in Trollope's novels proper. Trollope's Thackeray is another example of that vacillating, self-doubting, overscrupulous, overgenerous, improvident, vulnerable, somewhat foolish, not worldly-wise, and wholly attractive sort of hero Trollope presents in so many of his best novels. Trollope's Thackeray is of the brotherhood of Phineas Finn, of Plantagenet Palliser, of Josiah Crawley, and even of Johnny Eames, different as they all are from one another. It is likely that such characters in one way or another express an aspect of Trollope's sense of himself, as he presents himself, for example, in the pages about his adolescence and young manhood in *An Autobiography*. In his novels Trollope excels in describing from the inside what it feels like to be such a person, as in the expression of the inner life of Plantagenet Palliser in *The Prime Minister*, or of Josiah Crawley in *The Last Chronicle of Barset*, or of Johnny Eames, hopelessly in love with Lily Dale, in *The Small House at Allington*. The best part of Trollope's *Thackeray* is his presentation of Thackeray as such a person:

> Unsteadfast, idle, changeable of purpose, aware of his own intellect but not trusting it, no man ever failed more generally than he to put his best foot foremost. Full as his works are of pathos, full of humour, full of love and charity, tending, as they always do, to truth and honour, and manly worth and womanly modesty, excelling, as they seem to me to do, most other written precepts that I know, they always seem to lack something that might have been there. There is a touch of vagueness which indicates that his pen was not firm while he was using it. He seems to me to have been dreaming ever of some high flight, and then to have told himself, with a half-broken heart, that it was beyond his power to soar up into those bright regions. I can fancy, as the sheets went from him every day, he told himself, in regard to every sheet, that it was a failure. (19)

The reader of Trollope's *An Autobiography* will know how much he cared for punctuality, hard work, careful counting of words, and the delivery to the publisher of what had been promised. Trollope's story of the unselfconfident Thackeray has, however, a happy ending, as, in one way or another, do the stories of most such people in Trollope's novels. The happy ending is the formal triumph of *Henry Esmond.* This is Thackeray's best work, in Trollope's view, the only novel on which he labored hard from beginning to end to make it a fully crafted, wholly finished work of art. In Trollope's opinion, the writing of one such novel makes up for the slackness present in all the others, even the best of them, and earns Thackeray a place "among the small number of the highest class of English novelists" (119). "His only work, as far as I can judge them," says Trollope,

> in which there is no touch of idleness, is *Esmond.* . . . All his full-fledged novels, except *Esmond,* contain rather strings of incidents and memoirs of individuals, than a completed story. But *Esmond* is a whole from beginning to end, with its tale well told, its purpose developed, its moral brought home – and its nail hit well on the head and driven in. (121)

All four of the ways of reading Trollope's *Thackeray* I have proposed come together in this passage. It tells the reader about Thackeray the man and about his work. It employs those Victorian ideas about what a good novel should be which I have identified. It reveals Trollope's criteria of judgment both of people and of literary works. It forms the climax of the little novel about Thackeray that Trollope hides within a book which seems on the surface no more than biography and criticism.

Notes

1. I have used my copy of the American edition of this: Anthony Trollope, *Thackeray*, English Men of Letters (New York, n.d.), p. 40. Further references are to this edition.
2. *Thackeray: Prodigal Genius* (London, 1977).
3. "Pauline de Browning: Extraits d'un Cours inédit," *Études Anglaises*, 7 (1954), p. 164: "*l'introspection d'autrui.*"

18

Theology and logology in Victorian literature

> All destructive discourses and all their analogues are trapped in a sort of circle. This circle is unique. It describes the form of the relationship between the history of metaphysics and the destruction of the history of metaphysics. *There is no sense* in doing without the concepts of metaphysics in order to attack metaphysics. We have no language – no syntax and no lexicon – which is alien to this history; we cannot utter a single destructive proposition which has not already slipped into the form, the logic, and the implicit propositions of precisely what it seems to contest.
>
> Jacques Derrida

> Men make their own history, but they do not make it just as they please; they do not make it under circumstances chosen by themselves, but under circumstances directly encountered, given and transmitted from the past. The tradition of all the dead generations weighs like a nightmare on the brain of the living. And just when they seem engaged in revolutionizing themselves and things, in creating something that has never yet existed, precisely in such periods of revolutionary crisis they anxiously conjure up the spirits of the past to their service and borrow from them names, battle cries and costumes in order to present the new scene of world history in this time-honored disguise and this borrowed language.
>
> Karl Marx

All interpretation, according to Nietzsche, is misinterpretation, the misappropriation of the traces of the past for some present purpose. Nevertheless, there is a difference, in scale at least, between the act of interpretation necessary to sustain large historical generalizations and that necessary to the reading of a single text or even the totality of works by a single author. My own work has been primarily of the latter kind. It seems likely to become even more exclusively so, though of course I know that one cannot take even the first step in the reading of a single text without making historical and literary–historical assumptions. Even so, I have puzzled a bit about the contribution I might make to this symposium.[1] In the end it has seemed that I might best try to raise the question of how one aspect of Victorian "counter-culture," in this case religious doubt, scepticism, or unbelief, entered into the intimate texture of important literary works of the Victorian period, even into those apparently affirming the official culture, that is, some form of Christianity.

Everyone who has studied nineteenth-century England knows of the wide range of religious conviction, or lack of it, represented in the period, from Roman Catholicism and High Church Anglicanism at one extreme through Evangelicalism, to various forms of Broad Church adherence to Christianity, to the Nonconformists, and finally to various sorts of liberals, modernists, humanists, agnostics, and outright atheists. The best studies of the important examples of these religious positions have of course recognized the complexity in the religious commitments of a Newman, a Browning, a Dickens, a Leslie Stephen. Noel Annan has magisterially identified the recurrent pattern in Victorian culture of early Evangelical upbringing followed by a loss of faith and a commitment to some form of agnostic humanism, but with the ethical patterns of Evangelicalism still remaining firm, as in the case of George Eliot or of so many others.

In spite of their recognition of this complexity, however, critics and intellectual historians have sometimes tended to pigeon-hole individual figures. Each has been thought of as representing one more or less unified religious position, the Scotist Catholicism of Gerard Manley Hopkins, the agnosticism of Huxley, the Feuerbachianism of George Eliot, and so on. Or the complexity of an individual figure has been seen as diachronic rather than synchronic. In the latter case the individual is represented as passing through a series of distinct stages of faith or unfaith, each in itself a unified and unequivocal position. An example of this perhaps inevitable pigeon-holing is the organization of the valuable new handbook, *Victorian Prose: A Guide to Research*. In this book, along with the separate sections on Newman, Arnold, Pater, Ruskin, and the rest of the major figures, there are sections on "The Oxford Movement: 1833–45," on "The Victorian Churches" (with subsections on "Church of England," "Nonconformists," and "Roman Catholics"), and on to "The Unbelievers" (Federick Harrison, Thomas Henry Huxley, John Morley, and Leslie Stephen).

This kind of organization, however necessary in a book of this sort, is misleading. It tends to imply that the quarrel among various forms of belief and unbelief was fought between individuals and sects, each with a well-defined and coherent position. Complexities in a given thinker are likely to be condemned as "inconsistencies" or "contradictions," as has often been the case, for example, in the abundant secondary literature on Matthew Arnold's religious writings. In fact, however, as I shall argue (it is the central point of this brief paper), the battle among various forms of belief and unbelief was fought within each individual mind, or, more precisely, within each individual text. Each text may have what Gerard Manley Hopkins called its "underthought," a submerged counterpoint to its manifest meaning, more or less opposed to that meaning. In Victorian England the "counter-culture" was present within the characteristic expressions of the official culture as a covert "counter-thought," a subversion not from the outside but from within. On the other hand, even the most extreme expressions of the "counter-culture," for example the deliberately provocative atheism of Swinburne, tend by an inevitable law to contain within themselves, as *their* counter-thought, exactly that system of concepts, figures, and myths which they are most concerned to reject.

I propose to test this hypothesis briefly in a few salient examples, chosen rather arbitrarily to represent a spectrum from fervent commitment to one form of Christianity to defiant rejection of Christianity. My hypothesis could only be genuinely tested by a full and intimate interpretation of the writers in question, something impossible to do in such a brief paper. In fact, one major desideratum in the study of Victorian literature and culture is a reinterpretation of major texts, an interpretation not governed by disabling presuppositions about the way texts have meaning. One such presupposition especially relevant here is the notion that a literary work has, or ought to have, a single, verifiable, unambiguous "meaning." The exegete who would undertake this difficult but necessary enterprise would find himself with an embarrassment of riches, since there is not one important Victorian writer who does not turn out to be another variation on my theme. In each some version of Christian–Platonic metaphysics is co-present with its undermining deconstruction. In fact I should say that a test of the importance of a writer, in the Victorian or any other age, is the presence together of the metaphysical system and its subversion. Only a writer who has not thought out his premises far enough to encounter the latent presence within them of their apparent opposite does not subvert himself in this way.

My examples are Carlyle, George Eliot, and Swinburne. After discussing each briefly, I shall try to draw a few tentative conclusions suggesting why it is that every distinguished literary text of the Victorian period turns out when examined closely to contain within itself both its manifest religious position (whether "official" or "counter") and the opposing position. In each case, the counter-culture is entangled within the official culture and undermines it from within, or, contrariwise, the counter-culture is unable to free itself from what it rejects and is forced to restate the old faith in spite of itself.

Carlyle's life and writings are a paradigmatic model in nineteenth-century English literature of the attempt to maintain the basic structure of the Christian faith without its essential dogmatic elements, such as the belief that the Bible is the single Scripture or the belief that Jesus was the Messiah. If some Victorians, like John Stuart Mill or George Eliot, develop a positivistic, even openly atheistical, faith to replace a lost supernaturalism, and if others, like Newman and Hopkins, go back to Roman Catholicism in order to preserve their endangered belief, others, of whom Carlyle was perhaps the most influential, develop some form of secular religion, or, as Carlyle called it, "natural supernaturalism." This enterprise is a continuation of Romanticism, or at least of one essential aspect of Romanticism. Such a secularized supernaturalism maintains in new forms the images, metaphors, concepts, and narrative patterns or "myths" of Christianity or of the Platonic idealism which is such a basic ingredient of post-Augustinian Christianity. Carlyle's natural supernaturalism differs from Christianity, however, in believing that these metaphors, concepts, and myths can be transformed, the old wine poured into new bottles, without being destroyed. As opposed to Christianity, with its notion of a single revelation and a single set of religious symbols and observances, Carlyle believes that all symbolic systems are inadequate to the divine reality, hiding it as much as revealing it. They quickly become fixed and dead, almost as soon as they are established, worn out old clothes which must be discarded, to be replaced by newly woven symbolic tissues, products of a fresh inspiration, in a never-ending sequence of creation followed by obsolescence, destruction, and a further creation again.

As subsequent literary and cultural history has suggested, Carlyle's attempt to naturalize supernaturalism was unstable. Like all contradictions or oxymorons, it expresses rather an unfulfilled yearning than a realized fact. It is difficult to change so much of a system of thought and belief without suggesting, whether one wishes to do so or not, that the whole structure may be a man-made fiction, not something based on eternal truth. That profound psychologist, Friedrich Nietzsche, felt that the rhetorical fervor with which Carlyle proclaimed his new secular faith betrayed his unfaith, the hollowness of his "Everlasting Yea." Carlyle was, said Nietzsche in *Twilight of the Idols*, an example of "pessimism as a poorly digested dinner (*Pessimismus als zurückgetretenes Mittagessen*)." He was

> a man of strong words and attitudes, a rhetor from *need*, constantly lured by the craving for a strong faith, and the feeling of his incapacity for it. . . . The craving for a strong faith is no proof of a strong faith, but quite the contrary. . . . At bottom, Carlyle is an English atheist who makes it a point of honor not to be one. (tr. Kaufman)

Ultimately destructive of the traditional faith Carlyle wanted to maintain in a new form are Carlyle's ultra-Protestant idea that every man can be his own priest or poet and his idea that each system of thought or belief, with its embodying symbols, is valid for no more than a time, since all such systems are fictions, "supreme fictions" as Wallace Stevens was to call them. Each is inadequate to the mystery it is meant to express, a veil as well as a revelation, and therefore it needs to be changed frequently. To take it as permanently valid is idolatry. It is only a step from this to that moment in Stevens' "The Comedian as the Letter C" when the whole fabric of occidental concepts, symbols, and mythological figures vanishes once: "Exit the whole / Shebang." To shift the attention, as Carlyle consistently does, from what is received in inspiration to the prophet, poet, statesman, or other hero who receives the inspiration, to shift attention from the content of a doctrine to its form, from meaning to language, is inevitably to imply that there is a radically inventive or constructive aspect of the hero's work. To see his work in this way is to see him as perhaps indeed no more than a maker of supreme fictions, as, like Carlyle himself, an atheist who makes it a point of honor not to be one.

Nietzsche may be cited again for his insight into the paradoxical structure of George Eliot's thought. She attempts to maintain the Evangelical virtues of self-sacrificing commitment to duty and a strong habit of fellow-feeling for one's neighbors in the absence of belief in the Christian God who had been the traditional basis for those virtues. In *Twilight of the Idols* Nietzsche speaks of those who:

> are rid of the Christian God and now believe all the more firmly that they must cling to Christian morality. This is an English consistency; we do not wish to hold it against little moralistic females à la Eliot. . . . We others hold otherwise. When one gives up the Christian faith, one pulls the right to Christian morality out from under one's feet. This morality is by no means self-evident: this point has to be exhibited again and again, despite the English flatheads (*den enlischen Flachköpfen zum Trotz*). Christianity is a system, a *whole* view of things thought out together. By breaking one main concept out of it, the faith in God, one breaks the whole: nothing necessary remains in one's hands. Christianity presupposes that man does not know, *cannot* know, what is good for him, what evil: he believes in God, who alone knows it. Christian morality is a command; its origin is transcendent; it is beyond all criticism; all right to criticism; it has truth only if God is the truth – it stands and falls with faith in God. (tr. Kaufman)

This seems to me an accurate judgment of one aspect of George Eliot. I should like, however, to affirm a counter truth. Insofar as George Eliot does in fact reaffirm the Christian morality in her novels, she inevitably drags in with that morality Christian metaphysics also. She affirms the existence of that transcendent deity who is precisely what she is determined to do without. I say "insofar as" because both the morality and the "ontology" of George Eliot's later novels are complex. In *Middlemarch* and *Daniel Deronda*, for example, the deconstructive effort of interpretation, based on a recognition of the role of language, especially figurative language, in shaping human convictions, extends beyond the undermining of belief in the basic metaphysical assumptions of origin, ending, and teleological movement between origin and ending. It ultimately also recognizes, however implicitly, that, as Nietzsche says, when belief in a transcendent deity vanishes a new kind of morality must replace the old. In Eliot's early work, however, for example in *Adam Bede*, there is a more straightforward attempt to maintain the peculiarly precarious Feuerbachian poise which says, in effect, "All the affirmations of Christianity are true, but not as the believers believe."

This attempt makes *Adam Bede* throughout a deliberately ambiguous text. It is intended to be taken in one way by the credulous and in another way by those who know that God, as Feuerbach defines him, "as the epitome of all realities or perfections is nothing other than a compendious summary devised for the benefit of the limited individual, an epitome of the generic human qualities distributed among men, in the self-realization of the species in the course of world history." "Theology," says Feuerbach in another place, "is anthropology, that is, in the object of religion which we call *Theos* in Greek and *Gott* in German, nothing but the essence of man is expressed." It accomplishes nothing, however, to affirm one's mastery over words in this way, Humpty-Dumpty-like, and so to say that the word "God" really means "man." The theological words, of which the word "man" is also to be sure an example, form a system which is stronger than the intention of any writer. The result is that certain key passages in *Adam Bede* vibrate before the reader's eyes like one of those Gestaltist diagrams which may be seen as duck or rabbit, or as inside out or outside in. The entire system of Christian metaphysics insinuates itself willy-nilly into George Eliot's expression of the Feuerbachian version of the counter-culture. It forces her to say both what she means to say and its tranquilly orthodox opposite.

An example of this is a passage in Chapter XLV where she says, "God . . . manifest[s] himself by our silent feeling, and make[s] his love felt through ours." Another example is four widely spaced echoing passages in Chapters III, XX, XXXIII, and L. Each of these asserts that there is a divine ocean of love which is the transcendent basis of individual human love and experienced in it. The divine ocean is also glimpsed in experiences of religious worship and in responses to nature and to works of art. "[I]t seems to be a far-off mighty love that has come near to us, and made speech for itself there," says the narrator of Adam's love for Hetty in Chapter XXXIII, and in Chapter III the narrator affirms that

> Our caresses, our tender words, our still rapture under the influence of autumn sunsets, or pillared vistas, or calm majestic statues, or Beethoven symphonies, all bring with them the consciousness that they are mere waves and ripples in an unfathomable ocean of love and beauty; our emotion in its keenest moment passes from expression into silence, our love at its highest flood rushes beyond its object, and loses itself in the sense of divine mystery.

Only in the almost unnoticeable words of qualification, "it seems to be," "consciousness that," "sense of," does George Eliot's Feuerbachianism, fully developed at the time she wrote these words, appear on the surface as a gentle ripple to disturb her reaffirmation of certain central concepts and metaphors of just that aspect of the official culture she was in her translations of Strauss and Feuerbach most concerned to counter.

Swinburne seems to fit perfectly that description Walter Pater gives of what he calls, speaking especially of William Morris, "aesthetic poetry." Pater means by that term what we should today call "Pre-Raphaelite poetry." "Greek poetry," says Pater,

> medieval or modern poetry, projects, above the realities of its time, a world in which the forms of things are transfigured. Of that transfigured world this new poetry takes possession, and sublimates beyond it another still fainter and more spectral, which is literally an artificial or "earthly paradise." It is a finer ideal, extracted from what in relation to any actual world is already an ideal. Like some strange flowering after date, it renews on a more delicate type the poetry of a past age, but must not be confounded with it. The secret of the enjoyment of it is that inversion of home-sickness known to some, that incurable thirst for the sense of escape, which no actual form of life satisfies, no poetry even, if it be merely simple and spontaneous. (213–14)

A poetry building itself not even on the "abolishing," to use Mallarmé's word, of physical nature, but on a further refinement or sublimation of a previous poetry which had already performed that effacement of the solid and earthly, a poetry metaleptically based on an earlier poetry and so annihilating any substantial presence or present within itself, perversely hungry not for home but for an ever more impalpable exile – Swinburne's version of "aesthetic poetry," so defined, and his greatness as a poet, take the form of an ability to use words as independent powers, powers liberated from their referential ties to "reality." Words, in Swinburne's hands, are like tones for the musician or colors for the painter. They can be repeated, modulated, and combined with other words to form new melodies or new chromatic sequences. To hazard a dangerous comparison between several arts, one might say that the effect of Swinburne's poetry is something like that of two artists whom he greatly admired, J. M. W. Turner in painting and Richard Wagner in music. If one adds to this creation of a self-sufficient realm of words in Swinburne's poetry the fact that the conceptual content of this poetry often takes the form of violent denunciations of Christianity, it would seem that Swinburne is an unusually pure example of what might be meant by "Victorian counter-culture" in its religious dimension. Moreover, in his notorious life and in the sado-masochistic aspects of his poetry he would seem to be also an example of other aspects of Victorian counter-culture.

When one turns to the most salient examples of his defiant rejection of Christianity, however, for instance in the celebrated chorus of *Atalanta in Calydon* where he speaks of "the supreme evil, God," one finds not atheism at all but a language heavy with the conceptual terms, the metaphors, and the narrative patterns of Graeco-Roman literature and the Bible. John Ruskin called *Atalanta in Calydon* 'The grandest thing ever yet done by a youth – though he is a demonic youth." According to W. B. Yeats' name as an initiate of The Order of the Golden Dawn, however, "Demon est Deus Inversus." To put a minus sign instead of a plus sign before the elements of western culture is not to liberate oneself from them but to remain entirely bound within their net. To define God as the supreme evil is as much an act of homage and belief as to define him as the supreme good. Far from establishing the subversive attitudes of a counter-culture or the dangerous freedom of a purely "aesthetic" poetry, Swinburne, one might argue, is as traditional as Job or Aeschylus, for example in these lines near the end of that famous chorus:

> Because thou hast bent thy lightnings as a bow,
>   And loosed the hours like arrows; and let fall
> Sins and wild words and many a wingèd woe
>   And wars among us, and one end of all;
> Because thou hast made the thunder, and thy feet
>   Are as a rushing water when the skies
> Break, but thy face as an exceeding heat
>   And flames of fire the eyelids of thine eyes;
> Because thou art over all who are over us;
>   Because thy name is life and our name death;
> Because thou art cruel and men are piteous,
>   And our hands labour and thine hand scattereth;
> Lo, with hearts rent on knees made tremulous,
>   Lo, with ephemeral lips and casual breath,
>   At least we witness of thee ere we die

That these things are not otherwise, but thus;
  That each man in his heart sigheth, and saith,
    That all men even as I,
All we are against thee, against thee, O God most high.
(ll. 1174–92)

I shall try in conclusion to identify one or two small consequences which follow from what has been said so far. One has already been formulated in my epigraph from Jacques Derrida. The counter-culture has no instruments with which to attack the official culture but those drawn from the twenty-five-hundred year old official culture. For this reason, the counter-culture turns out regularly and inevitably, in spite of itself, to be another version of what it attempts to destroy.

A second consequence is a recognition of the irreducible plurality of any cultural expression, such as a literary text. This plurality does not result from confusion on the part of the author, his inability to get his thoughts straight or to say what he means. Nor does it result from some remediable error or willful overcomplication of things on the part of the interpreter, though a new definition of the relation between reader and text would emerge from the problems I have been discussing. No, the plurality of meanings in each literary text, the presence of an underthought inextricably interwoven with each overthought, a counter-culture within each culture, arises from an intrinsic necessity of the literary texts themselves, insofar as they depend, as all texts in our language do, on conceptual terms, metaphors, and narrative patterns drawn from the finite reservoir of such elements in our Western family of languages. The counter-culture has always been present within the official culture, waiting to be brought out into the open in new ways by the George Eliots, Swinburnes, and Wildes of each new generation. Anti-Platonism was already present within the dialogues of Plato, not something added later by Plato's antagonists.

The final consequence of what I have said is a notion of history – of literary history, of cultural history, or of history as such – different from the familiar paradigm of a series of self-enclosed "epochs," each with its own intrinsic set of forms, its own "world picture." Not that there is no such thing as history, in the sense of intrinsic differences between epoch and epoch, country and country, individual and individual, text and text. Each text, person, country, and epoch are indeed different from one another, as no two signatures from the same hand are identical, no two copies of a text the same, no two performances of a play exactly congruent. The concepts of difference, of signature, of history are in fact integral elements within the cultural remains, such as literary texts, which they are used to investigate. Like the other elements, they must be solicited, interrogated. A more adequate concept of history must add to the notion of difference the notion of repetition. The problematic of repetition balances the problematic of difference, in an unstable equilibrium or oscillation. The writings and other cultural artifacts of the Victorians appear, in the light of these modes of interpretation, as latecomers in a long line of repetitions with a difference of concepts, figures of speech, and myths going back to Plato and the Bible, and behind them to their antecedents.[2] These elements contain within themselves the genetic possibility of both thought and underthought, both cultures and counter-cultures, in inexhaustible, though not unbounded, permutation.

Notes

1. This was first presented to a symposium on Victorian "counter-culture."
2. Compare the admirable opening of Pater's *Plato and Platonism* (London, 1893), so definitive a qualification, before the fact, of A. N. Whitehead's celebrated dictum that all Western history is a footnote to Plato: "Plato's achievement may well seem an absolutely fresh thing in the morning of the mind's history. Yet in truth the world Plato had entered into was already almost weary of philosophical debate, bewildered by the opposition of sects, the claims of rival schools. Language and the processes of thought were already become sophisticated, the very air he breathed sickly with off-cast speculative atoms. . . . Some of the results of patient earlier thinkers, even then dead and gone, are of the structure of his philosophy. They are everywhere in it, not as the stray carved corner of some older edifice, to be found here or there amid the new, but rather like minute relics of earlier organic life in the very stone he builds with. The central and most intimate principles of his teaching challenge us to go back beyond them, not merely to his own immediate somewhat enigmatic master – to Socrates, who survives chiefly in his pages – but to various precedent schools of speculative thought, in Greece, in Ionia, in Italy; beyond these into that age of poetry, in which the first efforts of philosophic apprehension had hardly understood themselves; beyond that unconscious philosophy, again, to certain constitutional tendencies, persuasions, forecasts of the intellect itself, such as had given birth, it would seem, to thoughts akin to Plato's in the older civilisations of India and of Egypt, as they still exercise their authority over ourselves" (pp. 2–3). In this exemplary rejection of any notion of origin or of originality, each text refers to some still earlier text, that to still another, and so on. Moreover, "influence" is not a matter of conscious borrowing, but something that, like a disease, in fact like "influenza," insinuates itself into the air we breathe, or something that is present, whether or not we know it or wish it, in the intimate texture of our material, in the words we must use to speak or write at all. If we are another footnote to Plato, Plato was himself already a footnote to still earlier footnotes, in an endless chain of footnotes to footnotes, with nowhere a primary text as such.

19

The two rhetorics:

George Eliot's bestiary

In an essay published in 1983, "Composition and Decomposition: Deconstruction and the Teaching of Writing,"[1] I argued that all good readers as well as all good writers have always been "deconstructionists." Deconstruction was defined as presupposing a methodical awareness of the disruptive power that figures of speech exert over the plain construable "grammatical" sense of language, on the one hand, and over the apparent rigor of logical argumentation on the other. I concluded from this that rhetoric in the sense of knowledge of the intricacies of tropes should be taught in courses in composition, along with grammar and rhetoric in the sense of persuasion. Knowledge of figures of speech should also be taught in courses in reading. In the process of arguing that more attention should be given in courses both in reading and in writing to knowledge of figures of speech and their disruptive power, I discussed briefly (as examples of the way the great writers are all "deconstructionists" before the fact) a passage from Plato and one from George Eliot. I propose here to analyze those passages in more detail in an attempt to identify their deconstructive rigor. It should be remembered that "deconstruction" is not something that the reader does to a text; it is something that the text does to itself. The text then does something to the reader as she or he is led to recognize the possibility of two or more rigorously defensible, equally justifiable, but logically incompatible readings of the text in question.

The passage from Plato comes from the *Phaedrus*. Plato's rejection in the *Gorgias* and in the *Phaedrus* of empty skill in writing well still has force. It is not enough to learn to write correctly and forcefully about any subject at all, taking any side of an argument, as a gifted lawyer can get the man on trial freed or condemned depending on which side has hired him. Writing well is not writing well unless it is guided by all of those ethical, political, and even metaphysical considerations that cannot be excluded from the teaching of writing. Such considerations involve true knowledge both of the human soul and of language. Here rhetoric as reading or as the knowledge of tropes comes in even for Plato. Plato's discussion of rhetoric in the *Phaedrus* contains a program for both kinds of rhetoric – rhetoric as writing and rhetoric as reading. The latter, too, must be guided by a knowledge of truth and conducted in the name of truth. Here is the crucial passage in the *Phaedrus*:

> *Socrates*: So contending with words is a practice found not only in lawsuits and public harangues but, it seems, wherever men speak we find this single art, if indeed it is an art, which enables people to make out everything to be like everything else, within the limits of possible comparison, and to expose the corresponding attempts of others who disguise what they are doing.
>
> *Phaedrus*: How so, pray?
>
> *Socrates*: I think that will become clear if we put the following question. Are we misled when the difference between two things is wide, or narrow?
>
> *Phaedrus*: When it is narrow.
>
> *Socrates*: Well then, if you shift your ground little by little, you are more likely to pass undetected from so-and-so to its opposite than if you do so at one bound.
>
> *Phaedrus*: Of course.
>
> *Socrates*: It follows that anyone who intends to mislead another, without being misled himself, must discern precisely the degree of resemblance and dissimilarity between this and that.
>
> *Phaedrus*: Yes, that is essential.
>
> *Socrates*: Then if he does not know the truth about a given thing, how is he going to discern the degree of resemblance between that unknown thing and other things?
>
> *Phaedrus*: It will be impossible.
>
> *Socrates*: Well now, when people hold beliefs contrary to fact, and are misled, it is plain that the error has crept into their minds through the suggestion of some similarity or other.
>
> *Phaedrus*: That certainly does happen.
>
> *Socrates*: But can anyone possibly master the art of using similarities for the purpose of bringing people round, and leading them away from the truth about this or that to the opposite of the truth, or again can anyone possibly avoid this happening to himself, unless he has knowledge of what the thing in question really is?
>
> *Phaedrus*: No, never.[2]

Rhetoric as reading, as the knowledge of tropes, is here defined as the only means of protection against the powers of rhetoric as writing, as illicit persuasion, as well as the essential means of composition for those who write successfully. A mastery of the truth about things and a mastery of the various forms of similitude turn out to be the two things that are needed by the rhetorician, both in his guise as writer and in his guise as reader. For Plato, too, reading and writing are intrinsically connected.

But what of Plato himself? What happens if we apply to Plato's discourse the method of reading that he himself advises? It is readily observable that Plato's own argument (or that of Socrates) proceeds by just that persuasion by means of similitude against which he warns – for example, when Socrates expresses his condemnation of rhetoric in the *Gorgias* in what he calls "the language of geometricians": "Sophistic is to legislation what beautification is to gymnastics, and rhetoric to justice what cookery is to medicine." A moment before, Socrates has condemned cookery and beautification as being mere semblances of medicine and gymnastics, respectively: "Cookery then, as I say, is a form of flattery that corresponds to medicine, and in the same way gymnastics is personated by beautification, a mischievous, deceitful, mean, and ignoble activity, which cheats us by shapes and colors, by smoothing and draping, thereby causing people to take on an alien charm to the neglect of the natural beauty produced by exercise" (*Gorgias*, 465b, 247). By the remorseless logic of the language of geometricians, then, if we condemn cookery and beautification, we must also condemn rhetoric and its brother in false similitude, sophistry. The language of geometricians, however, it is easy to see, is nothing but a somewhat misleading name for that reasoning by similitude which Socrates condemns in the *Phaedrus*.

A is to B as C is to D: this is just the paradigmatic form of a proportional metaphor as Aristotle gives it in the section on metaphor in the *Poetics*. The ship is to the sea as the plow is to the earth, and therefore we say that the ship plows the waves. The basic resources of rhetorical argumentative persuasion are, in Aristotle's *Rhetoric*, said to be the example and the enthymeme. An example is a synecdoche – part used for the whole and then applied to another part – with all the problems appropriate to that trope; and the enthymeme is defined as an incomplete syllogism – that is, once more, argument by similitude or trope, since a syllogism is a formally stated proportional metaphor.[3]

It is all very well for Plato to have Socrates claim that he is dividing things according to their essential nature, as a good butcher cleaves a carcass at the joints – for example, in the distinction between body and soul on which the comparison of cookery to rhetoric depends – but Socrates' argument proceeds as much by similitude as by division. Plato's "dear gorgeous nonsense," as Coleridge called it, is primarily a brilliant gift for arguing by means of similitudes or tropes – for example, in the famous condemnation of writing in comparison with speaking at the end of the *Phaedrus*. Writing is like the stupid farmer who sows his seeds in a barren garden of Adonis, while speaking is like the farmer who sows his seeds in suitable soil, that is, in the souls of living men (276b–77a, 521–2). The wise reader will remember this by-no-means-innocent metaphor of farming when I come in a moment to discuss a passage from George Eliot's *The Mill on the Floss*. In the *Gorgias*, Callicles responds to a metaphor from shoemaking proposed by Socrates, followed by another use of the figure of the farmer who sows seed, by saying in exasperation, "By heaven, you literally never stop talking about cobblers and fullers and cooks and doctors, as if we were discussing them" (490e, 273). That is to say, Plato never stops talking nonliterally, not least in personifying himself as Socrates, and the result is that readers of Plato need most of all a skill in interpreting arguments based on tropes.

Plato's writings, too, both in what he says about rhetoric and in how he says it, provide an example of the inextricable interinvolvement of the two kinds of rhetoric and of the impossibility of having one without the other. He also provides another example of the way in which the act of reading can uncover directions for reading the text at hand in such a way as to undermine or deconstruct the apparent affirmations of that text, if the reader is cannily attentive to the play of tropes in the text. This is just what Plato tells us to be, along with learning to use tropes cannily in our own compositions. The text warns against the argument by tropes on which the text itself depends. To put this in another way, all discourse about rhetoric, for example Plato's *Gorgias* or a modern textbook of freshman composition, is itself an example of rhetoric and demands to be read as such, if we are not to be bamboozled by its enthymemes. This is another argument for the necessity of teaching reading along with writing.

As an exemplification of what might be meant by a "deconstructive" or rhetorical reading or of a reading as such, along with a demonstration of the truth of my claim that all good readers have always been deconstructionists, I shall discuss a wonderfully penetrating and witty passage from George Eliot's *The Mill on the Floss*. The passage reads itself, or gives the reader directions for how to read it. It is not only a text to be read but also a lesson in how to read. Any careful reader of *The Mill on the Floss* is likely to notice this passage. It has not failed to elicit comment.[4] The passage gives oblique hints to the reader about how to read the novel itself, as well as hints about some dangers lurking in the pedagogy of grammar and composition. The passage has to do with poor Tom Tulliver's sufferings at school in the hands of Mr Stelling. It might have as title "The Beaver, the Camel, and the Shrewmouse":

> Mr. Broderip's amiable beaver, as that charming naturalist tells us, busied himself as earnestly in constructing a dam, in a room up three pair of stairs in London, as if he had been laying his foundation in a stream or lake in Upper Canada. . . . With the same unerring instinct Mr. Stelling set to

work at his natural method of instilling the Eton Grammar and Euclid into the mind of Tom Tulliver. . . .

[Mr. Stelling] very soon set down poor Tom as a thoroughly stupid lad; for though by hard labour he could get particular declensions into his brain, anything so abstract as the relation between cases and terminations could by no means get such a lodgment there as to enable him to recognise a chance genitive or dative. . . . Mr. Stelling concluded that Tom's brain being peculiarly impervious to etymology and demonstrations, was peculiarly in need of being ploughed and harrowed by these patent implements: it was his favourite metaphor, that the classics and geometry constituted that culture of the mind which prepared it for the reception of any subsequent crop. I say nothing against Mr. Stelling's theory: if we are to have one regimen for all minds, his seems to me as good as any other. I only know it turned out as uncomfortably for Tom Tulliver as if he had been plied with cheese in order to remedy a gastric weakness which prevented him from digesting it. It is astonishing what a different result one gets by changing the metaphor! Once call the brain an intellectual stomach, and one's ingenious conception of the classics and geometry as ploughs and harrows seems to settle nothing. But then it is open to some one else to follow great authorities, and call the mind a sheet of white paper or a mirror, in which case one's knowledge of the digestive process becomes quite irrelevant. It was doubtless an ingenious idea to call the camel the ship of the desert, but it would hardly lead one far in training that useful beast. O Aristotle! if you had had the advantage of being "the freshest modern" instead of the greatest ancient, would you not have mingled your praise of metaphorical speech, as a sign of high intelligence, with a lamentation that intelligence so rarely shows itself in speech without metaphor – that we can so seldom declare what a thing is, except by saying it is something else? . . .

At present, in relation to this demand that he should learn Latin declensions and conjugations, Tom was in a state of as blank unimaginativeness concerning the cause and tendency of his sufferings, as if he had been an innocent shrewmouse imprisoned in the split trunk of an ash-tree in order to cure lameness in cattle.[5]

This admirable passage rises from height to height by a continual process of capping itself or going itself one better, which is to say it constantly deconstructs itself. The passage speaks of the activity of reading, manifests a model of that activity, and invites us to read it according to the method it employs. In all these ways it is a fine example of the form of reading that I am calling "deconstructive" or of reading as such. Though good reading does not occur as often as one might expect or hope, it is by no means confined to any one historical period and may appear at any time, perhaps most often in those, like George Eliot, who are also good writers, masters of composition. The deconstructive movement of this passage is constituted by the proffering and withdrawing of one metaphorical formulation after another. Each metaphor is dismantled as soon as it is proposed, though the sad necessity of using metaphors is at the same time affirmed. No doubt, most teachers of English grammar and composition, like teachers of Latin, have experienced Mr Stelling's exasperation at the obduracy and denseness of their students' inability to remember the rules of grammar and idiom when they try to write or to grasp syntactical concepts, while at the same time they speak with fluency and force, just as Tom Tulliver "was in a state bordering on idiocy with regard to the demonstration that two given triangles must be equal – though he could discern with great promptitude and certainty the fact that they *were* equal" (215). Though Tom cannot learn Latin grammar, he uses English with devastating cruelty towards his sister.

It might seem that George Eliot is placing in opposition the use of literal language and the abuse of metaphorical language and that she is counseling the former in a way that recalls the late seventeenth- and eighteenth-century tradition alluded to in her Lockean figure of the mind as a sheet of white paper. In fact, the passage demonstrates that "rarely" or "seldom" seems to be "never." The only weapon against a metaphor is another metaphor, along with an awareness of our linguistic predicament in not being able – or in being so seldom able that "rarely" is "almost never" – to declare what a thing is, except by saying it is something else. Mr Stelling's problem is not that he uses the metaphor of plowing and harrowing for his teaching of Euclid and the Eton Grammar, but that he takes his metaphor literally, has no awareness of its limitation, and uses it as the excuse for a brutally inappropriate mode of instruction in Tom's case. Mr Stelling teaches "with that uniformity of method and independence of circumstances, which distinguishes the actions of animals understood to be under the immediate teaching of nature," such as that beaver who builds a dam "up three pair of stairs in London" in sublime indifference to the absence of water (213). The beaver, like Mr Stelling, is a literalist of the imagination. To take a metaphor literally is the aboriginal, universal, linguistic error, for as George Eliot says in an often-quoted passage in *Middlemarch*, "We all of us, grave or light, get our thoughts entangled in metaphors, and act fatally on the strength of them."[6]

The escape from this entanglement in the net of a metaphor (another metaphor!) is not a substitution of literal language for misleading figure, but is the replacement of one metaphor by another. The second metaphor may neutralize the first or cancel out its distortions. This is a cure of metaphor by metaphor, a version of homeopathy. So George Eliot replaces the metaphor of plowing and harrowing with a metaphor of eating. Forcing geometry and Latin grammar on Tom is like curing an inability to digest cheese with doses of cheese, or, the reader might reflect, like curing the disaster brought on by carrying the metaphorical basis in a pedagogical theory into practice by the application of another theoretical metaphor, replacing one kind of cheese with another kind of cheese. It is at this point that the narrator draws herself (himself?) up and makes the exclamation about how astonishing it is what a different result one gets by changing the metaphor.

To the other figures here must be added irony and prosopopoeia, irony as the pervasive tone of the narration and personification as the trope whereby the ironic discrepancy between narrator and character is given a name and a personality in the putative storyteller, "George Eliot." That narrator pretends to have made Mr Stelling's mistake, or the beaver's mistake – namely to have used a metaphor without reflection – and then to have been surprised by the results into having a metalinguistic insight into the role of metaphor in pedagogical theory. But of course the narrator, who has been aware of this all along, is manipulating the metaphors in full deliberate awareness. He only pretends to be astonished. The sentence is ironic in the strict sense that it says the opposite of what it means, or rather that it says both things at once. It is astonishing and not astonishing, and the reader is challenged to ally himself with one side or the other, though at the same time he is put in a double bind. If he is not astonished, he may be putting himself unwittingly in the same camp as the beaver and Mr Stelling, since another way to define a literalist is to say that he is incapable of being astonished by the workings of language. If the reader is astonished, then he is admitting that until a moment ago at least, he was a linguistic innocent, lagging behind the all-knowing narrator, who only ironically pretends to be astonished by something that he or she has known all along.

The digestive metaphor is then followed by two more traditional metaphors for the mind – the Lockean one of the white sheet of paper, and the figure of the mirror, which has had such a long history in expressions of "realism" in the novel: for example, in George Lukács or in George Eliot herself in the celebrated chapter 17 of *Adam Bede*, the *locus classicus* for the theory of realism in Victorian fiction.

The next metaphor, that of the camel as the ship of the desert, seems to be irrelevant or nonfunctional, not part of the chain, no more than a textbook example of metaphor.[7] It allows the bringing in of Aristotle and the opposition of the ancients who naïvely praised metaphor, on the one hand, and the moderns, such as Locke, who lament its presence in language and try (unsuccessfully) to expunge it, on the other. Aristotle, by the way, did not, strictly speaking, "praise . . . metaphorical speech as a sign of high intelligence," as George Eliot says. Aristotle said a "command of metaphor" was the "mark of genius," "the greatest thing by far," in a poet, the one thing that cannot be imparted by another."[8] A command of metaphor is for Aristotle not so much a sign of intelligence as an intuitive gift, "an eye for resemblances" (1495a, 87). The poet does not rationally think out metaphors. They just come to him in a flash, or they fall under his eye. In any case, the figure of a camel as a ship accomplishes three moves simultaneously in the intricate sequence of George Eliot's thought in the passage as a whole.

First move: The image of the camel more or less completes the repertoire of examples of metaphor that makes the passage not only a miniature treatise on metaphor but also, unostentatiously, an anthology, bouquet, herbarium, or bestiary of the basic metaphors in our tradition – that is, coming down from the Bible and from the Greeks. No choice of examples is innocent, and it is no accident that metaphors of farming and sowing (for example, in Plato's *Phaedrus* or in Christ's parable of the sower, with the sun lurking somewhere as the source of germination); metaphors of specular reflection, the play of light, of images, of reflection, and of seeing; metaphors of eating, of writing on that blank sheet of paper, and of journeying from here to there (that is, of transport, whether by camel back or on ship board) – all tend to reappear whenever someone, from Aristotle on down to the freshest modern teacher of composition, pulls an example of metaphor out of his pedagogical hat. These remain the basic metaphors still today, and though he will not necessarily have the poet's instinctive command of them, a good reader can learn to thread his way from one to another in their interchangeability and begin to master them as a deliberate reader if not as a writer. If the ship plowing the waves mixes the agricultural with the nautical region of figure, the sowing of seed, for both Plato and Jesus, is at the same time a form of writing, a dissemination of the word. And does not the assimilation of learning to eating appear in that extraordinary image of Ezekiel eating the scroll, as well as in Hegel's interpretation of the Last Supper in *The Spirit of Christianity*, not to speak of the Communion service itself, in which the communicants eat the *Logos*, or of a strange passage in George Eliot's own *Middlemarch*?[9]

Second move: The camel as ship of the desert is not just an example of metaphor. It is a metaphor of metaphor; that is, of transfer or transport from one place to another. This is not only what the word *metaphor* means etymologically but also what metaphor does. It effects a transfer. If George Puttenham's far-fetched Renaissance name for metalepsis is the "Far-fetcher," he elsewhere calls metaphor the "Figure of Transport."[10] Metaphor gets the writer or reader from here to there in his argument, whether by that "smooth gradation or gentle transition, to some other kindred quality," of which Wordsworth speaks in the "Essays upon Epitaphs,"[11] following the Socrates of the *Phaedrus* on "shifting your ground little by little," or by the sudden leap over a vacant place in the argument, of which George Meredith writes: "It is the excelling merit of similes and metaphors to spring us to vault over gaps and thickets and dreary places."[12] Pedagogy is metaphor. It takes the mind of the student and transforms it, transfers it, translates it, ferries it from here to there. A method of teaching, such as Mr Stelling's, is as much a means of transportation as is a camel or a ship. My own "passages" from Plato and Eliot are synecdoches, parts taken from large wholes and used as figurative means of passage from one place to another in my argument.

Third move: The sentence about the camel brings into the open the asymmetrical juxtaposition between the opposition of literal and figurative language, on the one hand, and the opposition of theory and practice, on the other. The reader may be inclined to think that these are parallel, but this probably depends on a confusion of mind. One thinks of literal language as the clear nonfigurative expression of ideas or concepts: for example, the "abstract" concepts of grammar, such as the relation between cases and determinations in the genitive and the dative, which Tom Tulliver has as much trouble learning as a modern student of English composition has in learning the rules of English grammar. At the same time, one thinks of literal language as the act of nonfigurative nomination, calling a spade a spade and a camel a camel, not a ship. We tend to think of figure as applied at either end of the scale – from abstract to concrete – as an additional ornament making the literal expression "clearer," more "vivid," or more "forceful." As George Eliot's sentence makes clear, however, the trouble with theory is not that it is abstract or conceptual but that it is always based on metaphor – that is, it commits what Alfred North Whitehead calls "the fallacy of misplaced concreteness."

If it is true that original thinking is most often started by a metaphor, as both Whitehead himself and such literary theorists as William Empson and Kenneth Burke aver in different ways, it is also the case that each metaphorically based theory, such as the alternative pedagogical theories that George Eliot sketches out, has its own built-in fallacious bias and leads to its own special form of catastrophe in the classroom. If a camel is not a ship, the brain is neither a field to plow nor a stomach nor a sheet of paper nor a mirror, though each of these metaphors could, and has, generated ponderous, solemn, and intellectually cogent theories of teaching. Neither theory nor literal meaning, if there is such a thing (which there is not), will help you with that camel. As soon as you try to tell someone how to manage a camel, you fall into theory – that is, into some metaphorical scheme or other. The opposition between theory and practice is not that between metaphorical and literal language, but is that between language, which is always figurative through and through, and no language – silent doing. If the praxis in question is the act of writing, the habit of writing well, it can be seen that there are going to be problems in teaching it, more problems even than in teaching someone how to drive a camel or to make a chair. That the terms for the parts of a chair are examples of those basic personifying catachreses, whereby we humanize the world and project arms and legs where there are none, may cause little trouble as the apprentice learns from watching the master cabinetmaker at work, but it might cause much trouble to someone who is writing about chairs.

After what has been said so far, the function of the final animal in George Eliot's bestiary, the shrewmouse – the vehicle for the last metaphor in the segment that I have excised from her narrative – is clear enough. Having seemingly aligned herself with those fresh moderns who would opt for an antiseptic "speech without metaphor," George Eliot, far from speaking without metaphors herself, goes on to present the most ostentatious and elaborate of all the metaphors in this sequence – ostentatious in the sense that the literal elaboration of the vehicle of the metaphor, a bit of Warwickshire agricultural folklore, seems far to exceed its parabolic application to Tom's suffering: "Tom was in a state of as blank unimaginativeness concerning the cause and tendency of his sufferings, as if he had been an innocent shrewmouse imprisoned in the split trunk of an ash-tree in order to cure lameness in cattle." This not only demonstrates once more that "we can . . . seldom declare what a thing is, except by saying it is something else." It also shows that the only cure for metaphor is not literal language but another metaphor that so calls attention to itself that no one could miss that it is a metaphor or take it as innocently "dead." If literal language is possible, it is likely, paradoxically, to occur in the elaboration of the vehicle of the figure, as in this case or as in the parables of Jesus in the Gospels. It is possible to speak literally about shrewmice in Warwickshire or about the details of farming, fishing, and household care in first-century Palestine, but this literal speech almost always turns out, by a kind of fatality intrinsic to language, to be the means of speaking parabolically or allegorically about something else. The most figurative language, it would follow, is the language that appears to be the most literal. The good reader is one who, like George Eliot, brings this sad fact into the open, as a secret writing in sympathetic ink beneath the writing on the surface is brought out by the application of heat or the right chemicals. Bringing it into the open, alas, is not an escape from it or a "cure" for it.

From where does my metaphor of "cure" come? Is it my own licit or illicit addition, the reader's license? No, it is of course already there as one of the places of passage in the quotation from George Eliot. I have said that the shrewmouse is the last animal in George Eliot's bestiary and that the literal details of the shrewmouse's suffering exceed its figurative application. Obviously, neither of these is the case. The last animals are those lame cattle, and they function to make the figure of the shrewmouse, at a second remove, a figure for the failure of teaching to cure lameness in the sense of linguistic incapacity – for example, an inability to write clear and concise English prose. Mr Stelling's pedagogy, based as it is on the magic literalization of a metaphor, is as much a piece of superstition as is the countryman's beliefs about shrewmice and cattle. Which of us twentieth-century teachers can be sure that our method is not another such blind belief in an unread metaphor?

In any case, the reader at the end of my sequence from *The Mill on the Floss* remains as trapped as ever within the linguistic situation of not being able to say what a thing is, except by saying it is something else. Tom is imprisoned within the obstinate rigors of Mr Stelling's pedagogy, rigors that result from the literal application of a metaphor. His situation makes him like a poor innocent imprisoned shrewmouse. The melancholy wisdom of this passage affirms that the reader or writer of any sort – you or I – is imprisoned as much as Tom, Mr Stelling, or the shrewmouse within the linguistic predicament that the passage both analyzes and exemplifies. The most that one can hope for is some clarification of the predicament, not escape from it into the free light of day.

In "Composition and Decomposition" I concluded my brief discussion of the passages from Plato and George Eliot with the claim that both teachers and students of rhetoric as persuasion or as composition must aim to become as good readers as Plato, George Eliot, or Jacques Derrida, as wise in the ways of tropes, or else they will not learn to be good teachers or practitioners of writing either. "Good courses in rhetoric as reading," I concluded, "must always accompany programs in composition, not only in preparation for reading Shakespeare, Milton, Wordsworth, and Wallace Stevens, but as an essential accompaniment to courses in writing." I draw now another, perhaps more radical or disturbing, conclusion. If the medieval trivium of grammar, logic, and rhetoric is indeed a place in which the pathways of those three disciplines come together or cross, as the etymology of *trivium* suggests (*tri-viae*, "three roads"), it may be that rhetoric is not so much the climax of a progressive mastery of language both for reading and for writing as it is the place in which the impossibility of mastery is definitively encountered.

The road called "rhetoric" is always marked "impassable" or "under construction; pass at your own risk" or, as it is succinctly put on signs in England, "road up!"

Paul de Man certainly thought this was the case with rhetoric as the wrestling with tropes. In an interview with Robert Moynihan, in answer to a question about irony, de Man asserted that "the claim of control, yes, when it is made, can always be shown to be unwarranted – one can show that the claim of control is a mistake, that there are elements in the text that are not controlled, that it is always possible to read the text against the overt claim of control."[13] And in another essay, "Semiology and Rhetoric," discussing Archie Bunker's question "What's the difference?" de Man asserts: "The grammatical model of the question becomes rhetorical not when we have, on the one hand, a literal meaning and on the other hand a figural meaning, but when it is impossible to decide by grammatical or other linguistic devices which of the two meanings (that can be entirely incompatible) prevails. Rhetoric radically suspends logic and opens up vertiginous possibilities of referential aberration. . . . I would not hesitate to equate the rhetorical, figural potential of language with literature itself."[14]

Certain notorious quarrels among literary critics or between philosophers and literary critics or among philosophers occupy the polemical field of humanistic study today. I am thinking, for example, of interchanges between Jacques Derrida and John Searle or between Paul de Man and Raymond Geuss or between me and Meyer Abrams, or of attacks on "deconstruction" in the name of history and straightforward referential language by Gerald Graff, Frank Lentricchia, and others.[15] The issues at stake in these various quarrels are complex, but it may be possible to understand them better by seeing them as disagreements about the proper relation among the three branches of the ancient trivium. A critic such as Meyer Abrams wants to make grammar, what he calls "construing" of the plain sense of a poem or a novel, the basis for literary study, to which the study of the "perfidious" language of tropes by deconstructionists might be added as an extra frill for a few specialists in advanced courses. Analytical philosophers or logicians (with a few honorable exceptions such as Wittgenstein and Austin) tend to minimize the effect that figures of speech might have on their enterprise, or to believe that logic might, so to speak, reduce, encompass, or master rhetoric. Such logicians or analysts tend to be violently and unreasonably hostile to a philosopher of rhetoric such as Jacques Derrida and even to deny him the name of philosopher (for is not philosophy purely a matter of logical reasoning?).

The claim of "deconstruction," by now patiently (and reasonably) demonstrated with a wide variety of philosophical and literary texts and patiently (and reasonably) argued in "theoretical" statements, is that language is figurative through and through, all the way down to the bottom, so to speak, and that rhetoric in the sense of tropes inhibits or prevents both the mastery of the plain sense of texts, which is promised by grammar, and the mastery of reasoning, which is promised by logic. "Rhetoric radically suspends logic and opens up vertiginous possibilities of referential aberration." If this is the case (and it is), rhetoric is not so much the imperial queen of the trivium and of basic studies in humanities generally, as it is the odd man out, the jack of spades or the wild card, who suspends the game or at any rate causes much trouble in playing it. This is not an argument against the kind of study of rhetoric that I have tried to define and exemplify in this essay. Far from it. Though the truth about language may be a dark and troubling one, it is better to know that truth than to fool oneself or others, since language is an edge tool, and much harm may be done by even the most amiable and well-meaning of mistaken assumptions about it, as the sad story of Mr Stelling demonstrates.

Notes

1. In *Composition & Literature: Bridging the Gap*, Winifred Bryan Horner, ed. (Chicago, 1983), pp. 38–56.
2. *Phaedrus*, 261d–62b, tr. R. Hackforth, in *Plato: The Collected Dialogues*, Edith Hamilton and Huntington Cairns, eds, Bollingen series 71 (Princeton, N.J., 1963), pp. 507–8. The citations from *Gorgias* are from the translation by W. D. Woodhead in the same volume, pp. 229–307.
3. See Aristotle, *The Rhetoric*, tr. Lane Cooper (New York, 1932), p. 10.
4. For example, by Joseph Litvak in a recent Ph.D. dissertation in Comparative Literature at Yale University.
5. George Eliot, *The Mill on the Floss*, Cabinet Ed., vol. 1 (Edinburgh and London, n.d.), bk. 2, ch. 1, pp. 213–17.
6. George Eliot, *Middlemarch*, Cabinet Ed., vol. 1 (Edinburgh and London, n.d.), ch. 10, p. 127.
7. The *OED* gives several examples under "Desert" and "Ship," the earliest dated 1615.
8. Aristotle, *Poetics*, tr. S. H. Butcher (New York, 1951), 1459a, p. 87.
9. *Middlemarch*, vol. 1, ch. 6, p. 86.
10. Cited by Richard A. Lanham, *A Handlist of Rhetorical Terms* (Berkeley, 1969), p. 100.
11. William Wordsworth, "Essays upon Epitaphs," in *The Prose Works*, W. J. B. Owen and Jane Worthington Smyser, eds, vol. 2 (Oxford, 1974), p. 81.
12. George Meredith, *One of Our Conquerors*, in *Works*, Memorial Ed., vol. 17 (London, 1909–11), p. 189.
13. Robert Moynihan, "Interview with Paul de Man," *Yale Review* 73, no. 4 (July 1984), p. 580.
14. Paul de Man, *Allegories of Reading* (New Haven, Conn., 1979), p. 10.

15. For the first see Jacques Derrida, "Signature Event Context"; John R. Searle, "Reiterating the Differences: A Reply to Derrida," *Glyph 1* (Baltimore, Md., 1977), pp. 172–208; and Jacques Derrida, "Limited Inc," *Glyph 2* (Baltimore, Md., 1977), pp. 162–254. For the second see Paul de Man, "Sign and Symbol in Hegel's *Aesthetics*," *Critical Inquiry*, 8 no. 4. (Summer 1982), pp. 761–75; Raymond Guess, "A Response to Paul de Man"; and Paul de Man, "Reply to Raymond Geuss," *Critical Inquiry* 10, no. 2 (Dec. 1983), pp. 375–90. For the third see M. H. Abrams, "The Deconstructive Angel"; and J. Hillis Miller, "The Critic as Host," *Critical Inquiry* 3, no. 3 (Spring 1977), pp. 425–47. For the fourth see Gerald Graff, *Literature against Itself: Literary Ideas in Modern Society* (Chicago, 1979); and Frank Lentricchia, *After the New Criticism* (Chicago, 1980). The literature about, for, and against deconstruction has since 1980 grown to impressive proportions.

20

"Hieroglyphical truth" in *Sartor Resartus*:

Carlyle and the language of parable

In gesture, rather than in speech . . .

Thomas Carlyle

Ralph Waldo Emerson made his second visit to England in 1847–8. One of the high points of his year there was his excursion with Thomas Carlyle in July of 1848 to see Stonehenge, Wilton, Salisbury and Winchester. In *English Traits* Emerson recounts the episode and tells the reader a bit of their conversation on the way to Amesbury by train and carriage. Carlyle attacked art generally and ornament in particular:

> Art and "high art" is a favorite target for his wit. "Yes, *Kunst* is a great delusion, and Goethe and Schiller wasted a great deal of good time on it:" – and he thinks he discovers that old Goethe found this out, and, in his later writings, changed his tone. As soon as men begin to talk of art, architecture and antiquities, nothing good comes of it. He wishes to go through the British Museum in silence, and thinks a sincere man will see something and say nothing. In these days, he thought, it would become an architect to consult only the grim necessity, and say, "I can build you a coffin for such dead persons as you are, and for such dead purposes as you have, but you shall have no ornament."[1]

I take this as a parable of a fundamental paradox about Carlyle. The man who rejects ornament, who praises sincere seeing and knowing above all, and who associates sincere knowing and seeing with silence, is at the same time far from silent, even in his praise of silence to Emerson. He publishes works that add up to thirty closely printed volumes in the collected edition, and, far from composing in a style like a plain coffin, enwreathes everything he writes with fantastic and ostentatious ornament.

In the case of *Sartor Resartus*, which I take here as my main focus and as the *locus classicus* in Carlyle's writing of "ornament," the ornament takes two forms. One is the local form of the openly elaborated style,

"Carlylese." Carlylese is mostly metaphor or other figure which displays itself, which calls attention to itself as figure, by its hyperbolic elaboration. Examples are legion, but would include these several not wholly compatible metaphors for the book as a whole: the image of a chaos of documents fitfully illuminated by intermittent flashes of light; or the image of Palingenesis, the image both of society and of Teufelsdröckh as a phoenix about to arise again from the flames of its own self-consuming; or the image of Teufelsdröckh's life as like a stream plunging over a waterfall and dispersing in vapor, to reform itself here and there in visible splashes and puddles; or the image of nature and the human heart as hieroglyphic writing to be deciphered; or, finally, the image, drawn ironically from Milton, of the Editor's reconstruction of Teufelsdröckh's life and opinions as the making of a bridge over chaos:

> Daily and nightly does the Editor sit (with green spectacles) deciphering these unimaginable Documents from their perplexed *cursiv-schrift*; collating them with the almost equally unimaginable Volume, which stands in legible print. Over such a universal medley of high and low, of hot, cold, moist and dry, is he here struggling (by union of like with like which is Method) to build a firm Bridge for British travellers. Never perhaps since our first Bridge-builders, Sin and Death, built that stupendous Arch from Hell-gate to the Earth, did any Pontifex, or Pontiff, undertake such a task as the present Editor. For in this Arch too, leading, as we humbly presume, far otherwards than that grand primeval one, the materials are to be fished-up from the weltering deep, and down from the simmering air, here one mass, there another, and cunningly cemented, while the elements boil beneath: nor is there any supernatural force to do it with; but simply the Diligence and feeble thinking Faculty of an English Editor, endeavouring to evolve printed Creation out of a German printed and written Chaos, wherein, as he shoots to and fro in it, gathering, clutching, piecing the Why to the far-distant Wherefore, his whole Faculty and Self are like to be swallowed up.[2]

The other mode of ornament in *Sartor Resartus* is the more comprehensive, large-scale, all-encompassing form of the complex narrative machinery which makes *Sartor Resartus* of great interest, among Victorian works, for contemporary narrative theory. *Sartor Resartus* is as complex and involuted a form of storytelling as, say, William Faulkner's *Absalom, Absalom!* or Conrad's *Nostromo*, *Lord Jim* or *Under Western Eyes*. In Carlyle's *Sartor*, as in novels by Conrad or Faulkner, the act of narration, in which someone retrospectively reconstructs the past from ambiguous evidence and ambiguous documents, is foregrounded as a problematic and uncertain enterprise. In all these cases the book becomes in part about the act of narration, about the act of achieving knowledge by a process of reminiscent retelling, retailoring the tailor, repatching the patcher, sartor resartus. Both in local style and in overall narrative conception Carlyle, in *Sartor Resartus*, does the thing that takes the most doing. The book, *Sartor Resartus*, about the book, Diogenes Teufelsdröckh's *Die Kleider, ihr Werden und Wirkung*, which purports to have been published by Stillschweigen and Co[gnie] [Keep Still and Company], is one of the noisiest books among the classics of English literature. I shall concentrate here on an attempt to answer the question: Why is this? What is the function of all that "ornament" and indirection in Carlyle? Why does this sincere man not keep silent or say the truth that is in him directly and plainly, like a coffin made of six flat slabs of wood, fit for his dead English readers, and have done with it? It will not do to say he could not help writing the way he wrote. The question is why he could not help it, given the circumambient condition he was in and the purposes he had in writing.

A clue to an answer or at least to a clearer definition of the question may be given by a passage from Chapter Ten of Book Second of *Sartor Resartus* entitled "Pause." It is the chapter which follows the grand climax of *Sartor Resartus*, "The Everlasting Yea":

> Here, indeed, at length, must the Editor give utterance to a painful suspicion, which, through late Chapters, has begun to haunt him; paralysing any little enthusiasm that might still have rendered his thorny Biographical task a labour of love. It is a suspicion grounded perhaps on trifles, yet confirmed almost into certainty by the more and more discernible humoristico–satirical tendency of Teufelsdröckh, in whom underground humours and intricate sardonic rogueries, wheel within wheel, defy all reckoning: a suspicion, in one word, that these Autobiographical Documents are partly a mystification! What if many a so-called Fact were little better than a Fiction; if here we had no direct Camera-obscura Picture of the Professor's History; but only some more or less fantastic Adumbration, symbolically, perhaps significantly enough, shadowing-forth the same! Our theory begins to be that, in receiving as literally authentic what was but hieroglyphically so, Hofrath Heuschrecke, whom in that case we scruple not to name Hofrath Nose-of-Wax [it means literally, of course, "grasshopper"] was made a fool of, and set adrift to make fools of others. (202)

This passage functions simultaneously as a real statement demystifying another set of statements as fictional and at the same time as a fictional statement working obliquely and ironically to give the reader directions for how to read the whole of *Sartor Resartus*, including the passage itself we are reading. The reader is invited to read the whole as hieroglyphical rather than as literal truth, as a "more or less fantastic Adumbration" or indirect "shadowing-forth" of the truth. It is the effect of the application to the passage itself which is hardest to see. It is able to be glimpsed only in the blink of an eye or out of the corner of the eye. This glimpse most concerns me here. In the following paragraph another purported deciphering, quotation and translation from a small slip of paper in one of those notorious paper-bags pins down in a few phrases as good a guide as the reader is ever given to the right way to try and read *Sartor Resartus*:

> What are your historical Facts; still more your biographical? Wilt thou know a Man, above all a Mankind, by stringing-together beadrolls of what thou namest Facts? The Man is the spirit he worked in; not what he did, but what he became. Facts are engraved Hierograms, for which the fewest have the key. (203)

The problem, the reader will see immediately, in a blink of the eye, is that though *Sartor Resartus* may indeed be engraved Hierograms shadowing-forth a transcendent meaning, those Hierograms, in this case, are not facts at all but outrageous and hyperbolic fictions. *Sartor Resartus* differs in this radically in its mode of language from most of Carlyle's other works, *The French Revolution*, *The Life of John Sterling*, *The Letters and Speeches of Oliver Cromwell*, *On Heroes and Hero-Worship* and the *History of Frederick the Great*. The latter have a solid historical or biographical base, however much they make that base the hieroglyphic vehicle of an otherwise invisible spiritual truth. That base is missing in *Sartor*, except by way of the exceedingly oblique and indirect presence of the facts of Carlyle's own life story behind the life of Teufelsdröckh. No one who did not already know those facts, however, for example the story of Carlyle's conversion experience in Leith Walk, could possibly extract them as such from *Sartor*. My questions here are the following: What, exactly, is the mode of language of *Sartor Resartus*? Why did Carlyle find it necessary to use such a fantastic mode of indirection to say the truth that was in him? What does it say about the nature of that truth that it needed to be said in such a roundabout and parabolic fashion?

That Carlyle's goal was to say that truth and convey it to his readers there can be no doubt. In his letter to *Fraser's* offering them the manuscript of *Sartor* he roundly affirms that, "The Creed promulgated on all these things [Art, Politics, Religion, and the rest], as you may judge, is *mine*, and firmly *believed*."[3] In his letter of August 12, 1834, to Emerson about *Sartor* he says, apologizing for the extravagancies of style, "My Transoceanic brothers, read this earnestly, for it *was* earnestly meant and written, and contains no *voluntary* falsehood of mine," and then adds,

> Since I saw you, I have been trying, am still trying, other methods, and shall surely get nearer the truth, as I honestly strive for it. Meanwhile, I

> know no method of much consequence, except that of *believing*, of being *sincere*: from Homer and the Bible down to the poorest Burns's *Song* I find no other *Art* that promises to be perennial.[4]

The question is why being sincere, speaking and writing sincerely, in Carlyle's case, requires such indirection, such recourse to fictions, to figures, to ironies and to rhetorical extravagancies of all kinds.

It is this element of sincerity, as of a man speaking directly to other men and women the truth that is substantially in him and makes up his substance as a person, since it is based on his God-given intrinsic nature, which Emerson emphasizes in his memorial address or brief character sketch of Carlyle presented in Boston in Emerson's old age, in February 1881. This was written just after Carlyle's death, but was primarily based on a letter written in 1848, after Emerson's second visit to Carlyle. "Great is his reverence for realities," says Emerson of Carlyle,

> for all such traits as spring from the intrinsic nature of the actor. . . . He preaches, as by cannonade, the doctrine that every noble nature was made by God, and contains, if savage passions, also fit checks and grand impulses, and, however extravagant, will keep its orbit and return from far. . . . His guiding genius is his moral sense, his perception of the sole importance of truth and justice; but that is a truth of characters, not of catechisms.[5]

Friedrich Nietzsche's view of Carlyle was very different, so different as to raise the question of whether they could have been speaking of the same person. Nietzsche, as is well known, greatly admired Emerson's work, carried a copy of Emerson's *Essays* in his knapsack, and when he lost it, went to some trouble to acquire another. In *Twilight of the Idols* (*Die Götterdämmerung*), Nietzsche praises Emerson for having that spiritual agility and gaiety, in the sense of *die fröliche Wissenschaft*, gay science or joyful wisdom, a power of constant self-renewal or self-transcendence, which Nietzsche most prized in himself and in others. Emerson, says Nietzsche, is

> one who instinctively nourishes himself only on ambrosia, leaving behind what is indigestible in things. . . . Emerson has that gracious and clever cheerfulness which discourages all seriousness; he simply does not know how old he is already and how young he is still going to be; he could say of himself, quoting Lope de Vega: "*Yo me sucedo a mi mismo* [I am my own heir]."[6]

Nietzsche's judgement of Carlyle, which just precedes his comments on Emerson in *Twilight of the Idols*, is strikingly different. It too uses the figure of eating and of digestion, certainly a maliciously appropriate figure for Carlyle:

> I have been reading the life of *Thomas Carlyle* [presumably he means Froude's *Life*],[7] this unconscious and involuntary farce, this heroic–moralistic interpretation of dyspeptic states. Carlyle: a man of strong words and attitudes, a rhetor from *need*, constantly lured by the craving for a strong faith and the feeling of his incapacity for it (in this respect, a typical romantic!). The craving for a strong faith is no proof of a strong faith, but quite the contrary. If one has such a faith, then one can afford the beautiful luxury of scepticism: one is sure enough, firm enough, has ties enough for that. Carlyle drugs something in himself with the fortissimo of his veneration of men of strong faith and with his rage against the less simple-minded: he *requires* noise. A constant passionate dishonesty against himself – that is his *proprium* [i.e. his propriety, what is proper to him]; in this respect he is and remains interesting. . . . At bottom, Carlyle is an English atheist who makes it a point of honor not to be one. (*Ibid.*, 521)

Which judgement is the correct one: Emerson's, which sees Carlyle as the type of the honest or sincere man, speaking from the heart, or Nietzsche's, which sees Carlyle's propriety as the impropriety of a constant passionate dishonesty against himself? My argument will be that Carlyle is both, or neither, that it is in principle impossible to tell which he is, for reasons which are essential to his situation as a human being, to his strategy as a writer, and to the meaning of the doctrine he preached. The reasons are the same as those which make it necessary for this admirer of sincerity and silence to write works which are so indirect in rhetorical strategy and so stylistically noisy.

In a letter to John Sterling Carlyle defends himself from the "*awful* charge" that he does not believe in a "*Personal*" God by imagining Teufelsdröckh replying to such a charge by laying his hand on his heart and making a gesture of "solemnest *denial*." "In gesture, rather than in speech; for 'the Highest *cannot* be spoken of in words'. . . *Wer darf ihn NENNEN?* I dare not, and do not."[8] If, for Carlyle, the highest cannot be spoken of in words, and if the aim of *Sartor Resartus*, which is precisely words, words on the page to be read, and by no means simply gestures, is to speak of the highest, which clearly *is* its aim, then that speaking must necessarily be of the most oblique and roundabout sort. It must be a speaking which, in one way or another, discounts itself in its act of being proffered.

Symbols, for Carlyle, are words or other signs, hieroglyphical emblems, which are used to name the highest, the unnamable. *Wer darf ihn nennen?* This infinite reality lies hidden behind the garment of nature, of words or other signs, and of human consciousness, all three. It might be said that for Carlyle the almost wholly metaphorical character of ordinary language loosens that language up. Ostentatious metaphor prevents language from being caught in a short-circuit of empirical naming of physical objects. The metaphorical nature of language makes it apt as an ingredient of symbol, but a symbol is not an ordinary metaphor. It is an oblique name for the unnamable. The traditional rhetorical name for such a use of language is "catachresis," the forced and abusive transfer of a name from its ordinary or at least seemingly literal use to a new realm. There it functions to name something which can be named in no other way, which has no literal name. Who dares name the highest? Such a word is neither literal nor figurative: not literal because it is carried over into a realm where it is improper, and not figurative because the definition, since Aristotle, of figure is that it substitutes for the proper name. In this case there is no proper name, no other name at all but the symbolic one. It can be said that all *Sartor Resartus*, all its exuberant ornament of local style and narrative involution, is both an example of symbol in this sense and written for the sake of making clear what symbols are. If Christ's parables are parables about parable, *Sartor Resartus* is an hieroglyphical work about hieroglyphs. It cannot be otherwise, for it is impossible to speak other than hieroglyphically in this region.

Carlyle makes a crucial distinction between two forms of symbol, the extrinsic and the intrinsic. His distinction is parallel but not quite identical to the one he makes elsewhere in *Sartor* between metaphor and those few primitive elements of natural sound. Carlyle's distinction corresponds closely to the distinction made by Hegel in paragraph twenty of the *Encyclopedia* and in the *Lectures on Aesthetics* between sign and symbol. This is not to argue that Carlyle was here influenced by Hegel but to indicate that the distinction was one he shared with his German Romantic contemporaries. For Hegel a sign is arbitrary and unmotivated. A sign is not similar to what it stands for. It is a proposition put forth by the human mind in its act of understanding. A sign is evidence of the power of the mind over what it thinks, in its endless process of appropriation and self-appropriation in the gradual fulfilment of spirit. A symbol, on the other hand, is similar to what it stands for. It participates in its meaning. It is, so to speak, the natural embodiment of its meaning. A symbol is found there already rather than proposed or arbitrarily set forth. In the *Encyclopedia* Hegel validates sign over symbol. In the *Aesthetics* he appears to validate symbol over sign in the section on symbolic art, but then, rather surprisingly, in the section on the sublime, which he makes parallel in functioning, again surprisingly, to allegory, fable, parable and other such indirect forms of language, Hegel gives the sublime a high place in aesthetic modes. The sublime is defined as a mode of sign rather than of symbol, since it is characterized by the distance and non-correspondence between the embodiment and what it stands for or expresses.

In a somewhat similar way, Teufelsdröckh, Carlyle's spokesman in

Sartor, distinguishes between two forms of symbol, those with an extrinsic and those with an intrinsic value, "oftenest the former only." Extrinsic symbols may be the glimmering expression of some divine idea of duty or daring, but there is no necessary correspondence between the symbol and what it symbolizes. Carlyle gives as examples the clouted shoe the peasants rallied round in the *Bauernkrieg* or the Wallet-and-staff which was the ensign of the Netherland *Gueux*, coats of arms and military banners generally, "national or other sectarian Costumes and Customs": "Intrinsic significance these had none; only extrinsic" (223). Even the Cross itself, the highest symbol of Christianity, is, amazingly enough, said by Carlyle to have "had no meaning save an accidental extrinsic one" (223). Examples of intrinsic symbols are "all true works of Art," "the Lives of heroic God-inspired Men," the body of a loved-one in death, and, highest of all,"those [Symbols] wherein the Artist or Poet has risen into Prophet, and all men can recognise a present God, and worship the same: I mean religious Symbols," of which "our divinest Symbol" is

> Jesus of Nazareth, and his Life, and his Biography, and what followed therefrom. Higher has the human Thought not yet reached: this is Christianity and Christendom; a Symbol of quite perennial, infinite character; whose significance will ever demand to be anew inquired into, and anew made manifest. (223–4)

Intrinsic symbols embody the infinite in the finite. The impetus for the conjunction comes from above not from below, and so the similarity between the above and the below, their intrinsic participation in one another, is guaranteed from above.

This seems clear enough and unequivocal enough, but is it? For one thing, it appears that in his highest example, Carlyle is talking not about Jesus himself, but about his biography, that is, I take it, the Gospels and the other books of the New Testament, and he is speaking of these books as human accomplishments: "Higher has the human Thought not yet reached." The Gospels are simply the highest form of the work of art generally, in which "Eternity look[s] through Time" and the "God*like*" (Carlyle's word, my emphasis) is "rendered visible" (223). Moreover, it will be noted that Carlyle does not speak of the intrinsic symbolic validity of anything Jesus said, for example in those parables which were a main mode of his teaching. It is Jesus himself, the man and his life, what he did, his wordless gestures, so to speak, which make him "our divinest Symbol." What aspect of that life, the reader might ask parenthetically, is intrinsically symbolic, if even the Cross itself, as he had said a moment before, is an extrinsic symbol? This displacement of symbolism from what a man said to what he did is reinforced by the inclusion of "the Lives of heroic God-inspired Men" in the hierarchy of intrinsic symbols, "for what other Work of Art," asks Teufelsdröckh, "is so divine?" (224). Most of Carlyle's writing in his long career after *Sartor* was, as any reader of his work knows, devoted to exploring various examples of "heroic God-inspired Men." Carlyle is primarily a biographical writer, even in *The French Revolution*.

Finally, though Carlyle (through Teufelsdröckh), speaks of Jesus as a symbol of quite perennial, infinite character, nevertheless the significance of the life of Jesus will ever demand to be anew inquired into and anew made manifest. I take it this means that, perennial and infinite though it is, Jesus as symbol will fade and become inefficacious if it is left solely as embodied in the lives of Jesus written by Matthew, Mark, and Luke. New Gospel-makers are constantly required to make even this symbol manifest for a new time. The new Gospel will, of course, to some degree at least be a new garment for the infinite. It will therefore be a transformation of the symbol depending absolutely for its efficacy upon the existence of what Teufelsdröckh calls a new "Poet and inspired Maker; who, Prometheus-like, can shape new Symbols, and bring new Fire from Heaven to fix it there" (225). It is difficult to discern the difference between an old symbol made new (old wine in new bottles) and an altogether new symbol (new wine in new bottles), since in both cases a new insight through the finite into the infinite is required.

This becomes especially evident when the reader confronts Teufelsdröckh's affirmation of a subdivision with the category of intrinsic symbols which complicates the apparently firm opposition between intrinsic and extrinsic symbols. There are perennial intrinsic symbols and others only "with a transient intrinsic worth" (224) even in that highest category of religious symbols. Moreover, the two categories of symbol will not stay neatly divided. The extrinsic is constantly superimposing itself on the intrinsic and contaminating it. Many even of religious symbols have "only an extrinsic" worth, for example the Cross, while to many works of art which have a genuine intrinsic value extrinsic meanings come in time to be added, man-made interpolations which cover over the original shining-through of infinity in time: "Here too," says Teufelsdröckh, "may an extrinsic value gradually superadd itself: thus certain *Iliads*, and the like, have, in three-thousand years, obtained quite new significance" (223–4).

The reader will see the problem here. Carlyle, or his spokesman Teufelsdröckh, is not confused. The difficulties are intrinsic, if I may use that word, to what he is trying to say. They arise from what is distinctive about Carlyle's theory of symbol. This distinctiveness is shared, of course, with others in the period called Romanticism. It even appears perennially in one way or another throughout the centuries in our tradition. One such distinctive feature is the introduction of the dimension of fleeting time or transiency. The other is the presentation of symbol as a form of catachresis, that is, as neither figurative nor literal, since, as I have said, it is the only possible expression of what it says and therefore may not be compared to any alternative form of expression, either figurative or literal. The difficulties might be defined by saying that on the one hand the distinction between arbitrary and motivated symbols, between extrinsic and intrinsic, is altogether clear and evidently necessary, while on the other hand the more carefully the distinction is analyzed the more difficult, even impossible, it becomes to make it. It becomes harder and harder to discern clearly between one kind of symbol and another. They merge into one another, or each turns out to be a version of the other, not its opposite. As soon as Carlyle allows for the notion of a symbol with "a transient intrinsic worth," and it is the essence of his doctrine to do so, then he is granting a particular place in time, a particular man, writer, hero or prophet, an essential role in determining the efficacy of the symbol. It is impossible, in principle, to distinguish this from the notion that the symbols are created or projected, by a kind of performative fiat, through the man himself who proffers the new symbol. This is especially true because there is, as I have said, nothing outside the symbols against which to test their authenticity. They must speak for themselves and carry on their own faces the testimonies or witnesses of their validity. For Carlyle no symbol retains its efficacy beyond its own time. It must be replaced by new ones or by a revalidation, a reinterpretation of the old which makes the old effectively new. Carlyle's vision of human history is of the constant appearance through the medium of particular men of transient new symbols, symbols which stand for a moment or a day. They then fade and vanish, to be replaced with new ones. These are brought into the world by new "Hierarchs," "Pontiffs," new "Poets and inspired Makers." Teufelsdröckh's image of the Phoenix, constantly reborn from its own immolation, expresses well enough this vision of human history as a perpetually renewed process of death and rebirth, as does the projected title of the second volume of his clothes philosophy: *On the Palingenesia, or Newbirth of Society*. Essential to this picture of human history is what Teufelsdröckh calls, in a phrase the Editor hesitantly quotes from one of the Professor's "nebulous disquisitions on religion," the "perennial continuance of Inspiration" (193).

It is all very well for Teufelsdröckh to distinguish between intrinsic and extrinsic symbols, but if no symbol can be counted on to remain permanently valid, then no symbol has the kind of permanent and logical relation to the kingdom of heaven ascribed to them, for example, in medieval Christian allegorical interpretations of the Bible. This both defines the Infinite as something incompatible with fixed symbols and breaks down the division between intrinsic and extrinsic symbols by indicating an arbitrary, impermanent, and not wholly adequate quality even to an intrinsic symbol. If it were wholly adequate, would it not go on being adequate? How could one tell, for sure, in a given case, whether a given symbol is intrinsic or extrinsic, since there is no conceivable yardstick or criterion outside their own force to distinguish them by and since the permanence of the intrinsic symbol has been abandoned as its distinguishing feature? Might makes right here,[9] as in Carlyle's later theory of the political leader, and the new right displaces the old right. The Professor may preserve the nominally Christian character of his speculations by distinguishing between transient intrinsic symbols and those of quite perennial, infinite character, of which the only example he gives is the life of Christ as recorded by the Gospel-makers. Nevertheless, if even Christ has to be "anew inquired into, and anew made manifest," presumably by new Gospels, then it is hard to see how Christ as symbol is not liable to transience like the rest. Without the new Gospel, product of the perennial continuance of inspiration, he would fade like the rest.

The center of Carlyle's chapter on symbols is an eloquent paragraph on the fundamentally temporal and temporary character of symbols. The paragraph rises to a hyperbolic climax in which *all* things, even the manifestations of the infinite and the finite, are said to be conditioned by time, valid only for a time. It is difficult to see how Christ as symbol would be exempt, any more than "many an African Mumbo-Jumbo and Indian Pawaw" from the sweeping inclusiveness of this "all":

> But, on the whole [writes Teufelsdröckh], as Time adds much to the sacredness of Symbols, so likewise in his progress he at length defaces, or even desecrates them; and Symbols, like all terrestrial Garments, wax old. Homer's Epos has not ceased to be true; yet it is no longer *our* Epos, but shines in the distance, if clearer and clearer, yet also smaller and smaller, like a receding Star. It needs a scientific telescope, it needs to be reinterpreted and artificially brought near us, before we can so much as know that it *was* a Sun. So likewise a day comes when the Runic Thor, with his Eddas, must withdraw into dimness; and many an African Mumbo-Jumbo and Indian Pawaw be utterly abolished. For all things, even Celestial Luminaries, much more atmospheric meteors, have their rise, their culmination, their decline. (224–5)

One final, or at least penultimate, question remains to be briefly asked and briefly answered. What of *Sartor Resartus* itself, which is one of those works that is obliquely about its own nature and efficacy? Is *Sartor* an example of extrinsic or of intrinsic symbol, transient or intransient? Or, if those distinctions indeed do not hold, what, exactly, is the result of this fact for our reading of *Sartor*? Any interpretation of *Sartor Resartus* must centre or culminate in a reading of the "Everlasting Yea," and to an explication of that chapter I turn before concluding.

It would seem that the answer to my question would be easy to give decisively. The conversion experience in the rue de l'Enfer, echo of Thomas Carlyle's own experience in Leith Walk and echo in turn of all those conversion experiences going back through Augustine to Saul of Tarsus, is followed by the "Centre of Indifference" and then by the ringing affirmations of the "Everlasting Yea." In that "Yea"-saying Teufelsdröckh asserts his divine vocation as a writer. He testifies that he is one of those God-inspired men through whom Eternity enters into Time. He is another "Poet and inspired Maker, who, Prometheus-like, can shape new Symbols, and bring new Fire from Heaven to fix it there [in the world]." "Feel it in thy heart and then say whether it is of God!" cries Teufelsdröckh. "This is Belief; all else is Opinion" (194).

The examples that Teufelsdröckh gives of God-inspired men are all of real historical personages, Jesus, for example. What difference does it make that Teufelsdröckh is a fictive character in a work of fiction, someone who never existed as such on land or sea, but in *Weissnichtwo?* Does that not make him rather a model or simulacrum of such men, proffered for the reader's better understanding of what they might be like when encountered in real life, though not really one himself, only the cunning image of one? Does that not discount, ironize or hollow out Teufelsdröckh's claim to present genuine Promethean Hieroglyphs or to be such a one in himself? He is not a real God-inspired man but a diabolical image of one, or worse, the mere detritus of such an image, its remnant written down on the pages of a work of fiction, in short, Teufelsdröckh, "devil's dung." On the other hand, Teufelsdröckh (and presumably Carlyle behind him) names the true work of Art, the *Iliad*, for example, as an example of intrinsic symbol, and I have suggested that in speaking of Jesus as an intrinsic symbol, it is impossible to know whether Carlyle means that life as such, in itself, or that life as written down by Matthew, Mark, or Luke, with whatever fictive additions and ornamentations. Might not *Sartor Resartus* obliquely claim to be another such divinely inspired work of art, even though from the point of view of historical reality it is fictive through and through? On the other hand again, insofar as *Sartor Resartus* is, in one way or another, Thomas Carlyle's own disguised or indirect autobiography, the story of his conversion and his saying yes to his vocation as a writer transmuted, redressed, as hieroglyphic myth, can the reader not see it as, in fact, historically based and having as much ground in reality as even the Gospels? Back and forth among these various possibilities the reader alternates, without being able by the utmost interpretative efforts to find evidence allowing a decisive choice among them. It is of the nature of ironic fictions like *Sartor* to be in this particular way undecidable.

Even if this oscillation is momentarily suspended and the "Everlasting Yea" taken "straight," a further undecidability emerges in the nature of that "Everlasting Yea" itself. Here the interpreter is aided by a now familiar modern distinction which is showing itself to be of great, but perhaps of dangerous or enigmatic, power for the interpretation of literature. I mean the distinction between performative and constative utterances. The distinction was introduced by Austin, developed by Searle, and has been criticized and appropriated for literary studies by, among others, Derrida, de Man and Fish.[10] The distinction between performative and constative language in turn echoes Nietzsche's distinction between *ersetzen* and *erkennen*, to posit and to know. A constative utterance expresses, accurately or inaccurately, a prior state of affairs, a state of affairs which exists independently of the language which names it. Such a statement records an act of knowledge and is to be judged by its truth of correspondence. A performative utterance makes something happen. It is a way of doing things with words. A performative utterance brings something new into the world, something which did not exist a moment before, as when the minister says, "I pronounce you man and wife," or when the proper person in the proper circumstances says,"I christen thee the Queen Mary." A performative utterance does not correspond to anything already there. It is not the result of an act of knowledge, but is a groundless positing, an *Ersetzung*, thrown out by the words themselves to change the world. A performative creates rather than discovers. Or rather, it should be said that whether or not performatives are groundless is just the point of most controversy about them. Into the intricacies of this controversy there is not enough space to enter here, but for me a grounded performative is an oxymoron, not in fact a true performative positing, but a species of constative utterance, based on a prior act of knowing, as in the case of God the Father's *fiat lux*. God already knows before he names.

In any case, which form of utterance is Teufelsdröckh's "yea"? My argument is that it appears to be a constative statement but is in fact performative, or, to be more precise, that on the basis of Carlyle's own language about it, ascribed of course to Teufelsdröckh, it is impossible to tell for sure which it is, in a systematic ambiguity which is, once more, not Carlyle's fault, but an essential feature of what he is trying to say.

At first Teufelsdröckh's "Yea" seems unequivocally constative, another version of Isaiah's answer to God's "Whom shall I send?": "Here am I, Lord. Send me." Has not Teufelsdröckh heard God's call in his own heart, and is not his "Yea" in answer to that a knowledge of his vocation which justifies what he is, what he does, and what he says? His speech is in answer to speech of the Eternal, and it is this which justifies his claim to express unconditioned truth hieroglyphically or environed with earthly conditions, to name the unnamable in symbols which are intrinsically valid rather than extrinsic or arbitrary. Teufelsdröckh's answer of "Yea" to the divine call makes him one of those working "to embody the divine Spirit of [the antiquated Christian Religion] in a new Mythus, in a new vehicle and vesture, that our Souls, otherwise too like perishing, may live" (194).

On the other hand, Teufelsdröckh makes it clear that his "Yea" is not to be a knowledge but an action, a gesture, if you will, a form of conduct not the result of speculation, in short, a performative. "But indeed Conviction," affirms Teufelsdröckh,

> were it never so excellent, is worthless till it convert itself into Conduct. Nay properly conviction is not possible till then; inasmuch as all Speculation is by nature endless, formless, a vortex amid vortices: only by a felt indubitable certainty of Experience does it find any centre to revolve round, and so fashions itself into a System. Most true it is, as a wise man teaches us, that "Doubt of any sort cannot be removed except by Action." (195–6)

Action or conduct precedes conviction and the knowledge (or conviction of knowledge) conviction brings, not the other way around. One must do before one can know. Performance precedes knowledge. What sort of conduct, action, or performance does Teufelsdröckh (or Carlyle) have in mind?

The famous paragraph immediately following about doing the duty that lies nearest you in the actual is given the widest applicability to constructive action of any kind:

> Yes here, in this poor, miserable, hampered, despicable Actual, wherein thou even now standest, here or nowhere is thy Ideal: work it out therefrom; and working, believe, live, be free. (196)

The terms Teufelsdröckh uses, however, his basic hieroglyphical figure here for conduct or action, as well as his account in the next chapter of his acceptance of "Authorship as his divine calling" (198), indicate that what is especially in question here is the proffering of language as gesture, action or conduct, in fact a form of action like Carlyle's in writing *Sartor Resartus*. Carlyle's basic figure for this, or the figure he attributes to Teufelsdröckh, is the analogy between a man's act of taking up the pen and writing a work like Teufelsdröckh's clothes philosophy or like *Sartor Resartus*, and God's act of creating the world through the divine fiat, "Let there be light." "Hast thou not a Brain," asks Teufelsdröckh in the chapter following "The Everlasting Yea,"

> furnished, furnishable with some glimmerings of Light; and three fingers to hold a Pen withal? Never since Aaron's rod went out of practice, or even before it, was there such a wonder-working Tool: greater than all recorded miracles have been performed by Pens. . . . The WORD is said to be omnipotent in this world; man, thereby divine, can create as by a *Fiat*. Awake, arise! Speak forth what is in thee; what God has given thee, what the Devil shall not take away. (199)

Teufelsdröckh's use of this same figure in the next to last paragraph of "The Everlasting Yea" shows what is problematic about it. In spite of the phrase "what God has given thee," it is impossible to tell whether the fiat of the man who holds the pen and wields it as a magic wand is a response to God's call or whether it is an autonomous act, a performance which on its own turns chaos into an organized world spinning round a center and making a coherent system. The ambiguity, or, more properly, undecidability, turns on the uncertain reference of the "it" in Carlyle's formulation "it is spoken." Is the "it" speech of God or is it speech of man the performative penwielder? If "it" is the first, then conduct for Carlyle is based on a prior knowledge, and it is God who brings light, intellectual illumination, and order. If "it" is the second then man's own autonomous act as a producing writer creates the order, posits it as a manbegotten fiction, along with the conviction that the conviction is Godbegotten. It is, I argue, altogether impossible to tell which it is. This impossibility is the essential meaning of the "Everlasting Yea," therefore of Carlyle's book or indeed of his work as a whole. "Divine moment," writes Teufelsdröckh,

> when over the tempest-tossed Soul, as once over the wild-weltering Chaos, *it is spoken* [my emphasis]: Let there be Light! Ever to the greatest that has felt such a moment, is it not miraculous and God-announcing; even as, under simpler figures, to the simplest and least. The mad primeval Discord is hushed; the rudely-jumbled conflicting elements bind themselves into separate Firmaments: deep silent rock-foundations are built beneath; and the skyey vault with its everlasting Luminaries above: instead of a dark wasteful Chaos, we have a blooming, fertile, heaven-encompassed World. (197)

The figure here is a good example of Teufelsdröckh's "Hierograms." The august figure of God's creation of the world out of chaos is applied to the ordering of man's inner world when he abandons speculation and acts, doing the duty that is nearest him, to make something, for example a book. This is then followed by the famous affirmation or self-exhortation of the last paragraph of the chapter. This, in the light of what has preceded it, would seem to tip the balance in the direction of saying it is man's unaided power of production, plunging blindly ahead to create something, which makes a world out of chaos, were it not for the phrase at the end, "in God's name." This could be no more than a strong expletive, or it could mean man's production of order out of chaos is valid only if it is sanctioned and justified by God's election of the writer. This returns the reader once more to that impossibility of deciding which I am trying to identify. "I too could now say to myself: Be no longer a Chaos, but a World, or even Worldkin. Produce! Produce! Were it but the pitifullest infinitesimal fraction of a Product, produce it, in God's name!" (197).

It will be seen now what I meant by saying that it is impossible to tell whether Emerson or Nietzsche is right about Carlyle. Both and neither are right. Surely no one has ever spoken more sincerely or more from the heart than Carlyle here in the guise of Teufelsdröckh, nor has anyone more persuasively praised the productive chaos-taming power of sincere speaking and writing. On the other hand, Nietzsche, with his astute and disquieting psychological insight, is right too. What Nietzsche names as Carlyle's passionate dishonesty against himself, his need to be a rhetor and speak in ostentatious ironic figures, we can see as an inescapable necessity of the position that Carlyle was affirming through Teufelsdröckh. Once any symbol of the infinite is seen as transient and as having that sort of inadequacy which is intrinsic to any catachresis, or name for the unnamable, then there is no way in which Carlyle can affirm one version of his doctrine of hieroglyphic truth without at the same time affirming the counter version. What Nietzsche calls Carlyle's passionate dishonesty against himself, I am calling the intrinsic, undecidability of his doctrine.

If this is the case, it will allow me to come, finally, full circle and to indicate the answer to the question with which I began. The justification for all Carlyle's "ornament," the stylistic ornament of "Carlylese" and the narrative elaboration of fictive narrator within fictive writer, ironies within ironies, wheels within wheels, is that only in this way can Carlyle be true to the double orientation of his doctrine of writing as production. Only a form of writing which constantly destroys itself and renews itself, as figure follows figure, like phoenix after phoenix in a constant process of palingenesis, will be true to Carlyle's fundamental insight, which is "that all Forms are but Clothes, and temporary" (267). And only the self-subverting irony of a fictive dramatization of this truth will be able simultaneously to be one of those works of art which may function as an intrinsic symbol, the Infinite embodied in the circumstantial dress of the Finite, and at the same time openly a fictive product, the positing of an imaginary world or worldkin, complete with a hero, places for him to live, and a life-story, with no grounds for their existence but the fiat of Carlyle's magic power of the pen. The Editor too is a narrative necessity. What does his activity do but mime the pontifical process of making order out of chaos, as the Editor more than once says? The chaos in this case is that monster book by Teufelsdröckh and the disordered contents of those six famous paper-bags, but these are in turn a "Hierogram" for Carlyle's own internal chaos, brought into order and made a worldkin by the production of *Sartor Resartus*.

Notes

1. Ralph Waldo Emerson, *English Traits, Works*, Concord Ed., v. (Boston, Mass., and New York, n.d.), p. 274.
2. Thomas Carlyle, *Sartor Resartus: The Life and Opinions of Herr Teufelsdröckh*, Charles Frederick Harrold, ed. (New York, 1937), pp. 79–80. Further citations from *Sartor* will be identified by page numbers from this edition.
3. *The Collected Letters of Thomas and Jane Welsh Carlyle*, Charles Richard Sanders, Kenneth J. Fielding, Ian Campbell, John Clubbe and others, eds (Durham, N.C., 1970–), VI, p. 396. (Hereafter cited as *CL*.)
4. *CL*, VII, p. 266.
5. Emerson, *Works*, X, pp. 494, 495.
6. Friedrich Nietzsche, *Twilight of the Idols, The Portable Nietzsche*, tr. Walter Kaufmann (New York, 1959), p. 522.
7. *Twilight of the Idols* was written in 1888. Froude's *Life* was published in two sections of two volumes each in 1882 and 1884, but probably Nietzsche was reading a German translation, *Das Leben Thomas Carlyles* . . . Übersetzt, bearbeitet und mit Anmerkungen versehen von T. A. Fischer, 3 vols (Gotha, 1887).
8. *CL*, VIII, p. 136.
9. But see Carlyle's clarifying comment in *Two Reminiscences of Thomas Carlyle*, John Clubbe, ed. (Durham, N.C., 1974), pp. 98–9.
10. For a penetrating discussion of what is problematic about applying the notion of performative utterance to literature, see Rodolphe Gasché, " 'Setzung' and 'Übersetzung': Notes on Paul de Man," *Diacritics*, XI (Winter 1981), pp. 36–57. It should be noted that what I say here significantly modifies and corrects what I said earlier about God's *fiat lux*, pp. 225–6.

Index